BEST PLACES®

ALASKA

Edited by
NAN ELLIOT

EDITION 2

D1021462

SASQUATCH BOOKS
SEATTLE

To all those who love the wilderness
May we all have the courage to protect it.

Printed in the United States of America
Distributed in Canada by Raincoast Books Ltd.

Second edition
03 02 01 00   5 4 3 2 1

ISBN: 1-57061-180-7
ISSN: 1095-9777

Series editor: Kate Rogers
Cover and interior design: Nancy Gellos
Maps: GreenEye Design, pp. vi, 364; Rohani Design, Edmonds WA, pp. 2, 98, 124, 156, 178, 220, 232, 258, 294, 314, 326, 348.

SPECIAL SALES

BEST PLACES® guidebooks are available at special discounts on bulk purchases for corporate, club, or organization sales promotions, premiums, and gifts. Special editions, including personalized covers, excerpts of existing guides, and corporate imprints, can be created in large quantities for specific needs. For more information, contact your local bookseller or Special Sales, BEST PLACES® Guidebooks, at the address below.

Important Note: Please use common sense when visiting Alaska's wilderness. No guidebook can act as a substitute for experience, careful planning, and appropriate training. There is inherent danger in all the outdoor activities described in this book, and readers must assume responsibility for their own actions and safety, even when using a guide or outfitter. Changing or unfavorable conditions in weather, roads, trails, waterways, wildlife, etc. cannot be anticipated by the editors or publisher, but should be considered by any outdoor participants. The editors and publisher will not be responsible for the safety of users of this guide.

SASQUATCH BOOKS

615 Second Avenue
Seattle, WA 98104
206/467-4300
books@SasquatchBooks.com
www.SasquatchBooks.com

CONTENTS

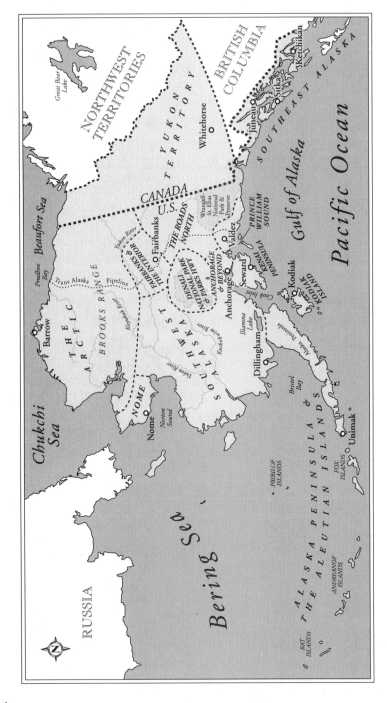

CONTRIBUTORS AND ACKNOWLEDGMENTS

Twenty-three of Alaska's best writers (including chefs, guides, and wilderness adventurers), plus one Scotsman and one transplanted New Yorker, have joined forces to bring you the land they love. It is a wild and wonderful team. Some are sober-minded, philosophical, and poetic. Others are hilarious, outrageous, and high-spirited. All have a great zest for life and together have won dozens of awards for their work—in many fields, not only for writing. They have paddled, filmed, climbed, mushed, fished, and swilled their way across and over Alaska. Two have stood on the summit of the highest mountain in North America, Mount McKinley (also known as Denali). One has rowed nearly the entire coastline of Alaska. The youngest is 28; the oldest is 83.

SOUTHEAST ALASKA: SUSAN "MEADOW" BROOK wrote about Gustavus, her adopted home for the last 20 years. She moved there, as she says, "in the old days before telephones, television, and tourists." She also writes about Icy Strait and the tiny outposts of Elfin Cove, the Hobbit Hole, and Gull Cove. A European-trained gourmet chef, she is co-author of *The Fiddlehead Cookbook*. **BARBARA ROSSOMANO**, a world traveler and social worker from New York state, recently moonlighted for a couple of years running a bed-and-breakfast in Haines. On one of her first extended trips on the Roads North into the Interior, she "rolled her rig." She wrote (while apologizing for missing a deadline): "I hear rolling your rig is a rite of passage in these Alaska parts, so I'm starting to feel more at home." Who better then to write about lodgings in Haines, her home-away-from-home? **MARILEE ENGE**, a professional journalist and member of one of the oldest Norwegian immigrant families in Petersburg wrote about her hometown.

THE ROADS NORTH: JOHN KOOISTRA is no stranger to life on the move. He first hitchhiked to Alaska in 1965 with two fishing rods—and got hooked on the place. A commercial fisherman for 28 years and a former professor of philosophy at the University of Alaska Fairbanks, John is also an ace carpenter, connoisseur of fine wines, and a charming essayist. Our bold Scotsman, **DAVID ELLIOT**, one of the last living members of the old British Raj in India, wrote about the "Circular Route" and Kennicott-McCarthy. After meting out justice under the banyan tree, he went to California as professor of history at Caltech. Now emeritus, he once again got hoodwinked into another Alaska project by his ever-loving daughter.

ANCHORAGE: CATHY RASMUSON and her Merry Band of Galloping Gourmets (who often included her daughters Laura and Natasha, representing our "daring young sophisticates" on the food scene) were the sleuths for Anchorage restaurants. Cathy is the ultimate hostess and entertainer. She thinks nothing of preparing for a dinner party of a hundred any night of the week. And she's no stranger to adventure either. In 1993, she mushed a team of dogs 1,049 miles down the Iditarod Trail with the Father of the Iditarod, Joe Redington, Sr, on his first Iditarod Challenge. **KIM SEVERSON**, who wrote the lively chapter on Anchorage, was once editor and food critic at the *Anchorage Daily News* until, alas, she was recently wooed away by the *San Francisco Chronicle*. **PETER PORCO**, editor and writer at the *Anchorage Daily News*, was the perfect person to write about the city's spectacular backyard, Chugach State Park. Peter has traipsed all over the Chugach Mountains and has served as base camp manager on Mount McKinley (and even climbed to its summit). **WANDA SEAMSTER**, woman of many talents—award-winning artist, graphic designer, editor, critic, writer, and wit—gives a sprightly take on the local arts scene.

PRINCE WILLIAM SOUND: NATALIE PHILLIPS is one of our "fast women," a formidable backcountry racer and marathoner. She just made the deadline before becoming the happy mom of a new little fast guy named Dash. A feature reporter for the *Anchorage Daily News*, Natalie has spent considerable time in the Sound, covering the 1989 *Exxon Valdez* oil spill, paddling a kayak, and fishing out of Cordova. Writing on kayaking, **JILL FREDSTON** is actually an ocean-going rower who disappears every summer on 3- to 5-month trips. For a "not-so-old salt," she has rowed about 20,000 miles of wild seas around the world, including much of the coast of Alaska. In winter she works as an avalanche expert and is currently writing a book about her adventures.

KENAI PENINSULA: LIZ RUSKIN, with her crisp, upbeat style, covered Homer and Kachemak Bay. On most days she covers the even wilder scene of Alaska politics for the *Anchorage Daily News*. A former reporter for the *Homer News*, Liz was born in Alaska, and, like Natalie, she is one of our fast women in running shoes and on skate skis. **JOAN DANIELS** is a saucy wit and a wilderness-savvy woman. She's equally adept at shooting a grizzly as serving him up for tasty hors d'oeuvres. She's cooked and catered everywhere in Alaska, from ski training camps high up on glaciers to dog mushing expeditions along the Iditarod Trail. Who else could serve oysters Rockefeller and German honey cakes outdoors on the banks of the frozen Yukon River at −30°F with panache, and still keep everyone laughing? "Well, you can't just go crashing through life eating sardines out of a can!" she'd say.

KODIAK ISLAND: CAROL MURKOWSKI STURGULEWSKI, a lifelong Alaskan, has written warm and engaging pieces from a kaleidoscope of remote outposts that she has called home, from Southeast to the Aleutians. Here, she writes about her two favorite places—Kodiak and Unalaska. Between packing and unpacking, she has been a writer/editor for the *Fairbanks Daily News-Miner, Anchorage Times,* and the *Aleutian Eagle and Dutch Harbor Fisherman.*

DENALI NATIONAL PARK AND THE PARKS HIGHWAY: KRIS CAPPS, now a freelance journalist, lives near Denali National Park. She came to Alaska 20 years ago, worked as editor of the *Kodiak Daily Mirror* and the *Valdez Vanguard* and was a reporter for nearly 10 years at the *Fairbanks Daily News-Miner.* In her "other life" she's a wilderness river guide in the Brooks Range, teaches whitewater kayaking, and is the founder of several whitewater races. She was the perfect choice to write about her home, the most popular national park in Alaska.

FAIRBANKS AND THE INTERIOR: DEBRA MCKINNEY has worked for the past 15 years (with a few hiatuses recently like a year in Teller, a village near Nome, and a year in Japan) as one of the star feature reporters for the *Anchorage Daily News.* In winter, she works in Anchorage. In summer, she escapes to her dream cabin in the hills west of Fairbanks. The Interior is full of characters and that's just what gets Deb's creative juices flowing. She wrote a wonderfully funny piece about Fairbanks (powering her computer off solar batteries). Read it for fun, even if you never intend to go there.

NOME: Deb McKinney also lent her wonderful flair to the town of Nome while she was staying in nearby Teller. **MARK GILLESPIE** wrote for us about his old home of Kodiak. But when Mark left "The Rock" for the wilds of the Interior, he ended up in Nome and happily became our writer there. An entertaining young fellow, Mark was born in the Blue Ridge Mountains of Virginia, but moved to Alaska because, as he says, "the mountains are bigger, the outhouses are nicer, and sled dogs are smarter than hound dogs." He's first of all a radio man—a former director of public radio on Kodiak and later a public radio reporter on the Iditarod Trail. Currently, he's gotten very white-collar as a college administrator for the Northwest Campus of the University of Alaska Fairbanks in Nome.

THE ARCTIC: Photographer **TOM WALKER** has spent nearly 35 years in Alaska and his photographs of this country are stunning. He is the author/photographer of more than a dozen books. He lives in a beautiful log cabin he built himself near Denali National Park. Only in the last few years did Tom hook into electricity, which he says is a great boon, since in the dark of winter he can now see "which boot goes on which foot." Tom wrote about the Arctic, a land he has photographed, guided in, wandered, and loved for many years. **DAVID HARDING,** another humorous radio man, wrote about Alaska's most northern town on the edge of the Arctic Ocean: Barrow. For 20 years, David bounced around the state—from Juneau to Bethel to Barrow—working in all forms of media. He is now testing his Alaska wiles in the Lower 48. He is a delightful, knowledgeable character who is proud to say that throughout his successful mixed-media career he has never owned a suit.

SOUTHWEST ALASKA AND THE ALEUTIANS: BILL SHERWONIT, freelance journalist and author, wrote the bulk of these two chapters. Bill has spent his career in Alaska (nearly 20 years now) writing about nature and the outdoors, and he teaches wilderness writing at the University of Alaska. He not only wrote a book entitled *To the Top Of Denali*, he also climbed to the top himself. **SEAN STITHAM**, an itinerant Bush doctor, wrote about Bethel, where he practiced medicine for many years with the Indian Health Service. He has doctored all over Alaska and the world, from Sri Lanka to Africa. With his Irish heritage, red hair, offbeat sense of humor, and fast repartee, he quickly slips into the heartbeat of any community. Born and raised in Alaska, **HENRY "TE" TIFFANY** built his first log cabin at the age of 16 and has hunted since he was a little boy. He is a licensed big game guide in Alaska and currently operates several expedition camps. At age 28, he is also the youngest writer in this book, but displays a wisdom some take a lifetime to find. He was taught to hunt and to love writing by his grandfather, our senior writer in this book, **EDWARD J. FORTIER**. Also known as "Fast Eddie," Fortier, as the last living spy from World War II in Alaska, is the perfect image of a sourdough Alaskan. No matter how turbulent life has gotten in his 83 years, he has never lost his sense of humor or his passion for Alaska. A small sign outside his door reads: "Come on in. Everything else has gone wrong." Don't let it fool you—he lives the frontier code. He's the first to give encouragement, lend a hand, and help you out of any jam. A reporter for the *National Observer* and editor of *Alaska Magazine* for many years, Ed revisits his old wartime stomping grounds in the Aleutians with a new take on the future.

THE YUKON: This chapter is a new addition and rightfully so, as there is a great deal of simpatico across the border in these northern regions. **DIMITRA LAVRAKAS** came from Boston to Barrow in 1994 as the editor of the *Arctic Sounder*. She spent nearly 3 years in America's northernmost city on the edge of the Arctic Ocean before she moved south to become the editor of the *Skagway News*. In the little town of Skagway at the head of the Inside Passage, she found "the best place I could ever possibly imagine." Tooling around the Yukon was like cruising the neighborhood. It's just over the pass from Skagway. So, from one neighbor to another, here are Dimitra's best tips.

Finally, as editor, I (**NAN ELLIOT**), couldn't resist writing several sections of the book myself—mainly the chapters on Southeast, the Kenai, parts of Denali, chunks of Southwest, etc. As they say, if no one else on the team avows knowledge, it's *mea culpa*. I've had the good fortune through my work as an author, journalist, filmmaker, radio producer, educator, and naturalist on the cruise ships to travel all over Alaska and the world. I first came to Alaska more than 25 years ago to teach Eskimos how to swim. And I fell in love with this country.

So here is my wish for all of you. No matter how long or short your stay, may it be as magical for you as it has been for all of us.

With a low bow and many popping of champagne corks, I would like to extend a very special thanks to my whole team and to so many others who gave generously of their humor, time, knowledge, opinions, and technical support: Rick Kool, Enid Elliot, Wendy Munger, Lenny Gumport, Amy Malcom, Carroll Hodge, Mary Kemppel, Sally Mead, Chip and Bucky Dennerlein, Al and Penny Meiners, Marla Berg, Bonnie Berg, Carol Berg, Lulu Belle, John Connolly, Debe Marshall, Graham Sunderland, Ed Rasmuson, Marty Beckwith, Ruth Ann Dickie, Max Hall, Harry Turner, Brian and Sharon Davies, Dr. Vacation (alias Jim Thompson), Peter McKay, Peggy Mullen, Marge Mullen, and Doug Fesler. Lastly, the warmest of thanks to "me dear faither" who is a sharp-eyed editor and a wise man.   —N. E.

About Best Places® Guidebooks

People trust us. BEST PLACES® guidebooks, which have been published continuously since 1975, represent one of the most respected regional travel series in the country. Each guide is written completely independently: no advertisers, no sponsors, no favors. Our reviewers know their territory, work incognito, and seek out the very best a city, state, or region has to offer. Because we accept no free meals, accommodations, or other complimentary services, we are able to provide tough, candid reports about places that have rested too long on their laurels, and to delight in new places that deserve recognition. We describe the true strengths, foibles, and unique characteristics of each establishment listed.

Alaska Best Places is written by and for locals, and is therefore coveted by travelers. It's written for people who live here and who enjoy exploring the state's bounty and its out-of-the-way places of high character and individualism. It is these very characteristics that make *Alaska Best Places* ideal for tourists, too. The best places in and around the state are the ones that denizens favor: independently owned establishments of good value, touched with local history, run by lively individuals, and graced with natural beauty. With this second edition of *Alaska Best Places*, travelers will find the information they need: where to go and when, what to order, which rooms to request, how to find the best guides and outfitters, where the best festivals, shopping, and other attractions are, and how to find the state's hidden secrets.

We're so sure you'll be satisfied with our guide, we guarantee it.

NOTE: *Readers are advised that places listed in the previous edition may have closed or changed management, or may no longer be recommended by this series. The reviews in this edition are based on information available at press time and are subject to change. The editors welcome information conveyed by users of this book. A report form is provided at the end of the book, and feedback is also welcome via email: books@ SasquatchBooks.com.*

How to Use This Book

All evaluations in this book are based on numerous reports from local and traveling inspectors. BEST PLACES® reporters do not identify themselves when they review an establishment, and they accept no free meals, accommodations, or any other services. Final judgments are made by the editors. Every place featured in this book is recommended.

STAR RATINGS Restaurants and lodgings are rated on a scale of zero to four stars, based on uniqueness, loyalty of local clientele, performance measured against the establishment's goals, excellence of cooking, cleanliness, value, and professionalism of service. Reviews are listed alphabetically, and every place is recommended.

★★★★ The very best in the region

★★★ Distinguished; many outstanding features

★★ Excellent; some wonderful qualities

★ A good place

NO STARS Worth knowing about, if nearby

(For more on how we rate places, see the Alaska Star Ratings box, below.)

PRICE RANGE Prices for lodgings are based on peak season rates for one night's lodging for two people (i.e., double occupancy). Off-season rates vary but can sometimes be significantly less. Prices for restaurants are based primarily on dinner for two, including dessert, tax, and tip. Call ahead to verify, as all prices are subject to change.

$$$ Expensive (more than $100 for dinner for two; more than $150 for one night's lodgings for two)

$$ Moderate (between expensive and inexpensive)

$ Inexpensive (less than $35 for dinner for two; less than $80 for one night's lodgings for two)

ACCESS AND INFORMATION At the beginning of each chapter, you'll find general guidelines about how to get to a particular region and what types of transportation are available, as well as basic sources for any additional tourist information you might need. Also check individual town listings for specifics about visiting those places. **ALASKA WILDER-NESS RECREATION AND TOURISM ASSOCIATION (AWRTA)** is a group of more than 200 outdoor-oriented businesses throughout the state. Their trip planner, *Alaska Source Book: Trip Planning Info for Independent Travelers to Alaska*, is available by contacting AWRTA (2207 Spenard Rd, Ste 201, Anchorage AK 99503; 907/258-3171, fax 907/258-3851; awrta@alaska.net; www.alaska.net/~awrta).

WILDERNESS LODGES For some visitors, the best way to experience Alaska is to stay at a remote wilderness or fishing lodge. There are hundreds of such lodges throughout the state, but we have tried to include here only those establishments that have proved to be dependable operations. They are not star-rated because they vary widely in terms of location and of overall experience versus fishing poundage. Please be aware that many of these places require expensive Bush flights to reach, minimum stays during the peak season, and charge an all-inclusive rate by the day or week.

ADDRESSES AND PHONE NUMBERS Every attempt has been made to provide accurate information on an establishment's location and phone

ALASKA STAR RATINGS

(A Disclaimer)

First of all, if you equate four stars to the best that Paris has to offer, be aware that our stars relate to nobody else's stars in the world! Our rating system is strictly "Alaska Bush Style." Character rates highly. In many places in this far northern state, assigning stars is like trying to compare Belgian chocolates and tropical mangos. Sometimes, the *best* place is the *only* place—and you're darn happy to be there, particularly if the rain is blowing horizontally in your face or the temperature has dropped to –50°F.

While we do have some wonderful places to eat and sleep—places which rival the best in the world—if you are on a serious four-star gastronomic mission and your toes cannot possibly be pampered outside a world-class hotel, we suggest you keep flying north over the pole to Paris. A singular quest for the finest food and lodging should not be the sole reason you come to Alaska.

While in most major cities you could learn a dozen different languages just by studying the menus, in Alaska, outside of a few towns, the only foreign word you'll see on a menu is *deluxe*—and it usually follows "cheeseburger." Ah, but do not dismay. There are also hundreds of places all over Alaska to eat (and sleep) which are so extraordinary and so outrageously magical that you will remember them all the days of your life. You cannot make a reservation. They have no maitre d' or concierge. They have no walls. As one of our writers so eloquently says, "The most exquisite meal is the country itself."

—The Editor

number. But it's always a good idea to call ahead and confirm. Please note that many Alaska businesses observe seasonal closures, operating only certain months of the year. The establishments in this edition are open year-round unless otherwise noted.

CHECKS AND CREDIT CARDS Most establishments that accept checks also require a major credit card for identification. Note that some places accept only local checks. Credit cards are abbreviated in this book as follows: American Express (AE); Carte Blanche (CB); Diners Club (DC); Discover (DIS); Japanese credit card (JCB); MasterCard (MC); Visa (V).

EMAIL AND WEB SITE ADDRESSES We've included email and Web site addresses for establishments, where available. Please note that the World Wide Web is a fluid and evolving medium, and that Web pages are often "under construction" or, as with all time-sensitive information, may no longer be valid.

MAPS AND DIRECTIONS Each chapter in the book begins with a regional map that shows the general area being covered. Throughout the book, basic directions are provided with each entry. Whenever possible, call ahead to confirm hours and location.

HELPFUL ICONS Watch for these quick-reference symbols throughout the book:

 FAMILY FUN Family-oriented places that are great for kids—fun, easy, not too expensive, and accustomed to dealing with young ones.

 GOOD VALUE While not necessarily cheap, these places offer you the best value for your dollars—a good deal within the context of the region.

 EDITOR'S CHOICE These are places that are unique and special to the Last Frontier and beloved by locals.

Appears after listings for establishments that have wheelchair-accessible facilities.

♿ **INDEXES** All restaurants, lodgings, town names, and major tourist attractions are listed alphabetically in the back of the book.

READER REPORTS At the end of the book is a report form. We receive hundreds of reports from readers suggesting new places or agreeing or disagreeing with our assessments. They greatly help in our evaluations, and we encourage you to respond.

MONEY-BACK GUARANTEE See "We Stand by Our Reviews" at the end of this book.

SOUTHEAST ALASKA

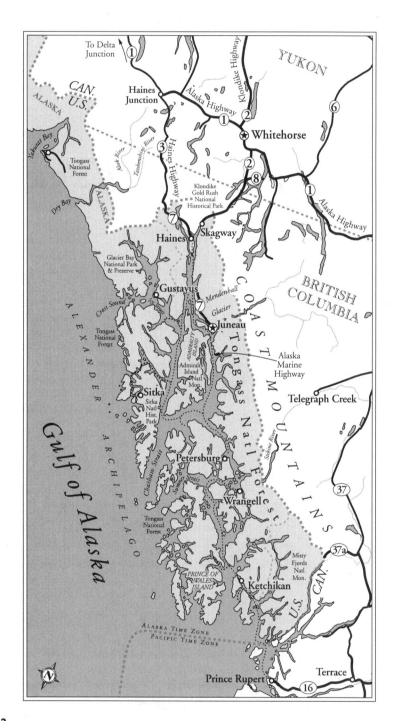

SOUTHEAST ALASKA

Named in 1867 for Alexander II, czar of Russia, the Alexander Archipelago is a series of islands and waterways that today define Southeast Alaska. Once, it was part of Russian America, when the double-headed eagle flew over this vast northern territory in the New World. For 126 years, Alaska was under the imperial Russian flag until Czar Alexander II sold his far-flung colony to the United States in 1867.

A narrow strip of coastline, bounded on the east by steep, icy mountains and on the west by the North Pacific Ocean, Southeast Alaska more recently was called "The Panhandle." You can see why if you look at a map of the rest of Alaska, which, if we carry the simile forward, looks like the frying pan itself. But that nickname, too, has gone the way of the czars.

Today, the region is spoken of and written about simply as "Southeast." (Note that you spell it with a capital "S.") If you were to fly over it, you would see islands, mountains, fjords, icefields, glaciers, more islands, and more ice-covered mountains rising like a crescendo to some of the highest summits on the North American continent.

Southeast is rich in culture. The original peoples to inhabit the land were predominantly Tlingit. Today, three major Native groups live in Southeast—Tlingit, Haida, and Tsimshian. Because the weather here is mild and the sea and forest rich with food, the peoples of Southeast Alaska had more time than the Eskimos and Indians of the north to create great art—carved totem poles, clan houses, wooden suits of armor, priceless blankets, great headdresses, masks, and silverwork. Many Native artists today are producing stunning works, blending both the contemporary and the traditional.

Although early inhabitants of Southeast Alaska considered the climate so mild that they did not have tailored clothing, this is not a wise custom to practice today. Southeast weather, even at the best of times, is usually cool. At its worst, it's downright bone-chilling. The sunniest months, although not necessarily the warmest, tend to be April, May, and June. Be forewarned: there is still plenty of snow then, at least in the mountains. But whenever you come, if you get 2 days of sun in a week, consider yourself fortunate. After all, there's a reason why all this country looks so green in the summer. You are traveling in a rain forest.

The Tongass National Forest, a temperate rain forest, covers most of Southeast Alaska. It is the largest national forest in the United States. There are nearly 1,000 islands under its banner. This is one of the country's last old-growth forests. The trees are primarily Sitka spruce and western hemlock interspersed with red and yellow cedar. The water between the islands and the mainland is known as the "Inside Passage"—

summer home for cruise ships, fishing boats, ferries, skiffs, kayaks, and rowboats of all sorts.

Water is an extension of everyone's life in Southeast. There are few roads and rarely do they link one community to another. So water serves not only as the transportation corridor, but also as the place of livelihood and recreation. Indeed, the official name of the ferry system is the Alaska Marine Highway. The only other way to get around is by air—bush plane, jet, or helicopter.

The land is dramatic. Carved by glaciers, the valleys have that telltale, U-shaped contour. Where the ice retreated, the sea rushed in to create deep, spectacular fjords. Today, those grand rivers of ice tumble down to the ocean. Warmed by the Japanese current, the sea itself does not freeze, even in winter, but glaciers are constantly kicking out icebergs, which you can see floating in the water or tossed up on a sandbar.

Magnificent whales, chubby harbor seals, swooping eagles, wild salmon, and the great Alaska brown bears are just a few of the alluring creatures that call Southeast home.

Towns and villages along the coast have their own special characters, founded on fishing, fur, gold, timber, or tourism. Native peoples have lived here for untold centuries. White settlers arrived within the past 300 years—Russian fur traders, Yankee whalers, European explorers, navigators, sailors, fishermen, and gold prospectors have all made their way here. Names on the map hint at the rich stories of a few of those early travelers who came before you.

Ketchikan

In the old days, long before the white man came, Tlingit people camped on the banks of Ketchikan Creek and fished for salmon, "the great swimmer." Southeast is home to many thousands of eagles, and spawned-out salmon is the bald eagle's favorite meal. "Ketchikan" comes from the Tlingit word meaning "thundering wings of the eagle." In the 1800s, settlers built a saltry at the mouth of Ketchikan Creek, and by 1930 Ketchikan was one of the world's largest exporters of salmon, with more than a dozen canneries in the area. Money and fish flowed fast and thick. Timber in the forests provided packing boxes for the canneries and, later, raw lumber for Japan and fodder for the local pulp mills.

Today, Ketchikan is the fourth-largest city in Alaska, with a population of more than 14,000. Fishing and tourism continue to keep the summer economy well greased. Folks in Ketchikan have always been inventive in promoting their town. In the heyday of salmon, it was the "Salmon Capital of the World." Then, when ferry service began in the 1960s, it was billed as "Alaska's First City," as it was the first stop on the ferry route from Seattle to Alaska. For a while, residents tried attracting curious travelers by calling the town the "Rain Capital of Alaska," since Ketchikan gets about 13 feet of rain a year.

Not so long ago, Alaska's First City was a rowdy, rough-and-tumble town of fishermen, loggers, and the occasional miner. But today Ketchikan has received a face-lift. Like the famous madams of yesteryear who waited for the return of the fishing fleet, the town has been getting all dolled up for the fleet of cruise ships sailing into port every summer. In the last few years, old weathered buildings have been spruced up and gaily painted with new names reminiscent of a saucier era, the dock has been extended to accommodate huge ships, and fancy new shops have been built along the wharf. In 1999, Ketchikan welcomed more than half a million cruise ship visitors alone.

"Sausalito of the North" may be stretching it a bit (particularly if the rain is blowing horizontally), but on a sunny day on the old boardwalk of Creek Street, while eating a fresh halibut sandwich and watching salmon jumping up the falls, one could easily slip into that feel-good, savory, pastoral feeling of old California. One look at the untamed, dramatic landscape all around you in the north country makes up in spades for what Ketchikan lacks in gourmet eateries and constant sun.

ACCESS AND INFORMATION

Ketchikan has daily **JET SERVICE** year-round via Alaska Airlines (800/426-0333). The best locally based air service for scheduled or charter operations is Taquan Air (1007 Water St; 907/225-8800 or 800/770-8800). Ketchikan is, of course, still Alaska's First City for the ferries. The cruise ships dock or anchor close to downtown. The ferries of the **ALASKA MARINE HIGHWAY SYSTEM** (907/225-6181 or 800/642-0066) dock at the ferry terminal 2 miles north of town. Just north of that terminal is the car ferry to the airport.

Once you get to Ketchikan, there are about 36 miles of road running north to south along the western edge of the island. Public buses run from the airport ferry to the southern edge of downtown, about 4 miles. If you want to drive to the ends of the road, you'll need to rent a car. Call **ALASKA CAR RENTAL** (2828 Tongass Ave; 800/662-0007 or 907/225-5000) for airport and town locations. They have a courtesy pickup and are open daily.

Be sure to stop first at the **SOUTHEAST ALASKA VISITOR INFOR-MATION CENTER (SEAVIC)** (50 Main St; 907/228-6214, fax 907/228-6234). Opened in 1995, the center is a stone's throw from the cruise ship dock. Once inside the door, you are met by three totem poles, carved to honor the Tlingit, Haida, and Tsimshian peoples of Southeast Alaska. Look up, not only to see the crests on top of the totems but to see salmon,

"OH, GIVE ME THE CRUISING LIFE!"

Once considered the domain of the very rich, cruising, it also used to be said, was for "the newly wed and the nearly dead." Not so today. Everybody cruises.

Some people sail for the food alone. On the big ships you can eat 14 meals a day if you choose, beginning with an early-bird continental breakfast and finishing up with the midnight buffet. As one cruise director joked, "You can come on as passengers and go off as cargo."

In summer, nearly 30 cruise ships ply the inland waterways of Alaska and even across the wild Gulf of Alaska up to Cook Inlet and Prince William Sound. A few smaller ships sail to the even more remote Aleutian Islands and up into the Bering Sea.

People sail to Alaska for every imaginable reason—food, romance, and scenery are just a few. So, how do you pick the ship that's right for you?

First of all, there are the big ships (1,000 to 2,000 passengers), which are more like floating hotels, sporting a different view each day, dominated by **Holland-America** and **Princess Cruise Lines**. The ships of both these companies are of similar size and itineraries, except the Holland-America ships still look—at least a little bit—as if they are actually real ships. Costs vary widely. If you're willing to take an inside cabin below decks, you can travel in the shoulder seasons (May and September) for less than it might cost you to travel overland and pay for a hotel every night. And that includes your meals. Your local travel agent will be the most helpful in securing the best deal for you.

Be aware that all shore excursions cost extra and often are very expensive. We highly recommend two kinds. Most of the towns you will disembark in are easily walkable, so, if you can walk at all, walk; don't take the bus tours. Save your money and spend it on a flight-seeing trip or on a marine cruise in a small boat going out to see whales, sea otters, and other marine life. The first will allow you to marvel at how vast

the lifeblood of these ocean peoples, swimming in a silver stream overhead through an architectural web of massive wooden beams. Like salmon swimming upstream, exhibits wind up the stairs and through various galleries and include "Native Traditions" and a re-creation of a temperate rain forest. There's a library, a trip-planning room, and a place to make reservations for public-use cabins. Admission fee is $4 per person or $12 per family; located at the southern end of the cruise ship dock. Open every day, May to September; and Tuesday through Saturday, October to April. For more information about Ketchikan, contact the **KETCHIKAN VISITORS BUREAU** (131 Front St; 907/225-6166 or 800/770-3300; kvb@ktn.net; www.visit-ketchikan.com).

this country is from the air—it's a whole different perspective. The second is so you can see some of the marine creatures up close. Many passengers on the big ships are disappointed to discover that whales do not constantly breach alongside, slapping their tails and frolicking in the sunshine. These ships, let us emphasize again, are *really big*, and if you see a whale, it's usually fairly far away or looks that way from your height on deck—about 10 stories up.

If you really want to see Alaska—to tuck into little bays and remote beaches where the big ships don't go, hang out and watch whales bubble feed instead of having to press forward on a set itinerary—then you need to think small. The small ships tend to be more expensive, more casual, and without a Broadway musical dancing through the dining room every evening. But you will see, hear, and feel more of the real Alaska. Some have teams of naturalists, lecturers, and specialists who take you by Zodiac into remote bays with unusual itineraries that allow you to jump on for various segments from British Columbia to the Bering Sea. **Lindblad Special Expeditions** (800/397-3348) mixes visits to small Southeast towns and expeditions by Zodiac into wilderness areas aboard the *Sea Bird* and the *Sea Lion*. They carry 70 passengers each. **Alaska Sightseeing Cruise West's** (800/770-1305) *Spirit* boats (50 to 75 passengers) sail through Prince William Sound and ports-of-call in Southeast Alaska. They also offer "daylight yacht cruises" where you cruise aboard the *Sheltered Seas* in Southeast and spend the night on shore in one of the small Alaska towns. **Clipper Cruise Lines** (www.clippercruise.com), with its 138-passenger *Yorktown Clipper*, also cruises the waters of Southeast Alaska with an itinerary including Tracy Arm, Glacier Bay, Elfin Cove, Petersburg, and Sitka.

However you choose to cruise to Alaska, images of grandeur—ice, mountains, glaciers, whales, brilliant red sunsets near midnight—are bound to linger a long time in your memory.

—Nan Elliot

Remember: Ketchikan is on an island (55 miles long and 35 miles wide) called **REVILLAGIGEDO ISLAND** (pronounced ruh-villa-hey-hey-do, or "Revilla" for short). It was named by Spanish explorers for the viceroy of Mexico in the 1800s. The island is also nicknamed "The Rock" as it has very little topsoil (only 2 inches to 8 feet deep) and is nearly all stone.

The **AIRPORT** is on another island called Gravina. There are no bridges or roads to Ketchikan from the airport, or from anywhere else, for that matter. The only way to get from Ketchikan to the airport—outside of hiring a helicopter or swimming—is by boat. The privately run Airporter to downtown is pricey (about $15), but convenient. A little public **FERRY** runs every 15 minutes or so in the summer and will take you and your rental car to the island. The trip across the water is only about 5 minutes, but allow an extra half-hour and some extra cash, as there's a toll for each person and vehicle. If you're on foot, you can pay the ferry toll ($2.50) and hop on the city bus for $1. In summer, the city bus runs about twice an hour.

EXPLORING

CREEK STREET / Creek Street is not really a "street" at all. When a revitalization of the area began in the early 1970s, it was, by some, discreetly billed (perhaps for funding purposes) as "Ketchikan's Historic District." But in 1925, its notoriety stretched all the way to the nation's capital, where Judge James Wickersham had another way of describing it: "The Barbary Coast of the North" or "Alaska's Tenderloin." This was, quite simply put, the red-light district of Ketchikan. Built on pilings, the former houses of the "Ladies of the Line" are linked by boardwalks over the rushing waters of the creek as it spills out into the ocean. In its heyday, Creek Street was called "the only place in the world where both fish and fishermen went up the creek to spawn." Today you can visit Dolly's House, a former bordello that has been turned into a museum. Most of the remaining houses are now little shops. Be sure and stop in at the old Star Building, Number 5 Creek Street, which houses **PARNASSUS** (907/225-7690), an eclectic little bookstore, and **SOHO COHO** (907/ 225-5954), the studio and shop of Ketchikan's infamous fish artist Ray Troll. Here you can buy local wearable art with humor from the deep, such as T-shirts emblazoned with "Ain't No Nookie Like Chinookie," "Salmon Enchanted Evening," and "Spawn 'Til You Die."

MARRIED MAN'S TRAIL / There are several ways to get to Creek Street. For the sake of history, particularly if you are of the male persuasion, take the "Married Man's Trail" to the right of the bridge over Ketchikan Creek on Park Avenue. In the old days, when a man wanted to visit one of the ladies on Creek Street but didn't want to be seen (for obvious reasons), he took this trail through the woods and approached the houses on Creek Street from the forest side rather than from the more public waterfront side. The trail in those days was just a muddy path through the forest, so even though he was trying to sneak into the bordellos incognito, the girls could tell which of the fellows waiting in the parlor were married by the mud on their trouser legs. This trail will take you right down to Creek Street, or if you veer off to the left you can walk up to the Cape Fox Hotel and take the short tram ride down to Creek Street.

DOLLY'S HOUSE: A LITTLE PLACE OF BUSINESS / The pale green house with the red trim, Number 24 Creek Street belonged to "Big Dolly" Arthur, Ketchikan's most famous madam. "I realized I could make a lot more money from the attentions of men than I could waiting tables," said Dolly, who plied her trade here for more than 30 years earlier this century. The government closed down the bawdy houses on Creek Street in 1953, but Dolly lived on there until shortly before her death in 1975. The house is now a museum. Be sure to read the old "Employment Application" posted in the window. How many job interviews have you been to where they asked you: "Are you currently in love?" "What is your unmentionable size?" and, when inquiring about the kind of men the gal preferred, "How small is OK? Tiny?" Open every day in summer; closed winter (October through April), when, as the sign on the door says, "Dolly is at the Policeman's Ball." For information, call 907/225-6329.

SAXMAN TOTEM PARK / Saxman is a Tlingit village 3 miles south of downtown Ketchikan on the South Tongass Highway. In the center of the village is the clan house and a very grand avenue of **TOTEM POLES** leading up the hill to the park. They say the totem poles here, which were moved from Pennock, Tongass, and Village Islands and from old Cape Fox Village at Kirk Point, represent the world's largest collection. The U.S. Forest Service directed a restoration project of the old totems beginning in 1939. Cape Fox Tours (907/225-4846; cftours@ktn.net) will take you on a 2-hour guided tour of the poles, the artists' carving shed, and the Beaver Clan House, where they will entertain you with songs and dances.

TOTEM BIGHT STATE HISTORICAL PARK / Ten miles north of town, Totem Bight is a lovely spot with a clan house and totem poles facing out to the sea. It is not an original village site, but rather a re-creation of one in a beautiful natural setting. A short walk through the forest with the smell of cedar and sea breezes brings you to the steps of the **RAVEN TRIBAL HOUSE**. Totem poles, carved from soft and durable cedar, were never meant to last forever. Their lifespan after being exposed to the wet and windy elements of Southeast weather is about 60 years. When people, for whatever reasons, left their villages, and moved to another, the poles were left to topple and rot. Totem Bight State Historical Park was founded in the 1930s, as part of a major restoration effort by the federal government to save, collect, and preserve some of these old poles. Tours are self-guided. The park is open year-round. For more information, call the Southeast Regional Office of the State Division of Parks in Juneau (907/465-4563).

ADVENTURES

WALKING TOUR / Towns in Southeast are not very big and are best explored on foot. "Streets" are often staircases up the hillsides, trails through the woods, or boardwalks over creeks and sloughs. Walking gives you a feel for the color, flavor, and people. Plus, if you're into flowers,

Alaska gardens are a knockout, and peering over the fence into someone's garden is free. (You might get lucky and be invited to a barbecue.) Don't be intimidated by the weather or you'll never get going. If you start your tour on the dock, there is a giant barometer there called the "LIQUID SUNSHINE GAUGE," which burst in 1949, they say, after nearly 18 feet of rain. Pick up a free copy of the "Ketchikan Walking Tour Map" from the visitor center, and begin at the CRUISE SHIP DOCK, a fun place to watch ships and boats. A walk from the dock up to the FRONT STREET OVERLOOK will get your heart pumping and give you a great bird's-eye view of TONGASS NARROWS. At the north end of Front Street, the street turns into stairs—about 130 of them. Go up, then stroll down to the end of the boardwalk. In order to build roadways along some of these steep mountainsides in the early days, residents used a braced framework of timbers called a trestle. The GRANT STREET TRESTLE is the only one still in existence in Ketchikan. Walk along KETCHIKAN CREEK to the sweet little CITY PARK, which has ponds and big trees. The creek is the heart of Ketchikan. Without this creek, there would be no town. Historically, its waters and creeksides have drawn in fish, fishermen, and flamboyant women. As you head down Bawden Street and turn left along Park Avenue, you'll cross a bridge over the creek. In the right season, you can often see salmon jumping up the falls or taking the easier route up the fish ladder to the left of the falls. On the right-hand side, after the bridge, you'll see a green street sign announcing the formerly covert "MARRIED MAN'S TRAIL," which is one way to return through the woods to CREEK STREET (more about these two locales, above). DEER MOUNTAIN TRIBAL HATCHERY (907/225-6760) was built in 1954 to help rehabilitate the severely depleted runs of chinook and coho salmon. Hatcheries are designed not to replace Mother Nature, but rather to enhance her efforts. About 300,000 salmon smolts are released every year into the wild. Only 2 percent will survive the hazards at sea to return here as adults after their journey through the ocean. The TOTEM HERITAGE CENTER (601 Deermount St; 907/225-5900) houses an extraordinary collection of old totem poles. They were carved by the Tlingit and Haida people who lived in villages around Ketchikan. (There is a short guided tour. Open daily in summer, and Tues–Fri in winter.) After a visit to Creek Street, en route back to the docks, stop in at the KETCHIKAN PUBIC LIBRARY, across the creek from Creek Street. The windows offer stunning views of the tumbling rapids of the creek.

FISHING CHARTERS / Dozens of charter-fishing operators take customers out of Ketchikan for half-day or daylong excursions. This is some of the best fishing in all of Southeast Alaska. Check the visitor center for a list of charter-fishing businesses. You'll need to buy a fishing license, but they'll direct you to the closest place in town for that. The most popular saltwater and freshwater fish available in the Ketchikan area are king (chinook) salmon, silver (coho) salmon, pink (humpback) salmon, red (sockeye) salmon, chum (dog) salmon, rockfish, halibut, Dolly Varden, cutthroat trout, rainbow trout, grayling, and steelhead trout. Fishing for Dolly Varden and trout starts in April. April and May are excellent for steelhead. You can fish throughout the summer for lingcod, rockfish, red snapper, and halibut. King salmon season is mid-May through early July, followed by runs of sockeye, coho, chums, and pinks well into August.

DEER MOUNTAIN HIKE / On a clear day, Deer Mountain dominates the skyline behind the city of Ketchikan. At 3,001 feet tall, it is also known as "Ketchikan's barometer." As the old saying around town goes, "If you can't see the top of Deer Mountain, it's raining. And if you can see the top of Deer Mountain, it's about to rain." Rain or shine, this is a popular hike. It gets you quickly into the rain forest experience. Listen particularly for the call of ravens. Ravens and eagles are plentiful. The first overlook can be reached in about 50 minutes at a steady pace. It is only a small break in the forest, but on a clear day it's a nice aerobic workout rewarded with a spectacular view of the ocean and islands below, leading to Dixon Entrance. You come out above tree line in another mile for even more spectacular views. Then it's on up to the top. The trailhead is a 30-minute walk from the cruise ship dock, or you can take a taxi to it.

TOURING THE ROADS BY CAR / Ketchikan has 36 miles of road, extending 13 miles to the south of downtown and 23 miles to the north— a mere drop in the bucket for those of you used to driving freeways back home. On a beautiful day, be Buddhist: take it slowly, and you will find a lovely view around each corner as you hug the edge of the sea. Within minutes, you'll even feel worlds apart from downtown Ketchikan. On the **SOUTH TONGASS HIGHWAY**, which is the road heading south from downtown, you can visit totem poles and a Tlingit cultural center, wet a fishing line, catch a salmon, barbecue it while sitting at the ocean's edge watching whales, and at the end of the road hike a trail into the mountains. If you travel north on the **NORTH TONGASS HIGHWAY**, traffic is busier. Totem Bight State Historical Park, at Mile 10, is a must (see above). Plan the day so you end up at **SALMON FALLS RESORT** for dinner near the end of the road.

TOURING TOWN IN AN OLD, OLD CAR / "Classic Tours in a Classic Car with a Classy Lady" is the billing for this fun, funny, informative, and personal tour in an old '55 Chevy with Lois Munch in her poodle skirt and oxfords regaling you with history and stories and legends of Ketchikan. She can squeeze in one to five passengers. Custom tours also may be arranged so you can feel just a little bit superior to all the big tour buses you pass. Call her at 907/225-3091.

TOURING BY BIKE / If you have only a few hours, rent a bike and head south toward Saxman Totem Park (see above). The South Tongass Highway is more peaceful than the road to the north, except for the tour buses going to Saxman. The road runs right along the edge of the water. If you want to avoid the buses, go in the late afternoon or evening. Bikes are available by the hour, half day, or full day from Southeast Exposure (907/225-8829).

PADDLING/MOUNTAIN BIKING / Take a guided 4- to 8-day trip into **MISTY FJORDS NATIONAL MONUMENT** or rent a kayak from Southeast Exposure (907/225-8829) for your own adventures. Before you head out, they give you a lesson in staying safe on the water. They also offer 3-hour guided mountain bike trips through the Tongass National Forest on old dirt logging roads. Located at 515 Water St.

FOREST SERVICE CABINS / The Ketchikan Area of the Tongass National Forest offers a diversity of recreational cabins available for rent. Some cabins you can hike or paddle to; some are great for fishing or have hot springs nearby; others land you in exquisite pristine wilderness. There are about 50 cabins near Ketchikan, in Misty Fjords National Monument, on Prince of Wales Island, and dotted around nearby islands. The rent is only $25 to $40 per night—one of the best deals in Alaska. However, be aware that the cost of getting to some of them could nick you up for to $1,000 for a round-trip charter flight to drop off you and your gear and pick you up again. For information and brochure on all the different cabins, go to the trip-planning room of the Southeast Alaska Visitor Center (50 Main St; 907/228-6214). For reservations, contact the national reservation system (877/444-6777; www.reserveusa.com).

FESTIVALS AND EVENTS

KING SALMON DERBY / This is the queen, or shall we say king, of salmon derbies in Southeast Alaska, held the last weekend of May and the first three weekends of June. In 1999, the winning salmon weighed in at 64.5 pounds, for a grand prize of $10,000 and 52 cents, since it was the 52nd annual contest. For more information, call the Ketchikan Chamber of Commerce (907/225-3184).

BLUEBERRY ARTS FESTIVAL / Every August, just about the time those huge Southeast blueberries get ripe, there's a hugely popular local celebration in their honor. There's a dance festival, four-poster bed races, and pie-eating contest. Kids bring slimy steeds for the annual slug race, and lots of talented artists display their creations with prizes for the best-designed booth and best costume. "Of course, if you dress up like a blueberry," said one local, "you'll probably win." For more information, contact the Ketchikan Arts & Humanities Council (907/ 225-2211; www.ketchikanarts.org).

FISH PIRATE'S DAUGHTER / Every Friday night in July and August, Ketchikan's First City Players put on this musical melodrama (sometimes called *Perfect Sweet William*) about the town's boisterous early days of bootlegging and prostitution on Creek Street. A spoof on the manners and mores of Ketchikan in 1932, the melodrama features such characters as Sweet William Uprightly, the fish commissioner, and Violette LaRosa, the Creek Street madam with a heart of gold. A whole lot of booing and hissing and oohs and ahhs go on and everyone has a great time. The performances are mobile—sometimes performed on the barroom floor of a local saloon. In recent years, they've even thrown in funny "gender-bender" performances at the end of the summer. The nonprofit theater group also gives other performances throughout the year. For further information, call their office at Main Street Theatre (338 Main St; 907/225-4792).

RESTAURANTS

Annabelle's Famous Keg and Chowder House / ★★

326 FRONT ST, KETCHIKAN; 907/225-6009

At this favorite of both locals and tourists, you can eat in the Bar, the casual side, or in the Parlor, the more elegant side of the restaurant, featuring "New York style dining circa 1927." With its floral-patterned carpet, heavy, dark-wood decor, and white tablecloths, the Parlor is reminiscent of those old 1920s mobster movies where the guys in pinstriped suits are drinking champagne, talking in low tones, and, as our mothers would say, "up to no good." Seafood, pasta, salads, sandwiches, and creamy thick pies are all favorites here. For dinner on the spicier side of life, try Tequila Prawns with Firecracker Rice or the rich and creamy tortellini with crab and Gorgonzola cheese or Annabelle's Brandy Peppercorn Filet. For dessert, the peanut butter pie is as good as its reputation. *$$$; AE, DC, DIS, MC, V; local checks only; breakfast, lunch, dinner every day in summer; lunch, dinner every day in winter; full bar; in the Gilmore Hotel.* &

The Edge

#5 SALMON LANDING MARKET, #116, KETCHIKAN; 907/225-1465

If you need a jolt of java before you head up Deer Mountain or whenever your spirits are flagging from running up all those stairs (also called "streets" here) or if you just want to sit inside with a peaceful water view out the window, head for the very end of the cruise ship dock. Where else will you find a cup of Ketchikan's favorite local espresso, Raven's Brew, but . . . on the edge? You can drink Czar's Blend ("fit for royalty") or their most popular, Deadman's Reach ("served in bed, raises the dead"). This is mainly a coffee place, although proprietor Joe Nichols does offer a selection of locally made bagels, Danishes, cinnamon rolls, and cookies. *$; MC, V; local checks only; breakfast, lunch every day; closed Sun in winter; no alcohol; inside Salmon Landing Market at the corner edge.* &

Heen Kahidi Restaurant / ★★★

WESTMARK CAPE FOX LODGE; 800 VENETIA WAY, KETCHIKAN. 907/225-8001
The name means "tree house on the creek." Nestled into the green branches of spruce, cedar, and western hemlock trees, with lovely views out to the Tongass Narrows, you'll feel as if you're eating outdoors with all the comforts of indoors. This is where local folks go for a special night out or to celebrate anniversaries. The service is warm and friendly. The menu is varied enough for any discerning palate: Belgian waffles, cheese blintzes, Tori Teriyaki with Yakisoba (teriyaki chicken with Japanese noodles and vegetables tossed in an exotic sauce), fresh oysters, Alaska king crab legs, and their classic Halibut Olympia, all topped off with a delicious Mud Pie or Bumbleberry Pie. *$$$; AE, DC, DIS, MC, V; local checks only; breakfast, lunch, dinner every day; on a hill overlooking downtown.* &

Polar Treats

410 MISSION ST, KETCHIKAN; 907/247-6527
Reminiscent of a 1950s diner, this very white, linoleum-floored eatery with bar stools at the window and four tables has made a splash hit in Ketchikan since 1997. You almost expect a juke box in the corner and poodle skirts to swirl through the door. With such frigid wet weather up north, it only figures that Alaskans have the highest per capita consumption of ice cream in the country, *n'est-ce pas?* And Polar Treats is doing its heroic part to keep up the quotas by serving dozens of flavors of handmade gourmet ice cream—go for the mocha chip or blueberry cheesecake in a waffle cone. On their deli side they serve sandwiches, huge wraps (ranch chicken is extremely popular), and panini or grilled Italian sandwiches. *$; no credit cards; checks OK; extended lunch (10am–5pm) Mon–Sat; no alcohol; located downtown near the corner of Main and Mission Sts.* &

Salmon Falls Resort / ★★

16707 NORTH TONGASS HWY, KETCHIKAN; 800/247-9059 OR 907/225-2752
On a sunny summer evening, it's lovely to go here for the drive and the setting alone. Perched at the edge of woods overlooking the water, Salmon Falls Resort is really a fishing lodge, but many locals go out here just for dinner. At the north end of the road, the resort has a rustic charm,

with flower boxes and log cabins—just what you'd expect Alaska to look like. From the windows of its huge octagonal restaurant, you can see water in all directions—to the east, a spectacular roaring waterfall, and to the west, Clarence Strait. Not surprising, the fare here is fish and more fish. And they do a very nice job with it. You can have halibut, cod, prawns, scallops, salmon, and crab, as well as steak. The average entree runs about $24. If you want to come for a 3-day/3-night fishing package (boat, skipper, cabin, and meals included), it will run you a tad more than dinner (about $1,350 per person). *$$$; AE, MC, V; local checks only; open mid-May–mid-Sept; full bar; www.ktn.net/sfalls; PO Box 5700, Ketchikan, AK 99901; 17.7 miles out along the North Tongass Hwy.* &

Steamers at the Dock / ★

76 FRONT ST, KETCHIKAN; 907/225-1600

Located downtown, right on the cruise ship dock with a view of the water (or the promenade deck of the ships when they're in port), Steamers is one of the newest, fancy additions to Ketchikan, opened in 1997. Everybody loves the long wooden bar, which wraps around one whole side of the restaurant. The alcoholic choices are wonderfully extensive and exotic—you can get anything from Pig's Nose Scotch and Pimm's Cup to from-scratch margaritas and Irish whiskey milkshakes. It can be quite fun and festive, especially if you're meeting someone for a drink and musicians are jamming up front, which usually happens daily in summer. The place is a bit cavernous and, thus, noisy. Although they specialize in seafood, many of their dishes get a mixed review, so we'd recommend going for their namesake—steamer clams—and fresh oysters from Prince of Wales Island. *$$; AE, DC, DIS, MC, V; local checks only; lunch, dinner every day in summer; dinner every day in winter; full bar; downtown at the cruise ship dock, restaurant is on the third floor, take the outside elevator.* &

LODGINGS

Blueberry Hill Bed & Breakfast / ★★★

500 FRONT ST, KETCHIKAN, AK 99901; 907/247-2583,
FAX 907/247-2584

Built in 1917, this historic and lovely home on Front Street has seen its share of gaiety and fun, says its charming proprietor, Elsan Zimmerly, who—not surprisingly, when you see her home—is quite creative (in her "real life," she's a naturalist, photographer, and writer). Her belief is that a home is meant to be restful, comforting, and restoring. And that's just what she and her husband, Hank Newhouse, a fisheries biologist, have created for travelers from all over the world who have had the good fortune to find their way to this doorstep. The B&B is more akin to a traditional inn. The four rooms upstairs—the Blueberry Suite, and the Salmonberry, Huckleberry, and Thimbleberry Rooms—all with private baths, are very sweet, light, and welcoming with lovely artistic touches everywhere, from Japanese-style curtains to colorful quilts to oak beds with futon mattresses. Elsan is a devotee of healthy, gourmet food from around the world and serves up wonderful breakfasts of fruits, scones (her favorite is the yam scones), Swiss muesli, a German spinach kugel, and a variety of homemade breads. You get an extra boost to your heart by hiking up the 117 stairs from the docks below to historic Nob Hill. Rates are $95 to $105 for a double, lower for a single person. Very good rates negotiable for winter. No smoking or pets. $$; AE, MC, V; checks OK; blubrry@ptialaska.net; www.ptialaska.net/~blubrry; PO Box 9508, Ketchikan, AK 99901; downtown.

Captain's Quarters Bed and Breakfast / ★★

325 LUND ST, KETCHIKAN, AK 99901; 907/225-4912
Within walking distance of downtown, the Captain's Quarters is a cheerful, airy home away from home, with picture-postcard views of the water from the large windows in the upstairs rooms. Tastefully furnished with a fun nautical theme, this little B&B has three rooms with views of the Tongass Narrows and the ships, boats, and floatplanes along the busy waterfront. For the best views, request either one of the upstairs rooms. No smoking allowed. A single/double is $85 in summer and lower in winter. $$; MC, V; no checks; captbnb@ptialaska.net; www.ptialaska.net/~captbnb; near downtown (a long walk or a short drive)—call for directions.

Ketchikan Bed and Breakfast Reservation Service

412 D-1 LOOP RD, KETCHIKAN, AK 99901; 800/987-5337 OR 907/247-5337
In Alaska, bed-and-breakfasts (or B&Bs) are more often than not rooms in people's houses. If you are a people person and curious about the local folks, this is definitely the way to go. You'll get a more personal glimpse into Alaska lifestyles. Some are very basic; some are quite special. Wanda Vandergriff at the reservation service can help you make a good choice. Room rates run about $60 to $85 for a single and $75 to $95 for a double. krs@ktn.net; www.ktn.net/krs.

New York Hotel and Café / ★★

207 STEDMAN ST, KETCHIKAN, AK 99901; 907/225-0246
This small hotel has a charm and simplicity all its own. For the price, location, and sense of history, it's a great deal. More like a traditional B&B or small inn, it has personalized service and is located right downtown, across from the small boat harbor at Thomas Basin. (In the old days, there was a baseball diamond on the tidal flats there. Action was often interrupted by the incoming tides. Undaunted, players used skiffs

to catch fly balls in the outfield.) The hotel once had 18 rooms with one bath available on Saturday nights only. Fred Ochsner took on the challenge of renovating and restoring it to historical authenticity in 1991. Now there are eight rooms, each with full bath (most have an old clawfoot bathtub), private phone, and television. As he says, "Come step into the past with all the amenities of modern-day living." The hotel is full most of the summer, so you'll need to call ahead for reservations. Singles are $69 per night and doubles are $79 per night (in summer), which includes a continental breakfast. Ask for the front rooms overlooking Thomas Basin. *$; AE, MC, V; local checks only; breakfast, lunch, dinner every day; no alcohol; downtown, 3 doors down from Dolly's.*

The Oakes House Bed and Breakfast / ★★

10409 POINT SUSAN RD, KETCHIKAN, AK 99901; 907/225-1705
This luxurious log home offers a more upscale experience. Opened in 1995, it is managed by owner Christine Oakes and her husband, Blair, both retired from the U.S. Navy. He was Ronald Reagan's personal guard. She was on the bomb squad—one of only seven women at the time to have that distinction. Now, they enjoy a different kind of ocean view with a sod-roofed sauna at water's edge. There are two guest rooms in their home, each with private entrance and bathroom. A "great room" stands between them with a big stone fireplace. Behind the house is a cottage with a loft, and while it has no direct view of the ocean, a path leads directly to the beach. Christine recommends guests make their reservations in summer at least 30 days in advance and rent a car. Guest rooms are $75 per night in summer, $55 per night off-season. The cottage rents for $110 per night in summer and $70 per night off-season. *$–$$; DC, DIS, MC, V; local checks only; oakes@ktn.net; 10 miles out of town.* &

Westmark Cape Fox Lodge / ★★★

800 VENETIA WY, KETCHIKAN, AK 99901; 800/544-0970, RESERVATIONS, OR 907/225-8001
This is one of the best hotels in all of Southeast Alaska—for its simplicity, warmth of interior, views, and peaceful charm. Sitting on the hill, it gazes down on the town of Ketchikan, the harbor, the islands, the floatplanes, and the boats sailing up and down the Tongass Narrows. Up above the treetops, where the eagles dip and soar, the hotel escapes most of the noise and huggermugger of Ketchikan's busy port, but you still have the fun of watching all the action (and, early in the morning, of hearing the fleet of planes roaring over the harbor to take cruise ship tourists to Misty Fjords). Out back, there are views into the forest and up Deer Mountain. Whatever your preference, trees or water, all the rooms are spacious, with warm pinewood furniture and wood accents. (The rooms that were looking a little ragged around the edges were scheduled for

renovations in winter '99-00.) Designed as a ski lodge, the hotel lobby is lovely and welcoming with its lofty views and stone fireplace. Blended into this theme are exquisite Southeast cultural motifs, from the totem poles in the front garden to a stunning carved screen on the second-floor landing by the distinguished Tlingit carver Nathan Jackson. *$$$; AE, DC, DIS, MC, V; local checks only; breakfast, lunch, dinner every day; on the hill, overlooking downtown Ketchikan. No courtesy van, so take a taxi from the airport or ferry terminal; if you're downtown, you can ride the tram up from Creek St.* ⅄ *(2 rooms)*

WILDERNESS LODGES

Alaska's Inside Passage Resorts

1170 COAST VILLAGE RD, STE 211, SANTA BARBARA, CA 93108-2717; 800/350-3474 OR 805/969-8780

This is a consortium of fishing resorts and companies offering luxury sailing adventures in the southern part of Southeast Alaska. Represented in the group are Yes Bay Lodge, Waterfall Resort, and Boardwalk Wilderness Lodge on Prince of Wales Island. They also offer cruising on a 70-foot yacht called the *Midnight Sun*, which can be chartered for up to six passengers at a weekly rate. Your itinerary is custom designed, running from Ketchikan to Juneau. The weekly rate for the yacht is $23,800. The fishing/yachting season begins in April or May and runs through mid-September. Call for more information, a promotional video, and reservations. For those who want to go yachting but at a more bargain price, there are Alaska Yacht Safaris, where you charter your cabin rather than the whole yacht and sail with a maximum of 21 other guests. The cost per person for 7 nights/8 days is $2,950. *No credit cards; checks OK; www.aipr.com.*

Salmon Falls Resort

16707 NORTH TONGASS HWY, KETCHIKAN, AK 99901; 800/247-9059 OR 907/225-2752

At the northern end of the road from Ketchikan, Salmon Falls Resort sits in a lovely spot on the edge of Behm Canal, with a spectacular waterfall cascading down the mountain behind it. It is the definition of rustic elegance. While it is expensive, it is not nearly as pricey as other fishing resorts listed here. Cost for 3 days/3 nights is $1,350 per person. *AE, MC, V; local checks only; open mid-May–mid-Sept; full bar; www.ktn. net/sfals; PO Box 5700, Ketchikan, AK 99901; 17.7 miles out the North Tongass Hwy.* ⅄

CRUISE THE INSIDE PASSAGE IN "THE BIG BLUE CANOES"

"The big blue canoes" is the nickname for the blue-hulled Alaska state ferries. Since you cannot drive to most towns or villages in Southeast, everyone travels by plane or boat. The water is the road. That's why the ferries are formally called the **Alaska Marine Highway System**. They're fun, colorful, local, and a cheap way to get out on the water to see fjords, whales, and fishing boats, and to catch up on the regional gossip—a cruise ship experience at bargain rates. Even the visiting circus travels by ferry, including the elephants. You can visit some of Alaska's major ports or tiny picturesque fishing hamlets and hot springs. (See also the section on Icy Strait.) For a recorded schedule, call 907/465-3940, and for reservations contact Alaska Marine Highway (1591 Glacier Ave, Juneau, AK 99801-1427; 800/642-0066, fax 907/277-4829; www.akferry.com).

—Nan Elliot

Waterfall Resort Alaska

PO BOX 6440, KETCHIKAN, AK 99901; 800/544-5125 OR 907/225-9461

If price is no object, then go where the Fortune 500 go and head to the west coast of Prince of Wales Island, about 63 air miles from Ketchikan. This resort is for serious fishermen, the kind who wouldn't look up even if a humpback whale did a backflip right in front of them. It also caters to squeamish fishermen: if you choose, you are so coddled that you need not handle your fish more than a nanosecond (for the photograph) before it is whisked away, filleted, boxed, and frozen for your departure. The humor of this now-luxurious resort, which caters to your every saltwater desire, is that you get to sleep where the cannery workers once slept. Built in 1912, Waterfall is actually an old salmon-packing house that operated for six decades. It reopened in 1981 (following renovation) for a fancier crowd. Accommodations serve 84 guests at a time with a 1:1 ratio of staff to guests. In 1912, cannery workers earned a pittance a day; you will pay considerably more than that for the privilege of staying here. The cost for 3 nights/4 days is about $2,960 per person; 5 nights/6 days is $4,150 (not including gratuities, spirits, or fishing licenses). Season runs from mid-May to early September. There is an early season rate of $1,862 per person for 3 nights/4 days from May 21 through May 31. *No credit cards; no checks; www.waterfallresort.com.*

Yes Bay Lodge

PO BOX 8660, KETCHIKAN, AK 99901; 800/999-0784 OR 907/225-7906, FAX 907/247-3875

Of the small, secluded wilderness lodges specializing primarily in fresh and saltwater fishing, Yes Bay Lodge is considered la crème de la crème when it comes to savoring the finest and most intimate of Alaska fishing and wilderness experiences. Yes Bay is casual elegance, only a 20-minute flight from Ketchikan. Its main attraction is that there are only 24 guests at a time, perfect for families (children 6 or older are welcome) or corporate getaways. Guests fish two to a boat with a guide and plan their own itinerary daily. (Catch-and-release is encouraged.) Prices run $2,500 per person for 4 nights/3 days. It's definitely a family operation, as some of the family live in Ketchikan in winter, but some live out at the lodge year-round. *No credit cards; checks OK; open late May–Sept; info@ yesbay.com; www.yesbay.com.*

Misty Fjords National Monument

Twenty-two miles west of Ketchikan by air, Misty Fjords National Monument is a lovely jewel set within the Tongass National Forest. In 1978, by presidential decree, it achieved fully protected wilderness status, although it is located within multiple-use national forest land. Carved out by glaciers during the last great period of the ice age more than 10,000 years ago, Misty Fjords is, as its name suggests, a series of deep-water fjords left by receding glaciers, tall granite cliffs, and almost perpetual swirling mist.

In **PUNCHBOWL COVE**, one of the more popular destinations, sheer granite walls rise to a height of more than 3,000 feet. Some have called it the Yosemite of the North. Special to the awe-inspiring beauty of Misty Fjords is its stillness and peace. With more and more visitors coming each year, particularly for quick visits via floatplane, this aspect may change radically—although for the benefit of all of us, let us hope not. There are many ways you can explore the monument—by plane, boat, kayak, and foot.

SOUTHEAST EXPOSURE (907/225-8829; www.southeastexposure.com) offers guided kayak trips to Misty Fjords for 4 to 6 days, ranging from $700 to $950 per person from May to September 15. **ALASKA CRUISES** (907/225-6044) offers day trips to Misty Fjords with several options such as flying one way and cruising back. **TAQUAN AIR** (800/770-8800 or 907/225-8800) offers a variety of tours, from flightseeing over Misty Fjords and LeConte Glacier to drop-offs for wilderness sportfishing, camping, or kayaking trips. Highly respected for its safety record and local pilot knowledge, Taquan has been in operation for 18 years. For information on trails and public-use cabins, write **U.S. FOREST SERVICE, KETCHIKAN RANGER STATION** (3031 Tongass Ave, Ketchikan, AK 99901) or consult the folks who staff the trip-planning room at the Southeast Alaska Visitor Center (50 Main St, Ketchikan; 907/228-6214) near the cruise ship dock.

Please note: this is a wilderness area. There are **NO VISITOR FACIL-ITIES**. You must bring with you everything you will need, from maps, nautical charts, and compass to food, tents, warm clothing, and plenty of rain gear. Consult local knowledge on weather, water, boats, safety, itinerary, and necessary skills.

Sitka

To fully appreciate this lovely town on the western edge of Baranof Island, it is important to know something of its rich history. When Chicago was merely a fort town in the middle of the prairies and San Francisco a small mission, Sitka was hailed as the "Paris of the West." Ships docked here from all over the world. Today only 8,500 people live in Sitka year-round. But that is a large part of her charm.

For many years, Sitka was the capital of Russian America. In the center of town, dominating the low skyline, is the onion-shaped dome of the old wooden church known as St. Michael's Cathedral. As the ironies of history often unfold, the fortunes and legacy of an empire here rose and fell on a funny, bewhiskered fellow—the sea otter.

Alaska was once a treasure chest of sea otters. To the Russian hunters, this creature's fur was known as "soft gold," and the pelts brought high prices in the courts of China. But as the sea otters began to disappear, hunted to near extinction, Russia's interest in her far-flung colony began to wane. In 1867, the advice given the czar was "Sell! Sell the colony before someone takes it by force." So after 126 years of rule in this wilderness outpost, Russia sold her colony to the Americans under a storm of controversy here at home. There were many who thought Russia had sold us "a sucked Orange," a land of icebergs and polar bears, a wasteland of no consequence. But history has proven much the contrary. The purchase price of Alaska—$7.2 million—has been recouped many times over—in furs, fish, timber, gold, oil, and, today, tourism.

Sitka was home to the Tlingits before the Russians, however, and today it is the blending and preservation of the history of both cultures that gives the town its unique flavor. Sitka's economy is now founded primarily on fishing and tourism. It has a beautiful setting, with sparkling waters, emerald islands, rocky beaches, and a safe harbor for ships. Even though thousands of tourists from the cruise ships land on her shores every week in the summer, Sitka manages to maintain her individual character and charm.

ACCESS AND INFORMATION

Sitka lies on the west side of Baranof Island. As with most Southeast towns, there are no roads to Sitka. Access is **BY AIR** or sea. Alaska Airlines (800/426-0333) has scheduled flights daily going both north and south, summer and winter. The **ALASKA MARINE HIGHWAY** (800/642-0066 or 907/747-8737) has ferry service to Sitka throughout the year from ports in Alaska, Canada, and Washington. (It takes about 3 days of cruising to reach Sitka from Bellingham, Washington, 88 miles north of Seattle, and about 18 hours from Prince Rupert in Canada.) The ferry terminal is located north of town, near the end of the road. From downtown Sitka, the road extends about 7 miles in either direction. Rental cars are available at the airport. The airport is only 5 minutes or so from downtown Sitka, and there is a limousine service that runs year-round ($5 round-trip). Experienced **AIR CHARTERS** are Taquan Air (800/770-8800 or 907/225-8800) and Mountain Aviation (907/966-2288).

Stop first at the **CENTENNIAL BUILDING VISITORS INFORMATION** (330 Harbor Dr; 907/747-3225). It is located in the heart of downtown, inside the Centennial Building at the edge of the harbor. For more information, contact the **SITKA CONVENTION AND VISITORS BUREAU** (303 Lincoln St, PO Box 1226, Sitka, AK 99835; 907/747-5940; www.sitka.org). **OLD HARBOR BOOKSTORE** (201 Lincoln St, Sitka, AK 99835; 907/747-8808) has a wonderful array of books on Sitka, Southeast, and Alaska, and also sells nautical charts. You'll be greeted at the front door with its now infamous permanent handwritten sign: "Please Do Not Drip On Our Books," which gives you an inkling of just how much rain Sitka gets.

SITKA RANGER DISTRICT (TONGASS NATIONAL FOREST) (201 Katlian St, Sitka, AK 99835; 907/747-4220; sitka.rd/r10_chatham@fs.fed.us) has information and a brochure about public-use recreational **CABINS** on beaches, mountain lakes, and remote islands in the national forest. Cost for cabin rentals is $25 to $40 per night—the best deal going in all of Alaska. For cabin reservations, call the national reservation line (877/444-6777). The **ALASKA DEPARTMENT OF FISH AND GAME** (304 Lake St, Rm 103, Sitka, AK 99835; 907/747-6688) is a good source of information on fishing and hunting in the area, regulations, seasons, and licenses.

EXPLORING

SITKA NATIONAL HISTORICAL PARK / Do not miss this gem of a national park. A **MUSEUM** houses beautifully displayed cultural treasures, but the real treasure is found along the 2-mile trail through the **TOTEM POLE PARK**, which weaves through the forest and along the beach. The carved cedar totem poles blend so well into the woods that the faces of frogs, ravens, whales, and other creatures appearing out of the mist seem almost magical. The **VISITOR CENTER** is also home to master artists from Southeast Indian clans. You can watch them working—

making mountain goat wool, spruce tree roots, abalone shells, and cedar bark into masks, ceremonial regalia, robes, jewelry, and other traditional artworks. The park and visitor center are open year-round and are located at the end of town, about a 10-minute walk from the cruise ship dock.

One of the few surviving examples of Russian colonial architecture in North America, **THE RUSSIAN BISHOP'S HOUSE** is also part of Sitka National Historical Park. It stands near the heart of downtown on Lincoln Street. Built in the 1840s by Finnish shipwrights, the house was elaborately restored in the 1980s at a cost of $5 million, all from private donations. The first resident of the house was Ivan Veniaminov, known as Bishop Innocent, and later canonized as St. Innocent. The bishop was an impressive man. Wherever he was, he learned the local dialects, paddled hundreds of miles by kayak to the farthest islands of his parish, and built chapels; later he built St. Michael's Cathedral. Note the clock he invented and built, which keeps accurate time with the dripping of water. From May to October, the Bishop's House is open daily; in winter, it is open by appointment. For more information, contact Sitka National Historical Park (106 Metlakatla St, Sitka, AK 99835; 907/747-6281; www.nps.gov/sitk).

SHELDON JACKSON MUSEUM / On the campus at Sheldon Jackson College, 5 minutes from Sitka National Historical Park, the Sheldon Jackson Museum is an octagonal treasure box crammed full of beautiful Native tools, art, boats, and clothing, the artistry of which you may not anywhere else in Alaska. The college and museum are named for the 5-foot-tall, feisty Presbyterian missionary Sheldon Jackson, who came to Alaska in 1877. He lobbied vigorously in Congress for funds to educate Native peoples; he was responsible for the "school ma'am schooner," which transported teachers into rural Alaska; and he helped import the first reindeer herds to what was then the Territory of Alaska to fend off widespread starvation in the villages. Many of the treasures in this museum come from his early journeys to Native villages. Open every day; 907/747-6233.

ALASKA RAPTOR REHABILITATION CENTER / Volta collided with a powerline. Contact hit an airplane. Elder got trapped in barbed wire while trying to steal ducks. Beauty is from Kodiak and Midi can't fly. While these five unfortunates are all bald eagles, many other raptors live here. "Help Us Help the Birds!" is the slogan used by the center, which receives no state or federal funding. Your contributions support the work here and help these "patients" return to the wild. About 80 percent of the injuries these birds have suffered are human-caused by such things as bullets, traps, oil slicks, and the like. Presentations and tours at the center usually coincide with cruise ship schedules. The center is located off

Sawmill Creek Road, a 10-minute walk from the historical park. Cost is $10 for adults; $5 for children. For more information, call 907/747-8662.

BALD EAGLE SIGHTINGS / OK, get ready. We're about to—gasp!— give **MCDONALD'S** "Golden Arches" its first four-star rating ever (at least in this guidebook series). It's not, however, for its Big Mac, but for its parking lot, which is the best place in town to see wild bald eagles. The tree and beach at low tide are often jammed with 30 or more eagles. Head north from town (about 1.5 miles) on Halibut Point Road. This area is also great for sunsets.

THE CLAN HOUSE: SHEET'KA KWAAN NAA KAHIDI / The name means "House for the People of Sitka." Owned by the Sitka Tribe of Alaska, the Clan House hosts dance and storytelling performances throughout the summer. As one young Native guide explained, "This was a 20-year dream of the Tlingit people of Sitka. We celebrated the first anniversary of the Clan House completion in 1998 with sacred songs and dances to thank the tree spirits since we had taken a lot of wood for the building. We try to stay in balance with nature—bad things happen when one is not in balance with nature." The building is lovely, with an impressive entrance and totems and carvings. Designed in the style of the traditional long house, it features tiered seating inside around a fire pit and a house screen in the back. In 1879, clan houses would have lined Katlian Street. Here, you will hear history from the Tlingit point of view. For instance, Castle Hill was known as "Noow Tlein" and used to have a clan house sitting on top before the Russians came. Old Sitka was known as "Gaa Jaa Heen," the name of the river where salmon return. Located at 200 Katlian St; 907/747-3770.

TLINGIT DANCE PERFORMANCES / In a replication of the old-style Tlingit long house called Sheet'ka Kwaan Naa Kahidi Community House, there are stories and dance performances by the Tlingit people of Sitka twice daily in summer. Cost is $6 per person. Once a week they do combined Tlingit and Russian performances with the New Archangel Dancers (see below). The cost is $8 per person. 200 Katlian St; 907/747-7290.

RUSSIAN DANCE PERFORMANCES / More than 30 years ago, so the story goes, eight women in Sitka who loved to dance started a Russian folk dance troupe and tried to entice men in town to join. No way, said the men! Undaunted, the women formed the **NEW ARCHANGEL DANCERS**, taking the old Russian name for Sitka (and taking on the men's dance parts as well). In the ensuing years, they also took their show on the road, performing all over the world. Now men ask to audition. But the dance troupe still preserves its all-women status—entertaining tourists in the summer with such popular dances as the Cossack Horsemen's Dance and the Moldovian Suite. Choreographers from New York,

Russia, and the Ukraine come to teach the group new dances every year. Performances are in Centennial Hall and coincide with the cruise ship schedules, beginning in early May. Call 907/747-5516 for dance times.

CRIMES / Gotham City has nothing on Sitka. This is a town that thrives on the **"POLICE BLOTTER."** Printed five days a week in the *Sitka Sentinel*, the column is sometimes so quaint that the *Anchorage Daily News* reprints selections for its readers statewide. Consider these top-of-the-list, heinous crimes: "June 12—Two boys apprehended playing hackysack in the middle of Lincoln Street. They promised never to do it again." "June 21—Police were unable to locate the vehicle which drove over the traffic cones at Sheldon Jackson College. An officer put the cones back in their upright position."

SHOPPING / Named for the Sitka rosebush that blooms out front, the **SITKA ROSE GALLERY** (419 Lincoln St; 907/747-3030) is a lovely little gallery situated in a quaint Victorian house on Lincoln Street, across from the harbor. The little turreted building is 100 years old and a piece of art in itself. The gallery features sculpture, painting, and Native art, representing more than 80 artists around Alaska. The owners are Eugene Solovyov and his wife, Barbara Kendall, both delightful folks. Go in and chat and browse. **"THE ROSE BUD"** (120 Lincoln St) is the nickname of a smaller version of the gallery located 4 blocks west.

For the best chocolate in Southeast Alaska, stop in the **CHOCOLATE MOOSE** (907/747-5159) for a little taste of heaven. They have a variety of freshly made fudge, chocolate fish, specialty teas, and good espresso. Located near the Sitka Rose Gallery's western branch, "The Rose Bud," on Lincoln Street.

With its rich assortment of Russian and Alaskan handicrafts, the **RUSSIAN AMERICAN COMPANY** (407 Lincoln St; 907/747-6228) is upstairs at the MacDonald Bayview Trading Company in downtown Sitka. A tribute to one part of Sitka's heritage, it has some gorgeous and colorful things, from hand-painted lacquered boxes and religious icons to nesting dolls and Russian candy.

PIES / Hands down, the **NUGGET RESTAURANT** (907/966-2480) at the Sitka Airport has the best pies in town. They are famous all over Alaska. You often will see folks boarding planes with the telltale bakery boxes tucked under their arms for pie lovers back home. The pies are baked in town but sold only at the Nugget. Here's a sampling of the most popular, available in season: strawberry, banana-coconut, blackberry-rhubarb, chocolate "moose," and cherry crisp.

MILK SHAKES AND COFFEE / Step into the old bowling alley, **LANE 7 SNACK BAR** (331 Lincoln St; 907/747-6310), in the heart of downtown and belly up to the bar for the best milkshakes in town. The atmosphere isn't overly seductive, so take them outside by the harbor to sip while drinking in the view at the same time.

At **HIGHLINER COFFEE CO.** (907/747-4924) you can drink fresh-roasted espresso (they roast their own coffee here) and tuck into a selection of yummy treats, while you check your e-mail and send a few messages around the world. The baked goods are homemade and delicious. Try Norwegian krumkaka, Pumpkin Extreme Cake, or the popular "mookies," which are a cross between a muffin and a cookie with cranberries, oatmeal, and walnuts. A **CYBER CAFE** as well as an upscale coffeehouse, Highliner, through both its name and the photos on the walls, is a tribute to Sitka's fishing industry. Its high-energy owner, Melissa Thorsen-Broschat, is a fifth-generation Alaskan and former fisherwoman from Petersburg. 1 block north of the Shee Atika Hotel, next to the fire station, on Oja Loop Rd.

ADVENTURES

SITKA WALKING TOUR (GUIDED) / This is not a generic title, so don't get confused. Of all the guided tours in Sitka, this is the best. With her love of stories and nature, longtime resident Jane Eidler gives her walking tours a personable and humorous twist. She worked for both the National Park Service and the U.S. Forest Service in Alaska as a ranger/naturalist before settling in Sitka 20 years ago to raise her family. The tour is historical and anecdotal, which, to quote that time-honored newsman Paul Harvey, tells "the rest of the story." Rain or shine, she and her business partner, Lisa Busch, will give you the behind-the-scenes of Sitka and then point you in the right direction to explore the Sitka National Historical Park on your own. Tours start at the Centennial Building; times vary. For information, call Jane at 907/747-5354.

SITKA WALKING TOUR (SELF-GUIDED) / If you miss Jane's tour and are on your own, here are a few of the highlights of any walk around Sitka. First, look for the unmistakable onion-shaped dome spires of **ST. MICHAEL'S CATHEDRAL** in the center of town. The cathedral burned to the ground in a terrible fire in 1966. Bucket brigades saved precious icons, and 10 years later it was rebuilt to the original design. The **CENTENNIAL BUILDING**, at the edge of the water, offers some wonderful shows throughout the summer, including the Sitka Summer Music Festival and the all-women New Archangel Dancers, who celebrate the town's Russian past with folk dances from the old country. Next door is **THE LIBRARY**, haunt of bookworms and brides. With a beautiful view of Sitka Sound through its windows, the library is popular for weddings as well as an attractive place to read or do research. A 5-minute walk along Harbor Drive and up the stairs to **CASTLE HILL** offers a commanding view of the sea, mountains, and islands. This was the original village site for the Tlingit people before the arrival of the Russian invaders. Old Russian cannons punctuate the circular stone wall where once stood the governors' residence known as Baranov's Castle, named for the first governor of Russian America. Baranov himself never lived here. But many of the 13 Russian governors who followed him to Alaska did. On October 18, 1867, the flag of the czars was lowered and the Stars and Stripes raised. The **PIONEER HOME** was built to honor this northern land's early pioneers. The gardens are brilliant with colorful flowers and visitors are always welcome. The old-timers here have stories to tell. Up the hill is the **RUSSIAN BLOCKHOUSE**, built of logs, a replica of the blockhouse that was part of the fort and stockade dividing the Tlingit and Russian sections of Old Sitka. Surrounding it is the peaceful **RUSSIAN GRAVEYARD**. Look for the old stone Russian crosses. **GOVERNORS WALK** is the old name for the promenade along Sitka's main street (Lincoln Street) from Castle Hill along the waterfront to the woods by Indian River. This area is now **SITKA NATIONAL HISTORICAL PARK**. The walk is lovely, about 15 minutes. On the way, you will pass The Bishop's House and Sheldon Jackson Museum before you arrive at the historical park with its scenic paths through woods and past totem poles.

LONGER HIKES / Whether you go on a short hike or a long one, plan for wet, cool weather. And remember: this is bear country. Don't let that keep you from enjoying the woods, but be alert. The buddy system always makes good sense. If you do go alone, sing, recite poetry, whistle, or make noise occasionally, particularly in deep grass, thick brush, bends in the trail, or when you can see the streams are filled with salmon and the hills covered with berries. Bears love both. Unless you surprise them, mistakenly get between a mother and her cubs, or have the great misfortune to encounter a bear with a toothache, for the most part, any bear will be more frightened of you than you are of it. With that in mind, here are some popular hikes in the Sitka area. The ranger station has a full listing of hikes and directions. For information, call the **U.S. FOREST SERVICE, SITKA RANGER DISTRICT** (907/747-4220).

GAVAN HILL TRAIL is a lovely hike that will get you up high. It takes about 3 hours to make the steep climb to the summit, at elevation 2,505 feet. A plank trail, mainly wooden stairs, has been built all the way up, and the kids in town call it "The Stairmaster." Watch your knees going up and down. You are pretty much in the trees until about three-quarters of the way up. But at the top are pretty alpine flowers and a beautiful view of the water and islands. (*Gavan* in Russian means "harbor.") The trail begins at the edge of downtown. The marked trailhead is just past the house at 508 Baranof Street.

HARBOR MOUNTAIN RIDGE TRAIL is the hike to do on a clear day. The views are spectacular. Drive 4 miles north of town along Halibut

Point Road, turn right, and go 5 miles up Harbor Mountain Road, which was built during World War II as an access to a military lookout. The trail begins where the road ends and wanders 2 miles along ridges and alpine meadows. It takes 2 hours one way. The end of the trail intersects with the Gavan Hill Trail. Here's where the fun can begin. If you really want to make it a day, you can continue down Gavan Hill and end up back in Sitka. If you have buddies who want to start from the opposite direction, you can pass car keys and meet back in town for a beer.

If it's a cloudy day, the **INDIAN RIVER TRAIL** is the perfect hike. You can walk to the trailhead from downtown. The trail is flat, wandering through typical rain forest and alongside muskeg meadows. Much of the time you are walking by the river. The falls are about 5 miles in. Walk softly and you may see deer or sometimes bear. Head east along Sawmill Creek Road to Indian River Road. This is the next road east of the Troopers Academy driveway. The trail begins just west of the pumphouse, about half a mile along the road.

MOUNT EDGECUMBE TRAIL leads to the top of Mount Edgecumbe, the volcano that is one of Sitka's most stunning landmarks. This hike is good on a sunny day. But don't try to do the whole journey and hike in one day. You need a skiff to get to the trailhead as the mountain is on Kruzof Island, about 10 miles west of Sitka. Ask at the visitor center in Sitka about rentals. The trail begins behind Fred's Creek Cabin and is wet and muddy in places and steep for the last 3 miles. It's about 7 miles one way and will take you about 5 hours to get to the summit. Reserve the cabin through the Forest Service's national reservation line (877/444-6777) for a few nights, so you won't have such a long journey back. The best time to go is mid-July, when the snow in the crater has all melted and leaves a warm, shallow lake for swimming. Too early, it's all snow; too late, and it's all evaporated.

TO THE ENDS OF THE ROAD / From downtown Sitka, the road runs about 7 miles to the north and 7 miles to the east. If you have access to wheels, it's great for biking or a scenic drive. To the north, follow **HALIBUT POINT ROAD**. Near the end of the road is the site of the Russians' first fort on the island. Nature and bird lovers won't want to miss the **STARRIGAVAN BIRD VIEWING PLATFORM**, on the right side of the road, just past Old Sitka. (*Starrigavan* in Russian means "old harbor.") There is a beautifully designed boardwalk and interpretive trail about the life of the estuary at Starrigavan Bay.

To the east of downtown Sitka, follow **SAWMILL CREEK ROAD**, which extends about 5 miles out to Herring Cove. Near the end of the road, there is a dirt road to Blue Lake, then, at the very end, another dirt road that continues to Green Lake. It's a beautiful mountain bike ride. **WHALE PARK**, 3 miles out, sits on the edge of the cliff and is an excellent spot for peaceful picnicking and whale-watching. Frolicking whale sculptures welcome you to a series of artful wooden gazebos, boardwalks, and stairways to the beach.

KAYAK RENTALS / Get out on the water. Go anywhere. With all the islands in Sitka Sound and the proximity to Olga and Neva Straits, the paddling around Sitka is more protected than many other places in Southeast. Rent a kayak from Larry Edwards at **BAIDARKA BOATS** (201 Lincoln St; 907/747-8996). In business since 1977, Larry has reasonable rates—"kayaks of all types for every budget"—and gives a good orientation on paddling and safety skills.

SCUBA GEAR RENTALS / The waters surrounding Southeast can be very colorful in spring, when the plankton are blooming. Visibility is best in winter months, though, say locals. The water is cold, but **SOUTHEAST DIVING AND SPORTS** (203 Lincoln St; 907/747-8279) can outfit and advise you. They also rent mountain bikes for knocking about town. The shop is near St. Michael's Cathedral.

BICYCLE RENTALS / If you love to bike and are looking for a different kind of adventure, call Bill Hughes, the enthusiastic and imaginative owner of **YELLOW JERSEY CYCLE SHOP** (907/747-6317). He'll rent you top-quality mountain bikes and gear and point you in the direction of some wonderful excursions where you'll pedal past black sand beaches and up the cylinder cone of an extinct volcano or bike some of the old logging roads watching for brown bears and nesting eagles. Bikes rent for $25 to $30 a day at this full-service bike shop. 805 Halibut Point Rd, just past Katlian St; 907/747-0670, after-hours phone/fax.

GUIDES AND OUTFITTERS

TLINGIT CULTURAL TOURS / Tlingit Indians have lived continuously in Sitka since the end of the last Ice Age. Through their eyes, "Sitka's history is a steady drumbeat, a rhythm, a song 10,000 years old." The Tlingit peoples of Sitka invite you to tour the area from their perspective of history and then enjoy the songs, language, and dance regalia of their peoples. The tours are 1 to 3 hours. Call **TRIBAL TOURS** (888/270-8687) or contact their umbrella organization: **SITKA TRIBAL ENTERPRISES** (429 Katlian St, Sitka, AK 99835; 907/747-7290, fax 907/747-3770; ttours@ptialaska.net).

HARBOR MOUNTAIN TOURS / If it's a beautiful day and you're not into serious aerobic activity, consider taking a ride with **HARBOR MOUNTAIN TOURS** (1210 Edgecumbe Dr; 907/747-8294). A former fisherman who survived one of Alaska's wildest fishing stories, your guide, Howard "Howie" Ulrich, is not only famous, but a character to boot. He also has the only Forest Service permit to drive you up the old military dirt road for spectacular views of Sitka and the surrounding jagged mountains and islands. The trip lasts about 3 hours. If you want, he'll drop you off so you can hike back down to Sitka on the Gavan Trail or he'll take you and your bike up to the top of the gravel road and you can fly "like a bomber on two wheels" back down to sea level. All combinations are possible.

SEA OTTER AND WILDLIFE QUEST / This tour, offered by **ALLEN MARINE TOURS**, cruises down Olga and Neva Straits toward Salisbury Sound. On the way, you'll see bald eagles, sometimes eaglets in the nest, Sitka deer, maybe a bear, very often a humpback whale, and almost always those "little old men of the sea," the sea otters. In fact, if you don't see an otter, a whale, or a bear, these guys will give you half your money back. Even in rainy or foggy weather, it's one of the best wildlife tours, and it's all in protected waters. Some years they offer a special excursion to St. Lazaria Island, famous for its nesting puffins and other seabirds. Trips depart from Crescent Harbor in downtown Sitka. Allen Marine caters primarily to the cruise ships but offers special evening and weekend voyages for Sitkans, so jump on one of these. Fare is $49 for adults; $30 for children 12 and younger; operates May through October. PO Box 1049, Sitka, AK 99835-1049; 888/747-8108 or 907/747-8100; www.allenmarinetours.com.

NATURALIST TRIPS / A favorite tour of local naturalist Bill Foster is a late-evening sunset cruise to **ST. LAZARIA ISLAND** to watch the petrels return from the sea. The beautiful island wildlife refuge with its steep, sharp cliffs is black with birds such as the little clown-faced puffins and common murres. (Be advised this trip is over open water if you are prone to seasickness.) The 30-foot vessel, equipped with underwater hydrophone for listening to whales, can take four people fishing or six people touring. Steller Wildlife and Exploring; 2810 Sawmill Creek Blvd, Sitka, AK 99835; 907/747-6157.

MARINE WILDLIFE TOURS / **RAVEN'S FIRE TOUR CONNECTION** offers several different tours, from 2-hour pocket cruises ($65 per person) to see sea otters and whales to full-day tours for wildlife sightings and cruising to Goddard Hot Springs (about 17 miles south of Sitka) for a soak to an overnight cruise ($175) to St. Lazaria Island to see the breeding ground for thousands of seabirds such as tufted puffins, murres, auklets, and storm petrels. They can even arrange kayak drop-off/pickups or custom-design the trip of your dreams. Their captains are longtime Sitkans who are also commercial fishermen, professional biologists, teachers, or blue-water sailors and can take you out in boats ranging from 24 to 60 feet. 403 Lincoln St, Ste 233, Sitka, AK 99835; 907/747-5777 or 888/747-4789; ravnfire@ptialaska.net; www.ravensfire.com.

NIGHTLIFE

PIONEER BAR / Also known as "The P-Bar," this is an old-time Alaska establishment. Windows overlook the harbor, and the walls are plastered with photos of boats and fish, with this maxim overhead: "There is nothing, absolutely nothing, half so much worth doing as simply messing about in boats." It can get smoky, but it's a friendly, down-home meeting place. And, as one resident says, "Any gossip you missed out at the Backdoor Cafe, you can pick up later at the P-Bar." For live action, go Friday night. 212 Katlian St; 907/747-3456; open every day.

FESTIVALS AND EVENTS

SITKA SUMMER MUSIC FESTIVAL / If you love music and beauty and beautiful music, come to Sitka in June. Internationally renowned musicians come back year after year and consider it an honor to be asked to play here. The people of Sitka love "their" musicians and they treat them like visiting royalty with down-home style. It's all very contagious. The grandeur of the stage at the Centennial Building frames the concerts to perfection. The backdrop is all windows out to ice-streaked mountains and Sitka Sound. Look particularly for the performances of a lively, bearded, elflike violinist who answers to the name of Paul Rosenthal. A former student of Jascha Heifetz, Paul is the genius behind the festival and a delightful character to boot. For tickets and information, contact PO Box 3333, Sitka, AK 99835; 907/747-6774; sitkamus@ptialaska.net; www.sitkamusicfestival.org.

SITKA SYMPOSIUM / This popular writers' gathering coincides with the music festival in the middle of June. You do not have to be a writer to participate. You just have to love ideas, the written word, and the discussion of the values and forces that influence our global village. Every year, the **ISLAND INSTITUTE** (PO Box 2420, Sitka, AK 99835; 907/747-3794; island@ptialaska.net) in Sitka pulls together a small faculty—usually writers, poets, and always one leader who is an Alaska Native—and organizes the weeklong forum around a current topic of interest. Writers are welcome to bring their manuscripts for a critique.

WHALES AND HERRING / From mid-September to mid-January, Sitka is a seaside cafe for dozens and dozens of **HUMPBACK WHALES**. These huge creatures make winter migrations to the warmer climates of Hawaii and Mexico, but they hang around the rich marine waters of Sitka Sound, bulking up for the journey by feeding on herring. The first wave of humpback whales returns to Alaska in March from the whales' winter breeding grounds. By the third week or so of March, there is another marine-life extravaganza when the **HERRING** return—millions and millions of herring. The Department of Fish and Game sometimes opens this fishery to fishermen for just a matter of minutes. Dozens of boats congregate in anticipation in the Sound, like runners waiting for the starter's pistol to go off in the 100-yard dash. The opening is calculated to occur at the moment before the female herring is ready to release her eggs, and fortunes are made and lost with one set of the net. The Japanese particularly prize the eggs as a delicacy that is salted and eaten on New Year's Day. You can view the fishery from Halibut Point Road or charter a boat into the Sound to watch the action.

RESTAURANTS

The Backdoor Cafe / ★

104 BARRACKS ST, SITKA; 907/747-8856

This is "the real Sitka," as one resident says—"a verbal message board" and the best place for coffee and gossip in town. At the back door of the Old Harbor Bookstore, the little cafe is somewhat dark, but anybody who's anybody in Sitka comes in here. There's an array of coffee drinks, make-your-own bagel sandwiches, and baked goods such as cranberry-walnut scones or poppy seed cake. *$; no credit cards; checks OK; breakfast, lunch every day; no alcohol; walk through the Old Harbor Bookstore or go around the alley to the back door.*

Bayview Restaurant / ★

407 LINCOLN ST, SITKA; 907/747-5440

This bright, pleasant cafe has large windows overlooking a million-dollar view—the islands, mountains, boats, and sparkling waters of Sitka Sound. You can keep in the Russian theme here with samplings from the old country such as a hearty bowl of borscht or piroshki. Or go American with good soup-and-sandwich fare and a wide choice of burgers. There's something for everyone's taste buds here. The morning menu features yogurt and fresh fruit; dinner includes locally caught seafood. *$; AE, DIS, MC, V: local checks only; breakfast, lunch, dinner every day; beer and wine; downtown on the second floor of the MacDonald Trading Company building.* &

Channel Club / ★★

2906 HALIBUT POINT RD, SITKA; 907/747-9916

Seven miles from downtown, the Channel Club is for serious carnivores. They serve the best steaks in town. As one resident said, "If you really want to stuff yourself, this is the place to go." Bill and Dotty Aragon have owned it for more than 25 years. They serve "corn-fed Nebraska beef, which is fresh cut on the premises and has never been frozen." They also serve plenty of fresh seafood and boast a salad bar with 35 salads. The windows look out to Sitka Sound and the interior is "bush Alaska," complete with moose antlers, crab shells, and glass fish balls hanging from the walls. Limited seating for nonsmokers. *$$; AE, DC, MC, V; local checks only; dinner every day (closed 3 weeks in Jan for maintenance); full bar; 7 miles out along Halibut Point Rd (call a taxi or the Channel Club's courtesy van).*

Mad Greek Bistro / ★★

104 LAKE ST, SITKA; 907/747-6818

With authentic Greek food and simple charm, this little bistro downtown made a hit in Sitka when it opened in 1997. The owner, Kosta Alexandropoulos, is a warm, exuberant host and chef, who was born in Corinth, Greece, and raised in Munich, Germany, so the atmosphere is not only fun, but multilingual. "Our food is simple—no leaves or fancy flowers on the plates. My favorite place in Greece is the market where they have these big grills and make shish kebab," he explains. So he is grilling "Sitka-bobs" from locally caught salmon, halibut, and the throats of black cod. And the locals love him. (He says he got his nickname—and thus the name of his restaurant—when he was commercial fishing out of Sitka and jumped into a net filled with 100 pounds of squid to rescue a baby seal tangled in there. "He nipped me a few times, but he lived," he grins.) His most popular dishes are the Mad Greek gyros made with roasted beef and lamb—very spicy, with his own special bread—and the Garlic Garlic Platter, featuring heads of baked garlic with hummus, tzatziki, and Mad Greek bread. Also Greek-style pizzas and burgers. *$; MC, V; local checks only; beer and wine; downtown.* ⅋

Mojo's / ★★

256 KATLIAN ST, SITKA; 907/747-0667

Mojo's and the Backdoor Cafe are really hand-in-glove operations, even though they are a half-mile apart. All the baked goods for the Backdoor Cafe are made at Mojo's and bicycled over early in the morning. Mojo's is situated in a tiny, unpretentious yellow-and-blue concrete-block building that sits right on Katlian Street. The interior is quite chummy, with bar stools by the window and a few cheerful tables. They serve all kinds of coffee drinks—espresso, lattes, and the powerful Buzzsaw—along with baked goods. But it is lunch at which they excel, with a menu rich and inventive in soups and sandwiches, flavored with Asian and Indian spices and chutneys. The sandwiches are huge; half is plenty. They also have fresh juices such as carrot, ginger, and celery. The owners, Bernadette Rasmussen and Darryl Rehkopf, say their specialty is that they make everything from scratch using as many organic ingredients as possible, from biscotti to soup stocks. Nonsmoking. *$; no credit cards; local checks only; breakfast, lunch Mon–Fri, dinner Fri–Sat; no alcohol.*

The Raven Dining Room (Westmark Shee Atika) / ★★★

330 SEWARD ST, SITKA; 907/747-6465
If you want a romantic candlelit dinner, the Raven Room is your best choice. In the heart of town, the restaurant has a spectacular view of the mountains and harbor and reflects Sitka's friendly, small-town atmosphere. The staff is welcoming, the service prompt, and, considering the lack of real competition in town, the menu is quite inventive. They serve reindeer sausage and the best eggs Benedict in town. Seafood dishes include tiger prawns coated with almonds with an orange marmalade dip, a shrimp and crab fettuccine, broiled tropical halibut topped with pineapple salsa and a splash of tequila, the local favorite of beer-batter halibut, and salmon, cucumber, and spinach salads. *$$$; AE, DC, DIS, MC, V; local checks only; breakfast, lunch, dinner every day; full bar; in the center of town.* &

Van Winkle and Daigler Frontier Cuisine / ★★

228 HARBOR DR, SITKA; 907/747-3396
This cheerful yellow restaurant by the sea has been a distinctive landmark in Sitka for several years, with a mural of its owners—Van Winkle and Daigler (who are cousins)—adorning the outside. Usually, they have the freshest fish in town—halibut or rockfish caught just that day. They often grill them, which adds an extra flavor of the outdoors. Their fish-and-chips is by far the most popular and their Mud Pie is famous—the best in town. Our tip: go midafternoon and eat Mud Pie. Why? When the restaurant is full, it's far too smoky. The second reason is that the scene is classic Bush Alaska. The sea view is terrific, but at busy times you'd never know it, because pickups park right in front of the windows. *$$; AE, MC, V; checks OK; lunch Mon–Sat, dinner every day; full bar; a 5-minute walk from the Centennial Building.* &

LODGINGS

Crescent Harbor Hideaway–Bare Island Charters / ★★

709 LINCOLN ST, SITKA, AK 99835; 907/747-4900
A stone's throw from the water, this charming historic home overlooks Crescent Harbor. It has two guest units equipped with private bath and entrances. Devotees of Steller sea lions or pelagic birds should opt to stay here and join their B&B hosts on an ocean adventure. Walt Cunningham and Susan Stanford are experienced commercial fishermen, biologists, and marine mammal researchers. They offer custom-designed, small boat charters and educational marine tours for their guests under their aegis of Bare Island Charters. Nonsmoking. *$$; no credit cards; checks OK; bareis@ptialaska.net; www.ptialaska.net/~bareis; directly across from Crescent Harbor, downtown.*

Karras Bed and Breakfast / ★

230 KOGWANTON ST, SITKA, AK 99835; 907/747-3978
The Karrases' home reflects a delightful mixture of Greek and Tlingit cultures, homey atmosphere, unique foods, and some great views. It's like having Santa Claus and Earth Mother running a B&B. Bertha is Tlingit and gathers traditional food from the woods and seacoast to bring to her table. Pete is Greek, and at Christmas he sometimes moonlights as Jolly Old Saint Nick. In summer, he wields a fishing rod and a spatula. He's a great breakfast cook. No smoking or alcohol allowed. *$$; MC, V; checks OK; breakfast every day; up the hill from the Pioneer Bar.*

Raven's Nest House–Berry Island Adventures / ★★★

3 MILES SOUTH OF TOWN, SITKA, AK 99835; 907/747-5165
On a private island 3 miles south of town in Sitka Sound is a sweet, magical cottage perched on the edge of the water. First named by the Russians in 1806, Berry Island is known for its abundance of blueberries, salmonberries, huckleberries, blackberries, and Russian currants. The cedar cottage, hexagonal in shape, with windows in all directions, can accommodate up to four people, with a captain's berth downstairs and a little sleeping loft for two tucked at the top of a ship's ladder. While the cottage is tiny (500 square feet), it has a wraparound deck of 1,000 square feet sitting above the water in a lovely natural setting of trees and moss and berry bushes for the plucking. Down by the water is your own private hot tub. There's a fully appointed kitchen and grill. All you need to bring are the groceries. Your hosts, Signe and Al Wilson, who own the entire island (10.5 acres) and live in the old fox farm house, will pick you up and ferry you over and back to town. They also rent kayaks. Al and his daughter Kim Elliot are both charter boat captains and through Berry Island Adventures can take you sailing or fishing or sightseeing. Cost of the Raven's Nest House is $225 per night for two (2-night minimum). Each extra person (up to four) is $50. Honeymooners and anniversary couples particularly love it. *$$$; no credit cards; personal checks OK; open in summer; berryisl@ptialaska.net; www.ptialaska.net/~berryisl; PO Box 597, Sitka, AK 99835.*

Rockwell Lighthouse / ★★★

SITKA SOUND, SITKA, AK 99835; 907/747-3056
One of Sitka's most famous landmarks, the picturesque white-and-red lighthouse sitting on a small rock island out in the bay was not originally designed as a beacon for ships but built as a mock lighthouse back in the 1980s by one of Sitka's most eccentric and well-loved characters, Burgess Bauder, the local veterinarian. Four stories high, the lighthouse, made of brick, cedar, fir, mahogany, and black walnut, can bunk two people on each level. With two bathrooms and a fully equipped kitchen, if you have

eight in your party, it's the cheapest place to rent in town. Locals rent it for all kinds of events and celebrations. Renting a skiff costs extra, but Bauder will take you over and pick you up, and the ride with him is worth the price of admission. It's good for those who enjoy relaxing. There's no television and the hot tub is often broken. Winter rates run $125 to $200 for two to eight people and in summer $150 to $340 for two to eight people. Warning: it books up fast in summer. *$$–$$$; no credit cards; checks OK; PO Box 277, Sitka, AK 99835.*

Westmark Shee Atika / ★★

330 SEWARD ST, SITKA, AK 99835; 907/747-6241

"Shee Atika" is an old name for Sitka. It is the name the Tlingit people gave to their home here, long before the arrival of the Russians. "Shee" is Baranof Island. "Shee Atika" means roughly "the settlement on the outside of Shee." Some translate it as "the village behind the islands." Today, this friendly downtown hotel is owned by the Tlingit people of the region, under the aegis of the Shee Atika Corporation, and managed by Holland-America/Westours. The hotel is decorated with Tlingit motifs and artworks. For the best views, reserve a room on the fourth or fifth floors, middle to the west wing, overlooking the water. The fifth floor is nonsmoking. *$$$; AE, DC, DIS, MC, V; checks OK; breakfast, lunch, dinner every day; in the center of town.* &

WILDERNESS LODGES

Baranof Wilderness Lodge

BARANOF WARM SPRINGS BAY, BARANOF ISLAND, AK 99835; 800/613-6551 OR 907/738-3597

This lodge is located 20 air miles over the mountains from Sitka, on the east side of Baranof Island, and the flight alone will stop your heart from beating. Jagged peaks, glaciers, and mountain passes sail past the cockpit windows until you descend, swooping over a roaring river and a spectacular waterfall, to land on floats at the head of Warm Springs Bay. You'll fall in love with this bay and the lodge, originally built in the 1980s by the grandson of Alaska's most beloved territorial governor, Ernest "Pop" Gruening. Cabins sit close to the water, meals are family style and delicious, and the fishing is great. Mike Trotter owns it now and offers remote fishing expeditions as well as lodge stays. Trotter and his professional guides encourage catch-and-release fishing. *No credit cards; checks OK; flyfishalaska.com; PO Box 2187, Sitka, AK 99835 (June–Sept); PO Box 42, Norden, CA 95724; 916/582-8132 (Oct–Apr); east side of Baranof Island.*

Wrangell

At the northern tip of Wrangell Island, far from the popular Love Boat circuit of the Inside Passage, nearly 90 miles north of Ketchikan and 150 miles south of Juneau, the tiny community of Wrangell (pop. 2,500) sits amid wilderness splendor. It's an unpretentious little town that, until recently, relied heavily on the timber industry for its livelihood. This is the more typical Southeast Alaska town of the not-so-very-long-ago when only a few small cruise ships and the Alaska ferry tucked into the dock. (Today the number of passengers on the cruise ship fleet tied up at the docks or anchored out in the harbors can double—even triple—the population of some of these small Southeast towns on any given day.)

Wrangell is older than its neighbor, Petersburg, a fishing town, with a history that weaves together threads of the ancient Tlingit culture and the cultures of three world powers—Russia, Britain, and the United States—who have occupied the region in more recent times. When Wrangell's sawmill, the largest private industry in town, closed in 1994, it took a big chunk out of the local economy. Recently, the mill has been revived on a smaller scale, exporting the main woods of the forest here—cedar, spruce, and hemlock—and supporting independent woodsmen and artisans in town. The small fishing fleet still pulls in salmon, halibut, shrimp, crab, and herring. While the town is trying hard to develop a tourist industry, it still retains its gritty mill-town character.

Although Wrangell was founded by Russian traders in the early 1800s, the Tlingits long dominated the region. Perhaps the greatest carver in the history of the Tlingit nation lived here 200 years ago. The museum holds four of his totem poles, thought to be the oldest Tlingit house posts in existence. A replica of a clan house on Shakes Island, in the city harbor, contains copies of the old posts, crafted by modern master carvers.

Wrangell is the gateway to the Stikine River, a wild and spectacular waterway with headwaters in Canada. The Tlingit people named it Stik-Heen, which means "great river." Nearby is the Anan Creek Black Bear Observatory, which is becoming so popular with visitors the Forest Service is currently pondering a lottery system to limit the number of people per day.

ACCESS AND INFORMATION

Wrangell has daily **JET SERVICE** year-round via Alaska Airlines (800/426-0333). One of the two flights per day goes north; the other south. The state ferries also make frequent stops here; call the **ALASKA MARINE HIGHWAY SYSTEM** (800/642-0066) for reservations.

Pick up information at the **WRANGELL CHAMBER OF COMMERCE** (PO Box 49, Wrangell, AK 99929; 907/874-3901; www.Wrangell. com/Chamber/Commerce.htm), located at the end of the city dock, on Stikine Avenue.

EXPLORING

CHIEF SHAKES HOUSE / Chief Shakes House, situated on Shakes Island in the city boat harbor, and built by a Civilian Conservation Corps crew in the 1930s, is a wonderful replica of an original clan house. There were eight chiefs named Shakes. Shakes House is open when cruise ships are in port or by appointment.

WRANGELL MUSEUM / It's worth a visit to see the original Shakes totem poles and artifacts from the early days of Russian, British, and American settlement. The museum is open Monday through Saturday from early May to the end of September or "whenever the ferries and cruise ships are in for more than an hour." Fee for adults is $2. On the lower floor of the Community Center, 318 Church St; 907/874-3770.

PETROGLYPH BEACH / About a 10-minute walk north of the dock is a beach where ancient artists—for reasons unknown today—carved symbols, faces, fish, and seashell spirals into the rocks. Several thousand years old, these carved rocks perhaps served as territorial markers or pointed the way to good fishing on the Stikine River. Perhaps they were ritual carvings to invoke the spirit helpers of the animals killed in the hunt. Many shapes are geometric; others are recognizable as fish or whales. Along the way, you may meet local children peddling garnets from Garnet Ledge near the mouth of the Stikine River.

ADVENTURES

ANAN BLACK BEAR OBSERVATORY AND CABIN / Thirty miles southeast of Wrangell, large runs of pink salmon returning to Anan Lake attract a bevy of black bears, brown bears, bald eagles, and harbor seals. The Forest Service maintains a popular **RENTAL CABIN** here. There is also a **DAY OBSERVATORY** at the falls, a mile upstream from the cabin, so that visitors can watch the bears feeding in relative safety. Anan is accessible only by boat or floatplane. Several air and boat charter companies in both Wrangell and Ketchikan offer trips. The best times to go are from the end of June through the end of August. For more information, contact the U.S. Forest Service, Wrangell Ranger District (907/874-2323), or the Petersburg Ranger District (907/772-3871).

STIKINE RIVER / From its headwaters in British Columbia, the Stikine River flows for 400 miles, entering salt water about 5 miles north of Wrangell. It is a popular destination for birders, fishermen, and river runners. Depending on the time of year, you can see hooligan running, sea lions feeding, and thousands of bald eagles perched on trees and stumps. The river served as a transportation route into Canada during the Stikine, Cassiar, and Klondike gold rushes that took place here between 1861 and 1898. Sixteen miles upriver, the Forest Service maintains CHIEF SHAKES HOT SPRINGS, where you can soak in the hot tubs. Near the mouth of the river is GARNET LEDGE, where the children of Wrangell mine the garnets they sell you in town. The Stikine is fast flowing, averaging 8 knots per hour. River runners (see Guides and Outfitters, below) who venture onto the Stikine usually start at Telegraph Creek (pop. 300), in British Columbia. It is the only town along the river and about 130 miles from Alaska tidewater. Above Telegraph Creek is the Stikine's spectacular Grand Canyon, where cliff walls jut straight up from the river edge, reaching up to 1,000 feet in elevation. The canyon is about 55 miles long and considered dangerous and unnavigable.

STIKINE RECREATIONAL CABINS / The U.S. Forest Service, Wrangell Ranger District, maintains many primitive cabins along the lower Stikine River. These can be reserved for $25 to $35 a day. The Forest Service also sells $3 maps showing Stikine River canoe and kayak trails. For information, contact U.S. Forest Service (PO Box 51, Wrangell, AK 99929; 907/874-2323). For reservations, contact the National Recreation Reservation Service (877/444-6777; www.ReserveUSA.com).

GUIDES AND OUTFITTERS

ALASKA WATERS / This company offers custom-designed jet boat tours and adventures on the Stikine River. They provide flotation suits, refreshments, guided history, and as much excitement or relaxation as you want. Captain Jim Leslie is the owner and guide. 800/347-4462 or 907/874-2378; infor@alaskawaters.com; www.alaskawaters.com.

STIKEEN WILDERNESS ADVENTURES / Billed as "the oldest operating business on the Stikine River," this company provides water-taxi services, "mild or wild" jet-boat excursions of the Stikine River area, overnights up the river to Telegraph Creek in British Columbia, and more. They're available for individual or group tours. Todd Harding, licensed by the Coast Guard since 1981, is the owner/operator. Sign up for one of his offerings at their desk inside the Stikine Inn (800/874-2085 or 907/874-2085; wildside@akgetaway.com; www.alaskagetaway.com).

RESTAURANTS AND LODGINGS

Stikine Inn–Waterfront Grill

1 BLOCK FROM THE FERRY TERMINAL, WRANGELL, AK 99929; 888/874-3388 OR 907/874-3388, FAX 907/874-3923
Located right downtown next to the city dock and overlooking the water, the Stikine Inn, with 33 rooms, offers simple, motel-like lodgings, but half the rooms do have a water view. Room rates begin at $75 for a single and $80 for a double. The service is friendly and its restaurant, the Waterfront Grill, gets a thumbs-up from teenagers and adults alike with such favorites as chicken teriyaki, fettuccine, and calzone. *$$; AE, DIS, MC, V; checks OK; breakfast, lunch, dinner every day; no alcohol; inn@stikine.com; www.stikine.com; PO Box 990, Wrangell, AK 99929.* &

Petersburg

The fishing town of Petersburg (pop. 3,200) is quite prosperous, capitalizing on its abundant salmon, natural beauty, and Scandinavian charm. While Petersburg welcomes visitors, like Wrangell it is not a mainstay on the cruise ship circuit.

Petersburg was founded just before the turn of the century by sturdy Norwegian immigrants who were drawn here by plentiful salmon and halibut and an inexhaustible supply of natural ice from nearby LeConte Glacier, in which they packed their catch. Many of them were fishermen from the fjord country of western Norway who found a landscape of tall mountains and deep waters remarkably like their homeland. A century later, Petersburg is still dominated by a Scandinavian aesthetic and work ethic. The homes are square, wooden, and solid. Descendants of the early immigrants are raising their families here, and some of the boats you see in the harbor are operated by fourth- and fifth-generation Petersburg fishermen and -women.

Above all, Petersburg is an authentic fishing community, untouched by the big-business tourism that has radically changed such places as Juneau and Ketchikan. You won't find mega-cruise ships, shops filled with trinkets, T-shirts, or gourmet ice cream. Instead, you'll experience a bustling seaport going about the business of catching, processing, and selling seafood. For that reason, Petersburg has never worked very hard at attracting tourists, and services are a bit thin.

If you are comfortable in rain jacket and rubber boots, you're sure to enjoy Petersburg. More than 100 inches of rain falls every year, moisture that nurtures salmon streams and gives the rain forest a thousand shades of green. Consider yourself blessed when the sun breaks through and reveals the stunning coastal mountain range with its jutting pinnacle, Devil's Thumb.

ACCESS AND INFORMATION

Petersburg is served by Alaska Airlines (800/426-0333) daily **JET SERVICE**. It's possible to leave San Francisco in the morning and arrive in Petersburg in the afternoon. The **ALASKA MARINE HIGHWAY** (800/642-0066) vessels also make frequent stops here.

Stop in at the **PETERSBURG VISITOR INFORMATION CENTER** (907/772-4636; www.petersburg.org) at the corner of First and Fram Streets in downtown, to pick up information; open daily in summer. **SING LEE ALLEY BOOKS** (907/772-4440) is open daily, featuring field guides, Alaska-specific books, and lots of other good reading.

ADVENTURES

WHALES, ICEBERGS, AND MOUNTAINS / Classic Petersburg excursions are whale-watching in **FREDERICK SOUND**; a visit to **LECONTE GLACIER**, the southernmost tidewater glacier in North America; and flight-seeing around **DEVIL'S THUMB**. Viking Travel (101 N Nordic Dr; 800/327-2571 or 907/772-3818; www.alaska-ala-carte.com) books charters and tours with such offerings as humpback whale-watching, LeConte Glacier Bay boat tours, Helicopter flight-seeing and glacier walk, and Tongass kayak adventures. Pacific Wing (907/772-4258 or 907/772-9258) is the best for flight-seeing or air charters.

WALKING EVERYWHERE / Stroll the boardwalks that cross Mitkof Island's muskeg meadows. Wander along the harbor. Get up early, buy a caffe latte at **HELSE**, and park yourself on a bench overlooking the **OLD BOAT HARBOR**, a block off Main Street. During salmon season, you'll see cannery laborers hurrying to jobs, fishing crews readying their gear, and boats of all kinds coming and going. All this activity may inspire the more adventurous to rent a skiff and motor down **WRANGELL NARROWS**—really the best way to get a feel for how people live here.

HIKING / There are several good hiking trails. **THREE LAKES TRAIL** is a delightful hike, mostly on boardwalk, that connects three lakes named Sand, Hill, and Crane. Go to Mile 21 on Mitkof Highway, then turn on Three Lakes Road. The trail begins at the sign for Crane Lake. The **OHMER CREEK TRAIL** starts a couple of miles beyond the Three Lakes turnoff on Mitkof Highway. You walk 2 miles one way through a deep, green, old-growth forest, across a floating bridge over a series of pools, and into a wildflower meadow. The **RAVEN'S ROOST TRAIL** is more challenging. It's 8 miles round-trip to a rustic cabin, and views of Frederick Sound are great. The trail begins 2 miles from downtown, near the airport. The cabin, about $30 per night, requires a permit and may be reserved by calling the U.S. Forest Service's national reservation line (877/444-6777).

KAYAKING / Rent a boat or take a guided trip. With **TONGASS KAYAK ADVENTURES**, trips range from afternoon paddles to Petersburg Creek ($55 per person) to multiday trips to LeConte Glacier or weeklong tours. For information, contact Tongass Kayak Adventures, PO Box 2169, Petersburg, AK 99833; 907/772-4600.

MOUNTAIN BIKING / Pedal remote roads with Terry's Unforgettable Charters and Expeditions (Mile 9.7, Mitkof Hwy; 907/772-2200).

FESTIVALS AND EVENTS

LITTLE NORWAY FESTIVAL / This festival takes place the third weekend of May and commemorates **SYTTENDE MAI** (May 17), the day in 1814 when Norway declared its independence from Sweden. The celebration includes smorgasbords for sampling Scandinavian delicacies, displays of traditional crafts, and a community-wide pageant that's a kitschy mix of old-country dancing and corny Norwegian humor.

PETERSBURG'S SALMON DERBY / This fishing derby takes place Memorial Day weekend. What sets it apart from all the other derbies in Southeast is the level of competition. Casual sportfishers will find themselves competing with the most competitive and successful commercial fishermen anywhere. But that doesn't mean the skipper of a 78-foot seiner has a leg up. It's still a matter of luck. For more information, call 907/772-4636.

RESTAURANTS

Helse / ★★

17 SING LEE ALLEY, PETERSBURG; 907/772-3444

This cozy little cafe in the heart of Petersburg's historic district is the best place to eat in town, bar none. Unfortunately, it offers only coffee and lunch. Deli sandwiches are huge, and specials run from grain salads to enchiladas. A bowl of soup and fresh, homemade bread is always a good choice here. *$; no credit cards; checks OK; breakfast, lunch Mon–Sat; no alcohol; downtown.*

Homestead Cafe / ★

206 NORDIC DR, PETERSBURG; 907/772-3900

The local fishermen are in their element in this little cafe. The Homestead serves good, standard American breakfast fare: eggs, bacon, blueberry pancakes, and omelets. You can't go wrong with burgers the rest of the day. Fish is always available but mostly comes fried. They also serve homemade pies and banana splits. Coffee refills are endless, and that's what keeps the old-timers on their breaks coming back day after day at 10am and 3pm on the nose. Note that the stools nearest the door are unofficially reserved for the town elders. You'll have to endure uncomfortable stares if you happen to be sitting there when coffee time rolls around. **ON-THE-RUN** is a take-out version of the cafe open from 5am–9pm and is located behind the restaurant. *$$; AE, DIS, MC, V; checks OK; breakfast, lunch, dinner Mon–Sat; no alcohol.*

Pellerito's Pizzeria / ★

1105 S NORDIC DR, PETERSBURG; 907/772-3727
Pellerito's is conveniently located across from the ferry terminal, half a mile from downtown. The pizza is good but service can be slow sometimes. If possible, call ahead with your order. They serve hand-thrown pizzas, whole or by the slice, spaghetti, lasagne, sandwiches, and calzone. A large "crab bait" pizza (a.k.a. "the works") is $35. *$$; MC, V; local checks only; lunch, dinner every day in summer (reduced hours in fall); full bar; across from ferry terminal.*

LODGINGS

Broom Hus / ★

BETWEEN THE FERRY TERMINAL AND DOWNTOWN, PETERSBURG, AK 99833; 907/772-3459
Sylvia Nilsen's house is one of the solid old Norwegian places that make Petersburg distinctive. The location is terrific—midway between the ferry terminal and downtown—making it a short walk in either direction. You get the basement suite with a pretty garden entrance. From the boat harbor across the street, you can walk to town entirely on the floats. The rate is $65 for a single and $80 for two, but with the addition of bunk beds, the suite can sleep six. *$$; no credit cards; checks OK; broomhus@alaska.net; www.alaska.net/~broomhus; PO Box 427, Petersburg, AK 99833.*

Scandia House

DOWNTOWN, PETERSBURG, AK 99833; 800/722-5006 OR 907/772-4281
When the Scandia House burned down in 1994, Petersburg lost its oldest, funkiest hotel. But the new Scandia House is clean, quiet, and comfortable and retains the central downtown location. There are rooms of every configuration. All have baths; many have kitchenettes. Rates are $80 to $175 for a double. *$$; AE, DC, DIS, MC, V; checks OK; PO Box 689, Petersburg, AK 99833.*

Water's Edge Bed and Breakfast / ★

SANDY BEACH RD, PETERSBURG, AK 99833; 800/868-4373 OR 907/772-3736
Barry and Kathy Bracken's bed-and-breakfast is on the bottom level of their split-level seaside home on Sandy Beach Road, about 1.5 miles from downtown. They have two rooms—the Beach Room, with a panoramic view of the Sound, and the Creekside Room, tucked in the woods with a partial view of the beach. The Brackens are located on the edge of the water and have a spectacular view of Frederick Sound and the mountains on the mainland. Barry is a former biologist who offers naturalist excursions on his 28-foot cruiser. Rate is $80 to $90 for a double. *$$; no credit cards; checks OK; bbsea@alaska.net; www.alaska.net/~bbsea; PO Box 1201, Petersburg, AK 99833.*

WILDERNESS LODGES

Rocky Point Resort

PO BOX 1251, PETERSBURG, AK 99833; 907/772-4405
Only 12 miles from town, this lodge still feels remote. It caters to serious sportfishers. From June to September, guests fish for the region's best: salmon, lingcod, halibut, and trout. The price of $265 per person per day includes three hearty meals a day, guided fishing, gear, and use of skiffs. *No credit cards; checks OK; open June–Sept; 12 miles from Petersburg.*

Juneau

Flying into Juneau over islands and the Coast Mountains, dipping between mountain peaks to make a landing on Juneau's runway, in full view of the Mendenhall Glacier on a spectacular, bluebird day, you'll look below at sparkling waters, fishing boats, and the occasional multi-million-dollar yacht, and you'll wonder, "Why doesn't everyone in the world live here?"

Not to give away too many family secrets, but an average 90 inches of rain per year and Taku winds that can blow bricks off buildings in the wintertime are a few small clues. As in the rest of Alaska, the cold and dark seem to chase away the snowbirds. But that's what makes it a grand place for those of us on the far edges of sanity and for visitors from saner climates who want to see how the other half lives.

Still, there are a million other reasons that make Juneau a wonderful place to live, work, and play. With the ocean at their front doorstep and mountains rising steeply out the back bedroom window, Juneauites love to play—and they play hard. They paddle, hang glide, sail, parasail, ice climb, kayak, and row in all kinds of wild weather. The sun comes out, and they're off to hike the ridges. They helicopter pianos to the top of Mount Roberts, while the party folks scramble up through the mud with tuxedos and ball gowns in their knapsacks, and then dance till dawn. This is the capital city of Alaska. It was gold in "them thar hills" that lured a couple of unsteady old prospectors here more than 100 years ago, and it was oil that sucked in a lot of the present-day generation in their younger years. Not the raw stuff itself, but what oil money could buy. That whole, heady, high-adrenaline environment came from having, as one young lawyer described it, "all that raw meat on the table." Alaska was rolling in dough from the late 1960s to the early 1980s. Oil was discovered at Prudhoe Bay on the North Slope in 1968; then in the 1980s the price of oil took a nose dive and the oil reserves began tapering off. However, 90 percent of the state's budget is still run on oil, and the seat of state government is in Juneau. Only 30,000 people live in Juneau today. A few thousand less were here in the 1970s, but that kind of money put Juneau on the world map.

True to the city's frontier character, many of the high-flying deals were cut in the old Bubble Room in the Baranof Hotel, under the capricious eye of the Bubble Lady, a painted portrait of a saucy gal dressed in strategically placed bubbles. (Alas, although the new bar there is still called the Bubble Room, the fair lady went up in flames during a fire several years ago.)

The Bubble Lady's place of honor is not surprising given the town's founding fathers. Joe Juneau and Dick Harris, two down-on-their-luck and much-in-their-cups prospectors, tottered off the boat in Sitka in the fall of 1880 and were grubstaked by an old mining engineer named George Pilz. But they did not impress their employer with their high moral character. "Sinful was the way they spent their days," Pilz complained. Between hooch and women, they squandered nearly everything he gave them. They dragged themselves back to Sitka empty-handed.

Pilz knew there was gold up north. The Indians had told him so. But winter was coming, and there was no one else but these two ne'er-do-wells to send out. If not for their guide, Chief Cowee of the Auk Indian tribe, Juneau's history might have been quite different. The chief led them to a small tributary flowing into Gastineau Channel, soon to be known as the legendary Gold Creek. The rush was on!

"I broke some rock with a hammer," wrote Harris later. "Juneau and I could hardly believe our eyes. We knew it was gold, but . . . so much!" News of the fabulously rich strike spread like wildfire. Prospectors poured in from all over the Territory of Alaska. Harris named the region Silver Bow. The miners, in turn, named the town Harrisburg. But then, one day, they got mad at Harris and renamed the town after his partner, Joe Juneau. Both founders died penniless—Harris in a sanitorium in Oregon and Juneau in Dawson City, where he went following the Klondike Gold Rush. Both are home now, buried in Juneau in Evergreen Cemetery (as is Chief Cowee). Alaskans have a special fondness for their homegrown characters.

While some made fortunes panning in Juneau's rivers and creeks, the big money was in hard-rock mining. Three big companies had large-scale mining operations going full tilt here at one time. The mountains behind Juneau are a honeycomb of old mining tunnels. The first and most profitable mine, though, was on Douglas Island, just across Gastineau Channel from downtown Juneau. Over the course of 35 years, $66 million worth of gold was taken out. At its zenith, there were four mines, 2,000 workers, and diggings 2,000 feet beneath the surface of the earth. Safety standards were not high priority. The first big gold came out of the Glory Hole, which was not named because of "hallelujah-there's-gold-here!" but because it sent so many men on that one-way road to glory.

While Juneau was booming as the first really big gold strike in the Territory of Alaska, Sitka's star was waning with the declining fortunes of the fur industry. So, in 1906, the capital of the territory moved from Sitka to Juneau. There it has stayed—despite several attempts in recent years by many vociferous parties to move it northward to the whistle-stop of Willow.

For such a small town in a fairly remote location, Juneau has a highly educated, well-traveled, articulate, and artistic populace. Even with wilderness only moments away, the town fosters professional theater and music, a strong sense of community, a university, and one of the most prize-winning high school drill teams in the world—no fooling. In the summer of 1998, many residents enjoyed the thrill of seeing themselves on film as movie "extras," when Juneau was used as the setting for *Limbo*, a film about a Southeast fisherman, written and directed by John Sayles.

Somewhat like the weather here, Juneau has two distinct seasons: the political season or the convening of the state legislature, called "the session," which runs from January to May; and the tourist season, which starts with the arrival of the first cruise ships toward the middle of May and lasts until the beginning of October, when the last ship sails out of Gastineau Channel. The average high temperature in July is 65°F and the average low temperature in January is 20°F.

ACCESS AND INFORMATION

You can get to Juneau only by air or sea. There are no roads to the state's capital. However, Juneau has regularly scheduled, daily **AIR SERVICE** on Alaska Airlines (800/426-0333). Air North (867/668-2228 or 800/764-0407) has scheduled service, year-round, between Juneau and White-horse. Juneau is also a regular stop on the ferry system. For a booklet with times, schedules, rates, and reservations, contact the **ALASKA MARINE HIGHWAY SYSTEM** (PO Box 25535, Juneau, AK 99802-5535; 800/642-0066; fax 907/277-4829; www.dot.state.ak.us/external/amhs/ home.html). The ferry links up with Alaska's road system about a 5- to 7-hour ferry ride north from Juneau to Haines or Skagway. Juneau is also on the regular itinerary of Alaska ports of call for more than 20 cruise ships. Within town, there are public buses, taxis, and rental car agencies available. **ALLSTAR PRACTICAL RENT-A-CAR** (907/790-2414 or 800/722-0741) has economical rates and a nonsmoking fleet. **RENT-A-WRECK** (907/789-4111; damian@ptialaska.net) has a courtesy pickup from all Juneau locations and low-cost autos and trucks.

The Alaska Division of Tourism has information online (www.visitalaska.com; www.travelalaska.com). The **JUNEAU CONVENTION & VISITORS BUREAU** (888/581-2201; www.juneau.com) can be reached for local community information. For information on the north country, visit www.north-to-alaska.com. If you're already in town, you can pick up information in several places. The **DAVIS LOG CABIN VISITORS INFORMATION CENTER** (134 3rd St, Juneau; 907/586-2201 or 907/586-JUNO) is housed in a replica of an old log cabin built in the late 1800s, which once served as a church, an office for the city brewery, and a soda works. In summer, there are also visitor information booths at the cruise ship docks.

Tucked into a corner of Centennial Hall on Egan Drive, the **U.S. FOREST SERVICE AND NATIONAL PARK SERVICE INFORMATION CENTER** (907/586-8751, fax 907/586-7928) has films; displays; notebooks about backcountry travel, trails, and public-use cabins in the Tongass National Forest; and information on all of Alaska's national parks system, including nearby Glacier Bay National Park. This is also where you obtain a permit for bear viewing at Pack Creek on Admiralty Island. The information center is open daily in summer.

As one notable bush pilot once said, "Alaska has some of the worst weather that God inflicts upon this earth." Take note. Winter or summer, you can get weathered in (or out of) all Southeast communities. Even in the height of tourist season, **FOG** can keep you grounded or stranded. So make your plans accordingly. It is not uncommon, given **WINTER STORMS**, to board the plane in Seattle, overfly Juneau, land in Anchorage, fly back to Juneau, overfly Juneau, and end up where you started from. If you think it's funny, just wait. This routine can sometimes go on for days. In that vein, note rule number one for flying in small planes: if the pilot says, "We don't go," do not insist on going if you value your life, no matter what your high-powered schedule says.

EXPLORING

ALASKA STATE MUSEUM / Permanent exhibits take you on a journey through the history of Russian America, the stories of the diverse Native peoples here, and the rich natural history of Alaska. Open daily in summer. Around the corner from Centennial Hall; 395 Whittier St; 907/465-2901.

MENDENHALL GLACIER / A stunning view as you fly in on a clear day, the Mendenhall Glacier, along with the surrounding mountains, is the jewel in Juneau's crown. While it may not be the most spectacular glacier in Alaska—a vast land covered with thousands of glaciers—it is one of the most dramatic so close to civilization. Hiking trails wind up the rocks on either side of the glacier. There is a newly renovated U.S. Forest Service **MENDENHALL GLACIER VISITOR CENTER** (907/789-0097), located at Mendenhall Loop Road only 15 miles from downtown Juneau, with a magnificent view of the ice and information about walking and hiking trails near the glacier. (See below for different ideas about how to visit the glacier.)

GASTINEAU SALMON HATCHERY VISITOR CENTER / This hatchery is also known as Douglas Island Pink and Chum (DIPAC), which locals pronounce "die-pack," and that is how it is popularly known. Stop here to learn about the life cycle of the salmon; open daily in summer. On the edge of Gastineau Channel; 2697 Channel Dr; 907/463-4810.

ALASKAN BREWERY CO. / Famous for their handcrafted ales— Alaskan Amber, Alaskan Pale Ale, and Alaskan Frontier—this is one of the best small breweries in the United States, with several ales and beers winning awards year after year. There are free tours (and samples) May to September, every afternoon except Sunday. Open Thursday to Saturday in winter. In Lemon Creek, a few minutes' drive from downtown; 5429 Shaune Dr; 907/780-5866.

SHOPPING / **HEARTHSIDE BOOKS** (254 Front St; 907/586-1726) has a full array of Alaska books and the latest best-sellers. It has two locations, one downtown and one in the valley. If you're into recycling books, **RAINY DAY BOOKS** (113 Seward St; 907/463-BOOK), next door to Valentine's Coffee, has half-priced, used books (they specialize in Alaska field guides), as well as new books, while **THE OBSERVATORY** (235 2nd St; 907/586-9676) specializes more in rare books, maps, and prints.

A visit to **WILLIAM SPEAR DESIGN** (165 S Franklin St; 907/586-4132; www.wmspear.com) is a hilarious experience, from the art itself down to the folks running the shop, who include Bill (the wacky artist), his classy wife, Susan, and Deanne, a Tlingit comedienne of inexhaustible good humor. Bill's a pin designer. But these are no ordinary pins. Some are exquisite colorful jewelry (birds and fish), some are renegade (the death-and-sex series), and some are autobiographical ("The night my goddamn drink caught on fire"). And they're sold everywhere from Chamonix, France, to Barrow, Alaska. Bill has lately turned many of his most popular pins into zipper-pulls for all your friends who don't sport pins or jewelry.

The emphasis at **THE RAVEN'S JOURNEY** (175 S Franklin; 907/463-4686) is on diverse, high-quality Alaska Native artwork—wonderful masks, carvings, baskets, Chilkat weaving, whalebone carvings, earrings, and more. John and Kathy Ellis, the owners, are delightful and informative—they know every artist whose work they display—and their shop is a fun stop in your downtown ramblings.

PORTFOLIO ARTS (493 S Franklin St, Ste 203; 907/586-8111; ~artak@alaska.net; www.alaska.net/~artak) is one of the few galleries in Alaska where you can see not only beautiful Native art from Southeast but also intriguing Inupiat and Yup'ik Eskimo art from the north. Everything is one of a kind. Located across from the cruise ship dock on the second floor.

Rie Muñoz's bright and cheerful work depicts village people and everyday life in Alaska and is on display in Mendenhall Valley at the **RIE MUÑOZ GALLERY** (2101 N Jordan Ave; 907/789-7411; info@riemunoz.com; www.riemunoz.com). A popular, longtime Juneau artist, Rie creates silkscreens, prints, posters, tapestries, books, and cards, and her work graces homes all over Alaska.

ANNIE KAILL'S FINE CRAFTS GALLERY (244 Front St; 907/586-2880) offers friendly, fun, and affordable gifts from Alaska. Open daily, year-round; located downtown.

If you're headed on an outdoor adventure, **FOGGY MOUNTAIN SHOP** (134 N Franklin St; 907/586-6780) sells top-of-the-line, expensive, but rugged outdoor clothing and gear. Located downtown, across the street from the Baranof Hotel. **NUGGET ALASKAN OUTFITTER** (8745 Glacier Hwy, Ste 145, 907/789-3635; 800/478-6848; www.ptialaska.net/~nugget), however, is where the locals shop for good, affordable outdoor gear and work clothing. This is where you can buy the ubiquitous "Juneau sneakers" otherwise known as knee-high rubber boots. Or outfit yourself in an "Alaskan Tuxedo"—rubber boots, wool hat, and wool shirt.

ADVENTURES

WALKING TOUR OF TOWN / In all Southeast towns, you will learn the most by walking. In Juneau, that takes particular stamina, because streets and stairways (which serve as streets) go straight up the sides of mountains. Pick up a free walking tour map at the visitors center. The following are a few highlights of any self-guided tour of Alaska's capital city.

Starting from the waterfront, note the **JUNEAU CITY LIBRARY** (292 Marine Wy; 907/586-5324), which has a commanding view of Gastineau Channel. It is built on top of a parking garage and has windows facing in almost all directions. Up the hill, on Main Street and Fourth Avenue, stands the **STATE CAPITOL BUILDING** (907/465-2479), with its marble pillars. The Governor's Office is on the third floor and, when the legislature is in session on the second floor, you can sit in and watch the show. Tours of the capitol are available. Across the street is the **STATE OFFICE BUILDING** (referred to in Juneau as "The S.O.B."). The State of Alaska Historical Library (333 Willoughby Ave, 8th Fl; 907/465-2925), yet another Southeast library with a great view, resides in the S.O.B., off a large airy atrium where free organ recitals happen at noon on Fridays. The **GOVERNOR'S MANSION**, white-columned, with a mosquito totem pole in front, is a few blocks around the corner, on Calhoun Avenue. It is not open to visitors. However, if you happen to be in Juneau in early December, you may be in time for the governor's holiday open house. All are welcome. Make your way back to 213 Seventh Avenue, above the capitol, to the **WICKERSHAM HOUSE** (907/586-9001), former home of one of Alaska's important early-day pioneers, Judge James Wickersham. He was Alaska's first territorial delegate to Congress. His grand old house with its commanding view of Gastineau Channel was once a beacon to ships at sea charting their course home. It is now a museum. Tours ($10) begin on the hour, 10am to 3pm, Tuesday through Sunday. If you're up for more exercise, a lovely walk up **BASIN ROAD** from Seventh Avenue takes you along famous **GOLD CREEK** and into the historic **SILVER BOW** mining area between Mount Juneau and Mount Roberts. **PERSEVERANCE TRAIL** continues up from here to **EBNER FALLS**, about a 45-minute walk one-way from the Wickersham House.

MOUNT ROBERTS TRAMWAY / Ride on the wings of a raven or eagle in tram cars painted in traditional Tlingit motifs. Start from the cruise ship dock and soar up the steep slopes of Mount Roberts. This is the easy, nonaerobic way to climb halfway up the mountain into breathtaking scenery and a bird's-eye view of the peaks and fjords surrounding Alaska's capital city. On a clear day, the view from this alpine lookout is spectacular. Take a short walk on the Interpretive Loop Trail or, if you want a more vigorous workout, continue on foot from the **GASTINEAU GUIDING COMPANY'S NATURE CENTER** (at 2,000 feet above sea level) to the summit of Mount Roberts (3,819 feet) along steep, rocky ridges and flower-filled meadows. These meadows are favorite launching sites for Juneau's colorful parasailers. (For a truly vigorous workout, walk up and ride down. You can climb to the tram station on the mountain in about an hour from town through lovely, steep, often wet woods and then continue on to the summit. The trail begins on the southeastern edge of downtown Juneau. For only $1, you ride down.) The tram generally runs 9am to 9pm, seven days a week, May through September, and costs $18 per person, or if you're in town a while you can buy a season's pass. For information, contact 907/463-3412; www.alaska.net/~junotram. &

HELICOPTER–FLIGHT-SEEING TOURS / Although, it's pricey, at least once during your trip to Alaska you should splurge and get up in the air, if only to experience the vastness of this magnificent land. To do it by helicopter adds an extra thrill. **NORTHSTAR TREKKING** (907/790-4530), led by Bob Engelbrecht, one of the pioneers of the now-classic Mendenhall Glacier helicopter tours out of Juneau nearly 20 years ago, offers the popular "Helicopter Glacier Discovery" and the "Helicopter Icefield Explorer," where Bob and his experienced team of pilots and mountain guides swoop you over mountaintops and cascading rivers of ice, then land you on the Mendenhall, Taku, Norris, Gilkey, or Lemon Glacier. **TEMSCO HELICOPTERS** (907/789-9501) offers a 1-hour Mendenhall Glacier tour during which you land on the glacier, which flows down into the heart of Juneau, and glimpse the enormous reservoir of ice in the Juneau Icefield that feeds so many of Southeast's rivers. **ERA HELICOPTERS** (907/586-2030) which has been dubbed the "Indiana Jones" of the helicopter services, takes you up Taku Inlet. One passenger described it as "more of a rollercoaster ride, very exciting, where you actually fly down inside a glacier." **WINGS OF ALASKA** (907/789-0790) flies fixed-wing aircraft, departing on floats from Juneau's downtown waterfront for flight-seeing adventures over the Juneau Icefield or to Taku Glacier Lodge. Prices run about $165 per hour.

HELICOPTER GLACIER HIKES / NorthStar Trekking (907/790-4530, fax 907/790-4419) offers an energetic adventure—combing helicopter flight-seeing with a 2-hour guided hike on the wild, still, icy terrain of the glaciers. Experienced mountain guides will fully outfit you with the proper clothing, gear, ice axes, and crampons for a surprising journey. You'll land by helicopter, climb amidst towers of ice, leap over tumbling blue-water streams, and peer into deep crevasses of startling blue. It's a magical world, where the forces of nature are constantly changing the landscape. Participants need not be experienced, just moderately agile with a sense of curiosity and adventure. Distance covered is about 2 miles. Cost is about $290 per person for a total of 4 hours.

WHALE-WATCHING / While Alaska is home to many of the great whales, the **HUMPBACK WHALES** are probably the most visible and acrobatic of the great whales and can be seen throughout the summer, swimming through Southeast and the Gulf of Alaska. Whether you're on a ferry or a charter fishing boat, keep your eyes open. Many outfits advertise and offer daily boat trips out to watch whales. **AUK NU TOURS**

(76 Egan Dr; 907/586-8687 or 800/820-2628) offers an excellent whale-watching trip daily to Point Adolphus with a naturalist on board. Since the company is Native-owned, you get a delightfully different naturalist/historian narration. The boat sails via Gustavus, so you can make it a 1-day trip out of Juneau or overnight in Gustavus—call or stop by their office on the waterfront downtown to make reservations. Their tours depart daily from Auke Bay. A number of smaller boats take folks whale-watching too from downtown at Merchant's Wharf. DOLPHIN TOURS (907/463-3422 or 800/770-3422) has been in operation for several years, taking up to 16 passengers on their jet boats for a 3-hour ride out to watch for whales; tours run April through October. Also, ORCA ENTERPRISES (907/789-6801 or 888/733-6722; www. alaskawhalewatching.com) takes passengers on small boats for whale-watching or charter fishing.

SEA KAYAKING / At ALASKA PADDLE SPORTS (907/789-2382), in 1-day intensive sessions in single kayaks, instructors drill you to help ensure a safe journey on the water. You spend the day in a dry suit, in and out of the water, flipping boats, learning paddling skills, how to get in and out of a capsized boat, and how to rescue yourself or your buddy. Nancy Peel, the owner, has been a ski instructor for 20 years at Eaglecrest and has been involved in sea kayaking for 17 years as a guide/instructor/expedition leader on trips for Alaska Discovery and Alaska Paddle Sports. Her prime focus is education for locals (including park rangers, Alaska Discovery, and Auk Ta Shaa guides), but they welcome all tourists too. You can take the class, then rent one of her fleet of boats. Call for classes and rental reservations. AUK TA SHAA DISCOVERY (800/820-2628 or 907/586-8687) offers a 6-hour Channel Islands sea kayak adventure for $95 per person every day, May to September, which includes round-trip transportation from Juneau, lunch, and all gear.

MENDENHALL FLOAT TRIP / No self-respecting Alaskan would call this a wilderness trip when you float through several subdivisions and underneath the highway bridge, but tourists love it, and a lot of cruise ship passengers choose to take this trip. It's not wild water, but there are a few thrills and chills, and it's still beautiful country, as you start off in Mendenhall Lake at the foot of Mendenhall Glacier. The 4-hour excursion costs about $90 per person and is offered through Auk Ta Shaa Discovery (800/820-2628 or 907/586-8687).

FISHING / Small fishing charters abound in Juneau. Once featured on Charles Kuralt's *America*, Butch and Sarah Laughlin offer a combination of freshwater fishing, bear watching, and floatplane adventures with ALASKA FLY'N'FISH CHARTERS (907/790-2120; akbyair@ptialaska. net; www.alaskabyair.com). David and Cynthia Hansen, both captains

in their own right, run **ACCESS ALASKA CHARTERS & TOURS** (907/
780-2232 or 888/432-4282; www.juneaucharterboats.com), which specializes in salmon and halibut fishing. They promise: "You'll arrive a
client and leave as a friend." If you are into fly-fishing, you're in luck!
Richard Culver of **FLYWATER ADVENTURES** (907/789-5977; www.fly-
wateradventures.com; flywater@alaska.net) is one of the best. He and his
guides host programs out of two Southeast lodges and run multiday
expeditions out to the coastal islands of Southeast Alaska and into Glacier Bay National Park.

HIKING / Juneau has wonderful hiking. Trails and ridges abound. The
trailheads to a few favorites—**PERSEVERANCE, EBNER FALLS, MOUNT
JUNEAU, GRANITE CREEK BASIN,** and **MOUNT ROBERTS**—are all
within easy walking distance of downtown. The most mellow route
takes you to Ebner Falls; a more energetic hike takes you farther, past
the falls, to Granite Creek Basin. Mount Juneau is the steep mountain
rising behind the city. Steep is the watchword here, so be careful. Mount
Roberts rises to the west of downtown and is not as steep an ascent as
Mount Juneau. **MOUNT JUMBO** is also a popular climb. This is the
highest peak on Douglas Island, which can be seen by looking across
Gastineau Channel from city center.

BIKING / Located downtown, **MOUNTAIN GEARS** will rent you mountain bikes by the hour ($6) or for the day ($25) and point you in the
direction of fun trips whether out to Douglas Island or the 24-mile
round trip to the Mendenhall Glacier. Rentals include lock, helmet,
map, water bottle, and directions. 126 Front St; 907/586-4327; open
Monday to Saturday.

GOLFING / The idea of golf in Alaska is amusing and a relatively new
sport in the Far North. Teeing off here more closely approximates what
the first Scots (who invented the game so many years ago) found so exhilarating. The roughs are truly rough, and at high tide you'll need your
knee-high rubber boots. Hazards abound—dirt, mud, spawning salmon,
and ravens that fly off with brightly colored golf balls. At the nine-hole,
par-3 Mendenhall Golf Course, "winter rules" are played all year long.
While the fairways are not smooth carpets of grass, there is a certain
charm here found on few other golf courses in the world. And, if you're
here to see Alaska, you'll see it all from the golf course—mountains, glaciers, eagles, salmon. You can rent clubs and tee off any day of the week.
At the end of Industrial Blvd, near the Juneau airport; 907/789-1221.

ROAD TRIP / Get on **EGAN DRIVE** downtown and just head north.
Technically Egan turns into another name like Glacier Highway, but
everyone just calls it "The Road" or "Going Out the Road." About 13
miles out is the turnoff for the **MENDENHALL GLACIER,** which John

Muir, who originally named it Auk Glacier after the Indians who lived here, called "one of the most beautiful of all the coastal glaciers." Past Auke Bay, there are a number of good sites for picnicking or strolling the rocky beaches. At Mile 23 is the lovely **SHRINE OF SAINT THERESE**, a little chapel on an island, which is a peaceful place to watch for sea lions, seals, and eagles. Farther along is **EAGLE BEACH**, a fun walk, but keep in mind the high fluctuation of tides in Southeast. You'll see stunning views of the Chilkat Mountains and the waters of Lynn Canal, which is not really a canal at all, but a deepwater fjord.

PUBLIC-USE CABINS / The U.S. Forest Service (877/444-6777) has four public-use cabins in the Juneau area for rent at Peterson Lake and along the Eagle Glacier, John Muir, and Dan Moeller Trails. Each has a propane stove, plywood bunks, and costs $25 to $40 a night. The State of Alaska Division of Parks (907/465-4563) also maintains three public-use cabins—Blue Mussel and Cowee Meadow cabins at Point Bridget, 39 miles out the road (Glacier Hwy), which may be reserved for $35 a night;

ADMIRALTY ISLAND: FORTRESS OF THE BEARS

To the Tlingit Indians, the long, forested island to the west of Juneau is known as *Kootznoohoo* or "Fortress of the Bears." Amidst one of the last great stands of old-growth forest and one of the densest populations of nesting bald eagles, there roams at least one magnificent, formidable brown bear for every square mile. It is not surprising, then, that early Russian explorers called this island "The Island of Fear." It is 100 miles long and 22 miles wide and today is designated and preserved as **Admiralty Island National Monument.**

When Captain George Vancouver sailed into these waters in 1789, charting the coast and looking for the fabled Northwest Passage, he named this island Admiralty in honor of the English Admiralty. But he, too, had a moment of reckoning near Point Retreat, the northern tip of the island, where today a stately lighthouse stands. When he sent a mapping party into Auke Bay on the mainland coast, the boats were met by Tlingits in their war canoes and regalia. Their spruce-wood armor and spruce-wood hats made them look very large and tall indeed. Wisely, Vancouver did not want trouble with these Native people and so he commanded his boats to retreat around the point. Thus, the name.

Today, most people go to Admiralty for a wilderness experience, to kayak, canoe, camp, watch bears, and experience the peace and solitude.

The **Stan Price Brown Bear Sanctuary** at Pack Creek on Admiralty Island has become a popular destination. Named for a marvelous old homesteader who, with and Oliver Inlet cabin, which is on Seymour Canal, 23 miles south of Juneau, accessible only by boat or plane.

TAKU GLACIER LODGE / Picturesque Taku Glacier Lodge (907/586-8258) lies at the end of a spectacular flight over the mountains and up Taku Inlet, a deepwater fjord south of Juneau. Wings of Alaska flies seaplanes from Juneau's downtown waterfront for a 3-hour tour that includes a salmon barbecue at the lodge (1 hour of flight-seeing, 2 hours at the lodge). Built in 1923, 30 miles from Juneau, Taku Lodge once was used as a hunting and fishing camp. Today, the lodge entertains folks for lunch and dinner all through the summer, from mid-May to October. The historic log cabin sits across from the Hole-in-the-Wall Glacier, and even has a resident black bear named Scarface, whom you often can see nosing about the premises. For more information, contact Wings of Alaska (8421 Livingston Wy, Juneau, AK 99801; 907/789-0790, fax 907/789-2021).

TRACY ARM ADVENTURE CRUISES / A day trip sailing out of Juneau, Tracy Arm will take you thousands of years back into the Ice Age. Be out

his wife, lived here among the bears until his death in 1989, the sanctuary is only 28 miles from Juneau. To protect Pack Creek from its own popularity, the Forest Service has now initiated a permit system, designating two places for watching bears: a gravel bar near the mouth of the creek and an observation tower deeper into the woods. Both offer wonderful opportunities to observe bears in their natural habitat. You will see the crumbling remains of Stan and Esther's cabin, floathouse, and gardens. No camping is allowed near Pack Creek, only on nearby islands. Permits are required from June 1 to September 10. Depending on the time you go, there is also a fee. For more details, and lists of guides and charter services to Pack Creek, contact the U.S. Forest Service Information Center (101 Egan Dr, Juneau, AK 99801; 907/586-8751) or Admiralty Island National Monument (907/586-8790).

Thayer Lake Wilderness Lodge was the essence of "wilderness experience" long before ecotourism became a trendy idea. Situated on the edge of Thayer Lake, it is remote, rustic, peaceful, and has been in operation for more than 40 years. The lodge can accommodate up to six people in two simple cabins by the lake and a room in the lodge. The Nelson family, who built the lodge and still run it today, offer two packages—one for hard-core hikers and the other for those interested in brown bear viewing and photography. Contact them for reservations or more information (PO Box 8897, Ketchikan, AK 99901; 907/789-5646, fax 907/247-7053; alaskabearviewing.com).

—Nan Elliot

on deck when you "cross the bar," the terminal moraine of the glacier, which now lies at the head of this 2,000-year-old jewel-like fjord. From here, it is 25 miles of steep canyon walls, intense blue-green water, and intricate maneuvering through icebergs to get to the north and south faces of the **SAWYER GLACIER**. The *Keet* (meaning "killer whale"), a 78-foot, custom catamaran designed for sightseeing, departs daily from downtown Juneau mid-May through mid-September at **AUK NU TOURS** (76 Egan Dr; 907/586-8687 or 800/820-2628) and costs about $100 per person with lunch included. There are also other smaller boats which cruise out to the enchanting glaciers in Tracy Arm, such as **WILDERNESS SWIFT CHARTERS** (907/463-4942; tongass@alaska.net). Reservations are recommended for all-day cruises. A family operation that runs the 56-foot *Adventure Bound* also takes folks on daily cruises into Tracy Arm and is concerned not only for your comfort but also for the environment. Call Steven and Winona Weber at **ADVENTURE BOUND ALASKA** (907/463-2509 or 800/228-3875).

EAGLECREST SKI AREA / Juneau is the home and training ground of Olympic downhill skier and silver medalist Hillary Lindh. She grew up skiing the slopes of Eaglecrest, high up on Douglas Island—a ski resort with 30 alpine trails, 8 kilometers of Nordic ski trails, and a vertical drop of 1,400 feet. Skiing here is geared to the intermediate and advanced skier. For information, contact Eaglecrest Ski Area (155 S Seward St, Juneau, AK 99801; 907/790-2000; 907/586-5330, for ski conditions; www.juneau.lib.ak.us/eaglecrest/eaglcrst.htm).

RENT A LIGHTHOUSE / Dotted along the coast of British Columbia and Southeast Alaska are dozens of lighthouses, for nearly a century now a beacon to seafaring men and women. Only a few in British Columbia are still manned; in Alaska they are all automated. But all are in remote, breathtakingly beautiful spots. A few near Juneau are being prepared as remote bed-and-breakfast rentals, such as the **FIVE FINGER LIGHTHOUSE**, which is now a decommissioned Coast Guard property. It is located on a 3-acre private island south of Juneau. Call the Juneau Lighthouse Association (907/790-3339; fax 907/586-2636; www.5fingerlighthouse.com) for reservations. **SENTINEL ISLAND LIGHTHOUSE** (907/586-5338, fax 907/586-5820) is a historic art-deco-style lighthouse, built in 1902 north of Juneau with a view of the Chilkat Mountains. It is open for group tours and events. A nonprofit group in Juneau also has been working to renovate and restore the **POINT RETREAT LIGHTHOUSE** at the northern tip of Admiralty Island and rent it out as a B&B. Call the Alaska Lighthouse Association (907/364-2410) for more information.

GUIDES AND OUTFITTERS

ALASKA DISCOVERY WILDERNESS ADVENTURES / This is one of the oldest and most respected wilderness expedition guiding companies in the state, with quality trips led by knowledgeable and enthusiastic guides. The company emphasizes "leave no trace" camping and donates 10 percent of its profits to environmental organizations working toward the preservation of Alaska's special places. Southeast is home, and the company offers 1- to 12-day canoeing, sea kayaking, and rafting trips to see glaciers, wild rivers, bears, and other wildlife. Canoe Admiralty Island, kayak through Glacier Bay, and raft the Tatshenshini and Alsek Rivers. 5449 Shaune Dr #4, Juneau, AK 99801; 907/780-6505 or 800/586-1911; akdisco@alaska.net; www.akdiscovery.com.

GASTINEAU GUIDING COMPANY / They will take you on adventure hikes, rain-forest nature walks, or trekking on the Juneau Icefield. Stop in for details at the Mount Roberts Nature Center (907/586-6421) at the top of the tram. PO Box 240576, Douglas, AK 99824; 907/586-2666, fax 907/586-3990; hikeak@ptialaska.net.

ALASKA RAIN FOREST TOURS / This outfit offers trip-planning services for the independent traveler—a one-stop shopping guide for wilderness travel, whale-watching, remote lodges, bed-and-breakfasts, charter fishing boats, kayaking trips, and more. They are conveniently located at the Juneau International Airport. 1873 Shell Simmons Dr, Juneau, AK 99801; 907/463-3466 or 800/493-4453; artours@alaska. net; www.alaska.net/~artour.

MARINE ADVENTURE SAILING TOURS (MAST) / The very rich, the very fun, the very talented, and the very smart have sailed with Captain Andy Spear on the *Adventuress*, a 50-foot Down East cutter. You can charter the entire boat for four people with full service—that means captain, crew, and gourmet meals—for $7,500 for a 6-day week. Some of the most popular custom-designed, weeklong voyages are to Glacier Bay and Tracy Arm–Ford's Terror. Captain Spear had so much fun as "Bad Guy #1" in John Sayles' film *Limbo*, that he's moonlighting in the movie business now with sailing ventures more limited. So book early. If he's available, you'll have a wonderfully entertaining time. 945 Fritz Cove Rd, Juneau, AK 99801; 907/789-0919; info@alaskasail.com; www. alaska.net/~mast.

WILDERNESS SWIFT CHARTERS / Andy and Kristen Romanoff take visitors on affordable 1-day trips to Tracy Arm ($125 per person) or multiple-day voyages (starting at about $499 per person) to watch whales, bears, and glaciers—"the best of Southeast Alaska." 6205 N Douglas Hwy, Juneau, AK 99801; 907/463-4942; tongass@alaska.net; www.alaska.net/~tongass.

AUK NU TOURS / If you want to see Alaska in an intimate and informative way with quality service, Auk Nu Tours, owned by Goldbelt Native Corporation, is a top-flight operation. Many of their own companies and partnerships have some of the best guides and tour operators in Southeast Alaska. With warm and personable service, they can create diverse itineraries of land and sea packages such as whale-watching, cruising into Glacier Bay, or rafting rivers, from 1 day to several weeks. They are especially proud of sharing their cultural history with you and creating quality tourist opportunities while at the same time respecting the environment and preserving their cultural heritage. 76 Egan Dr; 800/820-2628 or 907/586-8687; www.auknutours.com.

NIGHTLIFE

PERSEVERANCE THEATRE / This is community, regional, professional, and multicultural theater at its best. From its first Juneau production, *Pure Gold*, with local old-timers retelling gold-rush stories and grizzly bear encounters, to the staging of *Yup'ik Antigone*, a Yup'ik Eskimo rendition of the famous Greek tragedy, which toured New York and Paris, Perseverance Theatre has vaulted into the hearts of Juneau and all of Alaska. (Molly Smith, founder and former director of Perseverance Theatre for 18 years, is currently the artistic director of the prestigious Arena Stage in Washington, D.C.) Call for performance schedules. The theater is located on Douglas Island. 914 3rd St, Douglas, AK 99824; 907/364-2421.

BAR SCENE / Tourists go to the **RED DOG SALOON**, locals go to the **ALASKAN HOTEL**, old-time Juneau (young and old) goes to the **TRIANGLE**, and the politicians schmooze in **THE BUBBLE ROOM** at the Baranof Hotel (but the story is they loosen up later at the Triangle). The Red Dog, the Alaskan, and the Triangle are all within shooting distance of each other on Franklin Street in downtown Juneau. You can't miss 'em—ask any local. The Baranof Hotel is a couple of blocks up the hill on Franklin Street.

FESTIVALS AND EVENTS

FOURTH OF JULY / In the early days of Juneau's history, the Fourth of July was the highlight of summer. There were canoe races, rock-drilling contests, and firemen battling each other with fire hoses. The firemen today throw buckets of saltwater taffy to all the children during the parade and are still dousing each other (and the crowd) with fire hoses, to the beat of local bands, in an all-day street dance on Douglas Island. That's after the parade and the sand sculpture contest, a race against the tides. This is the height of old-fashioned, rip-roaring good fun found everywhere in Southeast on the Fourth. But it is the spectacular fireworks over the harbor at midnight on July 3 that sets Juneau apart.

GOLDEN NORTH SALMON DERBY / This is a big deal, not just for silvers, but for gold. The derby runs for 3 days on the third weekend in August. The record silver salmon weighed in at 51 pounds. If you catch a tagged fish, you can win $1,000. If you catch the record fish for that year, you can win $10,000. And if you catch the special tagged fish, you've not only landed dinner, but a $100,000 prize. Call 907/789-2399 for details.

ALASKA FOLK FESTIVAL / A springtime, cabin-fever, musical jamboree that goes on for 10 days in April, this event attracts talented musicians and bands from all over Alaska. Alaskans know how to make music, and they know how to party. This is a good time. Call the visitors center for details (907/364-2658).

JUNEAU JAZZ & CLASSICS / On the last two weekends of this festival features live professional jazz and classical performances, musical workshops, special cruises, and events for the whole family. Tickets may be bought at Hearthside Bookstores. 907/463-3378; music@juneau.com; www.juneau.com/music/.

THE GALLERY WALK / If you happen to be in Juneau the weekend after Thanksgiving, this is an opportunity you shouldn't miss. It starts after work on Friday and the streets downtown are packed until late at night. Annie Kaill started it years ago and "it's a real party." All the galleries feature a couple of artists and there are special shows and refreshments. Call Annie Kaill's at 907/586-2880.

JUNEAU-DOUGLAS HIGH SCHOOL DRILL TEAM / From little Juneau, Alaska, they've dazzled the world. In 1995, going toe to toe with the best on the planet, they swept the competition in Nagoya, Japan, to steal three world championships in the International Dance Drill Competition. There's even a proud subsidiary known as Drill Team Dads. If you're in Juneau during the school year or on the Fourth of July, check them out. The team performs throughout the winter at all Juneau-Douglas High School basketball games and at special events around the state. For a schedule of performances, call the high school (907/463-1923).

RESTAURANTS

Armadillo Tex-Mex Café & Brewery / ★★

431 S FRANKLIN, JUNEAU; 907-586-1880

"Armadillo's" (interchangeably known as "The Tex Mex") is a big-time favorite in Juneau. Why? It's cheap, and you get a lot of food. It's basic, but that's the charm of the place—friendly people, easy banter, and casual dining. The food ranges from nachos, chalupas, fajitas, and tacos to Armadillo specialties such as Enchiladas Azteca, Pollo Loco, and huevos rancheros. They recently added their own mini-brewery. *$; MC, V; local checks only; lunch Mon–Sat, dinner every day; beer and wine; across from the cruise ship dock.*

Buzz's Paradise Lunch & Bakery / ★★

245 MARINE WY, JUNEAU; 907/586-2253

Follow those warm, happy smells floating out the door to this tiny cafe near the water. Everything is baked from scratch—from morning pastries to birthday cakes to order such as "The Grand Duchess" (chocolate and raspberries)—but lunch is their particular specialty. Buzz and Monica Ritter have lived in Juneau for 25 years, and Buzz worked many years as a chef at the Fiddlehead. A day's sampling might be fresh soups such as chicken with lime, cilantro, and chile, or Paradise Sausage Soup with black olives and zucchini. He makes fresh breads, pasta and potato salads, all kinds of tortilla wraps, and roasts his own meats for sandwiches. *$; no credit cards; local checks only; breakfast, lunch every day in summer; breakfast, lunch Mon–Fri in winter; no alcohol.* &

The Channel Bowl Café / ★★★

608 W WILLOUGHBY AVE, JUNEAU; 907/586-6139

Tucked into a spare corner of the old bowling alley, this little cafe has been tickling the funny bone of Juneau for years. Master humorist and owner Laurie Berg runs a "full-service cafe," a throwback to the old diners of the 1940s. Almost everyone in Juneau has flipped burgers here—including the governor of Alaska. This is the ultimate breakfast spot, and local gossip is free; note the offbeat humor on the walls. Order the Mount Jumbo plate, "Breakfast to Match our Mountains," or another hometown favorite, Blueberry-Pecan Fancy Pancakes. If you love chocolate-chunk cookies, the hands-down, melt-in-your-mouth, best in the world are here. Pray that Laurie has baked some that day. *$; no credit cards; checks OK; breakfast, lunch every day; no alcohol; a stone's throw from the Fiddlehead.*

Chan's Thai Kitchen / ★★

11820 GLACIER HWY, JUNEAU; 907/789-9777

When this tiny restaurant opened in 1997, there were lines out the door. The menu is long, each dish very distinctive and tasty, and the portions are big, which is always endearing to Alaska hearts. It's definitely a local experience. The ambience is that there is no ambience. It's very basic, with simple dinette tables and chairs and little decor. But you look out on Auke Bay, so the combination is perfect in most Alaskans' book—good view and good food. Heavy-hitting favorites are the cashew chicken, spring rolls, and pad thai. *$; MC, V; local checks only; lunch Tues–Fri, dinner Tues–Sat; closed for 2 weeks in Dec; no alcohol; in Auke Bay on the Glacier Hwy.* &

The Fiddlehead Restaurant and Bakery / ★★★★

429 W WILLOUGHBY AVE, JUNEAU; 907/586-3150

Homey and folksy, the Fiddlehead Restaurant and Bakery has been a welcome oasis for Southeasterners for more than 20 years. It blends an informal natural foods restaurant downstairs with elegant, candlelit dining upstairs in the Fireweed Room. The Fireweed Room features a piano bar with live jazz and folk music. The menu varies from homemade soups and pastas, served with the unique Fiddlehead Pesto (made from the tender tips of the ferns for which the restaurant is named), to the freshest of seafoods, homebaked breads, and rich desserts. *The Fiddlehead Cookbook* (St. Martin's Press, 1991) shares some of the restaurant's secrets. *$$–$$$; AE, DIS, MC, V; local checks only; breakfast, lunch, dinner every day; full bar; around the corner from the Alaska State Museum.* & *(downstairs only)*

Hangar on the Wharf / ★★

#2 MARINE WY, STE 106, JUNEAU; 907/586-5018

Located in a reconverted floatplane hangar, sitting out on pilings at the edge of Gastineau Channel, this is one of the few restaurants in Juneau that really has an expansive water view. It has had many reincarnations in its lifetime, but this latest version, capitalizing on its view, history (with old photos), casual atmosphere, and affordable tasty menu (a step above "bar-grub" fare) has made it one of Juneau's most popular hangouts for the 25- to 45-year-old crowd. They specialize in seafood here and the portions are huge—like the popular halibut taco, coconut prawns, jambalaya, and clams steamed in pale ale. They are also fond of beer, with 108 varieties and styles with 24 of them on tap. "It's the largest beer selection in Southeast outside of some people's refrigerators at home," jokes owner Murray Damitio, whose father was a bush pilot up north. *$; AE, DIS, MC, V; local checks only; lunch, dinner every day; full bar; downtown in Merchants Wharf.* &

Heritage Café / Heritage Coffee Company

174 S FRANKLIN ST, JUNEAU; 800/478-JAVA OR 907/586-1087

Close to the cruise ship dock, Heritage is a well-known coffee haunt in Juneau. In summer, it is populated more by tourists than by locals. The front windows are good for people watching. The cafe features a selection of pastries, soups, salads, and sandwiches. *$; AE, DIS, MC, V; local checks only; breakfast, lunch, dinner every day; no alcohol; midway between the cruise ship docks and the State Capitol.*

The Hot Bite

AUKE BAY BOAT HARBOR, JUNEAU; 907/790-2483

"Out the road" at the Auke Bay Marina, the Hot Bite is a good place to know about. After a hard day fishing, or if you're biking round-trip to

Mendenhall Glacier from downtown Juneau, tank up here. It's just a shack in the parking lot, with picnic tables in a screened-in porch, and it's high on the grease quotient—but locals love it. Try the grilled chicken or great halibut burgers, with a side of tart vinegar chips, and wash them down with a thick, creamy milkshake. *$; no credit cards; local checks only; lunch every day in winter; lunch, dinner every day in summer; no alcohol; on the road to Auke Bay at the Auke Bay Boat Harbor.*

Olivia's de Mexico / ★

222 SEWARD ST, JUNEAU; 907/586-6870

Take a tip from Olivia's countrymen. The Mexican crews off the cruise ships all eat at Olivia's. During the legislative session, there are standing lines at lunchtime. Even though it's in the basement, it's colorful and festive. Here, diners get the genuine article—the distinctive taste from south of the border—because that's the way Olivia cooked it at home. Chili verde and chiles rellenos are popular, and Olivia makes daily specials such as posole, a meat and hominy stew. *$; MC, V; local checks only; lunch Mon–Fri, dinner Mon–Sat; beer and wine; downtown.*

Pizzeria Roma / ★

#2 MARINE WY, STE 104, JUNEAU; 907/463-5020

This small Italian cafe has the best pizza in town. It's a little pricier, but it's worth it. Try the thin-crusted Montecatini pizza with capers, red peppers, and feta cheese. Or dive into a huge Insalata Roma with fresh garlic, artichoke hearts, and Greek olives. The aroma of garlic is heavy here. Evening deliveries are available. *$–$$; MC, V; local checks only; lunch Mon–Fri, dinner every day; beer and wine; on the corner of Merchants Wharf near the Hangar.* &

The Twisted Fish / ★★★

550 S FRANKLIN, JUNEAU; 907/463-5033

Large neon fish hang from the wood beams of this airy, light restaurant at the end of the cruise ship dock. Their elegant fresh seafood and nice-quality wines served with a view of Gastineau Channel is reason enough to make the walk down the dock, rain or shine. They also serve a kaleidoscope of pastas, burgers, salads, and pizza pies—one which evokes an era gone by, the popular Georgio's Pie. (Georgio's was the original name of the restaurant, built in the mid-'90s.) The wine bar is quite extensive, with 30 wines available by the glass (including champagne) and five beers on tap. Smoking in the bar only; it can be quite noisy. *$$; AE, MC, V; checks OK; lunch, dinner every day; open May–mid-Sept; full bar; at the end of the cruise ship dock.* &

Valentine's Coffee House & Bakery / ★★

III SEWARD ST, JUNEAU; 907/463-5144

A bright, savory aroma-filled gathering place, this little coffeehouse has a cheerful atmosphere. Everything is baked from scratch. There are good coffee drinks, exceptional coffee cakes, and interesting and tasty sandwiches (their Italian Summer Garden Sandwich on focaccia is a favorite). Tempting desserts include great "snaps" (as in ginger snaps and ginger crinkles). *$; no credit cards; local checks only; breakfast, lunch, dinner every day; closed Sun in winter; no alcohol; downtown Juneau.* &

LODGINGS

The Baranof / ★★

127 N FRANKLIN ST, JUNEAU, AK 99801; 800/544-0970 OR 907/586-2660, FAX 907/586-8315

For years, the Baranof (built in 1939) was *the* hotel in Juneau, in more ways than one. As its finery began to fade, its character continued to grow. During the legislative sessions of old, this is where a lot of horse trading went on, and deals were sealed on the back of cocktail napkins. It's still a popular haunt during the legislative session. But in summer, it's all tourists. It's been remodeled in recent years; the rooms are still quite small, though, and the street side can be noisy. We recommend the corner, water-view suites on the sixth and seventh floors. *$$$; AE, DC, DIS, MC, V; checks OK; near the State Capitol.*

Goldbelt Hotel Juneau / ★★★

51 EGAN DR, JUNEAU, AK 99801; 888/478-6909 OR 907/586-6900, FAX 907/463-3567

If it's traditional comfort and a lovely view you're looking for, this hotel, which overlooks Gastineau Channel, is just the ticket. Formerly a Westmark Hotel, it is now owned by Goldbelt, the local Native corporation. They have opened up the lobby so that it is airy and bright with a simple elegance. Magnificent carvings, masks, and beautiful art adorn the entrance, reflecting the local heritage of its owners. A cheerful restaurant, Chinooks, serves a variety of seafood, pepper steak, omelets, burgers, and salads. It is open daily for breakfast, lunch, dinner and brunch on Sunday. There are 105 rooms, fairly spacious, with a color scheme of peach and green. Choose a water view, the higher up the better. Five of the six bedroom floors are nonsmoking. Lower rates are featured in winter. *$$$; AE, DC, DIS, JCB, MC, V; checks OK; www.goldbelt.com; downtown, directly across from the wharf.* &

Juneau International Hostel / ★

614 HARRIS ST, JUNEAU, AK 99801; 907/586-9559 (BETWEEN 8–9AM AND 6–10:30PM)
For budget traveling, this is one of the best hostels in Alaska and has gotten rave reviews from visitors around the world. Located in a historic home in downtown Juneau, the cheerful yellow building has accommo-dations year-round: 46 beds in two separate dorms for men and women, showers, and a common room. In summer there is a midnight curfew and the hostel is closed during the day from 9am to 5pm. Reservations via mail with deposit are definitely recommended in summer. Cost is $10 for adults, $5 for children, $7 for Hostel International members, and children under 5 are free. *$; no credit cards; no checks; at 6th and Harris, downtown.*

BED-AND-BREAKFASTS

There are more than 100 B&B homes around Juneau which range from historical to Victorian to classic Alaska log cabins. You can be by the water, in the mountains, or right downtown. Note that B&Bs in Alaska are less likely to be inns, but rather rooms in someone's home and therefore the "burn-out factor" is about 5 years. That said, here are a few that have been in business a few years and gotten rave reviews. For more information, contact the Bed and Breakfast Association of Alaska (369 S Franklin St, Ste 200, Juneau, AK 99801; www.wetpage.com/bbaaip).

DOWNTOWN JUNEAU / A block from the State Capitol, is the historic **MULLINS HOUSE BED & BREAKFAST** (526 Seward St; 907/586-3384), with three rooms where you are "pampered in an old-fashioned way"; $80 for a double, and guest pets are welcome. **CASHEN QUARTERS** (315 Gold St; 907/586-9863, fax 907/586-9861; www.cashenquarters.com) has five private apartments with their own kitchens, located at the foot of Mount Roberts; $100 per unit. **MOUNT JUNEAU INN BED & BREAKFAST** (1801 Old Glacier Hwy; 907/463-5855; www.mtjuneauinn.com; mtjuneauinn@alaska.com) is friendly and hospitable with a nice view of Gastineau Channel. A couple of miles from downtown, the inn has seven rooms and a cottage with private phones, gourmet breakfasts, and a guest kitchen; $85 to $120 for a double, nonsmoking.

DOUGLAS ISLAND / ENTRANCE POINT HOMESTEAD (11260 N Douglas Hwy; 907/463-2684; www.wetpage.com/entrancept/) is classic Alaska—a gracious log cabin home on 10 wooded acres with a waterfront view. Two cozy guest rooms with goose down comforters share a bath. Breakfasts are full of Alaska touches, from smoked salmon to rhubarb sauce for your pecan-yogurt pancakes. **BLUEBERRY LODGE BED & BREAKFAST** (9436 N Douglas Hwy; 907/463-5886;

www.wetpage.com/bluberry/) has five rooms and the entire lodge is often rented for special events such as retreats or family reunions. The lodge sits in the woods with views of mountains and water.

MENDENHALL GLACIER–AUKE BAY AREA / For the loveliest view of the Mendenhall Glacier and delightful hosts, rent a car and drive out to **GLACIER TRAIL BED & BREAKFAST** (1081 Arctic Circle; 907/789-5646; www.wetpage.com/glacier) with its Victorian and French country touches. Hot entrees like crab quiche, strawberry waffles, or oven omelets are served for breakfast; $120 for a double, nonsmoking. **AUKE LAKE BED & BREAKFAST** (11595 Mendenhall Loop Rd; 907/790-3253; www.AdmiraltyTours.com) is a large gracious home on the edge of Auke Lake with a hot tub for family and guests out on the front deck. The guest rooms are two-room or three-room suites, with private phones, and private entrance shared by other guests. About 3 miles from the airport, ferry dock, and glacier; $115 for a double. **PEARSON'S POND** (4541 Sawa Circle; 888/658-6328; www.juneau.com/pearsons.pond) is the place to go if you have money to burn and want all the conveniences of home and then some. The guest rooms share two hot tubs on the edge of a duck pond in the woods near Mendenhall Glacier. Located en route to the glacier; $229 for a double.

Gustavus and Glacier Bay National Park

Gustavus is unique in Southeast, tucked into the forest and spreading out on a flat outwash plain created by glaciers that receded more than 200 years ago. It is also on the edge of **GLACIER BAY NATIONAL PARK**. A 10-mile road connects the tiny town and park headquarters at Bartlett Cove. If you are flying into the park, you land in Gustavus.

Tlingit Indians built camps and smokehouses here for many generations. Then, in 1914, the first wave of white homesteaders arrived and called the settlement Strawberry Point because of the abundance of wild strawberries. A second wave of homesteaders arrived in the 1960s and 1970s, armed with *Whole Earth Catalogs* and a desire for back-to-the-land lifestyles. Gustavus (pop. 400) exudes small-town friendliness. People wave at each other, and pickup trucks still outnumber cars.

BARTLETT COVE, 10 miles down the road at Glacier Bay National Park, offers a very different experience from Gustavus. Gustavus appeals to independent travelers who want free time along with sightseeing, while visitors who stay at Bartlett Cove generally are on package tours designed to put the maximum amount of wilderness scenery in front of their video camera viewfinders.

Besides park headquarters, Bartlett Cove is home to the only developed campground in the area, as well as the Glacier Bay Lodge, where all manner of excursions may be arranged.

When Captain James Cook, on his voyages of discovery, sailed up Icy Strait more than 200 years ago, there was no Glacier Bay, only a huge wall of ice stretching across the opening to what we know today as Glacier Bay. In this blink of geologic time, the ice has receded and opened up a treasure of fjords and cascading rivers of ice—one of our most precious national parks. You can now travel 60 miles upbay into the West Arm, which is the most dramatic and glacially active area of the park. This is the route the cruise ships take. But the best way to see the bay is slowly, over 10 days or 2 weeks, by small boat, paddling or under sail. Watch for seals, puffins, whales, and bears.

ACCESS AND INFORMATION

Air taxis in Juneau, Sitka, Skagway, and Haines offer scenic flights to Gustavus. For those who prefer to do their flight-seeing in a Boeing 737, Alaska Airlines (800/426-0333) has daily jet service in the summer. **AUK NU TOURS** (800/820-2628 or 907/586-8687), based in Juneau, operates a daily ferry from Juneau and Gustavus. It takes a little more than 2 hours. A one-way fare on plane or ferry will cost you about $50. If you need taxi service while in Gustavus or Bartlett Cove, call **TLC TAXI** (907/697-2239). They'll even rent you a bike or a kayak to get around. **BUD'S CAR RENTAL** (907/697-2403, fax 907/697-2789) is also available and makes more sense ($60 a day) if you're a group of four.

You can contact the **GUSTAVUS VISITORS ASSOCIATION** (PO Box 167, Gustavus, AK 99826; 907/697-2475; gustavusvisitors@hotmail. com; www.gustavus.com) for more information. **GLACIER BAY NATIONAL PARK** (907/697-2230) has an interesting Web site: www. nps.gov/glba. Headquarters for the national park and visitor information are located in Bartlett Cove, 10 miles by road from Gustavus.

ADVENTURES

EXPLORING BY BIKE / At the hub of Gustavus is a re-created 1930s-era gas-station-cum-English-cottage-flower-garden, the perfect symbol of Alaskans' two loves—the internal combustion engine and Mother Nature. **THE GUSTAVUS DRAY** (907/697-2481) has lots of petroleum memorabilia inside as well as doughnuts and ferry tickets. Most bed-and-breakfasts have old one-speed cruisers for biking through town. Pedal about a half mile north from the gas station to **FIREWEED GALLERY** (907/697-2325), open afternoons in summer. Bill Locher, a retired engineer turned stone carver, has a small gallery displaying local and Alaska sculpture and paintings. Go a half mile south from the gas station to

GUSTO BUILDING SUPPLY, where you can pick up a fishing license, and stop in at the **BEARTRACK MERCANTILE,** a well-provisioned general store, to pick up a visitor's map or the booklet *Trails of Glacier Bay and Gustavus* for a list of off-road hikes. For another splash of local color, cycle over to artist Carole Baker's **FLAMINGO GALLERY** (907/697-2283). Go south off Main Road just west of the Salmon River Bridge and turn right at the flamingo sign. Pedal another mile to the dock, which juts into Icy Passage and offers a 360-degree panorama of everything Southeast—mountains, islands, forests, dunes, and ocean surf. The Gustavus dock is the best place to watch the sunset and sunrise. The salt air is a good tonic but bracing.

FISHING AND WHALE-WATCHING / The chief attractions in Gustavus, besides relaxing, are fishing and whale-watching. One of the world's-record **HALIBUT** (400-plus pounds), caught on sport gear, was hooked just a few miles from the Gustavus dock. Nearby **POINT ADOLPHUS** is summer home to **HUMPBACK WHALES.** You may want to book your outdoor trips once you arrive and check the weather; kayaking or sailing in rain or heavy ocean swells can be miserable.

GOLFING / Within walking distance of the ferry dock, the nine-hole, par-3 **MOUNT FAIRWEATHER GOLF COURSE** (907/697-2214) is certainly not hoity-toity golf, but a good old seaside game nonetheless. There's beach, rampant weeds, and even real grass. Put your money in the coffee can and grab a set of old mismatched clubs. If the Fairweather Mountain Range is out, you won't find a prettier course in all of Alaska. Watch out for bears and moose and be forewarned that the first hole in mid-July might take at least 2 hours as everyone is down on their knees picking wild strawberries.

GUIDES AND OUTFITTERS

ALASKA'S GLACIER BAY TOURS AND CRUISES / Offers day cruises, on the *Spirit of Adventure*, into Glacier Bay National Park where the magnificence of the last great period of the Ice Age 10,000 years ago is still at work. Cost is about $160, including lunch. 800/451-5952; www.glacierbaytours.com.

AUK NU TOURS / One of the many special offerings from Auk Nu in addition to their ferry service between Gustavus and Juneau is a wonderful half-day wildlife and whale-watching tour in Icy Strait. Cost is $78 per person. 800/820-2628 or 907/586-1337.

CAMPER–KAYAKER FERRY SERVICE / The MV *Crystal Fjord* will run from mid-May to early September ferrying campers, kayakers, and their boats in and out of Glacier Bay. The vessel is operated by Glacier Bay Tours and Cruises and provides service for 34 passengers and exterior racks for 24 kayaks. The boat will make a round trip between Bartlett Cove and these four drop-off/pickup points: Geikie Inlet, Rendu Inlet, Mount Wright, and Bear Track Cove. Cost one-way is about $85 per person. Reservations may be made at the front desk of the Glacier Bay Lodge in summer or on the reservation line out of Seattle (800/451-5952).

GLACIER BAY SEA KAYAKS / Rent seaworthy kayaks and gear for exploring the waterways around Gustavus. This is the National Park Service concession in Glacier Bay for "do-it-yourself" camping and kayaking trips. The fiberglass kayaks rent for $40 per day for singles and $50 per day for doubles. Prices drop $10 to $15 per day for 3 days or more. They also will arrange drop-offs in the West and East Arms of Glacier Bay. 907/697-2257; kayakak@he.net; www.he.net/~kayakak.

ALASKA DISCOVERY / The fully equipped, guided sea kayak tours of Bartlett Cove and the Beardslee Island Archipelago are for adventurous, but inexperienced, day trippers; $119 per person. Evening paddles ($49) and longer trips are also available. 907/697-2411 or 800/586-1911.

SPIRIT WALKER EXPEDITIONS / This outfit offers complete 1-day, guided sea kayak excursions to Pleasant Island in Icy Strait, just outside Glacier Bay, and longer trips to nearby wilderness areas. 907/697-2266.

SEA OTTER KAYAK / Rents single and double Necky kayaks and gear for half-day paddles or longer expeditions. Reservations are recommended. Located near the Gustavus dock on Dock Road. 907/697-3007; www.he.net/~seaotter.

PONY CART RIDES / For those who prefer a more festive arrival in Gustavus or a special honeymoon trot down the beach, Kate Boesser (wife of Fritz Koschmann of Woodwind Sail Charters) can often be enticed to garland up her pony cart with flowers and meet your plane or take you on a sunset ride. 907/697-2282.

SEA WOLF WILDERNESS ADVENTURES / Whisks passengers to Point Adolphus in its 65-foot motor yacht with four private staterooms. Once there, you can paddle in double kayaks for up-close whale-watching, then paddle back to the yacht for a hot shower and gourmet meal: $200 per person per day with kayak usage. Overnight custom charters to various points, including Glacier Bay: $300 per person per day. Your hosts, Rusty Owen and Pamela Jean Miedtke, are both U.S. Coast Guard, 100-ton license holders with years of experience piloting the waters of Southeast. 907/697-2416.

GUSTAVUS MARINE CHARTERS / Captain Mike Nigro runs these highly recommended trips, excellent for small yacht tours of Glacier Bay National Park and Icy Strait. If at all possible, set aside a minimum of 3 days to fully absorb the wonder and the subtlety of the park. 907/697-2233, fax 907/697-2414.

KELLY BAY YACHT CHARTER / This outfit is the first choice for those who want the ultimate custom trip—picnicking on a wilderness beach overlooking Icy Strait, gunkholing, or serious fishing for trophy salmon or halibut—you name it. You can do it in complete comfort on their motor yacht, equipped with skiff for beachcombing excursions. They can also put you up in their sweet little log cabin lodge, Spruce Tip Lodge. Your hosts are Mike and Connie Mills. 907/697-2215.

RESTAURANTS

Bear's Nest Café

WILSON RD, GUSTAVUS; 907/697-2440
Tucked into the forest, this little cafe is the home (upstairs) to artist Lynne Morrow and her husband, musician Philip Riddle. Downstairs is a warm, creative cafe with special artistic touches such as straw baskets hanging from the ceiling, handmade paper menus, lots of windows, and green plants. They serve fresh crab, vegetarian enchiladas, salmon stir-fry, hot sausage sandwiches, almond butter and jam sandwiches, espressos, and Italian sodas, along with decadent desserts. They even have a fun B&B a stone's throw away, a round wooden cabin that is called just that: The Round House (sleeps four for $85 a night for the first two people; $10 more for each additional person; includes breakfast). *$$; DIS, MC, V; checks OK; lunch, dinner every day; no alcohol; bearsnest@ hotmail.com; a quarter mile down Wilson Rd.*

LODGINGS

Glacier Bay's Bear Track Inn / ★★

255 RINK CREEK RD, GUSTAVUS, AK 99826; 888/697-2284, FAX 907/697-2284
At the Bear Track Inn, bears are not just the edible or huggable ones decorating the interior of this huge log lodge, newly opened in 1997, but very much alive, lumbering through the meadows and down to the slough to feast on salmon. (In the early days, the National Park Service wanted to make all of Gustavus a black bear preserve because there were so many bears here.) Sitting on 17 acres at the end of the road, this lodge is peaceful, but on a grand log scale—a huge lobby with walk-around fireplace, great expansive windows looking out on Icy Strait and Pleasant Island, and 14 spacious guest rooms with double beds. This is not your cozy intimate kind of wilderness lodge experience. Rather, they cater mainly to groups of tourists on package deals—all of which they will arrange, from saltwater fishing to corporate meeting spaces to sailing into Glacier

Bay. Dining is primarily family style with a few separate tables. Entrees always feature a choice of fresh seafood, beef, or steak, with desserts a medley of homemade berry ice creams, apple tarts, or Whiskey Fudge Pie. Dinner is open to the public ($30 per person; call an hour ahead for reservations). One night's lodging is about $350 per person, double occupancy. All activities are extra. As part of the package price, the inn provides all ground transportation to and from the inn and all activities. *$$$; AE, DIS, MC, V; checks OK; open May–mid-Sept; beer and wine; beartrac@aol.com; alaskaone.com/beartrac.* &

Glacier Bay Country Inn / ★★★★

4 MILES FROM TOWN, GUSTAVUS, AK 99826; 800/628-0912 OR 907/697-2288, FAX 907/697-2289

The original owners of the inn once dreamed of having a hay farm here, but it wasn't very practical, so they turned it into a country inn and welcomed visitors from around the world. The cleared hay fields—in summer beautiful meadows filled with flowers—give the inn a very unusual pastoral setting with lovely views of the Bear Track and Chilkat Mountains. The current owners, Sandi and Ponch Marchbanks, former onion farmers from Colorado, have done a wonderful job to enhance the charm of the original inn. There are four guest cabins and six rooms in the inn. Tea is served on the big outdoor deck. The personable young chef, Jon Emmanuel, who trained at the California Culinary Academy of San Francisco, enhances the bounty of the sea and vegetable garden with a variety of light Asian flavors such as tea-smoked duck over jasmine leaves, and is fond of adorning his creations with exquisite sauces, glazes, and fresh salsas. The focus is on fresh Alaska seafood and duck, albeit with intriguing twists such as a Greek-inspired sautéed halibut mouffaletta or the visually lovely salmon roulade where the fish is cut open, stuffed, and rolled into spirals. All manner of activities may be arranged through the inn, such as fishing, whale-watching, kayaking, and day trips to Glacier Bay. Someone from the lodge will meet you at the airport or dock. *$$$; AE, DIS, MC, V; checks OK; open May 18–Sept 10 (until Sept 30 for fly-fishers only); beer and wine; info@glacierbayalaska.com; www.glacierbayalaska.com; PO Box 5, Gustavus, AK 99821.* & *(with limitations)*

Glacier Bay Lodge / ★★

GLACIER BAY NATIONAL PARK, GUSTAVUS, AK 99826; 800/451-5952 OR 907/697-2226

A handsome cedar, glass, and stone structure with wide porches and a massive stone fireplace, the Glacier Bay Lodge is the only lodge located within Glacier Bay National Park and Preserve. A boardwalk connects the guest rooms to the lodge. All manner of excursions are available as part of package tours sold by the lodge operator or can be arranged once you get to the lodge. Nature walks, fireside programs, guided and unguided kayaking, sportfishing, whale-watching, day and overnight cruises into Glacier Bay, and flight-seeing are some of the options. In the warmth of a sunny summer evening it's a pleasure to sit out on the deck for drinks and hors d'oeuvres, since sunny days are a special commodity in the rain forest here. There are rustic, modern rooms ($165 for a double) but also a dorm for six men and six women ($28 per person) for campers who've spent one night too many in the rain. $–$$$; AE, DC, DIS, MC, V; checks OK; open mid-May–mid-Sept; full bar; www. glacierbaytours.com.

Good River Bed and Breakfast / ★

OFF GOOD RIVER RD, 4 MILES FROM THE GUSTAVUS AIRPORT, GUSTAVUS, AK 99826; 907/697-2241

On part of the old homestead once settled by the Reverend Good, this homespun guest house is made of timbers salvaged from an old fish trap. Each log has been painstakingly chiseled with a decorative bevel and perfectly dovetail-notched at the ends. Inside, hand-thrown ceramic tiles surround the woodstove, and simple homemade quilts top the beds. The craftsmanship continues at breakfast: homemade granola, flapjacks served with spruce-tip syrup, wild berry jams, and smoked salmon. The four guest rooms are not spacious, but the living room (with harpsichord) and deck are cheerful places to relax. For those who desire more privacy, a snug, rustic cabin with cooking facilities is also available. The cabin has no indoor plumbing, but many guests think of the "one-holer" as another addition to their life list of Alaska experiences. Rooms run around $95 for double occupancy, $85 for a guest cabin. They also have wild rainbow-painted bicycles for the borrowing or to ride in the Fourth of July parade. $; no credit cards; checks OK; open mid-May–mid-Sept; bandb@ goodriver.com; www.goodriver.com; PO Box 37, Gustavus, AK 99821.

Gustavus Inn / ★★★★

I MILE FROM THE GUSTAVUS AIRPORT ON THE SALMON RIVER, GUSTAVUS, AK 99826; 800/649-5220 OR 907/697-2254, FAX 907/697-2255

More than 25 years ago, Jack and Sally Lesh began the transformation of a homestead on the Salmon River into a small, comfortable country inn—no mean feat considering there was no electricity, no telephone, no stores, only sporadic mail and barge service, and eight children to raise. At the time, Gustavus was considered a featureless backwater, but Sal's good cooking and the unpretentious charm of the old homestead earned the inn a loyal following among Alaska cognoscenti. Today, their son Dave and his wife, JoAnn, continue the tradition of offering the best of country living. Guest rooms look onto the stunning garden or across hay fields to the ocean. They might serve their popular Halibut Caddy Ganty, a concoction of halibut and sour cream, or black cod steamed in sake and topped with morel mushrooms from the woods nearby. Dessert might be homemade ice cream or lemon meringue pie with sweet red raspberries from the garden. This is one of Alaska's very best. $140 per person per night, double occupancy, which includes all meals and local transfers; singles pay $200 per night with private bath. *$$$; AE, MC, V; checks OK; open mid-May–mid-Sept; beer and wine; dinner for nonguests by reservation; PO Box 60, Gustavus, AK 99826.* &

Meadow's Glacier Bay Guest House / ★★★

2 MILES FROM THE GUSTAVUS AIRPORT ON THE SALMON RIVER, GUSTAVUS, AK 99826; 907/697-2348, FAX 907/697-2454

In a lovely open setting overlooking the Salmon River, Icy Strait, and the mountains of Chichagof Island beyond, this is a beautifully designed, gracious home on a grand scale, yet with the feel of a summer cottage. The four guest rooms are charming and spacious with touches of basketry furniture, fresh flowers, and saltwater taffy by your pillow. Two have views of the water; two look out on the forest. Susan "Meadow" Brook, a gourmet chef and delightful hostess, and her husband, Chris Smith, pilot and airplane mechanic, set a trend in this little Southeast town when they moved out of the trees and into the open, designing their home "to be attractive from all sides" with stunning views. One of the authors of *The Fiddlehead Cookbook*, Meadow is also a European-trained chef. She whips up classic dishes for her exquisite breakfasts using new twists and fresh ingredients from her beautiful garden. A little bit of heaven may arrive on the table in the guise of a Swedish yogurt cardamom cream custard topped with kiwis and raspberries, chocolate rhubarb bread, fresh strawberries in cream, or garden omelets. Double occupancy runs $99 to $179, including breakfast. *$$$; MC, V; checks OK; meadows@glacier-bay-alaska.com; www.glacier-bay-alaska.com; PO Box 93, Gustavus, AK 99826.* &

Spruce Tip Lodge / ★★

IN TOWN, GUSTAVUS, AK 99826; 907/697-2215

Open year-round, this small charming log cabin lodge, designed barn-style, is cozy, warm, and friendly—just what you'd expect in a picture postcard of Alaska. Much of the furniture is handmade from local wood, with cheerful quilts on the beds. Prices start at $120 per person per day, which includes three meals a day and all ground transportation. The lodge is within walking distance of the beach, the dock, and the heart of town. The owners, Mike and Connie Mills, also run a first-class boat charter business called Kelly Bay Yacht Charters, and they provide ground transportation. *$$; no credit cards; checks OK; no alcohol; sprucetiplodge@hotmail.com; PO Box 299, Gustavus, AK 99821.*

Icy Strait

Icy Strait is the watery divide separating Glacier Bay National Park and Gustavus from Chichagof Island. Icy Strait area has escaped much of the hype surrounding Glacier Bay, although in many people's minds it's every bit as beautiful, and has just as much wildlife, as the national park. The tiny outposts of Elfin Cove, the Hobbit Hole, and Gull Cove in Icy Strait are beginning to look toward tourism, but commercial fishing, subsistence, and rugged self-reliance are still their heart and soul.

Until a few years ago, **ELFIN COVE** (winter pop: 50) could have passed for the set for the *Popeye* movie, with its handful of weathered houses perched on a boardwalk and rafts of fishing boats in the harbor. Unfortunately, plywood siding has made significant inroads in the local architecture in recent years, and a small cruise ship occasionally drops anchor here in the summer. Still, its setting is wild and magnificent. Trophy-size salmon and halibut are abundant, and enough salty ambience remains to charm the most jaded tourist. You can buy the best smoked salmon in Icy Strait at Patti Lewis' smokehouse above the inner harbor, and a short walk down the boardwalk brings you to Augusta Clement's cabin, where she sells homemade jams. Look for the faint handwritten sign on an old cabin saying "Jams for Sale" or ask directions from anyone on the boardwalk. (The jams are self-serve, honor system, outside her cabin.)

On a small, forested island, in a sheltered bight, lies the **HOBBIT HOLE** (see review, below), named in the 1970s for the Hobbit Hole in Tolkein's mythological stories. As you approach, the only sound you may hear is the haunting song of a hermit thrush deep within the forest. Wood smoke curls from the stovepipe of a rustic home, perfuming the air with cedar. The land was originally homesteaded in the 1920s by F. R. Townsend; the current owners recently began welcoming visitors to their Alaska paradise.

After a day on the water if you are kayaking, the two lodges at **GULL COVE** are a welcome sight. On a private inholding in the Tongass National Forest, the lodges are the only development between Elfin Cove and Hoonah, a distance of about 35 miles. Although they are next to each other and have similar layout (three cabins with baths on the beach and a main cookhouse), the personalities of the owners make each place unique. You can't go wrong staying at either place (see Lodgings, below).

ACCESS AND INFORMATION

For **AIR SERVICE** from Juneau, try Alaska Seaplane Services (800/478-3360 or 907/789-3331), Alaska Fly 'n' Fish (907/790-2120; akbyair@ ptialaska.net), or Wings of Alaska (907/789-0790). From Gustavus, try

Air Excursions (907/697-2376) or Wings of Alaska. If traveling in a group of three or more, it's usually cheaper to charter the entire aircraft than buy individual seat fares. **CROSS SOUND EXPRESS** (888/698-2726 or 907/697-2726; csexp@seaknet.alaska.edu) can take up to 22 passengers and gear to Icy Strait destinations from Juneau or Gustavus. Doug Ogilvy (907/697-2409) and **GUSTAVUS MARINE CHARTERS** (907/697-2233, 907/697-2250, or 907/697-2232; gmc@mars.he.net) can quickly transport people and kayaks anywhere in Icy Strait from Gustavus. The kayak drop-off services in Juneau don't usually run all the way to Elfin Cove—too far and not enough demand.

ADVENTURES

SEA KAYAKING / If you have good outdoor gear and sea kayaking or skiffing experience, you can enjoyably explore Icy Strait on your own. Be aware that under certain conditions South Inian Pass becomes a nightmare of standing rooster tails and whirlpools, and the crossing from Point Adolphus to Pleasant Island also can be treacherous. In Gustavus, rent kayaks from **GLACIER BAY SEA KAYAKS** (907/697-2257 or 907/697-3002; kayakak@seaknet.alaska.edu; www.he.net/~kayakak) or **SEA OTTER KAYAKS** (907/697-3007; seaotter@he.net; www.he.net/~seaotter). Both companies give thorough instructions before turning paddlers loose on the water.

GUIDED TRIPS / **SPIRIT WALKER EXPEDITIONS** (907/697-2266; 800/529-2537; kayak@he.net; www.seakayakalaska.com) leads small groups on lodge-to-lodge kayak trips in Icy Strait. For hardier sorts, they offer 2- to 7-day camping/kayaking expeditions along the northern shore of Chichagof Island and to Point Adolphus. **ALASKA DISCOVERY** (800/586-1911 or 907/780-6226; akdisco@alaska.net; www.akdiscovery.com) also leads multiple-day kayak trips to Point Adolphus. If you'd rather use horsepower instead of arm power to explore Icy Strait, the businesses mentioned above or any of the charter operators in Gustavus, Pelican, Elfin Cove, or Hoonah can arrange custom trips in their cabin cruisers.

LODGINGS

Gull Cove / ★

ELFIN COVE, AK 99825; 907/789-0944 OR 907/697-2720
Paul and Tammy Johnson's lodge, Gull Cove, features guided sportfishing and hunting trips, although nonhunters and nonfishers would feel comfortable here too. It is, perhaps, a little less rough around the edges than South Passage Outfitters. Gull Cove is 56 miles west of

Juneau on Icy Strait; guests arrive by charter aircraft or boat. *$$; no credit cards; no checks; open mid-May–mid-Sept; PO Box 22, Elfin Cove, AK 99825, 22891 summer; Glacier Hwy, Juneau, AK 99801, winter.*

The Hobbit Hole Guest House / ★★

INIAN ISLANDS, ELFIN COVE, AK 99825; 907/723-8514 OR 907/697-2580

Guests stay in a bright and airy cabin, named the Hobbit Hole Guest House, on the beach and can either prepare their meals in the cabin or join owners Jane Button and Greg Howe for delicious home-cooked meals. Jane is a treasure and a great cook. The setting is quintessential Southeast Alaska and offers visitors a unique glimpse at modern homestead life. Typically Alaskan, and homestead too, is the fact that there is always some gear and construction materials on the dock and beach. So don't be put off on first impression. They rent skiffs and kayaks too and are very savvy about local waters and weather conditions to advise you. The Hobbit Hole is on the largest of the Inian Islands near Elfin Cove, and someone will meet guests at Elfin Cove with prior arrangement. If you're arriving by boat, call VHF 14 or 16 for directions. *$–$$; MC, V; checks OK; PO Box 9, Inian Islands, Elfin Cove, AK 99825.*

South Passage Outfitters / ★

ELFIN COVE, AK 99825; 907/697-2507, SUMMER, OR 360/385-3417, WINTER

Peggy McDonald and Dennis Montgomery of South Passage Outfitters cater to experienced campers, fishers, and kayakers. They rent skiffs and kayaks and are extremely knowledgeable about local waters. This is a remote, pristine setting—still a little rough around the edges. Indoor plumbing and a futon seem luxurious when you've been kayaking for a week but would seem pretty basic if you've been traveling by private yacht. Guests arrive by charter aircraft or boat. *$–$$; no credit cards; checks OK; open mid-May–mid-Sept; spo@olympus.net; www.olympus.net/southpass; PO Box 48, Elfin Cove, AK 99825, summer; PO Box 1967, Port Townsend, WA 98368, winter.*

Tanaku Lodge / ★★

ELFIN COVE, AK 99825; 800/482-6258

At the entrance to the inner harbor, Tanaku Lodge is the best bet for quiet accommodations for the independent traveler, although sportfishermen are the big kahunas here. Ask for a room overlooking the water. Cushy guest rooms have views of both harbor and town. Easy-maintenance decor is the theme of the lounge, with a wraparound window looking out over the town and the Fairweather Mountain Range. Tanaku is on the opposite side of the "gut" into the inner harbor from downtown Elfin

Cove, hence quieter and less congested. The philosophy here is ecotourist friendly. Lodge staff will meet guests; if you're coming by boat, the lodge dock is clearly marked. *$$$; no credit cards; checks OK; open May–mid-Sept; tanaku@msn.com; www.tanaku.com; PO Box 72, Elfin Cove, AK 99825.*

Haines

Haines has what every Southeasterner often pines for—*sun!* (On the average, Ketchikan gets 160 inches of rain a year, Juneau gets 90 inches, and Haines gets 60 inches. Skagway gets only 30 inches, but beware the wind.) Both Haines and Skagway are in the rain shadow of the Fairweather Mountain Range, which catches much of the precipitation blowing off the Gulf of Alaska.

This is one of the most picturesque towns in all of Southeast, sleeping peacefully in unbelievable mountain splendor, where road meets sea. From the 1940s until the 1980s, when Skagway was linked to the Alaska-Canada Highway, Haines had a unique position in Southeast life: it had a road—a road that actually went somewhere. In its commanding position at the head of the Inside Passage, Haines was the beginning (or the end, depending on your perspective) of the road to the Interior. It sits on the edge of the forests and fjords of Southeast Alaska and the wide glacial valleys, mountain kingdoms, and more severe climates of the north. Its population is one of resilient old-timers who've done it all and young adventurers who are trying to do it all with boundless enthusiasm for all that this mountain-ocean playground offers.

The architectural centerpiece of Haines is striking and one-of-a-kind. Sitting just up the hill from the water, framed by breathtaking snowy mountains, is a grassy parade ground ringed by old Victorian buildings. This is historic Fort William H. Seward, once known as the Chilkoot Barracks, a former Army post built in the early part of the century and deactivated in the 1940s. A group of returning World War II veterans bought the fort years ago. Today the buildings include private homes, a hotel, and an art center. In the old days, the parade ground was the place where new recruits, on skis for the first time, learned to discharge their firearms (preferably without killing anyone). Now, this grassy arena serves as a popular summer location for salmon bakes, dance performances, and informal football.

At 90 miles north of Juneau—the same latitude as Oslo, Norway—Haines lies on a peninsula between the mouths of two rivers, the Chilkat and the Chilkoot. Situated at the edge of a deep fjord called Lynn Canal, the town and surrounding Chilkat Valley have a population of about 2,300. The Tlingit people called it *Dei-shu*, or "End of the Trail." Traders called it "Chilkoot"; the missionaries called it "Haines."

Haines is so picturesque that in recent years the Walt Disney Company, the National Geographic Society, the British Broadcasting Corporation (BBC), and wildlife photographers from around the world have "discovered" it. Jack London's classic story *White Fang*, which was filmed here in 1990, is one of Haines' latest claims to fame in the movie business. Almost everybody in town was an extra and had a jolly good time.

ACCESS AND INFORMATION

Haines is linked to the Alaska Highway, also known as the Alaska-Canada (Alcan) Highway, by a 160-mile road built in the 1940s called the HAINES HIGHWAY. This means that from Haines, you can drive anywhere the roads go in Alaska or, at Haines Junction, turn right and go back to the Lower 48 (through Canada, of course). Be aware that you will pass through U.S. Customs at Mile 42 on the Haines Highway. Haines is also linked to the state ferry system. The MV MALASPINA (all state ferries are named after glaciers) runs throughout the summer between Juneau, Haines, and Skagway (call 800/642-0066 for reservations, or 907/766-2111 for the Haines office; www.akferry.com). If you want to sail between Haines and Skagway, CHILKAT CRUISES (907/766-2100 or 888/766-2103; www.chilkatcruises.com) has daily passenger shuttle service in summer (May through September) with a resident Native naturalist/interpreter on board for about $35 round-trip. HAINES-SKAGWAY WATER TAXI (907/766-3395 or 888/766-3395) also has daily passenger service. Several small FLIGHT SERVICES fly in and out of Haines. The best are Haines Airways (907/766-2646) on Main Street, which has scheduled service to Haines, Juneau, Gustavus, and Hoonah, as well as Glacier Bay flight-seeing and charters in Alaska and Canada, and Skagway Air (907/983-2218).

The HAINES VISITOR INFORMATION CENTER (907/766-2234, fax 907/766-3155; www.haines.ak.us) is located on Second Avenue, near Willard Street in downtown Haines and is open daily in summer. For information year-round, contact the HAINES CONVENTION & VISITORS BUREAU (PO Box 530, Haines, AK 99827; 800/458-3579 or 907/766-2234; hainesak@wwa.com; www.haines.ak.us). For a copy of the *Visitor's Guide To Haines,* published annually, write the *Chilkat Valley News* (PO Box 630, Haines, AK 99827). For WEATHER FORECASTS AND MARINE CONDITIONS around the clock, call 907/766-2727.

If you want to see Haines the way it was, put your speed shoes on. This town is fast becoming discovered as an outdoor mecca not only by the young and go-for-the-gusto crowd, but also by seniors aboard the huge cruise ships that started to dock here in 1995. Their arrival doubles or even triples the population of the town in a single day.

EXPLORING

CHILKAT DANCERS AND SALMON BAKE / Performing in traditional regalia, with narration and a marvelous touch of humor, these Native dancers have been an inspiration to other Southeast Native communities in reviving their arts through performing for tourists. Sometimes they perform onstage at the **CHILKAT CENTER FOR THE ARTS** (907/766-2160) on the west side of Fort Seward, and sometimes in the longhouse in the center of the parade grounds. Call for a schedule of performances. The dance performance and salmon bake, billed as the **PORT CHILKOOT POTLATCH**, is a fun combo at the parade grounds. Grilled over an alderwood fire, the all-you-can-eat salmon is truly delicious. For times, call Hotel Halsingland at 907/766-2000 or 800/542-6363.

AMERICAN BALD EAGLE FOUNDATION / This small museum is truly a labor of love. A tribute to the bald eagle, it's also filled with the wildlife of the Chilkat Valley (once alive, but now stuffed) and resides just around the corner from the Mountain Market, close to the center of town. Cost is $2. PO Box 49, Haines, AK 99827; 907/766-3094.

SHELDON MUSEUM AND CULTURAL CENTER / One of five accredited museums in the state, this tiny museum will give you a feel for the history of Haines, its Native peoples and their traditional art, shipwrecks along the Inside Passage, early pioneers of the region, and more. Open daily in summer. Located at the corner of Main and Front Streets. PO Box 269, Haines, AK 99827; 907/766-2366.

SHOPPING / Haines has a wealth of artists and a lovely blend of traditional and contemporary art. There are probably 100 artists making a living off their art here in Haines (quite extraordinary in a town of only a few thousand). Spend some time poking around. Here are a few places to start. **ALASKAN INDIAN ARTS** (907/766-2160) and **WILD IRIS** (907/766-2300) are both located in the historic building on the west side of the Fort Seward parade ground. **SEA WOLF GALLERY** (907/766-2540) on the parade ground, and **WHALE RIDER GALLERY** (907/766-2540), on Portage Street, feature the work of Tresham Gregg. His signature style can be seen in wonderful masks such as the mythical sea wolf, a tiny mosquito mask, a raven encircled with rabbit fur, or a wolf head mask with fur tails. A block or so from the visitors center, **CHILKAT VALLEY ARTS** (907/766-2990), owned by artist Sue Folletti, features other outstanding local talent. Next door is **INSIDE PASSAGE ARTISANS** (907/766-2539). Most of these shops and galleries are open year-round. Locals say, "It's a Haines tradition" (in contrast with Skagway, where artists head south for winter). For a small town, Haines also has a charming little bookstore on Main Street called **THE BABBLING BOOK** (907/766-3356).

ADVENTURES

ALASKA CHILKAT BALD EAGLE PRESERVE / Located between Mile 10 and Mile 26 on the Haines Highway, this area is known as the **VALLEY OF THE EAGLES**. About 200 eagles reside here year-round. But in the fall and early winter, their ranks swell to nearly 4,000, lining the sandbars and filling the cottonwood trees. Warm water, which wells up from the bottom of the Chilkat River, keeps part of the river ice-free all winter, allowing these birds to feast on the carcasses of salmon. It's the largest gathering of eagles in the world. A 5-mile stretch along the Chilkat River between Mile 18 and Mile 22 is the main eagle-viewing area and is called the **EAGLE COUNCIL GROUNDS**. The greatest concentrations of eagles gather in the fall, peak in November, and taper off by February. 907/766-2202.

TOUR TOWN IN A LLAMA TAXI / You may be surprised to see those woolly South American creatures padding down the waterfront, but **ALASKA LLAMA GUIDES AND TOURS** (888/765-5262 or 907/766-2065; kcd.com/alaskallama) offers a different kind of taxi service and town tours for about $25 per person. They also encourage you "to take a llama to lunch" on one of Haines' beautiful hiking trails with a tasty campfire meal as part of the package deal for about $30 an hour.

KAYAKING / Experienced paddlers can rent kayaks, after a safety checkout, from **DEISHU EXPEDITIONS** (12 Portage St, Fort Seward; 800/552-9257 or 907/766-2427; paddle@seakayaks.com; www.seakayaks.com). They run the gamut from guided trips to kayak rentals to skills instruction.

FISHING CHARTERS / Just to be out on the water is a treat. Haines and Skagway are not the richest fishing grounds in Southeast Alaska, but they're still good compared to most other places in the world. Several charter companies offer trips for both saltwater and freshwater fishing. A couple are **JIM'S JAUNTS** (907/766-2935) and **MCCORMICK CHARTERS** (907/766-2450). For more information, call the **ALASKA DEPARTMENT OF FISH AND GAME IN HAINES** (907/766-2625).

BIKING / Haines is so small, and the country around it so grand, that you'll find biking is a nice way to get around from Chilkat Inlet to the west to Chilkoot Lake to the north. You can't lose. Both directions provide intense beauty. Rent mountain bikes or road bikes at **SOCKEYE CYCLE** (Portage St, Fort Seward; 907/766-2869).

HIKING / The mountain that rises directly behind Haines, **MOUNT RIPINSKI** (3,610 feet), is a rigorous but wonderful climb on a clear day. Make noise in the forest, as bears abound. A smaller mountain, also with good views, **MOUNT RILEY** (1,760 feet), the highest point on the Chilkat Peninsula, rises south of town in Chilkat State Park. For a forest and beach walk, head to Chilkat State Park and the 6.5-mile **SEDUCTION POINT TRAIL**, which has beautiful views of water, glaciers, and mountains and the chance to see bears, whales, seals, and sea lions. Check tides before setting out on this trail.

SAILING / MCCORMICK CHARTERS not only offers fishing charters but will teach you to sail so you can in short order (depending on wind and weather) be sailing a single-person WindRider trimaran. 907/766-2450 or 800/330-7245; www.sailak.com.

CAMPING / Two exquisite campgrounds lie at the ends of the roads running out of town. To the northwest is **CHILKOOT LAKE STATE RECREATION SITE** at the head of Lutak Inlet. To the south, across the peninsula and along Mud Bay Road, is **CHILKAT STATE PARK**. It sits at the edge of the ocean and has knockout views across to the water to the Davidson and Rainbow Glaciers.

VISIT A GOLD MINE / If "moiling for gold" stirs your imagination, **PORCUPINE GOLD MINE TOURS** (144 2nd Ave S; 907/766-3100) will take you on a 4-hour journey along the old Dalton Trail, 26 miles out of Haines, through the Chilkat Bald Eagle Preserve, across the Klehini River, and into the valleys that produced more than 3 tons of gold in their heyday. They'll tour you around an operating placer gold mine, you'll meet today's prospectors, and even get a chance to pan for gold yourself ($75 per person). The tours begin at their headquarters downtown.

THE GOLDEN CIRCLE ROUTE / You'll find 360 miles of indescribable beauty by road and 15 miles of scenic cruising over water along the Golden Circle Route. You can drive a car, or go slow and savor the scenery while riding a bicycle. If you want a **GUIDED BIKE TOUR**, call Sockeye Cycle (907/766-2869). The company runs a summer expedition along this route, which takes 9 days. By car or bike, follow the Haines Highway to Haines Junction, on the rim of Kluane National Park; turn right on the Alaska Highway, head toward Whitehorse in the Yukon, and then ride back through the mountains to Skagway in Alaska. At this point, just a few miles of water at the head of Lynn Canal separate you from Haines. You can take the ferry or one of the water shuttles back to Haines.

FLIGHT-SEEING / Flights over Glacier Bay National Park, which lies a short distance to the west, are offered by **HAINES AIRWAYS** (907/766-2646) on Main Street in downtown Haines. **MOUNTAIN FLYING SERVICE** (132 2nd Ave; 907/766-3007 or 800/954-8747), a small company that gets special kudos from passengers and other Southeast pilots alike, can take you on several unusual aerial adventures, such as beach landings in the remote wilderness of the Gulf Coast or glacier landings in their fixed-wing aircraft equipped with skis.

GUIDES AND OUTFITTERS

ALASKA MOUNTAIN GUIDE AND CLIMBING SCHOOL INC. / For those looking for a guide service, climbing school, and custom expedition outfitter, the Alaska Mountain School is your best bet. Its instructors and guides have worked in mountains all over the world. The school offers a 5-day Mountain School as an introduction to the basics of safe mountaineering. The groups are small (about four to six people), with one instructor to a maximum of four participants. Activities include glacier travel and guided climbs. Longer mountaineering and wilderness trips will take you on the Tsirku Icefield Traverse or combine sea kayaking, glacier trekking, and river rafting. PO Box 1018, Haines, AK 99827; 907/766-3366 or 800/766-3396; ams@alaskamountainguides.com; www.alaskamountainguides.com.

CHILKAT GUIDES / The folks at Chilkat Guides specialize in river trips. They offer a half-day float through the Chilkat Bald Eagle Preserve along the Chilkat River. It's scenic, peaceful, and departs daily. (Note: The eagles follow the salmon; therefore, you may not see many eagles during the early part of the summer. The greatest concentrations of the birds are found in the fall and early winter.) Chilkat Guides also offers 2-day adventures, but their crème de la crème trips are the 10-day and 13-day expeditions down the Tatshenshini and Alsek Rivers, which flow through two spectacular wilderness areas and the Stikine River, which flows farther south. PO Box 170, Haines, AK 99827; 907/766-2491, fax 907/766-2409; RaftAlaska@aol.com.

DEISHU EXPEDITIONS / For kayaking adventures to suit all comers, look no further. This company—"dedicated to safety, ecotourism, and preserving the Alaska wilds"—offers half-day, full-day, or even overnight trips to the Davidson Glacier and even "guaranteed whale trips" (mid-July through September) in search of the great whales. 12 Portage St (just up from the cruise ship dock); 800/552-9257 or 907/766-2427; www.seakayaks.com.

RIVER ADVENTURES / If you prefer jet boat and rafting trips, River Adventures will take you on the upper Chilkat River. Trips depart daily in summer. 800/478-9827 or 907/766-2050.

NIGHTLIFE

The **OFFICER'S CLUB LOUNGE** (907/766-2002) is a dignified bar in the Hotel Halsingland (see review, below) and a popular watering hole for locals. After all, this used to be the purview of the commander, so it feels like drinking in somebody's home with big windows and a nice view. Located down by the water is the **LIGHTHOUSE RESTAURANT** (Main and Front Sts; 907/766-2444) whose claim to fame is its buttermilk pie—

"Alaska slices at Alaska prices." (That translates as big and expensive.) Thirty-three miles "out the road" toward the Interior (otherwise known as the Haines Highway) is the historic **33 MILE ROADHOUSE** (907/767-5510). Everybody in Haines goes to Milepost 33 for the "best burgers in town." The pies are pretty good, too. Since it's 9 miles before the Canadian border, they also advertise it as "the last gas in America." Open every day; closed Tuesday in winter.

FESTIVALS AND EVENTS

MAYFEST / Mother Nature puts on this show. In May, everything is waking up after a long winter's sleep. It's a great time to be anywhere in Southeast, but particularly in Haines. Long days make for great cross-country skiing in Chilkat Pass. The first two weeks of May, hooligan are running upriver, followed by a whole bevy of sea lions; the sky is white with sea gulls. Whales are returning. Native folks dip-net for fish. People from the Yukon come to the coast with moose meat for trading. Hooligan oil is a prized commodity. The Native peoples of the Interior use it for dipping meats and dried fish. (In the old days, it was so valuable that the routes to the Interior were often called "The Grease Trail.") Good places to watch nature's show, particularly the hooligan and sea lions, are at Mile 4 on the Haines Highway, alongside the Chilkat River, and at the bridge over Lutak Inlet, on your way to Chilkoot Lake.

KLUANE TO CHILKAT INTERNATIONAL BIKE RELAY RACE / Held on the weekend closest to the summer solstice (June 21), this bicycling event has taken off like a rocket since its inception in 1993. More than 1,000 pedalists participate, either as individuals or in bike relay teams of two to eight people. Racers roar off in a mass start from Haines Junction in the Yukon, then follow the road over the pass to the ocean at Haines, about 153 miles. The terrain is rugged and demanding, but competitors like the nice local flavor and say the race has not yet been invaded by big-time serious racers from Outside (meaning non-Alaskans). For information, call the Haines Visitor Bureau (800/458-3579).

SOUTHEAST ALASKA STATE FAIR (AND BALD EAGLE MUSIC FESTI-VAL) / For five days near the beginning of August, folks from all over Southeast and the Yukon gather in Haines for a good old-fashioned fair, featuring big names in the music world and talented musicians from around the state. There are also the famous pig races, contests from logrolling to ax throwing, a parade, great food, and dancing, of course. Never mind that it often rains some of the days; everybody loves the fair. For more information, call 907/766-2476.

ALASKA BALD EAGLE FESTIVAL / The gathering of bald eagles on the Council Grounds of the Chilkat River from October to December is the largest concentration of eagles in the world. In their honor, Haines puts on a festival of local artists and musicians, usually the second weekend of November, but the really big-name, flamboyant performance artists here are white-headed, wear more than 7,000 feathers, and weigh in at about 13 pounds each. For more information, contact the Haines Chamber of Commerce (PO Box 1449, Haines, AK 99827; 800/246-6268 or 907/766-2202).

RESTAURANTS

The Commander's Room Restaurant / ★

HALSINGLAND HOTEL, FORT SEWARD, HAINES; 907/766-2000, FAX 907/766-2445

The commander of the fort once lived here; today you can eat here. The menu, titled "Military Dining Portfolio," is a replica of the original writing portfolios used by the Army at Fort Seward. The original menu items used to celebrate past characters such as a beer-guzzling bear, a dog named Gus who once flew co-pilot with the commander and wolfed down steak every night, and the commander's wife, Eleanor, who either through stroke of genius or perverseness composed the music to Alaska's Flag Song. (Genius? Because only the best voices in the state can actually sing this song. Perverse? Because the rest of us make it painful to your ears.) The new menu has sadly left off the old characters, but added many more choices such as seafood enchiladas and vegetarian burgers. Still, their specialties are locally caught fresh seafood. Our recommendation is the fresh Dungeness crab—it's entertainment unto itself. *$$; AE, DC, MC, V; local checks only; breakfast, dinner every day; closed Oct–April; full bar.* ♿

Fort Seward Lodge Restaurant & Saloon / ★

MILE 0, HAINES HWY, FORT SEWARD, HAINES; 800/478-7772 OR 907/766-2009

The seasonal specialty is all-you-can-eat crab, plucked right from the waters of Lynn Canal. Service is friendly, the atmosphere cozy, and from some tables you have a view of the water. While you're waiting for dinner, make a homemade dart with an autographed dollar bill and fire it at the ceiling. It is wise here to go for the house specialties—prime rib or crab. *$–$$; MC, V; local checks only; dinner every day in summer; dinner 5 nights in winter, days vary; closed for a few weeks in Jan; full bar; part of historic Fort Seward.*

Just For The Halibut

142 BEACH RD, HAINES; 907/766-3800 OR 877/766-2800

On a pretty day in Haines, if you're waiting for the shuttle ferry to Skagway or even if you're not, this is a fun place to eat out on the sunny deck just off the dock, but over the water, looking out at beautiful Lynn Canal. This little fish-and-chips cafe boasts a simple, tasty menu: ale-battered fish and chips ("best in town" say many residents), grilled halibut kebabs, espresso drinks, and a local Tlingit specialty of Native fried bread. *$; MC, V; local checks only; lunch, dinner every day; closed winter; no alcohol; portage@klukwan.com; www.portage.klukwan.com; on the dock at the Portage Cove Adventure Center.* &

Mountain Market / ★★

151 3RD AVE S, HAINES; 907/766-3340

Thoughtful, wholesome food is served, in this combination deli-health food store. Except for the sandwiches, the cuisine is largely vegetarian, with great muffins, good soups, daily specials such as enchilada bake, Singapore Stirfry, and basil-pesto pasta, and the best coffee drinks in

town or creations such as Mocha Margaritas, which taste just like a milkshake. It's a grab-and-go kind of place, but also on any given day fishermen, kayakers, mountain climbers, cabin dwellers, artists, and alternative-lifestyle folks may be found holding court here. *$; MC, V; local checks only; breakfast, lunch, dinner every day; no alcohol; corner of 3rd Ave and Haines Hwy.* &

Weeping Trout Sports Resort

144 2ND AVE S, HAINES; 907/766-2827, FAX 907/766-2824

On Saturday evenings in summer, the lodge has a special dinner open to the public. The resort is in a beautiful location on the edge of Chilkat Lake. Getting to dinner—which takes about half an hour from town—is half the fun and adventure as you bump over roads by car and then jump from boat to boat; or you can fly in. Set menus are published a month ahead and posted in Haines, so if you're staying for a while you can choose your favorite repast. Many Haines residents say it's a fun outing for a special dinner. For the price of about $50 per person, the meal is a set entree, which varies from lamb to seafood, with salad, dessert, a good wine list, and a full bar. Seating for dinner is at 6pm and the dining room looks across the lake. You can always go earlier on Saturday morning—fish, golf (Alaska-style), hike, and then eat dinner if you want to make a day of it. *$$–$$$; MC, V; local checks only; dinner Sat in summer; full bar; kcd.com/weepingt/; PO Box 129, Haines, AK 99827.*

The Wild Strawberry / ★★

138 2ND AVE S, HAINES; 907/766-3608

In a charmingly handcrafted wood house with scalloped gables, turrets, large deck, and gazebo, the Wild Strawberry is a delightful new addition to Haines' cuisine. A fishing family for more than 25 years, the owners, Jim and Pam Moore, specialize in seafood from the barbecue, fresh halibut sandwiches, homemade soups, an array of meat and vegetarian sandwiches served on focaccia, and, for dessert, giant ice cream cones or a beautiful selection of chocolates like a "Mount Ripinskiy." They also serve Belgian waffles, espresso, and decadent "candy bar drinks." *$; MC, V; local checks only; breakfast, lunch, dinner every day; closed Jan–March; no alcohol; downtown, 4 doors south of the visitor center.* &

LODGINGS

Hotel Halsingland / ★★

FORT SEWARD, HAINES, AK 99827; 800/542-6363 OR 907/766-2002, FAX 907/766-2445

Overlooking Lynn Canal, with mountains in all directions, the hotel is part of historic Fort Seward. The old Victorian buildings have a kind of faded gentility to them, and so do the rooms. The hotel itself was once home to the commanding officer of the fort. It has 35 rooms with private baths and 4 economy rooms with shared baths. The former owner, an immigrant from Sweden, named the hotel after a province of her native homeland. The complex includes the Officer's Inn Bed and Breakfast, which has 13 guest rooms and is up the hill from the hotel (economy rooms, $49 for a single; Officer's Inn B&B, $89 for a double). *$–$$; AE, DC, DIS, MC, V; local checks only; closed Nov–May; full bar; halsinglan@aol.com; www.haines.ak.us/halsingland/; PO Box 1589, Haines, AK 99827; on the east side of the Fort Seward parade ground.* &

Pyramid Island Bed & Breakfast / ★★

MILE 1.5, MUD BAY RD, HAINES, AK 99827; 907/766-2771

On a lovely hill overlooking the Chilkat River and Chilkat Mountain Range, this home has wraparound decks on two levels, making it an excellent place for relaxing in the sun while spotting eagles, bears, and mountain goats. Binoculars and spotting scopes are provided by your hosts, Dick and Wanda Aukerman, longtime residents of Haines. If you plan to spend a few days in Haines, this is a swell place. They have three bedrooms with private baths—two bedrooms share a kitchen and living room, but the third is really a private apartment with full kitchen and living room. Phones are available. A continental breakfast is provided in your own kitchen, but if you wish you can opt to have breakfast in town at the Chilkat Restaurant, provided by the hosts. Your hosts recommend you have a car, although they provide transportation to and from the ferry. *$$; MC, V; local checks only; PO Box 604, Haines, AK 99827; directly across from Pyramid Island (you'll know it when you see it).*

River House Bed & Breakfast / ★★

I MILE OUTSIDE OF TOWN, WHERE THE CHILKAT RIVER RUNS INTO THE SEA, HAINES, AK 99827; 907/766-3215 OR 888/747-RHBB
A sweet, private cottage beside the Chilkat River has a third-floor tower bedroom with skylights for watching the stars, and a private garden, deck, and sauna. This lovely oasis with views of mountains, glaciers, and river is a happy getaway for a night ($135 for two) or a week ($800 for two). The cottage is fully equipped with espresso machine, VCR and video library, telephone, and stereo. It can accommodate up to five people. No smoking allowed. *$$; no credit cards; checks OK; PO Box 1173, Haines, AK 99827.*

A Sheltered Harbor Bed & Breakfast / ★

57 BEACH RD, HAINES, AK 99827; 907/766-2741
With big picture windows, this B&B offers waterfront accommodations on Portage Cove, which lies at the foot of Fort Seward in downtown Haines directly across from the Port Chilkoot cruise ship dock. Several of the rooms have excellent views of the Lynn Canal and the surrounding mountains. As the rooms are located two flights over the Orca Arts & Crafts Gift Shop, you get an extra workout hauling your luggage upstairs. The rooms are cozy, tidy, and nicely decorated. Each has private bath and phone. Your hosts, Byron and Laura Rettinger, serve a hot, all-you-can-eat Alaska breakfast each morning. *$$; AE, MC, V; checks OK; www.geocities.com/TheTropics/Resort/6522/index.html; PO Box 806-B, Haines, AK 99827; on the waterfront across from cruise ship dock.*

Summer Inn Bed and Breakfast / ★★

117 2ND AVE, HAINES, AK 99827; 907/766-2970
A five-bedroom historic house, this simple, but charming inn has pretty views of Lynn Canal from the upstairs front bedrooms. It was built by Tim Vogel, a member of Soapy Smith's notorious gang of hoodlums, who skedaddled out of Skagway when Soapy was gunned down around the turn of the century. Quite a dandy, and known as a ladies' man, Vogel was a colorful character in the history of Haines. In the evening, you can take a bubble bath in the scoundrel's original tub, circa 1912. The inn is cheerful, homey, and a great location. They serve a hearty breakfast here and in the afternoon offer homemade cookies and tea. Summer rates are $70 for a single, $80 for a double, and $100 for a triple; winter rates are

lower. *$–$$; MC, V; checks OK; PO Box 1198, Haines, AK 99827; downtown, 2 blocks off Main St.*

Skagway

In the fall of 1896, a prospector named George Washington Carmack was panning for gold on a tributary of the Klondike River in Canada. Something glittered. He brushed away the gravel. And there, lying "like thick slabs of cheese" in a sandwich, was the first taste of the gold that would electrify the world. "I felt," he said later, "like I had just dealt myself a royal flush in the game of life."

The rush was on. Skagway, on the Alaska side of the coastal mountains, provided access to the quickest route into the Canadian Klondike, up and over Chilkoot Pass. From bank presidents to lowly clerks, oyster pirates to boardinghouse matrons, everywhere around the globe, people lured by gold walked out of their jobs, bound for the Klondike. Most of the gold claims were already staked by the time the masses had clambered and clawed their way over glaciers and peaks to get there. But not a soul forgot the glory days of the gold rush and its grand, unparalleled adventures as immortalized in Robert Service's poem "The Spell of the Yukon."

For every soul who came to dig gold out of the ground, hundreds more followed to dig gold out of the other guy's pocket. In those wild days, it was written about Skagway that a man could come into town from the Klondike with a fortune in his pockets and the next morning not even have money for a meal. "I have stumbled upon a few rough corners of the globe in my wandering, but I think the most outrageously lawless quarter I ever struck was Skagway," wrote a visitor in 1898.

One of the most lawless fellows could be found in Clancy's Saloon, headquarters for the notorious Soapy Smith gang. As a two-bit con man down south, Soapy picked up his nickname, as well as some extra cash, by using a trick involving soap to swindle the unsuspecting out of their dough. But when he arrived in the north, he hit the big time, and locals were soon calling him the King of Skagway. It was a glorious but brief reign, for Soapy eventually pinched one poke too many. On July 8, 1898, *The Skagway News* headlines read: "Soapy Smith's Last Bluff; Shot Through the Heart by Frank Reid."

Skagway has always been known for throwing a good party. But don't believe all you hear, particularly about winter in Skagway, because most of the people you're bound to meet don't live here, including the shopkeepers. When the last cruise ship sails down Lynn Canal in late September, folks start boarding up their shops and heading for Bali, Boston, Washington, or Tahiti.

That leaves about 700 people when the snow flies. And they love it!

ACCESS AND INFORMATION

Skagway can be reached year-round by scheduled and chartered **AIR SERVICES** out of Juneau and Haines. Skagway Air Service (907/983-2218), with the dance-hall queen doing the high-step on the tail flaps and the motto "We can can-can," is a good first choice. In summer, there's water transportation between Skagway and Haines: **CHILKAT CRUISES' HAINES-SKAGWAY SHUTTLE FERRY** (888/766-2103 or 907/766-2100) and **HAINES-SKAGWAY WATER TAXI** (907/766-3395 or 888/766-3395). The Alaska state ferry system has one ferry, the **MV MALASPINA** (800/642-0066; www.akferry.com), which runs between Juneau, Haines, and Skagway all summer. Call for recorded arrival/departure information in Skagway (907/983-2941). If you're coming by road, from the Alaska Highway, it's 110 miles on the **SOUTH KLONDIKE HIGHWAY**. To rent a car, contact **AVIS** (800/331-1212), located in the lobby of the Westmark Hotel, for day or weekly rates.

The best place to start is at the old railroad depot, now home to the **KLONDIKE GOLD RUSH NATIONAL HISTORICAL PARK**. Located in the heart of town, on Second Avenue and Broadway, the park's visitor center is open daily in the summer, with scaled-back hours in winter. The visitor center offers films, exhibits, walking tours, ranger talks, and the latest information on conditions on the Chilkoot Trail. **SKAGWAY VISITORS CENTER** (5th Ave and Broadway; 907/983-2854) has a great little brochure, "Skagway Walking Tour," for a do-it-yourself guided trip. The **SKAGUAY NEWS DEPOT** (264 Broadway; 907/983-3354) is the town's largest bookseller, open year-round. For more information, contact the **SKAGWAY CONVENTION & VISITORS BUREAU** (907/983-2854, fax 907/983-3854; www.skagway.org).

EXPLORING

Whether on foot, by buggy, or in a vintage car, tours abound. The National Park Service offers **WALKING TOURS OF HISTORIC SKAGWAY** (907/983-2921) that depart several times daily from its visitor center at the old railroad depot. A marvelous raconteur and performer, Steve Hites, runs a fleet of yellow vintage cars, **SKAGWAY STREET CAR COMPANY** (907/983-2908). His drivers are dressed in flamboyant costumes of the era and entertain you with story after story of yesteryear as they toot about town. If you want to get from here to there in a turn-of-the-century taxi, just flag down the **KELLER'S CURIOS LIMO**, a horse and buggy with costumed driver.

ADVENTURES

KLONDIKE GOLD RUSH NATIONAL HISTORICAL PARK / This park is unique among national parks in that it encompasses both historic downtown Skagway (the beginning—and the end—of the trail of gold) and the routes and mountain passes that thousands of gold seekers flowed over to get to the gold fields of the Canadian Klondike. It was certainly "the last grand adventure" of the 19th century. Over the years, the National Park Service has restored many of the old buildings and is working to renovate others, breathing life into the stories of the characters who once proliferated here. Visit, for instance, the OLD CABIN OF CAPTAIN WILLIAM MOORE, the founder of Skagway, who predicted gold would soon be discovered in the creeks of the Yukon River; THE MASCOT SALOON, a hop and a skip down Broadway; or nearby JEFF SMITH'S PARLOR, the gambling dive and hangout of the nefarious Soapy Smith. Two routes led into the Klondike from Skagway: the 33-mile CHILKOOT TRAIL, which you can still walk today, and the WHITE PASS TRAIL, the route followed by the trains of the White Pass & Yukon Railroad. The park is managed through the international cooperation of the national park services of both the United States and Canada.

HIKE THE CHILKOOT TRAIL / For those who love history and mountains, a hike along the Chilkoot Trail from Dyea to Lake Bennett is a wonderful adventure. Go prepared. While the distance (33 miles) may not look overly intimidating, the route is rugged and there's plenty of snow, even in July. The park service can give you maps, information, latest trail conditions, and an excellent brochure, "A Hiker's Guide to the Chilkoot Trail." The trail crosses the international boundary between the United States and Canada at the top of the infamous "Golden Steps"— Chilkoot Pass. Although you are required to register on the U.S. side, currently the permit is free. However, the Canadian permit currently costs $35 per adult and $18 for children younger than 15. Parks Canada limits the number of hikers on the Canadian side to 50 per day. This is for the protection of natural and cultural resources as well as the quality of visitors' experiences. If you are on a tight schedule or have an organized group, it is strongly recommended to make permit reservations in advance ($10 per person). Only eight permits per day are reserved for hikers who arrive with no reservations. Without reservations you need to be a little flexible with a few days to spare. Be aware the busiest season is July to early August. Currently, there's a train running twice a day, June through August, from the end of the trail at Lake Bennett back to Skagway for around $65 per person. But that service has not been consistent in the last several years, so be sure and check with the WP&Y Railroad or the park services so you'll know whether you have to hoof it back about 15 miles to the road or nearest train stop. For more information on FEES AND RESERVATIONS, contact Parks Canada (205–300 Main St, Whitehorse, YT, Y1A 2B5 Canada; 867/667-3910 or 800/661-0486, within Canada and U.S. mainland). On the U.S. side, contact Klondike

Gold Rush National Historical Park (PO Box 517, Skagway, AK 99840; 907/983-2921; www.nps.gov/klgo).

RIDE THE WHITE PASS AND YUKON RAILROAD / They said the route was "too steep for even a billy goat," but they hadn't counted on Michael J. Heney, a brilliant engineer. The route followed the old White Pass Trail and took miners into the Klondike. Heney was known for getting the job done. His famous rallying cry was "Give me enough snoose and dynamite, and I'll build you a road to Hell!" From the end of May to the end of September, the train departs twice daily for White Pass Summit, returning to Skagway 3 hours later. Round-trip fare is $80 for adults and $40 for children 3 to 12. 800/343-7373 or 907/983-2217, fax 907/983-2734; www.whitepassrailroad.com.

GO HIKING OR BIKING / The quickest and easiest trails up into the mountains are those that go to **LOWER AND UPPER DEWEY LAKES**. If you have only a few hours, hike to Lower Dewey Lake, a beautiful 2.5-mile jaunt and 600-foot elevation gain. The trail begins near the Westmark Hotel. Ask for directions. If time allows, continue to Upper Dewey Lake, a round trip of 7 miles. The **KLONDIKE SUMMIT TO SEA CRUISE** is a 2-hour guided bike trip offered by **SOCKEYE CYCLES** (907/983-2851). They'll drive you up to the pass; then you "coast" back down to the sea. You won't lack for speed or beauty on this trip.

GUIDES AND OUTFITTERS

THE MOUNTAIN SHOP/PACKER EXPEDITIONS / Here you can rent packs, tents, sleeping bags, camping, and climbing gear, fuel—everything you need to get up and over the Chilkoot Trail, just like in the old days of the gold rush. Stop into the Mountain Shop to sign up for a guided tour with Packer Expeditions, which has about 15 guides and focuses mainly on beginning rock climbing, hiking, and "heli-hiking," which is a combination of helicoptering and hiking out or getting picked up both ways and hiking in between. 907/983-2544, fax 907/983-3544.

NIGHTLIFE

Skagway's local character—**BUCKWHEAT DONAHUE**—with his merry grin and trademark howl ("Howling is good for you," he says) will dance, sing, and recite his way into your heart. Almost every summer, he has a one-man show, performing Robert Service favorites like "The Cremation of Sam McGee," along with other rousing tales of the north. Look for notices of his show about town or just follow a big guy with red suspenders who periodically bursts into howling like a wolf. The "Longest Running Show in the North," or so the town claims, is a historic musical comedy about Skagway and that legendary con man Soapy

Smith. The **DAYS OF '98** has matinee and evening shows, with mock gambling in the Eagles Hall on Sixth Avenue and Broadway. Join Soapy Smith and Squirrel Tooth Alice for a look at the wild days. (For tickets, call 907/983-2545.) Afterwards or before (or any other part of the day), head on down to the **RED ONION SALOON** (2nd Ave and Broadway; 907/983-2222) for toe-tapping honky-tonk piano or live music and dancing. This was once a brothel. Look up at the second-story windows and pay homage to the ladies. Legend has it there's a ghost roaming around up there. Dance- and music-wise, things really get revved up on a Saturday night. It's a good time. The **SKAGWAY BREWING COMPANY** (907/983-2294), first established in 1898, had a revival in its centennial year. It's now housed in the old Golden North Hotel on Broadway and lives again. With a microbrewery on the premises, they often have free beer samplings. The long wooden bar and back-bar mirror add distinctive character and elegance. So, stop in here for a step back in time and a pint of the local brew.

FESTIVALS AND EVENTS

VICTORIAN YULETIDE / As the dark and wintry days of December roll around, Skagway gets decked out in lights to celebrate an old-fashioned Victorian Christmas. Children set their shoes outside to be filled with treats at night. The tree is lit in the center of town, followed by a parade of lighted boats in the harbor. There are organ recitals, singalongs, teas, tours of restored Victorian homes, and a Yuletide Ball at the Elks Lodge. Festivities occur during the first two weeks of December. For more information, call the Skagway Chamber of Commerce (907/983-1898) or the Visitors Bureau (907/983-2854).

THE BUCKWHEAT CLASSIC / Started by one of the town's great characters, the classic is a cross-country skiing event (with associated hoopla) the third weekend of March for serious and the not-so-serious racers. Courses range from 5 to 50 kilometers. Rooms book up fast for the popular event, so book early and share! And don't miss the Miss Buckwheat Contest (no long-legged beauties need apply). For more information, call the Skagway Convention and Visitors Bureau (907/983-2854).

FOURTH OF JULY / Four days after Soapy Smith rode his white stallion down Broadway at the head of the Fourth of July parade in 1898, he lay dead, shot through the heart in a shoot-out with Frank Reid down on the docks. Skagway holds a wonderful small-town Fourth. Soapy, or his reincarnated self, still leads the parade on his white horse; the parade marches a few blocks down Broadway; and, just in case you didn't get a good look, it turns around and marches back.

KLONDIKE TRAIL OF '98 INTERNATIONAL ROAD RELAY / This is a wildly popular relay race (on foot), which starts at night and runs up and over the mountains the 110 miles from Skagway to Whitehorse. It's a fun team event for those who love to punish themselves through sleep deprivation and heavy, heart-pumping exercise. To commemorate the Klondike Gold Rush, the race began in 1983 with six teams. Now there are more than 130 teams from all over the country. Part of the competition seems to be coming up with the most unusual name for your team, such as Midnight Claim Jumpers, Take No Prisoners, Wild Women Do, Out of the Ooze & Born To Cruise, Food Factory Flamethrowers, Vestigial Appendages, and One Knight Stands. The relay usually takes place the first week in September. For more information, call the Skagway Convention & Visitors Bureau (907/983-2854) or Sports Yukon in Canada (867/668-4236).

RESTAURANTS

Olivia's at the Skagway Inn / ★★

7TH AVE AND BROADWAY, SKAGWAY; 907/983-3287
A charming little restaurant in the historic Skagway Inn, Olivia's specializes in fresh seafood and is renowned for its French onion soup with sherry, cognac, and lots of garlic; its broiled portobello mushrooms with fresh herbs and feta cheese; and, of course, its signature dessert—a delicious white-chocolate bread pudding soaked in rum sauce. The philosophy of chef Wendell Fogliani, a longtime resident of Skagway trained at the Culinary Institute of Nevada: "Simple is better. People still like seafood, meats, and greens, and we have more healthy ways now of preparing dishes with lots of herbs and olive oil." *$$–$$$; AE, DIS, MC, V; local checks only; lunch Mon–Fri, dinner every day; open June–mid-Sept; beer and wine; 5 blocks down Broadway from the old railroad depot.* &

Ristorante Portobello & Pizzeria / ★★

III BROADWAY, SKAGWAY; 907/983-3459
Want to practice your Italian, Arabic, Spanish, or French? Or just love the ambience of international flavors and spicy conversation? Stop in this popular gathering place. The pizzas and focaccia are as flavorful as the accents—full of the spices of the Mediterranean. No surprise, when you learn the warm, gregarious owner, Farid Hosni, who is of Tunisian and Italian descent, began his 26-year culinary career in Florence, Italy, and came to Skagway a few years ago via Paris, London, and Juneau. Originally he started his business as a small pizzeria, which became so popular he expanded into a brand new building on Broadway in the summer of '99 with full *ristorante* fare, from his own favorite—linguine with

fresh clams—to the town's favorite—peppersteak with cognac. The more than 50 offerings on the menu will suit any taste from Caesar salad, soups, sandwiches, and pizza to broiled seafood and an array of fancy appetizers including lox, scampi, and lightly fried calamari with aïoli sauce. *$$; MC, V; local checks only; lunch, dinner every day; open May–late Sept; beer and wine; on Broadway in the heart of town.* &

Stowaway Cafe / ★★

205 CONGRESS WY, SKAGWAY; 907/983-3463

If the sun's shining, sit out on the deck and enjoy waterfront dining. The food is tasty, creative, and thoughtful, from Mom's Incredible Spinach Salad and Hilbo's Hot Scallop and Bacon Salad to seafood file gumbo (as close to Louisiana gumbo as you're going to get this far north), mesquite-grilled halibut, and blackened salmon. You can start with pot stickers with orange-ginger dipping sauce or baked Brie with pesto and pecans. For dessert, there's a heavy Southern leaning with pecan pie and bread pudding in bourbon sauce. *$$–$$$; MC, V; local checks only; dinner every day; closed in winter; beer and wine; overlooking the small boat harbor, on the way out to the railroad/cruise ship dock.* &

Sweet Tooth Café

3RD AVE AND BROADWAY, SKAGWAY; 907/983-2405, PHONE/FAX

A comfy place for breakfast, this cheerful cafe is a gathering spot for locals. Buttermilk pancakes, homemade bread, doughnuts, and French toast are the main fare. For lunch, go for the halibut burger. Of course, if you have a sweet tooth, their specialties are sundaes and ice cream floats. *$; MC, V; local checks only; breakfast, lunch every day (shorter hours in winter); no alcohol.*

LODGINGS

At The White House / ★★

8TH AVE AND MAIN, SKAGWAY, AK 99840; 907/983-9000,
FAX 907/983-9010

A historic old building from 1902, the White House became a boardinghouse in the 1920s, then officers' quarters and a hospital during World War I, then a boardinghouse again until a fire destroyed it in 1978. The Tronrud family—two brothers and their wives—bought it, renovated it, and opened it as a B&B in 1997. It's quiet, with a lovely lawn and flowers surrounding it, and beautifully refurbished inside. The 10 rooms are fairly large so it's a good choice for families or for winter guests with a lot of gear. All rooms have private baths ($95 for a double, summer; $75 and up for a double in winter; $130 for four). The morning breakfast is a delicious selection of hot egg casseroles, French toast, bagels, muffins, and fresh fruit. *$–$$; AE, DIS, MC, V; checks OK;*

whitehse@ptialaska.net; www.skagway.com/whitehouse; PO Box 41, Skagway, AK 99840. ♿

Gold Rush Lodge / ★

6TH AVE AND ALASKA ST, SKAGWAY, AK 99840; 907/983-2831 OR 877/983-3509, FAX 907/983-2742
Simple and comfortable, this small lodge sits on the edge of Skagway's gravel airfield and the wilderness at the edge of town. It has rustic wood doors and pine-accented rooms with Appalachian and handmade quilts on the beds. The rooms are small but cozy, with phones, VCRs, and outside entrances. It's more like a motel but with the homeyness of a B&B, and guests are often pleased with the high level of personal attention. If you are fascinated by small bush planes, there's a whole flotilla, which take off down the runway for morning and evening adventures—a kind of Alaska entertainment while drinking your morning coffee or sipping an evening beer. *$; AE, DIS, MC, V; checks OK; grl@ptialaska.net; www.alaskaone.com/goldrush; PO Box 514, Skagway, AK 99840; at the edge of the airfield.* ♿

Golden North Hotel / ★★

3RD AVE AND BROADWAY, SKAGWAY, AK 99840; 907/983-2451 OR 907/983-2294, FAX 907/983-2755
With its golden dome and colorful decor, the Golden North is still a landmark on Broadway. Recently renovated, the wonderful old red velveteen lobby jammed with gold-rush paraphernalia is, alas, gone, but the upstairs rooms still flaunt luminescent floral brocade wallpaper laced with gold and silver. The hallways and bedrooms are filled with turn-of-the-century memorabilia, antique furniture, and pseudo antiques donated by many of the original gold-rush families. There are old brass beds, wonderful wooden carved headboards, appliqued hand-stitched quilts, old photos, and lace curtains. Each room is fun and unique. Some have claw-foot bathtubs so long that, if you're short, you may want to bring a snorkel. Number 30, under the cupola, is filled with roses; numbers 10 and 14 are also lovely. But beware, if you're superstitious at all (and even if you're not), there's still a ghost in Room 24. It can get noisy with the bar and a restaurant located downstairs, and of course the ghosts provide additional entertainment. A single room with shared bath runs $65; double rooms with private bath are $105 to $120. *$-$$; AE, DIS, MC, V; local checks only; gold nuggets and gold dust OK, too; open May–Sept; full bar; corrington@msn.com; PO Box 343, Skagway, AK 99840.*

Historic Skagway Inn Bed and Breakfast / ★★★

**7TH AND BROADWAY, SKAGWAY, AK 99840; 907/983-2289,
FAX 907/983-2713**

In 1897, this now-historic inn was a brothel that stood in the red-light district a few blocks off Broadway. Moved to its present location in 1916, the original inn has 12 rooms, each named for a different woman who might have once lived there; it is said that in two of the rooms, ghosts linger on. Men particularly get a bang out of their reservations when they are told, "Oh, you'll be spending the night with Hattie. She's up there waiting." They'll re-emerge for breakfast in the morning with a long sigh, "Lulu never showed up last night." Nor, for that matter, did Alice, Birdie, Cleo, Dottie, Essie, Flo, Grace, Ida, Kitty, or Mimi. But hope springs eternal. And while you're waiting for the spirits of these gentle, tarnished doves, this is as comfortable, friendly, and charming a place to tuck in as you will find anywhere in this part of the country. Six bathrooms for the 12 rooms are shared, and not just by ghosts. Make your reservations well in advance and ask for Alice, Flo, or Lulu ($105 for a double in summer and $75 per room in winter—prices include a full, hot breakfast at Olivia's). This past year, innkeepers Karl and Rosemary Klupar were in the process of adding on six rooms—with private bathrooms—but still in keeping with the nostalgia of the original inn. *$$; AE, DIS, MC, V; local checks only; sgyinn@ptialaska.net; PO Box 500, Skagway, AK 99850; 5 blocks down Broadway from the old railroad depot.*

Mile Zero Bed & Breakfast / ★★

**9TH AVE AND MAIN ST, SKAGWAY, AK 99840; 907/983-3045,
FAX 907/983-3046**

Built in 1995, Mile Zero has a warm and friendly atmosphere, halfway between a B&B and a motel. The rooms are bright, contemporary, and easily accommodate four people, with a few homey touches like an antique steamer trunk or bureau, but mostly quite simple and spacious, with phones and private baths. Each room has a private outside entrance, but there's also a front entrance and common room for socializing, which makes it convivial, especially in winter. As one happy guest said, "Mile Zero is user-friendly." In summer, the help-yourself continental breakfast is fresh fruit, cereals, and muffins. In winter, guests have kitchen privileges. Hosts prefer "mature" guests. No smoking. Rates are $70 for a single; $95 for a double in summer, lower in winter. *$–$$; AE, MC, V; checks OK; mile0@ptialaska.net; PO Box 165, Skagway, AK 99840.*

Westmark Inn / ★

3RD AVE AND SPRING ST, SKAGWAY, AK 99840; 800/544-0970 OR 907/983-6000, FAX 907/983-6100

With touches of the Gay '90s and a friendly atmosphere, the Westmark— with no original foothold in Skagway—does a good job of fitting in. Be forewarned: this is where the tour buses load and unload. But if you've opted for "character" accommodations in too much of Alaska already and you're looking for standard motel comfort where the bed is long enough to cover your feet and the shower is private, this could be your place. *$$; AE, DC, DIS, MC, V; no checks; open late May–mid-Sept; PO Box 514, Skagway, AK 99840.* &

THE ROADS NORTH

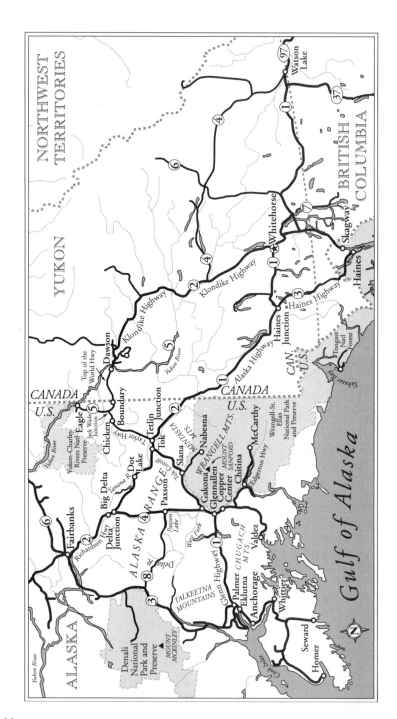

THE ROADS NORTH

When visiting Alaska, you will surely want to drive. Some people have the time to drive from the Lower 48 all the way to Alaska on the Alaska-Canada Highway (a.k.a. The Alcan). If you choose this option, you will be a road warrior by the time you cross the border. Others arrive in Haines or Skagway in Southeast Alaska via the Alaska Marine Highway and drive the 400 miles to Interior Alaska through Canada or the 800 or so miles to Anchorage. If you choose this option, be sure to reserve ferry space well in advance, as it is booked solid in the summer. You also can fly to Anchorage and rent a car.

Be sure to carry *The Milepost* with you. Billed—correctly—as the "Bible of North Country Travel," it takes you mile marker to mile marker down all the roads of Alaska. A note about lodging and food along the route: the watchword is "practical." Many of the operative words like "best" and "cuisine" become tongue-in-cheek in the Alaska outback. If you need to sleep and shower, there is probably a place to do it. One alternative to be considered for those with energy and equipment is camping. Not only is it cheap, but you can pick your spot and otherwise control your destiny.

The Alaska Highway

In the old days, the Alaska Highway nominally began in Dawson Creek, British Columbia, at Mile 0. It really began where the pavement ended in Fort St. John 50 miles later. From there on, the trip hovered between novelty and tedium, with novelty predominating in the beginning and intense tedium at the end. It was like being trapped inside a house that was being drywalled for 5 days. Dust hung in the air inside the vehicle. Opening windows only sucked it in faster through the trunk or tailgate. There was no way to get fresh air without stopping and getting out of the car. If you followed another car at any distance of less than half a mile, dust was a steady entree. The real knuckle-blancher was seeing a semi-truck bearing down, stones sparking out from the wheels as dust in great churning petticoats billowed out behind. These were both IFR (Instrument Flight Rating) situations with religious overtones.

The road was tightly wound around the contours of hills, lakes, and rivers, with sharp, steeply banked turns. One developed an empathy for the magnitude of this wartime project of 1942, which punched a road through some of the most unforgiving terrain and climate in the world in less than a year. Typically, the traveler prepared for the arduous journey with extra tires and gas. It was harder to prepare psychologically.

You knew that the trip was long and that none of it would be lost. So you tried to settle in behind the wheel and be patient. But after a couple of days, you just wanted to get it over. You drove faster and faster, taking on the turns by using both lanes, hoping no one else would appear. This backslide into recklessness was made even more palpable by the white crosses—little wooden obituaries that stood at the places where fatalities had occurred.

Now, the highway is paved. Where it used to resemble a dropped rope, the worst stretches have been eliminated. There are ample gas and amenities, and having a sign on your vehicle that states "Alaska or Bust" says more about you than the trip. Even the crosses are gone, removed after people complained that they gave the drive a macabre tone. Still, it is a long stretch of driving, and some of the same psychology that held in the old days colors your responses today. You become very anxious to arrive at the Alaska border, and it is a relief to see the solitary little customs compound show up in the middle of nowhere (unless either you or your car gets treated to a strip search).

Canadian Border to Tok

As if to say "Welcome back to the States," the road widens and becomes a flowing river of blacktop. Gas drops below two bucks a gallon and looks like a bargain. Tok, your first "real" Alaska town, is just 90 miles down the road. Things are looking up. If you're not immune to the spare beauty of the landscape by this time, there is lots to appreciate.

You are now in Alaska, a huge state that once spanned four time zones, since reduced to two. More precisely, you're in "Interior" Alaska. The destination no longer recedes like a carrot on the horizon, and there is time to take it all in. From the border all the way to Fairbanks, the Alaska Highway follows the Tanana River drainage. The climate is continental, protected from moderating ocean influences by the Wrangell-St. Elias Mountains to the south. Temperatures vary with the amount of daylight, reaching as high as 90°F in the summer and as low as -60°F in winter. Precipitation averages about 12 inches a year, only slightly more than arid. Any that falls as snow from early October on is part of the scenery until spring. In June and July, the sun makes a wide arc around most of the sky, rising in the north and setting there roughly 20 hours later. In winter, it's the other way around: the sun rises in the south and sets there perhaps 4 hours later, little more than an ornament for the cold.

For a relatively new civilization, the country has a strangely historical feel to it. The immensity and barrenness of the northern landscape lend a sense of timelessness that is unrelenting. Since each day lengthens or shortens by up to 6 minutes a day, one does not become absentminded. The sense of urgency is caught nicely by all the migrating waterfowl, as well as in the miner's reference to the first snow on the mountain tops as "termination dust." This usually comes in late August and used to mean that it was time to head out before the rivers froze and the last boat left for the south.

Speaking of miners, it was mining that opened up the Interior and that was the raison d'etre for almost every town here. What is a "real" Alaska town? The typical Alaska town was created around one natural resource and defined by it. A "real" Alaska town might, therefore, be a fishing town, a mining town, a trading town, or, more recently, a tourist town. Alternatively, it may have always been here, as in the case of aboriginal villages built around traditional food sources. If the reason for being here disappears, these towns become ghost towns. There are no ghost towns in Ohio, but there are plenty in Alaska. So there is a strong feeling for history in Alaska—for time inexorably moving on.

Tok

The first Alaska town you arrive in, after driving the Alaska Highway, is Tok. Its reason for being there is incorporated in its old name, Tok Junction. Not a town of obvious grace and beauty, Tok occurs in a floodplain of thousands of acres. The only defining characteristic is that two roads join, making it a logical place to sell needed things to travelers passing through on the way to or from mining districts such as Valdez, Anchorage, and Fairbanks, and from the Lower 48. A town naturally sprang up.

Tok had its beginnings as a construction camp on the Alaska-Canada Highway in 1942, when the road was being pushed through as part of the defense effort against an anticipated Japanese invasion. One story about the origin of Tok's name is that it is an abbreviation of "Tokyo Camp." The population today is 1,250, and the mean monthly temperature in January is truly mean: –19°F; in July, it is 59°F.

ACCESS AND INFORMATION

First, stop at **TOK MAINSTREET VISITORS CENTER** (Box 389, Tok, AK 99780; 907/883-5775 or 907/883-5887), located at the junction of Alaska Highway and Tok Cutoff. Open daily, May–Sept. **ALASKA PUBLIC LANDS INFORMATION CENTER** (907/883-5667) is next door to the visitors center and open daily in summer. Managed under the auspices of the U.S. Fish and Wildlife Service is **TETLIN WILDLIFE REFUGE** (907/883-5312), which is across the highway from the Public Lands Information Center and is open weekdays, year-round.

THE CIRCULAR ROUTE

Anchorage-Glennallen-Valdez-Whittier-Anchorage, with a side trip to Chitina and McCarthy

A journey by land and sea, this route combines a series of scenic dramas. You can go in either direction. In essence, this is a spectacular drive out of Anchorage to Glennallen along the Glenn Highway, turning right onto the Richardson Highway, peeling off shortly (if you have a few extra days for a side trip to historic Kennicott and McCarthy, reached by the Edgerton Highway), then back to the Richardson Highway and heading south to the port town of Valdez. Explore Valdez (see the Prince William Sound chapter), then take the ferry, part of the Alaska Marine Highway system, through Prince William Sound to the port town of Whittier (about 7 hours). Drive your car off the ferry and onto the train flatcars or, if the toll road is open, you can drive straight through the tunnel in the mountains and come out on the Seward Highway, just an hour or so south of Anchorage. And voilà! The circle is complete. Allow at least 4 or 5 days for the trip, the longer the better. The mountains and rivers beckon to the hiker, backpacker, fisherman, or rafter. And a side trip to McCarthy always offers a good time.

RESTAURANTS

Fast Eddy's

MILE 1313.3, ALASKA HWY, TOK; 907/883-4411

Fast Eddy's is connected with Young's Motel, one of the clean, modern motels in Tok. There's a salad bar, sandwiches, pizza, Alaska seafood, and steaks. No new wrinkles here, but the food is well prepared. The place is busy, always a good sign. *$; AE, DIS, MC, V; no checks; breakfast, lunch, dinner every day; beer and wine; PO Box 482, Tok, AK 99780; ¾ mile east of the junction.*

Tok Gateway Salmon Bake / ★

MILE 1313.1, ALASKA HWY, TOK; 907/883-5555

Like most places in Alaska, it's billed as a salmon bake, but the fish is grilled. No matter. Essentially, this is a barbecue with ribs, buffalo burgers, reindeer sausage, king salmon, and halibut. One advantage of a limited menu is that the establishment can pay attention to the few items it serves. Fresh salmon and halibut, grilled just right, are hard to top. *$$; lunch Mon–Sat, dinner every day in summer; MC, V; checks OK; no alcohol, but you may bring your own; PO Box 577, Tok, AK 99780; ⅞ mile east of the junction.*

LODGINGS

Cleft of the Rock Bed and Breakfast / ★★

MILE 1316.5, ALASKA HWY, TOK, AK 99780; 800/478-5646 OR 907/883-4219, FAX 907/883-5963

One of the first things you notice as you drive in is a real lawn and an absence of the usual Alaska collection of extra cars and odds and ends that might someday rise again like the old South. The guest rooms in the house are located in the daylight basement and share a bathroom ($80 to $115 for two). They are clean and acceptable, but the stars are awarded for the five log cabins you pass on the way in, complete with running water and bathrooms. The largest one sleeps up to five adults and has a kitchen, loft, and bath. The cabins are nicely situated on the lawn, among scattered trees, and come with lawn chairs begging to be used after a long day's drive. Reserve ahead. Full, hot breakfast served. The B&B also rents mountain bikes. *$$; AE, DIS, MC, V; checks OK; PO Box 122, Tok, AK 99780; off Alaska Hwy, 3 miles west of Tok, turn right on Sundog Trail and go ½ mile.*

The Tok Cutoff

Technically, this road is part of the Glenn Highway, running from Tok to Anchorage, but the first 125 miles have always been called the Tok Cutoff. It was built from Tok on the Alaska Highway to Gakona Junction on the Richardson Highway—a shortcut from one highway to another.

Be prepared for a lot of "frost heaves" and cracks on this portion of highway. It's nearly impossible to put a road surface down over permafrost that lasts beyond a couple of seasons. It isn't that Alaska refuses to put money into highways; it just can't keep up with ongoing deterioration.

The first 10 miles of road south out of Tok are straight, true, and well-surfaced. From there, you can kiss the straight and well-surfaced goodbye and the scenery hello, as you are in the mountains for about the next 50 miles. The road follows the Tok and Little Tok Rivers most of the way to Mentasta Summit. **EAGLE TRAIL STATE RECREATION SITE,** 15 miles out of Tok, has 40 campsites in a forest of large spruce. It's on the old trail that ran from Valdez to Eagle, a section of which has signed hiking trails.

The road continues on in quiet grandeur through the mountains. The food and lodging on this route, even though they do not merit stars, still can be part of a great adventure. **MINERAL LAKES B&B** (HC72, Box 830, Tok, AK 99780-9410; 907/883-5498), 35 miles south of Tok, has cabins overlooking the lakes, but with no running water or electricity.

You do get a memorable view of the Mentasta Mountains and a chance to go fishing. There's a canoe and motorboat for rent. **MENTASTA LODGE** (HC01, Box 585, Gakona, AK 99586; 907/291-2324), 47 miles south of Tok, has cabins and a bar and cafe. When people live year-round in such extreme climate and geography, a special resonance may occur that also deserves stars. Call it character.

Beyond Mentasta Lodge, the road runs beside the Slana River. On this side of Mentasta Summit, the rivers flow south into the Copper River and Prince William Sound instead of north into the Tanana River and then finally the Yukon. As you emerge from the Mentasta Mountains, if the weather is clear, you'll get your first glimpse of **MOUNT SANFORD** (16,237 feet). Welcome to the Wrangell Mountains. The country opens up, but the scene is always dominated by Mount Sanford, 35 miles away.

The **NEBESNA ROAD** branches off to the southeast at **SLANA** and allows access into the **WRANGELL-ST. ELIAS NATIONAL PARK AND PRESERVE** (see below). A park ranger station, a quarter mile down the road, offers information about the park and road conditions. The road is paved for the first 4 miles and gravel thereafter. Twenty-eight miles out, the road becomes rough and fords several streams. The area is open to camping. The road ends after 45 miles at the old mining town of **NEBESNA**, which is pretty much of a ghost town, although various population figures for the area say "less than 25." The last 3 miles are the roughest. Don't expect a chocolate shake at the end.

From Slana to Gakona Junction the road is less than exciting, unless you're looking for the perfect frost heave or road fissure to facilitate signature headprints in the roof of your vehicle. The highway is relatively straight, as there is nothing for it to go around and much of the country is permafrost. You come to Chistochina, one of the more beautiful Alaska names to the ear. Besides Mount Sanford and **MOUNT DRUM** (to the right of Sanford), startling scenery is absent, except if you travel at sunrise, sunset, full moon, first snow, first leaves, or first love, in which case the magic will be there with no help needed from terrestrial aberrations.

About 3 miles before the Tok Cutoff joins the Richardson Highway at Gakona Junction, the road drops into the shallow canyon created by the Copper River.

RESTAURANTS

Gakona Lodge / ★

MILE 2, TOK CUTOFF, GAKONA; 907/822-3482

Gakona Lodge is an old roadhouse, built in 1905. It was added to the National Register of Historic Places in 1977 and makes an interesting stop. It is one in a series of roadhouses that once ran up the old Richardson Trail, spaced about a day's travel apart. Most of the roadhouses have burned down now. Gakona Lodge and Rika's Roadhouse at Big Delta are still operating as historic places, while Black Rapids Lodge, at Mile 227.4, is standing but in serious decline. At Gakona, a cluster of mostly log buildings includes the old carriage house, which is now a restaurant, and the main lodge. The historic feel has been maintained. The dining room is dark and comfortable. The log walls come complete with mounted animal heads and old-time Alaska tools. The menu consists of steaks and seafood with salad bar. Bring your poke. *$$; MC, V; local checks only; dinner every day; closed in winter; full bar; PO Box 285, Gakona, AK 99586; by the bridge in Gakona.*

Tok to Delta Junction

The last chunk of the Alaska Highway runs from Tok to Delta Junction, where it joins the Richardson Highway for the trip into Fairbanks. It covers a scenic 100 miles. The road out of Tok runs for 15 miles, with hardly a bend until the road gets close to the **MENTASTA MOUNTAINS**.

A rustic and scenic camping spot, the **MOON LAKE STATE RECREATION SITE** comes at Mile 1331.9. A lovely spot, a quarter mile off the highway, it has swimming and a small sandy beach.

Jan Lake Road turns off to the south at Mile 1353.7. **JAN LAKE** is a half mile back, nestled among the mixed birch- and spruce-covered hills. It is a pretty location and a good picnic spot. The lake is small and stocked with small rainbows. In the fall, if you're lucky, you'll see hundreds of sandhill cranes fly over in wavering filaments, sun reflecting off their beating wings as if from waves.

The road crosses the Johnson River Bridge at Mile 1380.5. Most of the rivers have access roads that allow for a more intimate look and possible campsites (no amenities). **JOHNSON RIVER** is especially nice in this regard. In a few miles, the road leaves the mountains and goes straight over flat land for 40 miles, right into Delta Junction. It is still a beautiful drive, but the beauty now comes with distance. To the south, there's a line of mountains. The closer ones are soft, while those farther back are white and craggy—the beginnings of the Alaska Range. The rivers are glacial and run in braids across broad shallow beds. At Mile 1403.6, Sawmill Creek Road takes off to the north, right through the **DELTA BARLEY PROJECT**, an agricultural project. There's an interpretive sign explaining the project, and you can decide if you want to face a gravel road to see more.

Although you expect to see signs for moose and caribou crossings, it is a surprise to see a sign warning you to watch out for bison. A herd of bison was transplanted from Montana in the 1920s to see how they'd do. They've done fine, much to the chagrin of the farmers who have been feeding them whether they wanted to or not. The **BISON RANGE**, 70,000 acres of grassland for fall and winter grazing, was established south of the highway to reduce agricultural losses. The last 25 miles into Delta is all new blacktop and has wide shoulders, a welcome stretch after all the frost heaves one enjoys as part of the Alaska road package.

Delta Junction

Delta Junction was established as a construction camp on the Richardson Highway in 1919. It is the official end of the Alaska Highway, and from here you have the choice of Alaska 4 south or Alaska 2 on into Fairbanks. Delta Junction's population is listed at 736. If you want to put your finger on the pulse of the town, go to the **IGA FOOD CACHE** (907/895-4653), located on Main Street. It all happens here. Dog food in 40-pound bags is stacked up beside the plywood deli booths. There's an espresso cart and fresh-made doughnuts from the bakery. The homemade soups come after the coffee-and-doughnut rush subsides. No yuppies here, just farmers mumbling about getting the rest of the hay in and other folks in work clothes and quilted jackets. The weather is the topic in the fall, with all the geese and cranes filtering through in long strings; but it's also the topic the rest of the year because there's always weather.

The Taylor Highway

In Alaska, the road map, like the average menu, is limited to basics, and if you don't like the options, that's tough. Even Anchorage, Alaska's largest city, has just two roads: one going north and one going south. Fairbanks does better with three, but in deep winter many residents suspect that all three go in and none out. Indeed, when the temperature is –40°F or –50°F, a long car trip is serious business and one packs basic survival gear.

Alaskans know most of the roads by heart. They still excite us, but the prospect of a fresh road is like spring. One road not heavily traveled, even by Alaskans, is the road to **EAGLE**.

Eagle has a mystique about it. Alaskans know it as a checkpoint on the 1,000-mile Yukon Quest Sled Dog Race and as a town that cannot be reached by road in winter. It is a town for real Alaskans, for folks who don't need a bank or the security of an international airport within taxi distance. The name itself inspires. A town named "Finch" or "Dove" wouldn't have the same draw. **CHICKEN**, on the same road, catches the ear too, but its mystique is so bound by absurdity it never gets off the

CHICKEN

Chicken, at Mile 66, is an obvious draw. Who could resist such a burlesque name? And why "Chicken"? The story goes that early miners wanted to name the town "Ptarmigan" because of the bird's abundance there, but no one knew how to spell it. So they settled for Chicken. To our eye, a ptarmigan does not much resemble a chicken but then, that's the charm of the story.

The best thing to do in Chicken is to get the Chicken postmark on your letters at the post office, a small log building with flower boxes and a flagpole outside. Mail service to Chicken (pop. 37) is by air twice a week, weather permitting. If there is any more economic belt-tightening, Chicken's tiny post office, which was established in 1903, may be eliminated—a notion that worries the postmistress. So buy your year's worth of stamps in Chicken from someone who cares, and keep Chicken's mail service from getting fried.

—John Kooistra

ground. So Eagle it is, with a Chicken thrown in. If you venture down this road, your heart will soar like a hawk.

Most people travel to Alaska in summer, when the long, magic days open up possibilities limited only by stamina. If you drive to Eagle in late September with the days getting short, you get a sky full of stars in place of the same number of mosquitoes. And the Northern Lights! Also, a nearly empty road. Each summer season, more than 20,000 people take the Klondike Loop, leaving the Alaska Highway at Whitehorse, driving to Dawson City, then reconnecting with the Alaska Highway 12 miles east of Tok at Tetlin Junction. Heading west from Dawson, the road is gravel. The road that forms the Klondike Loop is better suited to heavy traffic than the spur road up to Eagle. The Canadian section has been improved, with heavy visitor traffic in mind.

The Taylor Highway (Alaska 5) runs from Tetlin Junction to Eagle, 160 miles of unpaved road, with the appropriately named Top of the World Highway branching off to Dawson City at Jack Wade Junction, 96 miles into the drive. The road is marked with mileposts. From Jack Wade Junction to Eagle, its 65 miles of narrow, winding, eminently cursable and memorable road. This stretch takes you back decades to the bad old Alaska Highway days, something to be considered before making the drive. The road is less than two lanes wide in those places where it hugs the mountainside in tight turns as it follows various river valleys. We cannot recall a single guardrail. It would not be a comfortable jaunt for a large motor home towing a getaway car. However, the scenery is terrific, and when the road is not brailling its way through the gorges and valleys, it is up on top of the world overlooking a landscape that goes on like a clear conscience. A sunset looks small up here: it's so far away and takes up so little of the horizon. If you want photos, bring a disposable panoramic camera. The wide-angle bite will still be too narrow, but several overlapping vistas can be put together to catch some sense of that space.

The road to Eagle from Jack Wade Junction was finally punched through in 1953, after 8 years of construction. One Eagle resident said the trip out to Tetlin Junction used to take 7 hours; now it takes 4, with more than half devoted to the Eagle spur. This is 4 hours for someone who has and means business, not someone who's there to savor the sights and the feel of the country. For touring, better stick with the original 7 hours with lots of stops.

The Alaska Highway parallels the **TANANA RIVER** and drainage, so it stays low. From Tetlin Junction, the road begins to ascend mountains appropriately called "domes." They are old and soft hills when compared to the brash, rugged, snow-covered Wrangell-St. Elias Range to the south, which contains some of the highest mountains in North America. Within 2 or 3 miles, you ascend enough to get a view of the hills, which is exciting after all the valley travel on the Alaska Highway. The vista is exciting in an ancient way, going out and out in layers of hills and distance. You truly start to feel "on top of the world," especially after about 25 miles, at the point where the road goes above timberline and skirts **MOUNT FAIRPLAY** (5,541 feet), the second-highest point on the way to Eagle.

Gold was discovered in this area in 1886. This is the **"FORTYMILE COUNTRY,"** named after the old town located where the Fortymile River enters the Yukon, a few miles east of the border. Chicken Creek and Wade Creek were also rich finds. In many places, the Taylor Highway runs right over the top of or right beside the old horse-and-wagon road that was built and used by the miners and freight haulers.

At Mile 34.4, there is a pullout on the left (west) and a mind-altering view. If you go in late September, there are no services until you get to Eagle, though food, gas, and "likker" are available in Chicken during the summer. Blueberries and crowberries are everywhere. Blue teeth, here we come!

Beyond Chicken, rivers are a big part of the scenery. From Mile 76 to Mile 80, the road rises high above **WALKER FORK**, which cuts an average of 800 feet into solid rock. It is one of the most scenic stretches of the highway. Pull over, peer into the canyon, and listen to the river far below. (During summer traffic this would not be a safe practice, so exercise due caution.)

Mile 96 brings a parting of the ways: east into Canada and Dawson City or north to Eagle. In either case, the road stays on top of the hills and you can see it winding around hilltops miles in the distance. After 10 miles on "the roof," the road descends toward the Fortymile River Bridge, a place for putting in your raft or canoe for running the river.

For much of the next 30 miles the road hugs O'BRIEN CREEK with lots of tight places and turns in the road. There are no guardrails and some of the drop-offs are precipitous. The views draw a fine line between prudence and curiosity. When the road leaves the valley around Mile 136, things open up and you're on top of the world again, traversing American Pass. A few miles away only one tiny building is visible, making it seem lonelier still. The sign in front announces "American Summit Liquor," surely one of the world's most isolated liquor stores.

The Taylor Highway is not maintained by the state beyond mid-October, the time of the general onset of serious snow. Before then, people from Eagle make their last drives of the year out to the big cities of Anchorage and Fairbanks for winter supplies.

Eagle

Eagle was named in 1897 for the eagles that nested on the nearby bluff. At the time there were only 28 miners, but by spring of 1898, there were 1,700 people in Eagle—10 times the number who live here today. In 1899, the Army established Fort Egbert, just west of the town, to maintain law and order; to build roads, trails, and the telegraph; and to help unfortunate civilians. Judge James Wickersham presided over the first federal court in the Alaska Interior: the Third Judicial District, which covers 300,000 square miles. Eagle was the commercial, judicial, and military center for the Interior during the Klondike gold rush.

Today, Judge Wickersham's original courthouse serves as a museum, and Fort Egbert's military buildings have been completely restored. And there's the town itself—a cluster of old buildings and cabins, an old school, and a library, as well as the Yukon River. Eagle Village is an Athabascan settlement on the banks of the Yukon, 3 miles upstream.

Eagle has charm. It is a real Alaska town—and one reason why you went to so much trouble and expense to come to Alaska in the first place. The town itself is attractive, squeezed down to the river by the mountains in two levels. Most of the town is on the second level—the sensible level—protected from the vagaries of the river.

Both the town and the residents have personality to spare. The impact of tourism is evident, but this community has not turned itself inside out catering to it. Few places take credit cards, and the nearest bank is in Delta Junction, 275 miles away, so come prepared. Most impressive, though, is the absence of a bar or liquor store, a notoriously profitable business in a state where many folks head for the bar to wait for spring.

If you go out to Eagle Village, you'll pass the town's primary airport, marked by signs displaying the silhouette of a Boeing 747, a droll touch. If a 747 ever lands in Eagle, it won't be a scheduled stop. Eagle Village is less than a mile down the road from the airport. The houses line the riverbank, and empty chairs sit waiting along the edge of the bluff. This is the best show in town. All the action is on the river.

Unless you want to winter in, start driving out before termination dust settles for good on Mount Fairplay. At night from your sleeping bag, watch the stars preen. That old ribbon of wonder, the Milky Way, will have you by the hair of your neck.

ADVENTURES

HISTORICAL TOUR / Given by the **EAGLE HISTORICAL SOCIETY**, the tours meet at the courthouse daily, 9am, Memorial Day through Labor Day. For more information, contact PO Box 23, Eagle City, AK 99738; 907/547-2325.

FLOAT TRIPS / Float the Fortymile or Yukon River. Canoes can be rented in Dawson City or in Eagle at **EAGLE CANOE RENTALS** (907/547-2203). You can float through the **YUKON-CHARLEY RIVERS NATIONAL PRESERVE** to Circle on the road system north of Fairbanks. Get any of your buddies driving north to pick you up.

RESTAURANTS

Riverside Cafe

FRONT ST, EAGLE; 907/547-2220
The best restaurant in town also happens to be the only restaurant. The log cafe with central woodstove is attractively situated, overlooking the Yukon. It is warm and friendly and supplies the town coffee table. You bring the conversation. Gravy-sogged rolls and canned fruit notwithstanding, the core of the dinners is straightforward and ample. Pies are homemade. *$; no credit cards; local checks only; breakfast, lunch, dinner every day; open mid-May–early Nov; no alcohol; Box 36, Eagle, AK 99738.*

The Glenn Highway

This route to Glennallen lies east out of Anchorage, a journey of about 200 miles. Half an hour out of town, the Athabascan village of **EKLUTNA** is on your left and a beautiful mountain lake of the same name is 14 miles up a dirt road, off the highway to the right. Just before the bridge, look to the left and you'll see sofas and chairs lined up on the bluff overlooking the highway, where the locals lounge around watching the traffic flow.

Right before the Knik River Bridge is the old road into **PALMER**, a scenic detour through this agricultural valley. After the bridge, you cross the **PALMER HAY FLATS**. Be on the lookout for moose, particularly in the early morning. **PIONEER PEAK** rises behind you, dominating the valley. It was named for the midwestern pioneers who came here in the 1930s to start a new life, fleeing the Dust Bowl during the Depression. Some of the most fantastic cold-weather vegetables are grown here—70-pound cabbages and foot-long carrots. If you're in the area during late August and the first of September, stick around for one of the state's most popular events—the **ALASKA STATE FAIR**. You'll pass the fairgrounds on the right as you head toward Palmer.

To visit the **MUSK OX FARM** (907/745-4151), turn at Mile 50.1, just past Palmer. These marvelous creatures can even be your namesake. For a modest donation of $50, you can have a musk ox named after you or your best friend. Contrary to their name, it's not the musk for which these animals are famous. In fact, they have no musk glands. Furthermore, they're not even oxen. They're really related to the goat and antelope family. But their great treasure is their underhairs, called qiviut, which are finer, lighter, and warmer than cashmere. Hats and scarves from qiviut make truly lovely, if expensive, gifts. The farm is open daily, May through September, with tours every half hour.

The next stretch of highway provides scenery of matchless beauty. The road follows the **MATANUSKA RIVER**, then climbs the outer fringe of the **TALKEETNA MOUNTAINS**, with the **CHUGACH MOUNTAINS** off to the right across the valley. As is true elsewhere in Alaska, many of the peaks in the Chugach are still unnamed, a reminder that this is still a young country, only recently explored. The stark and rugged mountains are interspersed with glaciers, including **MATANUSKA GLACIER**, which

THE DRUNKEN FOREST

At first sight, the trees seem to weave—first to the left, then to the right. No, it's not your eyes playing tricks on you. The trees really are leaning. Most of the land in northern Alaska consists of permanently frozen ground or "permafrost." During the summer, the top few inches of soil above the permafrost thaw out. It is in these few inches of moist soil that plants extend their roots. Trees growing in a permafrost zone can put down only shallow roots. The frozen soil inhibits further growth. Thus, their anchors are shaky and unstable. They often will grow at an angle, listing first this way, then that. Scientists call this "the drunken forest.")

—Nan Elliot

appears soon in this journey, off to the west. Meanwhile, you climb through a forest of aspen interspersed with evergreen: a lovely sight at any time, but if you hit it at the height of fall colors, it's a vision of golden beauty. **CHICKALOON** is summer home to **NOVA** (800/746-5753; www.novalaska.com), whitewater river-rafting guides who will take you on half-day trips down the Matanuska River. They offer everything from peaceful floats to wet and wild rides, depending on your thrills-to-chills quotient. Trips cost $60 to $90 per person; located at Mile 76 on the Glenn Highway.

KING MOUNTAIN, one of the few named peaks in the area, rises with majesty to the south. Up above the confluence of the Chickaloon and Matanuska Rivers, there is a fine view over the valley. The road follows the shore of Long Lake and brings you to Matanuska Glacier.

Beyond **SHEEP MOUNTAIN**, the road climbs to **EUREKA SUMMIT** (Eureka Lodge is a possible pie stop), and the scenery changes dramatically. The Chugach Mountains fall away to the south, as Mount Drum and the Wrangells appear in the east. A tundralike plain opens up, studded by several lakes and stunted trees—the "drunken forest" in local parlance (see "The Drunken Forest" in this chapter). The vast **NELCHINA GLACIER** interrupts the dark range of the Chugach and gives its name to the caribou herd that frequents this area. Keep a lookout for these wild reindeer.

LODGINGS

Sheep Mountain Lodge / ★★★

MILE 113.5, GLENN HWY, PALMER, AK 99645; 907/745-5121, FAX 907/745-5120

As you climb up to Sheep Mountain, the trees thin out and it's possible to catch glimpses of Dall sheep high up on the mountains. The best place to break your trip or, for that matter, to stop for several days of adventure is Sheep Mountain Lodge. The lodge is run by David Cohen and his wife, Diane Schneider. It is the best—and the only—place of this superb quality for many, many miles. Rustic and charming, the lodge is right on the highway. The entry is set off by a brilliant bank of lovingly tended flowers, which provide a special touch of class to this wilderness outpost. Individual cabins are sturdy and tastefully designed with comfort in mind. Views are stunning—wide-open country, glaciers, light woods. The hospitality is warm, and the lodge's dining room provides generous Alaska fare with a spicy Southwest touch. There is also a bunkhouse for larger parties or those on the cheap. *$$; MC, V; local checks only; open May–Oct (some years open earlier for spring skiing); sheepmtl@alaska. net; www.alaska.net/~sheepmtl; HC 03, Box 8490, Palmer, AK 99645.*

Glennallen

For a taste of local color, tune into the radio message board **CARIBOU CLATTER** on **KCAM** (790 on your AM dial during the news at 7am, noon, 5pm, and 9pm). In other regions of Alaska, this same radio message program has been called Ptarmigan Telegraph, Tundra Drums, and Cabin Trapline. The messages you hear are sometimes strange and wondrous, and always full of local color. Call to send a message on KCAM, 907/822-3306.

In Glennallen, at the junction of the Glenn and Richardson Highways, is the **GLENNALLEN VISITORS INFORMATION CENTER**, a charming log cabin, dripping with flowers, open only in summer.

LODGINGS

New Caribou Hotel

CENTER OF TOWN, GLENNALLEN, AK 99588; 800/478-3302,
IN ALASKA, OR 907/822-3302, FAX 907/822-3711
An attractive place to stay if you get sleepy in Glennallen. The rooms are standard motel, but cheerful. It is on the tour-bus circuit, so it can be a mob scene when the buses arrive. On the average, rooms run about $130/double. They do have a few suites and apartments to accommodate families or larger groups traveling together. Also, for bicyclists or hikers trying to make it on the cheap but wanting a shower and a bed, there is an economy section with beds for $49/night. The hotel is almost completely nonsmoking. *$$; AE, DIS, MC, V; local checks only; PO Box 329, Glennallen, AK 99588.* &

The Richardson Highway

Unless you are agoraphobic, it is hard to imagine not liking driving the roads of Alaska. There is space, something hard to get away from in Alaska. Most of the time, the scenery will knock your eyeballs out. But there are also miles of wet lowlands. The country around Glennallen has stretches of lowland permafrost stuff, marshy bogs with trees like pipe cleaners. You've got about 40 miles of this to drive through until you get to more exciting parts. The redeeming features are the distant regal mountains—**SANFORD** (16,237 feet), **WRANGELL** (14,163 feet), and **DRUM** (12,010 feet)—which form a postcard backdrop.

Glennallen to Fairbanks

For the first 30 miles, the Richardson Highway north from Glennallen is utilitarian. It's relatively straight with sections of generous frost heaves. The scenic attractions are caribou, if you're lucky, and views of the Gulkana River Gorge on the west side of the highway. The **GULKANA RIVER** is a good salmon and rafting river. It runs out of Paxson and Summit Lakes. The float from Paxson Lake to Sourdough Campground at Mile 147.6 is popular for experienced river runners.

Your first good look at the **ALASKA RANGE** comes when you round Hogan Hill, a row of shark's teeth running all the way across the horizon. The range begins near Tok, running west and then southwest through Denali National Park, ultimately becoming the Aleutian Chain. Mount McKinley (20,320 feet) is the highest mountain of this range and the highest in North America.

Here in the foothills of the Alaska Range, you can see the **TRANS-ALASKA OIL PIPELINE**, curving and silver, winding its way across the terrain like a sculpture, sometimes aboveground and sometimes under. **PAXSON LAKE** appears west of the highway—a long, deep lake, famous for lake trout.

Paxson Lake was named after the owner of **PAXSON LODGE**, at Mile 185.5, one of the early roadhouses. The original lodge burned, but the new lodge goes by the same name. The town of **PAXSON** has a population of 33. Before 1972, the year the George Parks Highway was completed, the only way to drive to Denali National Park, then known as Mount McKinley National Park, was to take the Denali Highway west from Paxson for 135 miles. If you wanted to drive to Fairbanks at that time, you also went through Paxson.

The road continues north from Paxson, climbing right alongside the Gulkana River, by now a sprightly creek that runs between Summit and Paxson Lakes. **SUMMIT LAKE** is at the divide, where the waters run either north or south. The elevation here is 3,210 feet. Midway along the lake, a blackened hole and standing chimney mark the spot where Summit Lake Lodge stood until 1993, another piece of history turned into firewood.

For the next 40 miles, the road makes its way through the Alaska Range. You'll find serious mountains and scenery here, and the road is some of the best highway in Alaska. A canyon curves alongside the headwaters of the **DELTA RIVER**, with the Alaska pipeline showing up here and there as if it were shadowing you. At Mile 204, there's a pullout where springwater gushes through a pipe out of the side of the mountain. Fill up there and save the freight from France.

At Mile 227.4, you'll see the old **BLACK RAPIDS ROADHOUSE** on the east side of the road. It was one of the roadhouses on the Valdez Trail, and the part now falling down dates from 1905. It originally was called

"The Black Rapids Hunting Lodge." The old roadhouses have been replaced by pump stations for the Alaska pipeline, a sign of the times.

The mountains get bigger. To the west, you see three of the great peaks of the Alaska Range: DEBORAH (12,339 feet), HESS (11,940 feet), and HAYES (13,832 feet). They don't look that big until you find out they're 40 miles away and dominate the horizon a good portion of the way into Fairbanks.

The last 20 miles into Delta Junction puts you down on the flats. It might sound like a letdown, but it's not. The scenery now comes as a marvel of straightness.

At the junction of the Richardson Highway and the official end of the Alaska Highway is DELTA JUNCTION. The Delta River, which you have followed from its source in the mountains down to the floodplains, runs right beside the town. People seem to be on their own time here, as well as having some to share.

The Richardson Highway continues into Fairbanks, 100 miles to the northwest, following first the Delta River and then the TANANA, which it joins at BIG DELTA, 10 miles down the road. If you have time, take the gravel road that runs along the river to Big Delta. There are good views of the milewide riverbed and the Alaska Range as the road follows the bluff. Take the first turn to the left after passing the sign for Jack Warren Road, 2 miles out of Delta.

Big Delta State Historical Park

In 1909, the Alaska Road Commission installed a ferry across the Tanana River on the old Valdez-to-Fairbanks trail to accommodate traffic to the gold fields. This was a natural place for a roadhouse, and John Hajdukovich built one that year. In 1917, he hired a Swedish immigrant, Rika Wallen, to run it for him. She bought it in 1923, and it became known as Rika's. She had a large garden and raised animals and poultry to supply the table. Rika operated the roadhouse into the late 1940s and lived there until her death in 1969, at the age of 94. After the ferry was replaced by a bridge, people no longer had to stop as they did in the past. More than 2,000 people crossed the river by ferry in 1925. Now, people don't even slow down.

In 1986, RIKA'S ROADHOUSE (Big Delta, Mile 275, Richardson Highway; 907/895-4201) was reopened as a living history homestead, after being restored by the Alaska Division of Parks and Outdoor Recreation. Admission is free. During the tourist season, the restaurant is open daily until 5pm and features home-baked goods. Just before crossing the Big Delta bridge, you'll see a parking area and interpretive display for the trans-Alaska pipeline, which makes an impressive sight as it crosses the river, especially in winter when it's all lit up. Only 90 miles remain to Fairbanks—Alaska's second-largest city with 50,000 people—and the terminus of the Richardson Highway.

Glennallen to Valdez

Turn right from the Glenn onto the Richardson Highway and head south. In a few miles you'll see the signs for the Copper Center Loop, a small road that swings you into the community of **COPPER CENTER** and back out to the main road again. Along the way is the ranger station for **WRANGELL-ST. ELIAS NATIONAL PARK**, open daily in the summer, with books, maps, and information. If you are going on to McCarthy and Kennicott, check here for McCarthy Road conditions.

Traveling south on the Richardson Highway alongside the **TONSINA RIVER**, the most intriguing sight—apart from spectacular nature—is a section of the oil pipeline, which transects Alaska, running 800 miles from the Arctic Ocean to the North Pacific, from Prudhoe Bay to Valdez. At various points, the pipeline parallels the road, crosses it, and recrosses it. Shortly before descending into the port town of **VALDEZ**, often called Little Switzerland because of the spectacular mountains and icefields, you'll pass the site of the World Extreme Skiing Championships, held in March every year at Thompson Pass (see the Prince William Sound chapter).

LODGINGS

Copper Center Lodge / ★★

MILE 101, RICHARDSON HWY, LOOP RD, COPPER CENTER, AK 99573; 888/822-3245 OR 907/822-3245, FAX 907/822-5035
In Copper Center, there's a very cozy hotel, an old historic roadhouse brought up to date for comfort and still in operation. The roadhouse, on the banks of the Copper River, opened its door to travelers in 1898 and has been welcoming them ever since. It's a warm, family-run enterprise. The owners say their sourdough starter is more than 100 years old—test it out. Try the sourdough pancakes or popular homemade berry pies. *$$; MC, V; local checks only; breakfast, lunch, dinner every day; open mid-May–mid-Sept; beer and wine; Drawer J, Copper Center, AK 99573.* ౬

Tsaina Lodge / ★★

MILE 34.7, RICHARDSON HWY, VALDEZ, AK 99686; 907/835-3500, FAX 907/835-5661
Even if you're not staying, stop in to sample the cuisine—it's adventurous and definitely a surprise from what you'd normally expect at the side of the road in Alaska. A historic old roadhouse, with hand-hewn logs on the interior, this little place has had new life breathed into it by its young,

enthusiastic outdoorswoman–proprietor Lisa Wax, who bought it in 1994. About 40 miles from Valdez, with the massive Worthington Glacier out the window and an array of breathtaking peaks, this is the land of extreme skiers, snowboarders, heli-hikers, and paragliders. You can rent a bed in a log cabin, yurt, or the bunkhouse; camping is free. Meals aim for healthy ingredients, with fresh seafood, pastas, and homemade soups high on the list. *$$; MC, V; no checks; breakfast, lunch, dinner every day; open for spring ski season, Feb–June; full bar; SR 80, Valdez, AK 99686.*

Wrangell-St. Elias National Park and Preserve

The Wrangell-St. Elias region is a mountain-and-ice kingdom of extraordinary beauty. It is the largest national park in the United States and has some of the highest peaks and the most extensive sweep of glaciers on the North American continent. It is mind-boggling. Thirteen mountains rise more than 14,000 feet; four of them are higher than 16,000 feet. Mount St. Elias (18,008 feet) is the second-highest peak in Alaska, next to Mount McKinley (20,320 feet). There are 75 named glaciers and many more unnamed glaciers. Together with its neighboring park in Canada, Kluane National Park, this region has been designated a World Heritage Site by the United Nations. Signed by 111 member nations, the World Heritage Convention declares such sites to be of such exceptional interest and such universal value that their protection is the responsibility of all mankind.

While several of the high peaks such as Mounts Sanford, Drum, and Blackburn and the still-active volcano of Mount Wrangell can be viewed from the highways that skirt the park's borders, this is just a hint of what lies beyond.

This is a park for the wilderness seeker. There are relatively few visitor facilities. Only two unpaved roads penetrate the park at all: the McCarthy Road in the west and the Slana-Nebesna Road in the north. The National Park Service stresses that in this mountainous region where help is often days away, visitors need to be skilled in backcountry travel and carry proper survival gear. You need to be both self-motivated and self-sufficient. **PARK HEADQUARTERS** is at Mile 105.5 on the Old Richardson Highway, near Copper Center. It is open daily in the summer and weekdays in winter. There is also a ranger station at Nebesna (907/822-5238), and one in the little town of Chitina (907/823-2205). For more information, contact Superintendent, Wrangell-St. Elias National Park and Preserve (PO Box 439, Copper Center, AK 99573; 907/822-5235).

The Edgerton Highway

A terrific side trip en route to Valdez begins when you peel off on the Edgerton Highway (at Mile 82.6, Richardson Hwy), which takes you to Chitina. From there, continue along the McCarthy Road to the Kennicott River, park the car, walk across the bridge, and visit the historic mines and old ghost town of Kennicott and the picturesque town of McCarthy nearby.

Chitina

Tundra gives way here to meadows and trees of middling size. **LIBERTY FALLS**, a short distance off the road, is quite lovely, with clear cascading water and a scramble up the hillsides for the more energetic. From here, head on to Chitina (pronounced chit-nah), which sits at the end of the gravel road under the shadow of Spirit Mountain. The year-round population here is about 50, but on a summer weekend, when the salmon are running in the Copper River and the dipnetters running right behind them, the population can sometimes balloon to 3,000 folks.

EXPLORING

TWO PROMISING WATERING HOLES / RAVEN DANCE (Mile 32.5, Edgerton Hwy; 907/823-2254) offers espresso and pizza at the near end of town, called "uptown Chitina." A little sign posted near the entrance gives the "Answers to the Top 10 Questions." Here are the first four: "1) 59 miles, 3 hours, bumpy, dusty; 2) 50, counting the kids and dogs; 3) Seldom below −30°F; 4) Haul water, chop wood;" and a Bonus Answer: "because the ones that run on weekends have all been fished out." Drive through town and stop at the far end, where the old fisherman stands with his dip net at the front door of the **IT'LL DO CAFE** (907/823-2244), open daily in summer.

SPIRIT MOUNTAIN ARTWORKS / Just across the street from the It'll Do Cafe is this charming art gallery, the creation of Art Koeninger. He bought the building for a song, intending to use parts for salvage, then became entranced by it, spent a fortune, renovated it, and now it's on the National Register of Historic Places. It's a fun gallery of fine Alaska art. "Husbands Welcome" says the sign out front. More than 100 Alaska artists are featured here. Art himself is a custom jeweler, working in silver and gold and other materials. He's also a storehouse of knowledge. Contact him at Main St, Box 22, Chitina, AK 99566; 907/823-2222; and uncleart@igc.org. Open in summers, call first in the off-season (Oct–May).

The McCarthy Road

Now the fun begins. As you drive through imposing walls of rock, you are entering the McCarthy Road, built along the old railroad bed of the Copper River and Northwestern Railway, 59 miles of dirt washboard and potholes. When you can spare time from the futile effort of trying to avoid these pitfalls, enjoy the lovely forest, but keep your eyes peeled for other drivers careening around the corners and for miscellaneous old railroad spikes. These are not good for your tires. Although it's only 59 miles, it will take you at least 3 hours. In the height of summer, it can be a long, dusty ride.

Above the trees, the Wrangell Mountains rise stark and bare, and you can spot the sharp division between the lighter limestone on top and the darker volcanic rock below. That division is where the metals—copper and gold—are to be found. On the ground, the erratic spruce hen or ptarmigan may scuttle across your path as you bounce along at a comfortable 20 mph. About 15 miles out, the road narrows somewhat just before you get to the **KUSKALANA BRIDGE**, but the change is not dramatic. The bridge is! It is an old railway trestle that has been reinforced. The view into the river gorge is heart-stopping and should be the biggest thrill you get on the way. If you want more thrills, some people bungee-jump here. Think of that!

If you avoid a flat (a minor miracle—so do carry mounted spares) or other mishap, you should reach the end of the road at **COPPERPOINT**, a minuscule encampment on the banks of the Kennicott River. Now you are faced with fording whitewater rapids. Do not attempt this in your car unless it is winter and 40 below zero.

The McCarthy Road ends at the whitewater of the Kennicott River, and the next stage of the journey involves a little more physical labor. Until only a few years ago, residents and visitors alike pulled themselves and their gear hand-over-hand across an open aerial tramway. But, sadly, the tram has slipped into a footnote of history and today you can see where it once reigned supreme. Now, there are two footbridges over the river to the other side.

McCarthy and Kennicott

Copper was discovered in these hills in the 1860s. Some mining took place in the last part of the century, but with the completion of the Copper River and Northwestern Railway in 1911, which ran from Cordova on the coast 200 miles into the mountains, business really boomed. The story of that railroad, built across the face of two moving glaciers by the brilliant engineer and wild Irishman Michael J. Heney, is a saga of great proportions. (So you will not be confused or think we are bad spellers, note that the spelling of Kennicott Glacier, named for Robert Kennicott, early explorer and geologist, is spelled with an *i*. The lodge spells its name the same way, as does the settlement of Kennicott. But you will see that any reference to the Kennecott Mines is spelled with an *e*. This is what is known as a historical mistake, now historical fact. Someone from those yesteryears misspelled Kennicott, and it stuck.)

The ore that came out of the Kennecott Mines high up on the hills here was about 80 percent pure copper in the early days. It was the richest and purest deposit of copper in the world. But the large costs of transportation required that it be further refined on the spot and, as the percentage of copper in the native ore declined in later years, refinement became increasingly important.

This was performed in the multistoried, red building that you can still see framed dramatically against the hillside today. The ore was brought down from the mines and decanted into a vertical process where, level after level, it was crushed, pulverized, shaken, washed, and sifted until it was ready to be tipped into waiting railroad cars. To this mechanical operation, the mine added a chemical separation process in the 1920s. This took place in a separate building across the road.

Both of these buildings, as well as the vast steam plant for generating electricity, can be seen on a guided tour (see Adventures, below), which takes a couple of hours. As you climb up the 192 steps in the processing plant, you will be astonished at the solidity of this rundown building. Much of the machinery has been ravaged by past salvage operations, but nonetheless this journey into the past is quite special. Kennicott was once a boomtown with more than 800 workers, until the price of copper fell and the operation was abandoned. Today it is a ghost town, with the exception of one or two hardy souls who live here in cabins year-round.

The little town of McCarthy sprang up at the edge of the Kennicott River, just across the tramway today. It was a place for miners' relaxation in the old days. Only a handful of folks live here now, but it is a popular destination for Alaskans all summer long, particularly for celebrations on the Fourth of July and Labor Day. Five miles up the hill is the ghost town of Kennicott and the Kennicott Lodge.

ACCESS AND INFORMATION

Drive the roads from Anchorage to McCarthy, or take the fast route with regularly scheduled **AIR SERVICE** from Anchorage through Gulkana to McCarthy on Security Aviation (907/248-2677 or 800/478-7880) or Ellis Air Taxi (907/822-3368). Service is year-round, Wednesday and Friday departures and return. McCarthy Air (907/554-4440) has two daily flights into McCarthy from Chitina. A van service, to save driving the

McCarthy Road, is available in summer, departing from Chitina, Glennallen, and Valdez. Call **BACKCOUNTRY CONNECTION** (800/478-5292 in Alaska, or 907/822-5292).

WRANGELL-ST. ELIAS NATIONAL PARK AND PRESERVE puts out an informative newspaper called *K'elt'aeni*, about travel in the park. For a list of mountaineering, rafting, backpacking, horsepacking, hunting, and fishing guides permitted to offer commercial trips into the park/preserve, contact park headquarters in Copper Center (907/822-5234).

ADVENTURES

FLIGHT-SEEING / In this mountain kingdom of castle peaks, glaciers, and stunning valleys, flight-seeing is a stunning experience not to be missed. A tempestuous sea of wild and jagged peaks spreads before you (and the pilot carefully misses them all) as you fly up bare rocky passes. The multicolored cliffs are reminiscent of southwestern deserts. Glaciers tumble from the brilliant snowfields down icefalls to black crushed rock below. As your eyes get used to the dimensions of aerial vision, you may spot herds of mountain goats. A good charter air service flying trips out of McCarthy is **WRANGELL MOUNTAIN AIR** (McCarthy #25, PO Box MXY, Glennallen, AK 99588; 907/554-4411 or 800/478-1160, fax 907/554-4400; Flywma@aol.com; www.WrangellMountainAir.com).

RIVER RAFTING / For whitewater thrills, head back across the Kennicott River and sign up with **COPPER OAR** (800/523-4453 or 907/554-4453; see also Guides and Outfitters, below), which offers half-day and multiple-day excursions. Their office is located in a little cabin at the end of the McCarthy Road.

TOURS OF THE GHOST TOWN / With headquarters in the Mother Lode Powerhouse in McCarthy, **ST. ELIAS ALPINE GUIDES** (907/554-4445) gives tours through the old buildings of the Kennecott Mines. This is a fascinating tour if you're into history or mining. The future of these old buildings is currently in the hands of the park service and it is not yet clear if the park will pick up these tours at a later date. It is a unique piece of history. Some of the guides live year-round in McCarthy and are as interesting as the buildings. The tour costs $25 per person.

GUIDES AND OUTFITTERS

COPPER OAR / If you want to go rafting for 1 day or 10 days, hop aboard with these experienced guides. They have a variety of trip offerings, from a 2-hour spin down the Kennicott River to 10 days down the Chitina and Copper Rivers (to Cordova on Prince William Sound). In operation since 1985, the company is owned by river guide Howard Mozen. Box MXY, Glennallen, AK 99588; 800/523-4453, 907/554-4453 (phone/fax May–Sept), or 907/566-0771, voice mail; HowMoz@aol. com; www.alaskan.com/copper_oar; operates May–mid-Sept.

ST. ELIAS ALPINE GUIDES / This highly respected guide service, owned by Bob Jacobs, who resides in Anchorage, will take you touring through ghost towns, climbing on glaciers, rappelling off mountains, or backpacking on long journeys and first ascents in the Wrangells. For a brochure, contact St. Elias Alpine Guides (PO Box 111241, Anchorage, AK 99511; 907/277-6867, in winter). In summer, call or stop in at the office at the Mother Lode Powerhouse in McCarthy (907/554-4445).

LODGINGS

Kennicott Glacier Lodge / ★★★

5 MILES UP THE ROAD FROM MCCARTHY, KENNICOTT, AK 99588; 800/582-5128 OR 907/554-4477, FAX 907/248-7975
This is a fine wilderness resort, dedicated to the pleasure of hikers, river rafters, and all outdoorsmen and -women. The veranda has a breathtaking view that extends from the Chugach Mountains to Mount Blackburn, the highest mountain in the Wrangells, and takes in Kennicott Glacier. Descended from the draftsmen's quarters or bunkhouse of the old mining days, it is still painted in the symbolic red and white colors of the day. Bathrooms are shared. Dining is family style with simple but hearty meals. And the staff couldn't be friendlier. The lodge accommodates only 50 guests, so book early. $$$; AE, MC, V; local checks only; open mid-May–mid-Sept; beer and wine; PO Box 103940, Anchorage, AK 99510; across Kennicott Glacier.

McCarthy Lodge / ★★

IN THE HEART OF MCCARTHY, AK 99588; 907/554-4402, FAX 907/554-4404
You can't get much more classic Alaska than this moose-horn-bedecked lodge in the center of town. It's the centerpiece of innumerable photos of McCarthy and boasts a more laid-back, easygoing, T-shirts-and-beer crowd than the lodge higher up on the road. Although built in 1916, the hotel does have modern bathrooms. It offers group bookings for winter getaways in the Wrangells. $$$; MC, V; local checks only; open mid-May–Sept; full bar; PO Box MXY, McCarthy, AK 99588; go over the river and through the woods, following the signs.

ANCHORAGE AND BEYOND

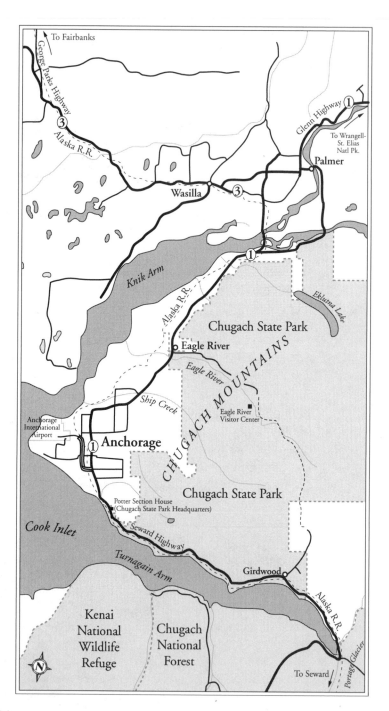

To Fairbanks

George Parks Highway

3

Alaska R.R.

To Wrangell-
St. Elias
Natl Pk.

Glenn Highway

1

Palmer

Wasilla

3

1

Knik Arm

Alaska R.R.

Eklutna Lake

Chugach State Park

Eagle River

Eagle River

CHUGACH MOUNTAINS

Ship Creek

Eagle River
Visitor Center

Anchorage
International
Airport

1 Anchorage

Chugach State Park

Potter Section House
(Chugach State Park Headquarters)

Cook Inlet

Seward Highway

Turnagain Arm

Girdwood

Alaska R.R.

Kenai
National
Wildlife
Refuge

Chugach
National
Forest

N

To Seward

Portage Glacier

ANCHORAGE AND BEYOND

For many people, the greater Anchorage area is where you can get it all: a city with a small, albeit enthusiastic, nightlife, good restaurants, and Broadway musicals—plus access to the half-million-acre Chugach State Park, an area packed with trails, streams, glaciers, bears, and moose. To the north, the wilderness playgrounds of the Susitna and Matanuska Valleys give way to views of the Chugach and Alaska Ranges. If the weather cooperates, Mount McKinley, which locals simply call Denali or "The Mountain," juts above the horizon. And in the right season, salmon run so thick you have to watch your step crossing a stream.

Seasons are alternately fleeting and harsh. Summer is short and intense. By September, the leaves are turning a vibrant gold. By October, frost has arrived and snow (euphemistically called "termination dust") is settling into the mountains. Winter hits hard and stays well into April. Temperatures can drop to below zero for a week or two at a time, but usually stay in the teens and 20s. By mid-May, the land comes alive again. The 6 hours of winter sunlight are nearly tripled. Summer is just a few weeks away. Not that the region has what most people from the Lower 48 would call "summer." Temperatures rarely get above 70°F, and rain is common. The average temperature in Anchorage in July is about 57°F. But on days when the sun shines until midnight and the Chugach Mountains scream with color, this place is spectacular.

Anchorage

People who live in Anchorage often say the best thing about it is that it's 20 minutes from the real Alaska. Built on the fortunes of the railroad, war, and oil, it began in 1915 as a tent city on the banks of Ship Creek. Today, half the state's population lives in this metropolis. A center for politics and the arts, it's also a gateway for adventures into Alaska's outback.

The Park Strip was once the very edge of town. In the 1920s, it was a combined airfield and golf course. Today it defines the edge of downtown. There, you can watch sunny, late-night softball games, during which an outfielder is as likely to watch the midnight sunset in awe as watch the play. Though few in number, highly trained chefs prepare the world's best seafood with aplomb. Anglers pull 40-pound king salmon out of Ship Creek, a river of wildlife in the shadow of downtown's glass-skinned office buildings. During the right season (early March), a visitor can see the start of the most famous sled-dog race in the world, cross-country ski to lunch, then go to a Broadway musical in the evening.

ACCESS AND INFORMATION

Most people fly to Anchorage. Some drive the Alaska Highway through Canada from the Lower 48. Others take cruise ships. Once here, as in all big cities, you can choose between rental cars and public transportation. The bus system, called **THE PEOPLE MOVER** (907/343-6543) will move you about town. **THE ALASKA RAILROAD** (907/265-2494), a 5-minute walk from downtown, will take you north to Denali National Park or south to Seward on Resurrection Bay. **ALASKA BACKPACKER SHUTTLE** (907/344-8775 or 800/266-8625) can take you north to Denali and Fairbanks or south to Seward. Call for friendly, reliable service.

With its cascades of flowers, the charming little **LOG CABIN INFORMATION CENTER** (907/274-3531) is located in the heart of downtown on Fourth Avenue and F Street, and is run by the Anchorage Convention and Visitors Bureau (907/276-4118). The first kiosk for a self-guided tour of old Anchorage's colorful past stands directly outside. Kitty-corner, in the old Federal Building, is the **ALASKA PUBLIC LANDS INFORMATION CENTER** (907/271-2737), with its marvelous displays and information on parks, refuges, forests, hikes, cabins, wildlife, and more. The *Anchorage Daily News* publishes an arts/entertainment guide that appears every Friday and contains information on food, music, theater, and special events around town. For another sprightly look at the local arts scene, pick up a free copy of *The Anchorage Press* at coffeehouses and outdoor boxes around town.

EXPLORING

ANCHORAGE MUSEUM OF HISTORY AND ART / The only major venue for sculpture and painting in the area is the Anchorage Museum of History and Art. The upper floor is devoted to the history of Alaska. During tourist season, the museum hosts major touring exhibits, such as the Smithsonian's "Crossroads of Continents" or glass art by Seattle artist Dale Chihuly. The Children's Gallery provides an interactive, hands-on exploration of the arts and is free admission for both children and adults. You can go on a treasure hunt, climb castle turrets, walk through Stonehenge, or be an animal in the zoo—each year there is a different theme show created by national and international artists. During the summer, Alaska Native groups perform songs and dances as part of the museum's cultural heritage program. The museum is located downtown (121 W 7th Ave; 907/343-4326).

ALASKA NATIVE HERITAGE CENTER / Opened in 1999, the Heritage Center provides an opportunity to appreciate the vastness of Alaska and the richness of her cultures. Situated on 26 acres on the outskirts of town, the Welcome House is filled with exhibits and demonstrations. Traditional village settings have been re-created around a small lake, one for

DRIVE-BY ART

For art lovers traveling with cultural couch potatoes, this is the tour for you. You can visit an art gallery in this city without ever leaving your car. The 1 percent for Art program in Anchorage requires that 1 percent of all construction funds for public facilities be spent on original art. The result? More than 260 pieces of artwork throughout the city liven up warehouses, schools, the bus station, convention center, university, parks, and other civic structures. You can buy a pocket guide, *Museum Without Walls*, in the gift shop of our museum *with* walls—the Anchorage Museum of History and Art (121 W 7th Ave). It directs you to art about town, providing background information on each. When imagining outdoor public art, most people picture large abstract sculptures. But you will be surprised, and often amused, at the diversity of this collection—an electrical lineman (made entirely of sheet metal) climbing up the side of a building, a bear trying to get a bite out of a bus driver's sandwich, and the unearthed "bones" of an ancient leviathan.

—Wanda Seamster

each of the five indigenous groups of people in Alaska, from the Inupiat in the north to the Tlingits of Southeast. This is a living museum with artists and craftspeople at work—building kayaks, carving totems, sewing mukluks, weaving baskets, drying fish, singing, and dancing. The original dream of the center was to celebrate, perpetuate, and share these traditions. The president of the center, Perry Eaton, who was born on Kodiak into the Aleut/Alutiiq culture, says, "Alaska is unique in American Indian experience because people still live in original traditional villages, not removed to reservations." The entrance fee is $20 for adults and $15 for children under 12. Open every day in summer; winter hours differ with educational programs offered. 907/330-8095 or 800/315-6608; www.alaskanative.net; at the intersection of Muldoon Rd and the Glenn Hwy. &

MUSIC AND THEATER / Located in Town Square, **THE ALASKA CENTER FOR THE PERFORMING ARTS** (800/478-7328) is the hub of dance, music, and theater performances in town. You can't miss it. In summer, the little park in front is ablaze with colorful flowers. In winter, it's lit up with Christmas lights. It covers the ground between E and G Streets and Fifth and Sixth Avenues. The box office has a display showing each season's events and sells tickets, or you can reserve them through **CARRSTIX** ticket outlets (907/263-2787).

Anchorage has its own symphony orchestra, opera company, and concert association. With the dark winters, community theater, too, has always been important in the far north. Some of the most successful and ambitious in recent years have been **VALLEY PERFORMING ARTS** (907/373-9500), headquartered in the Matanuska Valley; **CYRANO'S BOOKSTORE & OFF CENTER PLAYHOUSE** (413 D St; 907/274-2599); and the **UNIVERSITY OF ALASKA ANCHORAGE THEATRE/DANCE DEPARTMENT** (907/786-1792 or 907/786-4721 box office).

FRESH ART FIRST FRIDAY / The first Friday of the month features gallery opening receptions where you can meet some of Anchorage's finest artists, rub elbows with the up-and-coming, and purchase a piece of innovative Alaska art. Sometimes there are as many as 10 art openings about town on First Friday. The best local galleries include **DECKER/MORRIS GALLERY** (621 W 6th Ave; 907/272-1489), Anchorage's most professional gallery of original art, and **ARTIQUE LTD.** (314 G St; 907/277-1663), which offers original fine arts and crafts as well as prints. The best source of information on gallery openings is *The Anchorage Press*, which also lists addresses, phone numbers, and hours.

BOOKSTORES / For one of the largest selection of books on Alaska and the North, visit **COOK INLET BOOK COMPANY** (415 W 5th Ave; 907/258-4544). Around the corner is the small but intriguing **CYRANO'S BOOKSTORE** (413 D St; 907/274-2599). **BARNES & NOBLE BOOK-SELLERS** (200 E Northern Lights Blvd; 907/279-2373) is huge and located in Midtown. **BORDERS BOOKS & MUSIC** (1100 E Dimond Blvd; 907/344-4099) is also an event in itself, located at the south end of town.

SATURDAY MARKET / Every Saturday in summer on the old "buttress" area of downtown, Third Avenue and E Street, there is a huge outdoor market of vendors selling fresh produce, food, homemade crafts, and art. If you're sleuthing for the freshest vegetables, join chefs from all over town who do their shopping early Saturday morning (about 9am). As the summer progresses, farmers from the Matanuska Valley start hauling in their giant-size cabbages and zucchinis, huge sweet carrots, herbs, peanut potatoes, and delicious snap peas.

ADVENTURES

THE COASTAL TRAIL / Bike, walk, blade, jog, or ski the **TONY KNOWLES COASTAL TRAIL**, which runs for miles along the shores of Cook Inlet. This is one of the great treasures of the city, coursing like a lifeline from downtown neighborhoods to airport to wilderness trails. Everybody uses the trail, including porcupines, moose, and bears. Once you get to **KIN-CAID PARK**, the wilderness trails there are a mecca for running in the summer and skiing in the winter and are the site of world-class cross-country ski races. Bikes can be rented at **DOWNTOWN BICYCLE RENTAL** (333 W 4th Ave, #212; 907/279-5293). To buy a picnic lunch for the ride and also rent a bike, stop in at **ADVENTURE CAFÉ** (414 K

St; 907/276-8282), across the street from the Hotel Captain Cook. Skis can be rented at **REI** (1200 W Northern Lights Blvd; 907/272-4565), which has interesting weekly programs covering everything from mountain climbing to ski waxing.

HISTORIC WALKING TOUR / Look for the blue, three-sided kiosks downtown. An award-winning stroll from kiosk to kiosk is filled with gossip, stories, and photographs from yesteryear, which will take you on a self-guided journey through old Anchorage. The first kiosk stands in front of the Log Cabin Information Center on Fourth Avenue. Visit Silk Stocking Row and see where the fancy folks lived, or wander down by the water through Bootlegger's Cove, once honeycombed with whiskey tunnels. "The only thing more prevalent than the fine dust which clogs the air is the raw whiskey with which they wash it down," observed one disgusted federal bureaucrat in Anchorage's early days, thoroughly unimpressed by the new railroad town and the moral fiber of its inhabitants.

CHUGACH STATE PARK / Whether you have half a day or a week, head for the mountains. This is as wild as anywhere in Alaska. And it's in Anchorage's own backyard (see the Chugach State Park section in this chapter).

NIGHTLIFE

Spenard, once the racier part of Anchorage, is home to **CHILKOOT CHARLIE'S** (2435 Spenard Rd; 907/272-1010), a bar with the infamous motto "We cheat the other guy and pass the savings on to you." Chilkoot's has a loyal crowd and a lot of one-timers who come to catch live bands, drink beer, and walk around on wood chips in what's billed as a rustic Alaska saloon.

Don't miss the **FLY BY NIGHT CLUB** (3300 Spenard Rd; 907/279-7726), with *The Whale Fat Follies*, billed in their ads as "the show the Alaska Chamber of Commerce doesn't want you to see." It'll tell you more about the inside humor of Alaska than you'll learn anywhere else. After the show, a hoppin' little house band plays some rockin' blues.

GUIDES AND OUTFITTERS

For additional recommendations, see also the Chugach State Park section in this chapter.

ALASKA SNOW SAFARIS / If you have only a day or two in Anchorage, Rudi and Natasha von Imhoff, both lifelong Alaskans and outdoor enthusiasts, and their staff of experienced guides can take you out of the city into wilderness on your own snowmachine expedition for a few hours, a half day, or overnight. Prices range from $95 to $1,400 per person. They also can arrange dog-sledding excursions and heli-skiing packages. In the summer, they run guided sea kayaking tours in Prince William Sound with their summer business, **ALASKA OUTDOOR ADVENTURES**. Morning and day trips ($60 to $99 per person) begin out of Whittier. Their boats are top of the line, both single and double kayaks. Their tour offices are located in Girdwood at the base of Mount Alyeska and at the small boat harbor in Whittier. 888/414-7669 or 907/783-7669; www.akadventures.com.

NOVA / For 25 years, Nova (800/746-5753) has been taking folks rafting down Alaska's rivers on day trips. If your time is limited (and even if it's not), this is one way to experience the thrill and beauty of the outdoors a few hours away from Alaska's biggest city. North in the Matanuska Valley, they float the Matanuska River, Class II to Class IV rapids. South on the Kenai Peninsula, at Granite Creek and Six-Mile Creek, you can experience Class IV and Class V rapids. Choose your level of excitement.

FESTIVALS AND EVENTS

ALASKA STATE FAIR / The fair is a statewide party that dominates the tiny town of Palmer in the Matanuska Valley during the last week in August and the first weekend in September. The 10-day event is a cornucopia of music, rodeos, horse shows, carnival rides, food booths, and agricultural displays. Yes, they really do have 80-pound cabbages, 23-pound kale, and zucchinis as big as your arm. It's a good time. Everybody goes to the fair. Mile 40, Glenn Hwy; 907/745-4827.

IDITAROD TRAIL SLED DOG RACE / This famous race kicks off from Fourth Avenue in downtown Anchorage, the first Saturday of every March. The city is packed with television cameras, howling dogs, racing colors, and fur-clad mushers. For a brief moment, it all feels very glamorous. But in a couple of hours they are out of here and on their way across the wilderness, 1,049 miles to Nome, and the city quiets down again, although many people fly out along the trail to watch the teams or go to Nome for the grand finale. For information, call the Iditarod Trail Headquarters (Mile 2.2 Knik Rd, Wasilla; 907/376-5155).

FUR RONDY / To see the real Anchorage, visit in mid-February for the winter festival, formally known as the Fur Rendezvous. That's French, Alaska-style, for a fur get-together. Originally, trappers came in from the Bush to sell their pelts and spend some money. The cabin-fever festival today features all that's great and strange about Anchorage. On opening night, a spectacular display of fireworks lights up the winter sky. Anchorage goes all out here because on the Fourth of July the long daylight hours make fireworks nearly invisible. People participate in more than 100 contests ranging from ice bowling to oyster slurping. For more information, call 907/274-1177.

SKI FOR WOMEN / Held on Super Bowl Sunday in January, this is the largest cross-country ski race for women in North America, now in its fourth year. The race is 5 kilometers with both classic and skating divisions. All you need are some skis and a partner (any and all women are encouraged, whether beginner, recreational, racer, Olympian, mother, daughter, or grandmother). If you're shy or just visiting, race organizers will find you a partner. In recent years, the youngest competitor was 4 years old; the oldest was 77. The whole idea is to have fun. Participants come dressed in old prom dresses, hula skirts, racing silks, or black lycra if they succumb to that competitive edge. The spirit is enthusiastic and contagious and the effort draws attention to and supports a good cause— AWAIC (Abused Women's Aid In Crisis). Call for more information (907/279-9581 or 907/345-1913).

RESTAURANTS

Aladdin's Fine Mediterranean / ★★

4240 OLD SEWARD HWY, STE 20, ANCHORAGE; 907/561-2373
Aladdin's brings the warm touch of Middle Eastern and North African flavors to the cold far north. The smoky Casbah salad with fire-roasted bell peppers and eggplant is rich with olive oil. The *kefta* sandwich, with spicy, grilled ground beef, packs a garlic punch. Couscous with lamb and *tajin zitoun*—chicken with green olives and spicy tomato—are good too. In addition, there's a lovely selection of dips, including baba ghanouj, and hummus. If you can't make up your mind, taste them all in the Aladdin Sampler. *$$; AE, DC, DIS, MC, V; checks OK; lunch Tues–Fri, dinner Tues–Sat; beer and wine; in a strip mall off Old Seward Hwy, north of Tudor Rd.* &

The Bagel Factory

142 W 34TH AVE, ANCHORAGE; 907/561-8871
This isn't Manhattan. But if you're casting a critical eye around for a little taste of home, get your bagels here. They feature the "31 flavors" approach to bagel making (flavoring dough with jalapeños, cheese, pesto, and the like), but they also serve the tried-and-true favorites, such as onion, garlic, or sesame bagels. A nice spot for Sunday breakfast, with thoughtfully prepared frittatas and omelets. You'll see lots of local upwardly mobiles here on weekend mornings, reading the paper and planning the day's adventure. *$; MC, V; local checks only; breakfast, lunch Mon–Sat; in a strip mall off the corner of 36th Ave and C St.* &

BEST ESPRESSO

One of our favorite java joints is **Side Street Espresso** (412 G St; 907/258-9055) in the heart of downtown. Move over, Seattle. These guys probably serve the best lattes on the West Coast. The place is small, but the folks here are funny and friendly. They also pack people in for special concerts, art shows, and political discussions. Pay attention to their daily special announcements, delivered with a twist of artistic humor. The two big roasting companies in town are **Cafe Del Mundo** and **Kaladi Brothers Coffee Company**. First to truly launch Anchorage onto the coffee scene was roastmaster Perry Merkel with Cafe Del Mundo. He runs several cafes downtown and his main one in Midtown (341 E Benson Blvd; 907/274-0026). Kaladi Brothers Coffee Company's main operation (6921 Brayton Dr; 907/344-6510) has lots of great food, a warm atmosphere, and the characters at the classical radio station KLEF broadcasting there every morning.

—Nan Elliot

Campo Bello Bistro / ★★

601 W 36TH AVE, ANCHORAGE; 907/563-2040

Campo Bello (meaning "beautiful field") offers a fine menu featuring delicate pastas, chicken, and seafood dishes. Its gentle, white-tablecloth, candlelit interior offers a wonderful backdrop for fine art, promising food, and quiet conversation. The service is good with a friendly staff. The bread is delicious, baked next door at Europa Bakery. Appetizers are particularly inventive, and the lively calamari scallopine with capers and lemon comes to the table fork-tender. Follow a light meal of tasty homemade soup with a winning Caesar salad, filled with grilled chicken and roasted sweet peppers. Then kiss the evening good night with a celestial combination: their heavenly chocolate-raspberry cake. *$$; CB, DC, MC, V; local checks only; lunch Mon–Fri, dinner Tues–Sat; beer and wine; located in a strip mall near Arctic Blvd and 36th Ave.* &

Club Paris / ★★

417 W 5TH AVE, ANCHORAGE; 907/277-6332

If you look up at the dizzy Eiffel Tower, which has graced the exterior of the little Club Paris for decades, you will see the false-fronted architecture typical of an old Wild West frontier town. The idea was to make the building look grander and more permanent than it really was, as if folks were seriously planning on staying, when instead they would be moving on when the gold or work was gone. The funny thing is, the Club Paris has indeed stayed on and been a dining institution for more than 40 years. This is "old Anchorage," with a devoted clientele, and not even the new kid on the block can ruffle their feathers. Some of the staff from that "other steakhouse" even eat at the Club and sing its praises. The filet mignon with blue cheese stuffing is so tender and delicious it will melt in your mouth. But, if you top it off with their famous homemade Key lime pie and New York-style cheesecake, you'd better start your workouts now and hike a couple of mountains before dinner. *$$; AE, DC, MC, V; local checks only; lunch Mon–Sat, dinner every day; full bar; between E and D Sts on 5th Ave.*

Corsair / ★★

944 W 5TH AVE, ANCHORAGE; 907/278-4502

This is dining in the old-world style—a continental cuisine rich with sauces and butter, everything flamed or carved tableside. You slip down wide stairs and enter a dark restaurant where waiters in tuxedos do almost every dish at your table, from tossing salads to flaming after-dinner drinks. Go ahead, splurge on that good bottle of Burgundy; they've got probably the best cellar in town. Hans Kruger and crew also do nice rich things with oysters, such as topping them with pate and béarnaise sauce. The charbroiled rack of lamb "Armenonville" is exquisite. On Thursdays, Kruger does three-course German meals that are worth a visit—if only for his spaetzle and homemade sauerkraut. *$$$; AE, DC, DIS, MC, V; checks OK; dinner Mon–Sat; full bar; west end of 5th Ave, downtown.* &

Crow's Nest / ★★★★

939 W 5TH AVE (HOTEL CAPTAIN COOK), ANCHORAGE; 907/276-6000

The bird's-eye view, fancy service, feeling of elegance, and light French cuisine make dinner here a pleasure. The wine list is one of the finest in Anchorage. Feel pampered when they serve your entree from under a dramatic silver dome, and enjoy one of the best views downtown. Be sure to specify which view you'd like: take the inlet in the summer and the city in winter's darkness. If you're not ravenous, one of the loveliest places for a quiet tête-à-tête is the bar, which offers the same exquisite views and a fun sampling of exotic hors d'oeuvres such as Caspian Sea caviar; tartar of ahi tuna with avocado; citrus-cured salmon gravlax; or horseradish-marinated Dungeness crab. They also have the fanciest brunch in town. *$$$; AE, DC, DIS, MC, V; checks OK; dinner Mon–Sat, brunch Sun; often closed Tues or Wed in winter; full bar; at the top of the Hotel Captain Cook.* &

Downtown Deli and Cafe

525 W 4TH AVE, ANCHORAGE; 907/276-7116

One of the few spots to open early and close late, the comfortable Downtown Deli is often packed with summertime tourists. In winter, locals stop by for breakfasts of lox and bagels, omelets, and filling cheese blintzes, or schedule working lunches built around bagel sandwiches and matzoh-ball soup. Butcher-block tabletops, lots of room, and quick service are draws, but so is the fact that Alaska Governor Tony Knowles owns the place. He still drops by when he's in town, and the deli stands as a testament to how little space separates the average Alaskan from the pinnacles of power. *$; AE, DIS, MC, V; local checks only; breakfast, lunch, dinner every day; beer and wine; on 4th Ave, near the Log Cabin Visitors Center.* &

F Street Station / ★★

325 F ST, ANCHORAGE; 907/272-5196
For a quick, delicious meal at a good price, cruise into this freewheeling, casual bar. With a surprisingly good kitchen, F Street has redefined bar food in Alaska. The cheeseburgers, served with crisp, hand-cut fries, are the best in the city. Calamari is tender and the sauteed scallops worthy. Go for the daily special, whether it's a saffron-infused seafood chowder, a piece of halibut topped with black bean–fruit salsa, or a steak sandwich cooked rare and served with wild mushrooms on a baguette. A lot of pilots and lawyers hang out here and it can get a bit cliquish. Note the huge block of Tillamook Sharp cheese at the bar with the careful sign "For Display Only. Do Not Eat." Note also that everybody is eating it. It's a good conversation piece—ask for the story. Avoid crowds by heading in for a late lunch or supper. *$; AE, MC, V; local checks only; lunch, dinner every day; full bar.* &

Gesine's / ★★★

6700 JEWELL LAKE RD, ANCHORAGE; 907/243-0507, FAX 907/243-5110
Gesine Marquez creates fantastic lunches and elegant dinners in what started years ago as a corner soup-and-sandwich cafe. The presentation is beautiful, the appetizers delicious, and the entrees inventive. Start with the spicy softshell crab or the fabulous duck roll, tangy and full of fresh ginger. Enjoy one of the many fine wines with lively conversation. Then tuck into an exotic dinner entree of tender, grilled ostrich served over spaetzle, or the wild boar roast. For dessert, be daring. Try the Marzipan Potstickers served with warm plum sauce or the *Eierlikoer*, a flourless German hazelnut torte swimming in a vodka-egg sauce. Complementing the unusual cuisine is an atmosphere splashed with color—yellow and purple tablecloths. Ask for a table with a view of the Chugach Mountains. *$$; AE, MC, V; local checks only; lunch Mon–Fri, dinner Tues–Sat, brunch Sat–Sun; beer and wine; corner of Jewell Lake and Raspberry Rds.* &

Glacier BrewHouse / ★★

737 W 5TH AVE, ANCHORAGE; 907/274-2739

The Glacier BrewHouse's original claim to fame is that its entrance is next door to the infamous Orange Door. In fact, it was the smoke from this upscale brewpub's delicious pizza ovens that drove out all those endearing and colorful characters who used to live upstairs. But former residents aren't bitter; they even frequent the place. After all, the Brew-House is one of the most popular places to eat in town, with tasty food, award-winning beers, a nice wine list, and friendly bartenders. In fact, the whole atmosphere of this open warehouse–exposed beams interior is warm and inviting and packed year-round. (Don't go for quiet conversation.) Particular favorites on the menu are their barbecued silver salmon, herb-crusted chicken, spit-roasted pork loin chops, and all manner of pizzas. The bread alone will make you a convert. If you're a woman traveling by yourself, it's a happy, comfortable place to go sip a glass of wine at the bar and eat a Caesar or blue cheese salad. And, parents, kids will always find something they like on the menu here. *$$; AE, DC, MC, V; checks OK; lunch Mon–Sat, dinner every day; full bar; between G and H Sts.* ♿

Humpy's Great Alaska Alehouse / ★

610 W 6TH AVE, ANCHORAGE; 907/276-2337

Is it the location? Its boisterous nature? The 36 beers on tap? Or the bar food? Who knows? Ever since it appeared on the scene, Humpy's has been a smash hit. This dark, crowded brewpub has two time zones. At lunch and early dinner it is congenially filled with office workers and bicycle fanatics; later on in the evening and weekends, it's packed with 20-somethings and frat boys gone to seed. Stick with pub grub, which they do well, like the halibut tacos, Humpy Fettuccini, or Teriyaki Tid Bits. Live music every night. *$; AE, DC, DIS, MC, V; local checks only; lunch, dinner every day; full bar; across from the Alaska Center for the Performing Arts.* ♿

Ichiban Japanese Restaurant / ★

2488 E TUDOR RD, ANCHORAGE; 907/563-6333

Those in the know, including several distinguished chefs about town, sneak off to Ichiban to drink cold sake and eat what they deem "the best sushi in town." It has the freshest fish and the best prices. The Ichiban Roll is our favorite, made with eel, shrimp, *tabiko* (flying fish eggs), sprouts, and cucumber slices. The Super California Roll is delicious, stuffed with crab meat and cooked eel on top. If you want a momentary diversion from raw fish, try the Kalbi Ribs, which are fantastic. *$; AE, MC, V; local checks only; lunch Mon–Sat, dinner every day; beer and wine; on Tudor Rd near Lake Otis.*

Jens' Restaurant / ★★★★

701 W 36TH AVE, ANCHORAGE; 907/561-5367

Jens Hansen, of the restaurant that bears his name, is a wild Dane who is at once enchanting, zany, and incredibly knowledgeable about food. He'll eat caviar by the tablespoonful and dance on his wine bar, but when it comes to serious cooking, he's the man. No one else in the city has such a way with black cod, salmon, or halibut. His menu will always reflect his heritage: cabbage, root vegetables, smoked or cured fish, and light veal and pork meatballs called *frikadeller*. Mussels in mustard sauce make a nice nosh with a glass of wine, or go all out with a traditional rack of lamb or the pepper steak favored by locals. Inexpensive but tasty wines and crack waiters make for a nice evening. If you're feeling rich and rowdy, stick around after dinner and party with the well-to-do but silly crowd that pools in the wine bar next to the restaurant; the dining room is nonsmoking. *$$$; AE, DC, DIS, MC, V; local checks only; lunch Mon–Fri, dinner Tues–Sat; closed January; beer and wine; in the strip mall on the corner of 36th Ave and Arctic Blvd.* &

Kumagoro / ★

533 W 4TH AVE, ANCHORAGE; 907/272-9905

Kumagoro is one of the oldest Asian restaurants in downtown Anchorage and today serves primarily Japanese cuisine, although there are touches of other North Pacific cultures on the menu. They have a lovely little sushi bar where you can warm up from the winter cold with a bottle of hot sake and miso soup. Or sit at one of the little tables (which are all quite close together), and order a spicy appetizer of tasty meat dumplings called *gyoza*, dipped in a fiery hot oil. Kumagoro makes fresh udon and ramen noodles. The soups are big, hearty, and healthful. When the weather is chilly and you're up for a warm and lingering meal, try their shabu shabu, a marvelous dish for sharing with friends— vegetables, tofu, and meat in a broth that you cook at your own table. *$$; AE, DC, DIS, MC, V; local checks only; lunch, dinner every day; beer and wine; downtown.*

Marx Bros. Café / ★★★★

627 W 3RD AVE, ANCHORAGE; 907/278-2133, FAX 907/258-6279

For nearly two decades, this little historic house downtown, built during the early railroad era on Silk Stocking Row, has been home to some of the city's most innovative cuisine, a signature style of that flamboyant "galloping Greek," chef Jack Amon. In the summer, greens and edible flowers from the garden garnish delicious Alaska seafood such as halibut baked with a macadamia nut crust or roasted poblano chiles rellenos stuffed with Alaska king crab. In winter, fixed-price ethnic nights feature cuisine from the likes of Tuscany and Provence. Begin a delightful evening with a *melitzano salata,* roasted eggplant pâté with Greek olives and pita bread. Then try a Caesar salad whipped up tableside by master artist Van Hale, also co-owner and keeper of the impressive 10,000-bottle wine cellar, one of the top cellars in town. Don't miss the crème caramel made with rum and coconut milk. Candlelight and sweet views of Cook Inlet (ask for a view table when you make a reservation) only add to the panache. *$$$; AE, DC, MC, V; checks OK; dinner every day; closed Sun in winter; beer and wine; downtown.*

The Middle Way Cafe and Coffeehouse / ★★

1200 W NORTHERN LIGHTS BLVD, ANCHORAGE; 907/272-6433
This small cafe is very much into healthy, delicious, organic fare. Start off with a jolt from the espresso bar or a soothing mixture called Inner Balance (fresh orange juice, strawberries, banana and ginger) from the juice bar. Wraps here are a good choice. They have winning fillings such as hummus and pistachios, rounded out with red bell pepper–lemon yogurt dressing. Sandwiches and soups, both meat and vegetarian, are equally yummy. The atmosphere is mellow, with a crowd sporting everything from pierced body parts to pinstripes. *$; no credit cards; local checks only; breakfast every day, lunch Mon–Sat; no alcohol; Spenard Rd and Northern Lights Blvd.* &

Moose's Tooth Pub & Pizzeria / ★★

3300 OLD SEWARD HWY, ANCHORAGE; 907/258-2537
Two climbers, Rod Hancock and Matt Jones, started this popular pub in the summer of 1996 and named it after an extraordinary pinnacle of granite in the Alaska Range. At first it was chiefly a climbers' haunt, but today its popularity has skyrocketed off the charts, from the young and active to families with children to older professionals and outdoor types. It has a simple picnic-table approach, fresh salads, the best pizza in town, and handcrafted ales from their own microbrewery. Usually there's a long line at the door in the evening, but they'll take your name and usually can seat you in about 30 minutes. So order your pizza and sip a beer while you wait. There's pizza to suit everyone's fancy, from Aloha Escape to Pepperoni Supreme. A good choice for a post-hiking or -biking adventure with buddies or a quick bite before the movies. Nonsmoking. *$; DC, DIS, MC, V; checks OK; lunch, dinner every day; beer and wine; turn right off New Seward at 36th and backtrack on Old Seward Hwy.* &

Organic Oasis / ★★

2610 SPENARD RD, STE B, ANCHORAGE; 907/277-7882
For the growing population of vegans, this is a new haven, opened in the spring of 1999. An open, peaceful space with a long juice and espresso bar, the Oasis also has dining tables gathered around a fountain. You can get a shot of wheat grass juice and a Ginger Blast or a Palm Desert

Smoothie to go with the brimming-with-health salads, sandwiches, soups, and hot specials. Everything, with the exception of a few teas, is organic. And while you pay a little extra, it's definitely worth it. *$; DC, MC, V; local checks only; lunch, early dinner Mon–Sat; beer and wine; in a strip mall off Spenard Rd.* &

Sacks Café / ★★★★

328 G ST, ANCHORAGE; 907/276-3546 OR 907/274-4022
Consistently adventurous food built with top-notch ingredients makes Sacks a welcome oasis. Knockout starters include polenta with Gorgonzola, baked garlic, and sweet ahi tuna, barely seared on the outside and served over a healthy bed of Napa cabbage slaw with crisp-fried, grated ginger and a pat of hot wasabi. Chefs dream up a dish or two every night, centered on fresh Alaska finfish graced with some exotic combination of favorites like pecans, pine nuts, Oriental sauces, black beans, or ginger. Soups are standouts and include a slightly spicy African peanut, a cold cantaloupe soup kissed with cinnamon, and a hot salsa soup from south of the border. Locals love lunch here, returning for spinach salad with marinated Swiss cheese, the Thai chicken sandwich with spicy peanut dressing on a baguette, or the scrumptious vegetarian marinated olive sandwich. Always save room for dessert. The chocolate gateau, ginger crème brûlée, and chocolate chip carrot cake with rum sauce are close to ethereal. *$$; AE, MC, V; local checks only; lunch Mon–Sat, dinner every day, brunch Sun; beer and wine; next to Artique on G St between 3rd and 4th Aves.* &

Simon and Seafort's Saloon and Grill / ★★★

420 L ST, ANCHORAGE; 907/274-3502
Part of a West Coast restaurant chain that has honed its art to a fine edge, Simon's is probably the most popular place in Anchorage for steaks, salads, and seafood. The consistency, the opportunity for a beautiful view of Cook Inlet, and the occasional flashes of greatness with fish and shellfish make going here a fun, warm, and pleasurable occasion. Even in the height of tourist season, you can usually get a table if you're willing to wait and munch in the bar. It's light and airy with a bustling and upbeat atmosphere. Wild Alaska salmon is good, with cracked black pepper and honey, served over greens with artichoke tartar sauce. Try the made-from-scratch margaritas using fresh lime juice or sample one of the largest selection of single-malt scotches in Alaska. Their Brandy Ice is a marvelous "sipping dessert"—rich vanilla ice cream blended with Kahlua, brandy, and crème de cacao. *$$; AE, DC, MC, V; checks OK; lunch Mon–Sat; dinner every day; full bar; main floor of an office building on L St and 5th Ave.* &

Sullivan's Steakhouse / ★★★

320 W 5TH AVE, STE 100, ANCHORAGE; 907/258-2882, FAX 907/258-2808

Tell 'em Joe sent you. Step through the doors into the speakeasy days of 1930 Chicago. Sleek, sexy, and trendy, Sullivan's slipped into Anchorage two years ago and got the town hooked on martinis, cigars, steaks, and great live jazz. Ladies dress up; gents dust off their Panama hats. A spectacular bouquet of flowers adorns the center of a large, open room rich with mahogany and heavy white tablecloths. You are meant to see and be seen. The extensive cellar (more than 300 wines) is heavy into cabernets, reds, and merlots—all to complement those fabulous steaks. Here they do not have a wine steward; they have Nicki, "the wine goddess." Talented bartenders move like lightning. While there are no vegetarian entrees, they do tip their hats to Alaska's rich seafood tradition with a sampling from the Pacific and Atlantic—halibut, salmon, grilled tuna, and lobster tail. Nonsmoking. *$$$; AE, DC, DIS, MC, V; local checks only; dinner Mon–Sat; full bar; corner of 5th Ave and C St in the Anchorage Fifth Avenue Mall.* &

Tempura Kitchen / ★★

3826 SPENARD RD, ANCHORAGE; 907/277-2741

This little oasis for Japanese cuisine in Spenard has been a popular and tasty destination for years. The sushi is superb. Alas, the rest of the menu is disappointing in comparison, so stick with the sushi chefs. Try the artful displays of the spider roll, decorated with sprigs of daikon sprouts and waving crab legs, or the *unagi* (grilled eel). Take all the side-striped shrimp you can when they're in season. (Shrimpers start pulling them from Prince William Sound in mid-April and continue until the end of July. Some are caught during a short fall season, as well.) You can order them as sushi, with the heads deep fried on the side, or fried whole and served with a wedge of lemon. Try the sushi made with snapper and served with ponzu sauce, or simply trust the sushi chefs, who always know what's best. *$$; AE, DC, DIS, MC, V; local checks only; lunch Mon–Fri, dinner every day; beer and wine; off Spenard Rd, south of 36th Ave.* &

Thai Kitchen / ★★

3405 E TUDOR RD, ANCHORAGE; 907/561-0082

In 1987, a young Thai couple, Ben and Sommay Kitchpanich, opened a small convenience market with two tiny tables in the back for Alaskans to sample authentic, delicious, home-cooked Thai food. "Thailand is so hot," says Ben. "We wanted to see the coldest place. Here, there are more adventurous eaters than in the Lower 48." Their kitchen became so popular around town that they added a table a year. Now there are

12, with cheerful batik tablecloths, and the store is gone. "The Boss" (Sommay) still does all the cooking with the help of her sister Orathay. The heavy favorites include fresh spring rolls; Popeye Chicken, served with spinach and peanut sauce; garlic tofu; special eggplant sautéed with curry paste, coconut milk, and fresh basil; tom yum kai or lemon grass soup; and, of course, pad thai, the traditional thin rice noodles with peanuts, bean sprouts, and pork or shrimp. Nonsmoking. *$; MC, V; local checks only; lunch Mon–Fri, dinner every day; no alcohol; near Capri Theater in a strip mall off Tudor.* &

Villa Nova / ★★★

5121 ARCTIC BLVD, ANCHORAGE; 907/561-1660

Villa Nova is fun, continental, and homey, with wicker-nested Chianti bottles, braided breads decorating the walls, soft guitar music, and delicious aromas. This is the best Italian cuisine in Alaska! The charming host and chef, Giorgio Chirmat, welcomes his guests with an easy old-world charm. Fresh seafood, homemade pastas, and daily specials like the rich tournedos Gorgonzola or lamb osso bucco will melt in your mouth. For lighter fare try the surprising *cacciucco,* an Italian seafood stew, which is literally served in the kitchen pot, or Scampi da Jeff, a tasty pasta-and-grilled-prawn dish. The gnocchi and the seafood fettuccine are delicious. The wine list is quite diverse. The many elegant homemade desserts are not to be missed. We love the Domo, a cake laced with the flavors of oranges, chocolate, and raspberries, and Cassata da Grand Marnier, homemade chocolate cups filled with ice cream, marmalade, pistachio nuts, and liqueur. *$$; AE, DIS, MC, V; local checks only; dinner Mon–Sat; beer and wine; in a strip mall near Arctic Rd and International Blvd.* &

LODGINGS

Anchorage Hotel / ★

330 E ST, ANCHORAGE, AK 99501; 800/544-0988 OR 907/272-4553, FAX 907/277-4483

In the historic lodgings category, the Anchorage Hotel lays claim to being the city's oldest. Since its birth in 1916, many notables have stayed in its 26 rooms, including the famous painter Sydney Laurence, who once took up residence there. Guests step from busy E Street into a quiet, semiformal lobby with a fireplace and marble chess set. Renovated in the 1990s, the rooms are clean but lack a personality belying the hotel's past. Some rooms face the street, and traffic noise carries. Rooms 301 and 303 overlook Fourth Avenue and E Street, a terrific viewpoint for watching the start of the Iditarod Trail Sled Dog Race when you don't care if the howling of the dogs, people, and vehicles wake you up early. A continental breakfast is served in the lobby each morning. There are tea and coffee facilities and a minibar in the rooms. Bathrooms have nice amenities. The staff is young, very friendly, and accommodating. *$$$; AE, DC, DIS, MC, V; checks OK; downtown, corner of E St and 4th Ave.* &

Bed & Breakfast on the Park / ★★★

602 W 10TH AVE, ANCHORAGE, AK 99501; 800/353-0878 OR 907/277-0878

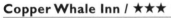

Your hostesses, Helen Tucker and Stella Hughton, preside over this former log-cabin church on the Park Strip in downtown Anchorage. The flower gardens get more beautiful every year at this quaint historic inn. You cannot help but be charmed. While peeling mangos for your breakfast, Tucker and Hughton will happily share tips on politics, gardening, old-time characters, or Chinese martial arts. They once owned the Willow Trading Post and made it an oasis on the way to Denali National Park. The same delightful spirit pervades their abode on the Park Strip. It's one of the best buys in downtown and a perfect location—quiet, but close to everything. The B&B has only five rooms, so book early. If you call their toll-free number direct, you get the lower price of $100 per night (otherwise, it's $111). *$$; MC, V; checks OK; downtown, between E and G Sts.*

Copper Whale Inn / ★★★

440 L ST, ANCHORAGE, AK 99501; 907/258-7999, FAX 907/258-6213

Something between a bed-and-breakfast and a country inn, the comfortable, Nantucket-styled Copper Whale is a rarity among Anchorage housing. It is charming and quaint, with a staff who are informal yet reserved. Most of the 15 rooms have beautiful picture-window views of Cook Inlet to the west (all but two with private bath). Redoubt is the nicest room in the inn, but you can't go wrong with any of them—they are simple and lovely. Rates run $120 to $165 per night with a hot breakfast; book early. If you rent a car, be aware that parking downtown is either an adventure or about $10 a day extra for a parking pass. *$$; AE, DIS, MC, V; checks OK; sometimes closed for a month in winter; cwhalein@alaska.net; www.copperwhale.com; downtown, corner of 5th Ave and L St.*

Hilton Anchorage / ★★

500 W 3RD AVE, ANCHORAGE, AK 99501; 800/245-2527 OR 907/272-7411

In the heart of downtown, the Hilton Anchorage is often packed with tourists and conventioneers. With 597 rooms, it's the biggest hotel downtown, and the lobby always feels more like Grand Central Station than a place for respite. But it's convenient. In the summer, the vendor-laden Saturday Market and the train to Denali are short strolls away. In the winter, the Iditarod Trail Sled Dog Race starts a block away, and the Fur

Rendezvous festival happens all around the hotel block. Locals like the rooftop view and panoramic sunsets in summer from the bar in the Top of the World restaurant. Rooms are nicely appointed but small. Try for a corner room in the Anchorage Tower, the original section of the hotel. *$$$; AE, DIS, MC, V; checks OK; dinner every day in summer, Tues–Sat in winter, brunch Sun; www.hilton.com; downtown, corner of 3rd Ave and E St.* ♿

Historic Leopold David B&B Inn / ★★

605 W 2ND AVE, ANCHORAGE, AK 99501; 907/279-1917,
FAX 907/279-1920

Once the grandest house on Silk Stocking Row in the fledgling frontier town of Anchorage, this home was built for Anchorage's first mayor in 1917 and is now on the National Historic Register. Restored with "European flair," it caters to both penny-poor climbers and fancy folk alike. The innkeeper, Maryvonne Guillemin, is French and speaks a variety of languages. Step back into Anchorage's fast-disappearing past in modern comfort. The six rooms and four suites, all with private entrances and phone lines, range from $45–$265/night. You can even rent by the week. Climbers and adventurers often will spend a night here before catching the train north to McKinley. The low-end price is the best in town for a comfortable and welcoming establishment, and the gourmet breakfast is luxurious. *$–$$; AE, MC, V; checks OK; welcome@AlaskaHoliday. com; www.alaskana.net; in the heart of downtown.*

Hotel Captain Cook / ★★★★

939 W 5TH AVE, ANCHORAGE, AK 99501; 800/843-1950 OR
907/276-6000, FAX 907/343-2298

This is the hotel that former Governor Walter Hickel built, and it remains the top of the line for Anchorage. When the big oil money was flowing in the 1970s and early 1980s, the Hotel Captain Cook and its elegant bars and restaurants (see Crow's Nest review, above) served as a backdrop for deal making and high-class partying. Towers Two and Three were renovated in the mid-1990s, so request a room in either tower. Ask for a view of Cook Inlet, available on the fifth floor and above, or a southwest corner room for a view of both water and mountains with morning and evening sun. It gets crowded with cruise-ship tourists in summer. Prices drop sharply in late September, once the ships sail south for the winter. *$$$; AE, DC, DIS, MC, V; checks OK; www.captain-cook.com; downtown, corner of 4th and 5th Avenues between I and K Sts.* ♿

Regal Alaskan Hotel / ★★

4800 SPENARD RD, ANCHORAGE, AK 99517; 800/544-0553 OR
907/243-2300

The Regal is located on Lake Hood, the busiest lake in Anchorage. Locals
scramble to get to the deck on sunny days to drink local ale and watch the
floatplanes vie for space with the ducks during takeoffs and landings. The
place is especially Alaskan in the winter, with leather chairs facing the fireplace and glass-enclosed stuffed bears. In March, as dogs and mushers are
racing from Anchorage to Nome, the hotel serves as the official Iditarod
Trail Sled Dog Race headquarters, and guests can follow the progress of
their favorite mushers on a frequently updated board in the lobby or from
printouts issued every few hours from the computer room. The rooms are
quite spacious, and the hotel has a restaurant, the Flying Machine, that
is open daily. *$$$; AE, DC, MC, V; checks OK; regal@alaska.net;
www.regal-hotels.com/anchorage; near the airport on Spenard Rd.* &

The Voyager Hotel / ★★★

501 K ST, ANCHORAGE, AK 99501; 800/247-9070 OR 907/277-9501

In the heart of downtown, the Voyager is an unpretentious, comfortable
little hotel with 38 large rooms (about 400 square feet each) with kitch-
enettes. Built in 1965, it is a low-rise, homey alternative to the big hotels.
All the rooms are nonsmoking and are a stone's throw away from the
water and the Coastal Trail. It has a loyal following and fills up fast. Best
to get your dibs in early. Folks often stay several days, even up to two
weeks. The location, friendliness, and prices (which are half of the other
downtown hotels) can't be beat. *$$; AE, DC, DIS, MC, V; checks OK;
rsvp@alaska.net; across the street from the Hotel Captain Cook, the
entrance is on K St.*

BED-AND-BREAKFAST SERVICES

Decide whether you want to be in town, on the hillside near the mountain wilderness, or somewhere in between. There are some wonderful
accommodations dotted around Anchorage in log homes, near water, or
with mountain vistas. For more information on the range of bed-and-
breakfasts, try one of these B&B services: **ALASKA BED AND BREAK-
FAST** (907/345-0923), **ALASKA PRIVATE LODGING** (907/258-1717), or
ALASKA SOURDOUGH BED AND BREAKFAST ASSOCIATION (907/
563-6244).

WILDERNESS LODGES

Within The Wild/Alaska Adventure Lodges

2626 GALEWOOD ST, ANCHORAGE, AK 99508; 907/274-2710, FAX 907/277-6256

For years, Kirsten and Carl Dixon have welcomed summer guests to RIVERSONG LODGE on the Yentna River, a 70-mile flight north of Anchorage by small plane. By day, they take guests to favorite salmon fishing holes; by night, they serve elegant Alaska seafood and wild game. Gourmets who love to catch their own fish and savor it should book a few days in here. Top winemakers from France and California, editors from fancy food magazines, and renowned national chefs have all eaten here. Do not expect luxury. The lodge is rustic—10 cabins, not all with private baths. However, there is a communal sauna and bathhouse so that you can get to know your neighbors while you primp for dinner. In recent years, the Dixons have expanded their repertoire and added two more lodges: WINTER LAKE LODGE, which is located on Finger Lake, a checkpoint along the Iditarod Trail Sled Dog Race route; and REDOUBT BAY LODGE, located across Cook Inlet from Anchorage in Lake Clark National Park and in prime bear-viewing country. Both these lodges have three guest cabins. Winter Lake Lodge is currently the winter home of the Dixons and is open year-round, except during freeze-up and breakup. Day rates are $325 per person, including transportation, guides, and lunch or dinner. Rates for a 3-day/3-night package to any of the lodges, which includes air transportation from Anchorage, guide services, lodging, and all meals (cost of fine wines and beers is additional), are $1,300 per person. Accessible only by plane, snowmobile, dog team, or snowshoes. *AE, MC, V; checks OK; open summer, part winter; beer and wine; alaskawild@gci.net; www.withinthewild.com.*

Palmer and Eagle River

PALMER, about an hour's drive northeast of Anchorage, sits at the center of what little agricultural life Southcentral Alaska has. The town's roots were put down during the Great Depression, when the federal government sent Dust Bowl farmers north. To this day, farmers still try to make the best of a short but intense growing season, raising huge cabbages and oversize zucchini. Stop at any number of farmers' stalls along the highway for sweet carrots, lettuce, and a cabbage so big you'll have to buy it a separate plane ticket home.

EAGLE RIVER, a town of 26,000, lies midway between Palmer and Anchorage. Sheer mountainsides and a river-scored valley dwarf any hint of suburban sprawl. This is one entrance to Anchorage's marvelous backyard: **CHUGACH STATE PARK** (see below). Eagle River Visitors Center (Mile 12 Eagle River Rd; 907/694-2108) is a wealth of information about the park. It offers daily programs of activities and good day hikes.7

RESTAURANTS

Vagabond Blues Coffeehouse / ★

642 S ALASKA ST, PALMER; 907/745-2233
With its warm wood floors and ambience, this is a delightful harbor for the gentle-hearted in Palmer. Great cinnamon rolls, espresso, pastries, bread, pasta salads, and bagel sandwiches top the menu. Soups such as a creamy broccoli with large florets are homemade and served in a local artist's handmade pottery bowls. The strawberry pie alone is worth the drive. Live music featuring local talent on weekends adds to the panache. *$; no credit cards; local checks only; breakfast, lunch, dinner every day; no alcohol; Koslosky Center in downtown Palmer.* &

Girdwood

This woodsy, ski enthusiasts' oasis about an hour's drive south of Anchorage, with funky little cabins tucked into the hollows and expensive condos facing the mountain, has long been a mecca for downhill skiers. Summer brings a wealth of spectacular views, from hanging glaciers to mountains covered with blueberry patches. High on the ski slopes is one of the more elegant dining experiences in the region.

The town was started by a gold miner who staked a claim on Crow Creek. Today, Girdwood is a little village of about 1,200 that swells to some 3,000 when the snow falls. In winter, skiers try their hand at challenging Nordic routes or schuss down breathtaking Mount Alyeska in the abundant company of snowboarders; there are seven lifts and an aerial tram. This is the only ski resort in the country where you plunge down powder-filled slopes while looking at the ocean below.

In summer, Girdwood is a good place for rafting trips, hikes, and live music featuring local performers. The pinnacle of the music scene is the **GIRDWOOD FOREST FAIRE**, a folk-music festival held the first weekend in July. It's also a fine time to see the town in its tie-dyed finest. In fall, the hillsides are filled with berry pickers; in spring, the same hills offer rare black morel mushrooms and fiddlehead ferns. But beware: anytime but deep winter, when they're mainly snoozing, you'll find bears also roaming these valleys and hillsides.

EXPLORING

While driving from Anchorage to Girdwood along the **SEWARD HIGH-WAY**, you enjoy wonderful views of **TURNAGAIN ARM**, one of the most scenic drives in all the world. Watch for bore tides, Dall sheep, and beluga whales. A tasty place for dinner along the highway is the cozy **TURN-AGAIN HOUSE** (907/653-7500), located in Indian, which has delicious seafood (try the silver salmon when it's in season or the Alaska scallops and shrimp in basil-saffron cream sauce). Often crowded in summer, but in winter it's a charming little dining room with a fireplace and view of the inlet.

If you're looking for something spicy, stop in at **TACO'S** (907/783-2155), a good spot for Arizona-style Mexican food in the strip mall located at the turnoff to Girdwood. The fresh salsa is first rate, the halibut fish tacos often sell out before dinner, and, for extra zip, they have an impressive array of 30 bottles of hot sauce from which to choose. Open daily for lunch and dinner.

At the base of **MOUNT ALYESKA** in Girdwood is a wonderful little bake shop, which has been catering to Alaskans for more than 20 years with its legendary sourdough bread, pancakes, farmer's breakfasts, tasty soups, and incredible sandwiches. You can eat in, picnic out amongst the flowers, or pack a sandwich in your rucksack for a climb up the mountain. **THE BAKE SHOP** (907/783-2831) is located on the Alyeska Boardwalk.

If you want to see an old gold mine and pan for a little paydirt in the creek yourself, bump 4 miles down Crow Creek Road in Girdwood to **CROW CREEK MINE** (follow the signs). A working gold mine in winter, it's open to the public, June through August, and is quite peaceful and beautiful—no flotilla of tour buses here.

RESTAURANTS

The Double Musky / ★★

CROW CREEK RD, GIRDWOOD; 907/783-2822
An old-time favorite among Alaskans, the Double Musky is known for its impeccable pepper steak and gargantuan Cajun portions. With remnants of Mardi Gras past hanging from the walls (as they say here, *"Laissez les bon temps rouler"*), the Musky is casual but expensive. The appetizer menu offers halibut ceviche, coconut salmon, Cajun-spiced shrimp peelers, and deep-fried zucchini. The dinner menu features mammoth steaks, seafood, and spicy Cajun and Creole dishes. Little loaves of bread, served with drinks, are studded with cheese and jalapeños, and the pepper steak is covered with a spicy coating of well-crushed peppercorns and Burgundy sauce. The fiery shrimp étouffée is flawless. For dessert, you can't go wrong with a slice of cool Key lime pie. (Be advised: they

don't take reservations, and sometimes the wait is long.) *$$$; AE, DC, DIS, MC, V; no checks; dinner Tues–Sun; closed Nov; full bar; www.doublemuskyinn.com; after the turnoff from the Seward Hwy to Girdwood, turn left on Crow Creek Rd (follow signs).* &

Seven Glaciers Restaurant and Lounge / ★★★

1000 ARLBERG AVE, (ALYESKA PRINCE HOTEL), GIRDWOOD; 800/880-3880 OR 907/754-2237

Opened in 1994, this elegant restaurant—with friendly wait staff and stunning views of the mountains—sits high on Mount Alyeska. To get there, you take a Swiss-built tram to the 2,300-foot level. Fresh, local ingredients such as blueberries, oysters, and boletus mushrooms often grace the menu, along with a sublime foie gras and scallop appetizer, the mesquite-grilled Alaska reindeer with blackberry sauce, or venison chops with roasted garlic mashed potatoes. Seafood and vegetarian dishes also shine. Alas, in a setting of such natural beauty, it's a pity the architect was more visually enamored by the inner workings of the tram wheels than the mountains, glaciers, and ocean outside as there are few tables positioned with a really spectacular view. So take a short walk after dinner and really drink in this exquisite location. To get there, take the tram from the Alyeska Prince Hotel. *$$$; AE, DC, DIS, MC, V; local checks only; dinner every day in summer; closed Oct, winter hours vary; full bar.* &

LODGINGS

Alyeska Prince Hotel / ★★★★

1000 ARLBERG AVE, GIRDWOOD, AK 99587; 800/880-3880 OR 907/754-1111

The Alyeska Prince Hotel is a grand, chateau-style resort hotel that rises eight elegant stories at the base of Mount Alyeska. Cherry wood and granite accent rooms and lobby. The hotel was opened in 1994 by the Seibu Corporation of Japan, and many rooms are geared for the Japanese visitor. Most rooms have two double beds only (few kings, no queens), but elegant, small touches—such as towel warmers, bathrobes, and fresh roses on room-service trays in the dead of winter—will win your heart. They'll even give you a wake-up call when the Northern Lights are visible. Two delicious restaurants are located in the hotel, the family-style Pond Café and a small fancy Japanese restaurant, Teppanyaki Katsura, where your chef grills your dinner of fresh seafood, meats, and vegetables while you watch, sipping hot or cold sake. The festive show is topped off with refreshing ginger ice cream and a huge almond cookie filled with crème brûlée. *$$$; AE, DC, DIS, MC, V; checks OK; www. alyeskaresort.com; at the base of Alyeska ski area in Girdwood.* &

BEST WAYS TO DIE

Bears, moose, sightseeing flights, cruise ship gangplanks, halibut fishing, calving glaciers, icy rivers—you name it, and someone's died from it in Alaska. Even the most humbly adventurous traveler to Alaska must be aware of the state's natural dangers. While you might have the street savvy to avoid a mugger back home, such skills are useless when a city-bound moose is angry and looking right at you.

To that end, here's a little guide to the best ways to die in Alaska.

Try to get close to the wildlife. Both bears and moose can cover an amazing amount of real estate in a short time, and they're likely to be on any number of popular trails around Anchorage. In the summer of 1995, two local people out for a day's jog on McHugh Creek Trail, minutes away from downtown Anchorage, were killed by a grizzly. Earlier that winter, a moose trampled a man to death as he tried to enter a building at the University of Alaska Anchorage Sports Center. The rule is simple: don't feed them, don't pet them, don't hang around them, don't harass them, and don't surprise them. If you see a creature in the woods, back away slowly. Wear bells on your pack, clap, or sing to let bears know you're coming. Don't get between a moose and her baby, and don't try to go around a moose.

Walk on the mudflats that surround Anchorage. That appealing shoreline is actually mud. And not just any mud. The consistency is more akin to wet cement or quicksand. You get a foot stuck and you'll have a hard time pulling it out. Matters get dicier if the tide is coming in or going out (and it's always doing one or the other four times a day). Anchorage has the second-highest tides in the world. Water levels can change several feet in a matter of minutes. People have gotten stuck and drowned while rescue workers tried to beat the tide. Don't go there.

Don't worry about your gear. Sure, that peak seems close enough to scramble up in an hour or two. Who needs water, good hiking boots, or emergency rations? You do. What was meant to be a short hike can turn into an overnight ordeal if you get lost or hurt. Remember, most of what surrounds Anchorage is wilderness. There are no park rangers or other hikers just around the bend. In all likelihood, you will be on your own. Basic emergency and survival gear should be tucked into your pack, including water, food, matches, fire starter, extra clothing, bug dope, a compass, a knife, a small first-aid kit, and a topographical map.

Don't respect the cold. Cold can creep into any Alaska day, even in the summer. And if you add cold to the problems outlined above, you can easily lose your life. Hypothermia may set in quickly if you get dunked in one of the many glacial streams, or simply get rained on or caught overnight at the right time of year. Dress for variable weather, and pack a space blanket and waterproof matches.

Panic, act macho, and don't follow your intuition. Fear is a warning. It means something is unsafe. Listen to it. It's sort of like the adage about anything that sounds too good to be true. If it seems dangerous, it probably is.

Don't do your homework. Even in Alaska, knowledge is power. Check out guidebooks and talk to locals. Learn about how to stay safe in the woods, avoid avalanches, and handle a bear attack. The Alaska Public Lands Information Center (605 W 4th Ave; 907/271-2737), in downtown Anchorage, has a variety of free brochures covering much of what you'll need to know.

—Kim Severson

Chugach State Park

Nowhere else does genuine full-blown wilderness lie so close to a major city. Chugach State Park is as raw as it gets. The peaks loom tall and jagged—up to 8,000 feet high. Valleys and rocks show abundant evidence of relentless scouring by ancient glaciers. Some of the world's last remaining icefields lie only a few dozen miles from downtown Anchorage. In any other state, Chugach State Park, created in 1970, would be a national park, not a state park. It is that much of a treasure.

This is one of Alaska's best-kept secrets. The remoter, more rugged regions see so little visitation that, even by Alaska standards, they are relatively empty. Statistically, July and August are Anchorage's rainiest months, while April, May, and June are the driest. Many of the trails are snow-covered or muddy even in April, but not the southernmost slopes facing Turnagain Arm. By June and July, most valleys have opened up, but then it's the height of mosquito season. (In Alaska, there's always a trade-off.) September, although cooler, offers some magnificent fall colors, berry picking, rutting moose, and fewer visitors.

Chugach is also an easy place to get killed. Whether by exposure, hypothermia, falls, avalanches, drowning, disorientation, or mauling by bears, people die here every year. Proximity to Anchorage offers only an illusion of safety. Only those with real outdoor savvy should venture beyond the trailheads and campgrounds. When you leave your car at the trailhead, even if you're planning just a short hike, take a small day pack with water, snack food, an extra coat and pants for wind or rain, hat, gloves, map/compass, matches and fire starter, first-aid kit, and pocket knife. Other items you may want to include are insect repellent, sunglasses, and headlamp or flashlight (except in midsummer). Also, be sure you know when and where the hunters are out. If in doubt, wear red. For a handy "cheat sheet" on hunting in the park, contact the Alaska Department of Fish and Game (907/267-2349).

ACCESS AND INFORMATION

Despite its rugged character, Chugach is eminently accessible along two sides of its triangular rim. Of 30 access points, however, only 15 offer a parking area and trailhead. But these are more than enough to put visitors in touch with the park's most outstanding features. Although the park has about 100 miles of trails, many valleys have no trails at all. Fording glacier-fed rivers and fighting your way through dense undergrowth without getting lost is a deterrent to many of the less adventurous. This is one reason why the remote regions of the park see few visitors. But the rewards are grand.

To get to the park you need a car, or a bicycle if you have legs of iron. However, be aware that within the park the use of mountain bikes is limited. Ditto for snowmobiles, all-terrain vehicles, and horses. Check with backcountry rangers (907/345-5014), or stop by the **CHUGACH STATE PARK HEADQUARTERS** (907/345-5014), located in the historic Potter Section House located south of Anchorage at Mile 115 on the Seward Highway. Another possibility to get to the Hillside or Turnagain Arm, which are two popular areas to access the park, is by cab, about a 20-minute ride or so from downtown—that is assuming you have a cell phone to arrange getting picked up again.

Operated year-round under a park permit by Friends of Eagle River Nature Center, the **EAGLE RIVER NATURE CENTER** (Mile 12, Eagle River Rd; 907/694-2108; www.alaska.net/~ernc) offers a wonderful variety of programs and activities throughout the year—from guided overnight hikes to talks on a myriad of subjects from bears and birch syrup to edible mushrooms and orienteering. The center is about 25 miles from downtown Anchorage; open daily, mid-May through Nov 1. In winter, call for hours. A new public-use cabin and yurt are a short walk from the center (1¼ miles) and may be rented for $45 per night; call for reservations. Be aware that all parking for Chugach State Park at access points is $5 per visit or $25 for a year pass.

ADVENTURES

Chugach State Park is a superb place to backpack, ski tour, or climb mountains. Most visitors come to day hike and gawk at the scenery. They also pick berries, run hills, scramble up mountains, canoe, kayak, study nature, and watch wildlife. The park is home to most mammal species in Alaska. Fishing is limited. Windsurfing is only for the experts. Ice climbers enjoy a number of good frozen waterfalls, though none are high.

One boundary of the park is the **SEWARD HIGHWAY**, one of America's National Scenic Byways. On one side is **TURNAGAIN ARM**, where, in the right season, you may spot beluga or killer whales, windsurfers, or unusual bore tides. On the other side of the highway, look for Dall sheep on the cliffs at **WINDY CORNER**. But be careful. When you want to rub-berneck at the beauty along Turnagain Arm, pull off the winding two-lane highway into a turnout, or you may end up as the kind of casualty that makes this one of the most hazardous stretches of roadway in the state.

Turnagain Arm offers a kaleidoscope of beauty and recreation. **BEL-UGA POINT** is a popular place to watch for beluga whales in summer. **MCHUGH CREEK TRAILHEAD**, renovated in 1998, has new hiking opportunities, interpretive panels, spotting scopes, and viewing decks. An interpretive overlook at **BIRD POINT** juts out into Turnagain Arm for some lovely view. The **BIRD POINT TO GIRDWOOD PATHWAY** (8 miles) is a fun use of part of the old Seward Highway, which was bypassed by new construction in 1998. There's a paved biking trail in the middle and soft trails on either side for joggers, walkers, and horseback riders. Plans call for bike rentals at either end of the trail, so check this out with the state park rangers (907/345-5014).

TURNAGAIN ARM TRAIL—sometimes referred to as "the old John-son Trail"—parallels this beautiful arm of water along the mountainside higher up from the Seward Highway. It was the mail route and trans-portation route in the old days before there was a road from Anchorage to Seward. This trail can be accessed at numerous trailheads along the highway. The section from **POTTER CREEK TO MCHUGH CREEK** is the easiest walking. From **MCHUGH CREEK TO RAINBOW AND ON TO WINDY CORNER** is more difficult but offers excellent views of Turnagain Arm and the mountains of the Chugach Range. A map for this interpre-tive trail is available at the Potter Creek trailhead. Those who want a strenuous climb, but not the bother of a long approach, should trek up **BIRD RIDGE** along Turnagain Arm (about 4,000 feet elevation gain). **FALLS CREEK** is another choice for a Turnagain Arm day hike that starts upward as soon as the car door is shut. Visitors enter a beautiful little alpine valley where, above tree line, they are almost sure to spot Dall sheep on the high escarpments.

Quick trips to the park from the city provide beautiful city and moun-tain views. There are three access points: the parking lot for **FLATTOP MOUNTAIN** at Glen Alps (20 minutes from the airport); the parking lot at Prospect Heights (again about 20 minutes from the airport and equi-distant from downtown) to climb **WOLVERINE PEAK** or amble up **POW-ERLINE PASS TRAIL**; and, finally, the **ALPENGLOW SKI RESORT** at **ARCTIC VALLEY** (40 minutes from the airport). Each destination is located on the front range facing Anchorage and all are exceptional for getting the visitor above tree line with not too much legwork. They provide awesome views. Note that there is a daily $5 parking fee at Glen Alps and other park facilities that supports maintenance of this beautiful wilderness.

Flattop is the city's most-climbed mountain. (It is also the most crowded, which means if you want a true Alaska experience, you might want to avoid it.) Shaped as its name suggests, it rises 3,510 feet above sea level. You start from the Glen Alps parking lot. Again, although it is popular, Flattop is not a cakewalk. It is quite steep, particularly toward the summit, and people have died on its flanks. Wear good shoes and pay attention. Across the valley and also easily accessible from the city, **WOLVERINE PEAK**, facing Anchorage, with beautiful views all around, is yet another easy-to-get-to trail that offers moderate hiking through spruce forest, tundra meadows, and alpine ridges and takes 6 to 9 hours round-trip. From the same trailhead, you can also take the route to Powerline Pass Trail, which is more of a stroll through beautiful mountains and a good place to picnic in the tundra alongside Campbell Creek.

Want to soak in exquisite natural wonders but don't want to walk very far? Try driving northeast of Anchorage to **EKLUTNA LAKE**, the largest lake in the park, which is glacially carved and has saw-toothed mountains rising to 7,000 feet above it. Want a more strenuous hike on the north side of the park? Try **TWIN PEAKS TRAIL**—it's a "huffer," but you get close to Dall sheep as well as see incredible views of Eklutna Lake. Also, its southern exposure loses snow earlier than other trails and is often warmer on a sunny day. A little further down the road, **PIONEER RIDGE–KNIK RIVER TRAIL** climbs the back of mile-high Pioneer Peak, which is a lovely mountain dominating the view of the little town of Palmer, which is about a 40-minute drive northeast of Anchorage. Each trail rises right out of the parking lot and quickly puts the hiker/runner in possession of an outstanding vista.

For river runners, **EAGLE RIVER**, northeast of Anchorage, is the only river in the park where there is any regular canoeing, kayaking, or rafting. An 11-mile segment can be managed by most experienced boaters. But unless you are very experienced and have scouted the rapids, do not go past the bridge on the highway. This can be a deathtrap. For those who want a taste of the river but don't have a boat, contact **MIDNIGHT SUN RIVER RUNNERS** (907/338-7238). Their 4-hour rafting tour costs $60 for adults, $30 for children (who must be 5 years old). A 30-minute whitewater add-on trip costs an additional $10 (children must be at least 8 years old). They run two tours daily in summer and will pick you up at your hotel.

For those who desire a deeper drink of Chugach splendors, a 28-mile backpacking trek, the **GIRDWOOD TO EAGLE RIVER TRAVERSE**, crosses from Girdwood over Crow Pass and down Raven Creek to the Eagle River Trail, northeast of the city. This cuts through the wilderness heart of the park, covering part of the historic Iditarod Trail that once carried travelers from Seward into the Interior before the advent of the railroad.

Another fun alternative to the Crow Pass trip is **GLEN ALPS TO INDIAN** via Ship Pass and Ship Lake. It's 12 miles, but the middle section is off-trail and easy to navigate with experience. The route from Ship Pass down to the lake is steep but safe if you take your time. A hiking stick or ski pole is highly recommended. You can camp overnight at the lake or at Indian Pass or do it in a day. Both routes require vehicle shuttles or willing friends to drop you off and pick you up.

PUBLIC-USE CABINS / YUDITNA CREEK CABIN, 4 miles or so from **EKLUTNA LAKE** parking area, is far from luxurious, but it is wheelchair-accessible and can accommodate as many as 8 people snugly. Bring all your own gear and food. Rent is $40 per night for a maximum of 3 nights and only one weekend a month. (Reservations must be made in person.) For information on this and other cabins, call the Alaska Department of Natural Resources Public Information Center (907/269-8400).

Hikers can rent a U.S. Forest Service cabin near **CROW PASS,** an A-frame that can sleep 10. It's bare bones: no bedding, no cooking gear, and no woodstove. Because of avalanche hazard, it is available only in summer for $35 per night; maximum stay is 3 nights. (For reservations, call 877/444-6777.) Finally, along the park's 40-mile **EKLUTNA TRAVERSE** are three A-frame huts that are free and require no reservations. The names of the huts are **PICHLER'S PERCH, WHITEOUT,** and **EAGLE RIVER.** They have no woodstoves or amenities. These backcountry cabins were built and are maintained by the Mountaineering Club for this extreme traverse and are meant to be shared by all travelers.

GUIDES AND OUTFITTERS

GREAT ALASKAN GOURMET ADVENTURES / With a motto and offerings of "A Menu of Extraordinary Beauty," Jennifer Johnston, a former Vermonter with 20 years of experience adventuring in Alaska, is the entertaining and delightful wizard behind this guiding adventure. If you're nervous going into the Chugach wilderness by yourself, she and her guides can custom-design a "soft" adventure with gourmet meals to fit your experience level for a day or overnight. If you're really up for a more dramatic adventure, join one of her 5-day trips in the Alaska Range in June to the granite spires and glaciers of Little Switzerland. In winter, Jennifer is a downhill ski instructor and Nordic ski coach, and in summer, a hiking and mountain guide. In 1993, she and her daughter Merrick, then 12 years old, made mountaineering history on Mount McKinley as the first mother-daughter team to climb the mountain, and today Merrick remains the youngest girl ever to scale North America's highest peak. So not only are you with an experienced hand, but Jennifer's personal philosophy is that all adventures are for fun and she creates them that way. 11090 Hideaway Lake Dr, Anchorage, AK 99516;

907/346-1087, fax 907/346-1356; jjohnston@customcpu.com; www. alaskan.com/akaadventures.

LIFETIME ADVENTURES (EKLUTNA LAKE) / This guiding outfit rents bikes and kayaks at Eklutna Lake in Chugach State Park. They give boat rides down the lake for up to 6 people and do day or overnight drop-offs around the lake. They operate a small information center near the trailhead at the lake. You can paddle up the lake (8 miles) and ride a bike back or do it the other way around. 907/746-4644.

FESTIVALS AND EVENTS

CROW PASS CROSSING / A 28-mile wilderness footrace held every July traverses the mountains from Girdwood to Eagle River. Winners complete the race in about 3 hours. Most backpackers, however, cover the same route in two or three days, parking a "getaway car" at one end, then driving around in a second car to begin at the other trailhead.

WINTER AND SUMMER SOLSTICES / Visitors who chance upon Chugach in the third week of June or December may want to join solstice celebrations on Flattop Mountain. In summer and winter, since the 1960s, solstice worshippers camp out all night en masse on the peak's huge summit field. Festivities, which sometimes even include bands playing to the glories of endless sunlight, are sponsored by the Mountaineering Club of Alaska and take place on the Saturday closest to the solstice. Legend maintains that not a single solstice has been missed. In winter, not surprisingly, the numbers are fewer. One December, only one soul proved hardy enough to brave the severe cold and wind so that the record could remain unbroken.

PRINCE WILLIAM SOUND

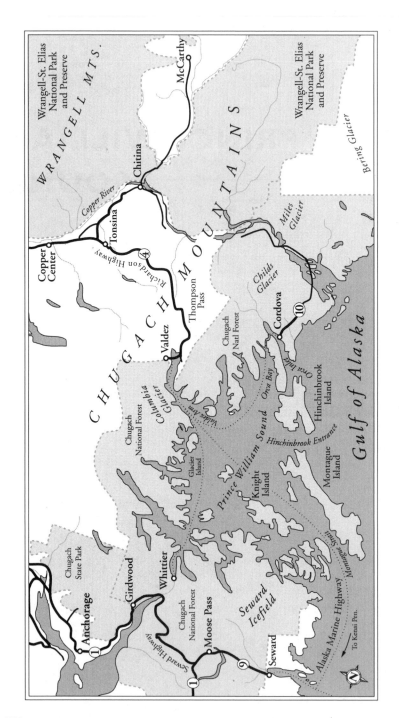

PRINCE WILLIAM SOUND

In the far northern Gulf of Alaska lies Prince William Sound, a marvelous wilderness of deep fjords, towering snowcapped mountains, rich blue seas teeming with wildlife, and chiseled tidewater glaciers. Only a few remote fishing towns and Eskimo villages dot the coast of this vast array of forest, islands, and waterways.

When the sun shines, there is nothing quite so exhilarating as paddling a kayak through bobbing icebergs and curious sea otters, watching huge chunks of ice break off the face of glaciers, feeling the crisp breeze, and riding the swell of waves created by falling ice.

Almost all of Prince William Sound—its 3,500 miles of coastline and 150 glaciers—lies within the boundaries of Chugach National Forest, which was established by President Theodore Roosevelt in 1907 and today ranks as the second-largest national forest in the United States. (The first is the Tongass National Forest, which encompasses most of Southeast Alaska.)

The weather and seas in the Gulf of Alaska are legendary and tumultuous. But the waters of Prince William Sound are mostly protected from storms in the Gulf by a series of islands. Standing guard at the entrance of the Sound are the two largest—Hinchinbrook and Montague. On the east side are Orca Bay and the little fishing town of Cordova. Continuing northeast, you'll find Valdez Arm, a long spectacular fjord leading through the Valdez Narrows to the head of the bay and the oil-boom town of Valdez. Anchoring the middle of the Sound are three tiny islands named Naked, Peak, and Storey. Just south of them is lovely Knight Island, with its myriad coves and bays.

On the west side of the Sound is the bunker town of Whittier, gateway to the railroad tracks and a new toll road that share a tunnel leading to the Seward Highway and to Anchorage. To the northwest, amid rafts of sea otters and seals, lie College and Harriman Fjords with glacier after glacier plunging into their waters. The 1899 Harriman Expedition named a number of glaciers here after the Ivy League and Little Ivy League colleges of the East Coast, such as Williams, Vassar, Smith, Harvard, and Yale.

When the great navigator Captain James Cook of the Royal British Navy first ventured into the Sound in 1778, he named it Sandwich Sound for the Earl of Sandwich. But by the time Cook returned to England, the earl had fallen from grace, so the name was changed to Prince William Sound after the king's third son.

ACCESS AND INFORMATION

The state ferry, **ALASKA MARINE HIGHWAY** (800/642-0066), can take you from Whittier to Valdez and Cordova, or from Seward to Valdez and Cordova, or vice versa. You can walk on, or take your car and drive the road system at your destination's end. Not only does the ferry provide transportation, but it's communal, fun, and a great way to view the remoteness of the Sound.

There are only two places from which you can access the Sound by road. Valdez on the east is at the beginning of the **RICHARDSON HIGHWAY**, and Whittier on the west is about an hour's drive south of Anchorage on the **SEWARD HIGHWAY**. From there, take a 30-minute train ride or pay to drive the new toll road (scheduled to open in summer 2000) that shares the railroad tunnel through the mountains. Otherwise, you need to take a boat or plane.

Dotted throughout the Sound are 25 **PUBLIC-USE CABINS** managed by the U.S. Forest Service and Alaska State Parks and available for roughly $35 per night. For more information about the U.S. Forest Service cabins, contact **CHUGACH NATIONAL FOREST** (3301 C St, Ste 300, Anchorage, AK 99503-3998; 907/271-2500) and ask for *Public Recreation Cabins: Chugach National Forest Alaska*, a 30-page pamphlet that describes each cabin and how to get there. For reservations, dial 877/444-6777 or check their Web site at www.reserveusa.com. For the state park cabins, contact **ALASKA STATE PARKS** (3601 C St, Ste 200, Anchorage, AK 99503-5929; 907/269-8400; www.dnr.state.ak.us/parks/parks.htm).

Whittier

South of Anchorage and through the mountains at the end of the tracks, where the road and railroad meet the sea, Whittier is the launching point for many Prince William Sound adventures. But Whittier itself is not a place to linger. The same mountains that isolate Whittier also trap storms over the town, which gets about 15 feet of rain and 20 feet of snow a year. If the sun does happen to shine, you will find yourself surrounded by mountains dripping with glaciers. But too often it is gray and dreary in Whittier, so the trick is to keep the visit short.

Until World War II, there was no Whittier. This may explain the rather unusual look of the town, which today depends primarily on fishing and tourism. Created as a major logistics center and built to be a self-contained U.S. Army community, much of the town is housed in a single gray, bunkerlike skyscraper. The Army pulled out in 1963 and left behind two towers; the other one is empty, its windows broken. The first couple of floors of the occupied 14-story war relic hold government offices, a

SHOREBIRD FESTIVAL

Cordova has joyfully celebrated for more than 10 years the return of the birds in early May, as the host of the Copper River Delta Shorebird Festival. The town is invaded by visitors in rubberized rain suits with notebooks in their pockets and binoculars around their necks. For 5 days, they take field trips and attend lectures, workshops, and slide shows. All the while, they engage in species-speak and general bird adoration. In town, shorebirds are everywhere—on signs, on T-shirts, and painted on store windows. Why the big whoop?

These are not just a few robins people are welcoming back. Waterfowl and shorebirds pass through the delta by the millions: western sandpipers, Canada geese, trumpeter swans, sandhill cranes, fork-tailed storm petrels, red-faced cormorants—more than 240 species live or stop here. At times, they come in intense gusts—as many as 200,000 geese, swans, pintails, sandpipers, and other waterfowl have been known to pass overhead in the course of an hour.

Most birds traveling to or through Alaska funnel through the delta, where six glacial rivers rendezvous with the sea. This heavily braided, 50-mile-wide delta is a mecca of meadows, marshes, ponds, mudflats, and sloughs. In the bird world it's like a 24-hour diner, offering an irresistible smorgasbord of fish and fly larvae after a nearly nonstop flight along the Gulf of Alaska's cantankerous coast. For most species, the last major rest stop was 900 miles back at the Stikine River in Southeast Alaska, or the Fraser River in southern British Columbia, more than 1,200 distant.

As former Cordova mayor Kelly Weaverling once put it, "The birds have been having a festival here for thousands of years. It's only recently that we figured out there was a party going on." Call for more information (907/424-7260).

—Debra McKinney

library, and local businesses. The upper floors are condominiums where most of the town's 200 residents live.

After years of debate and controversy, the state decided to build a **TOLL ROAD** to the tiny town. The road is scheduled to open in summer of 2000 (see Prince William Sound, Access and Information). More than half of the state's population lives less than an hour away from the tunnel to Whittier. In days of yore, the mountain and train tunnel provided a kind of natural selection and limited access to Whittier and the Sound.

The new road link has been likened to the opening of floodgates. In 1999, most of the 300-plus boats in Whittier's harbor were owned by Anchorage residents and annual visitors averaged 200,000. But there were only 100 parking spaces in the whole town and one public rest room. One year after the road opens, it is estimated that the average number of visitors to Whittier will leap to 1 million, and it is seriously doubtful that the Forest Service, state park system, and the small town of Whittier will be prepared to handle such an onslaught. So, be forewarned.

ACCESS AND INFORMATION

On the map, Whittier looks awfully close to Anchorage. But a wall of mountains in between makes it more remote and tricky to access. To get to Whittier, travel south on the Seward Highway from Anchorage for about an hour. Right before the Portage Glacier turnoff, there is a large parking lot on the left where an **ALASKA RAILROAD** (907/265-2607) train stops. You can drive your car onto the train, or park and ride as a passenger. The trip takes about 30 minutes and travels through the mountains to the edge of Passage Canal on Prince William Sound. To make reservations with the Alaska Railroad, call and ask for the Whittier schedule. If you choose **TO DRIVE** (and assuming the **TOLL ROAD** noted above opens on schedule), access is near the **BEGICH, BOGGS VISITORS CENTER** at **PORTAGE GLACIER**. Take the turnoff to Portage Glacier. (For more information on the glacier, see the Kenai Peninsula chapter.) It is expected the road toll will be somewhere between $10 to $20 round-trip. The new toll road shares the tunnel with the Alaska Railroad. Passenger trains will continue to run, but with less frequency when the toll road is open.

Much is up in the air as Whittier adjusts to the new toll road. For the latest information on services, accommodations, and other visitor information, contact the **CITY CLERK'S OFFICE IN WHITTIER** (907/472-2327).

Note that kayak and recreational boaters have more than doubled in Whittier and western Prince William Sound since the 1989 oil spill. July is the most heavily populated month to visit.

GUIDES AND OUTFITTERS

ALASKA OUTDOOR ADVENTURES / Two experienced and talented young Alaskans, Rudi and Tasha von Imhoff, offer kayak paddling in the Sound as part of a whole array of outdoor adventure offerings in the summer. In winter, they lead expeditions for those interested in dog mushing or snowmobiling. Their summer offerings in the Sound range from an early-morning, 2-hour paddle for beginners or enthusiasts with limited time to a full-day kayak trip out of Whittier watching for marine wildlife. Trips range from $60 to $99 each. Stop in at one of their two tour offices, either in Girdwood at the base of Mount Alyeska Ski Resort or in Whittier at the small boat harbor. They also can arrange a whole host of other activities in Alaska for you, from horseback riding to sailing trips. PO Box 241125, Anchorage, AK 99524; 907/783-7669 or 888/414-7669, fax 907/783-7670; info@adventures.com; www.akadventures. com; MC, V; checks OK; operates summer (operates winters for dog-sled tours, snowmobiling, and snowcat skiing as Alaska Snow Safaris).

HONEY CHARTERS AND ALASKA SEA KAYAKERS / These two businesses have teamed up to offer custom taxi charters and tours from fishing to whale watching to glacier viewing to guided kayak trips. The water-taxi service also provides drop-off service for kayak trips and overnight stays in remote cabins. The boat can carry small or large groups. Alaska Sea Kayakers rents boats and provides an hourlong orientation to new paddlers. In summer, their offices are located in the two-story log cabin in the Harbor Triangle in Whittier. PO Box 708, Whittier, AK 99770; 888/477-2493, Honey Charters, or 877/472-2534, Alaska Sea Kayakers; DIS, MC, V; checks OK; operates May–Sept.

LAZY OTTER CHARTERS INC. / Lazy Otter provides a water-taxi service for groups up to six people plus gear and is also available for sightseeing, photography, and drop-offs for kayakers, scuba divers, and campers. They will take you anywhere in western Prince William Sound. Perry Passage and southern Knight Island are good places for seeing orca and humpback whales. 15801 Amberwood Circle, Anchorage, AK 99516; 907/472-6887, summer; 907/345-3775, winter; www.alaska.net/ ~lazyottr; MC, V; checks OK; operates May–Oct.

SOUND ECO ADVENTURES / This charter is operated by retired marine biologist Jerry Sanger. He specializes in natural-history tours and birdwatching, but he also provides water-taxi services for kayakers or folks headed for remote cabins or campsites. PO Box 707, Whittier, AK 99693; 888/471-2312 or 907/472-2312; www.alaska.net/~sea/seasite. html; MC, V; checks OK; operates March–Nov. ᕗ

MAJOR MARINE TOURS / Offering a 6-hour round-trip out of Whittier to Blackstone Bay, this tour stays in fairly calm waters and travels past three tidewater glaciers, some quite dramatic and active. The boat holds 150 folks and the trip fare is about $110, which includes an all-you-can-eat salmon and prime rib buffet. They sometimes offer beginning- and end-of-the-season specials. PO Box 101400, Anchorage, AK 99510; 907/274-7300; www.majormarine.com; AE, DIS, MC, V; local checks only; operates May–Sept.

NATIONAL OUTDOOR LEADERSHIP SCHOOL (NOLS) / The school is based in Wyoming but has an outpost in Palmer, Alaska. It offers kayaking trips through the Sound. These trips (2 to 4 weeks) are not only paddling experiences but also are designed to train group leaders and teach outdoor skills. They are set up for different age groups, including a master's course for folks 50 and older. A 2-week trip costs between $2,000 and $2,600. PO Box 981, Palmer, AK 99645-0981; 907/745-4047; www.nols.edu; MC, V; checks OK; operates June–Aug.

PHILLIPS' CRUISES AND TOURS / The 330-passenger *Klondike Express* travels through protected waters in Harriman and College Fjords and offers a 6-hour, whirlwind tour of 26 glaciers. They've been in business for more than 20 years and have this trip down to a science. The $120 ticket includes lunch, but you have to make your own way to Whittier. 519 W 4th Ave, Ste 100, Anchorage, AK 99501; 800/544-0529 or 907/276-8023; www.26glaciers.com; AE, CB, DIS, JCB, MC, V; checks OK; operates May–Sept.

PRINCE WILLIAM SOUND KAYAK CENTER / In business since 1981, the center rents single and double kayaks at daily and weekly rates, offers guided day trips, or will provide an escort who serves as a group leader. But you're on your own as camp cooks. Prices run $45 per day to $275 per week. Make reservations well in advance. PO Box 233008, Anchorage, AK 99523; 907/472-2452; MC, V; checks OK.

RESTAURANTS

Hobo Bay Trading Company / ★

I WINDY PL, WHITTIER; 907/472-2374
Babs has been running this little joint for 22 years. She's a local renegade who usually can be found in the thick of local politics. Fishermen resupplying in Whittier will always treat themselves to a Babs Burger or a Buffalo Babs Burger made with real buffalo meat. Her burgers—beef or buffalo—have a bite. They come with a hot pepper on top. She also serves Alaska-made ice cream and pies. *$; no credit cards; checks "under protest," Babs says; lunch, dinner Wed–Mon; closed mid-Sept–mid-May; no alcohol; get off the ferry or train and head for the harbormaster's steel blue building.*

Valdez

This little oil town is known as the Switzerland of Alaska because of its jagged, snowcapped peaks and emerald green mountain slopes. The name is Spanish. But to pronounce it correctly is to mispronounce it to an Alaskan's ears. Here you say "Val-deez." It's home to 3,500 people, averages 26 feet of rain a year, and its record snowfall is more than 46 feet.

The town has seen its share of booms and busts. Around the turn of the century, Valdez was one port of entry to the rich gold fields in the Canadian Klondike. The gold route from Valdez to the Klondike was advertised all over the United States and drew about 4,000 hopeful gold seekers. A tent town sprang up and some of the miners stuck around. They later hacked a dogsled trail into the interior of Alaska, followed by a rough wagon route, which eventually became known as the Richardson Highway, to the gold-rush town of Fairbanks, some 400 miles away.

By the 1920s, the population was declining. It stayed that way through the greatest earthquake ever recorded on the North American continent. The epicenter for that quake was in Prince William Sound. On the Friday before Easter in 1964, late in the afternoon, a terrifying force let loose. It measured 8.6 on the Richter scale. The ensuing tsunami created waves that swept over the dock and town. Thirty-two people died, including two people aboard a steamer tied to the dock.

In the late 1960s, the town's population began to swell again. Oil was discovered on the North Slope and Valdez was chosen to be the terminus for the 800-mile trans-Alaska oil pipeline. Work on the pipeline began in 1974. The town's population skyrocketed to 10,000. When construction ended in 1977, the population plummeted to 3,500. It stayed there until 1989. Then, ironically, on Good Friday, exactly 25 years after the earthquake, disaster struck again. The *Exxon Valdez* oil tanker ran aground at Bligh Reef, spilling 11 million gallons of North Slope crude oil into the pristine waters of Prince William Sound. Alaskans were devastated. And yet, in one of those twists of fate that often occur, the ensuing cleanup effort ushered in another economic boom.

But don't expect to roll into this oil town today and get the latest environmental statistics on Prince William Sound. Oil is king here. So the spill is something most locals are not anxious to talk about. However, if you want to retrace a little history on your own, check out the Pipeline Club (see review below). It's the bar where Captain Joe Hazelwood of *Exxon Valdez* fame had that Scotch on the rocks before his ship ended up on the rocks at Bligh Reef that fateful night.

ACCESS AND INFORMATION

You can reach Valdez by driving from Anchorage. It's a long day, but a beautiful drive. Alaska Airlines (800/426-0333) has regularly scheduled flights. Or you can take the train or drive the toll road (see Prince William Sound, Access and Information) through the mountains to Whittier from Anchorage and board the ferry to Valdez on the **ALASKA MARINE HIGHWAY** (800/642-0066). A 7-hour trip through the Sound, this water route passes near the Columbia Glacier.

The **VALDEZ CONVENTION & VISITORS BUREAU'S VISITORS INFORMATION CENTER** (907/835-2984) is located at the intersection of Chenega and Fairbanks Drives. **ONE CALL DOES IT ALL** (907/835-4988) is a co-op of bed and breakfasts and boat/plane charters that offers free reservation and information services.

EXPLORING

ALYESKA PIPELINE TOURS / The Alyeska Pipeline Terminal, originally co-owned by eight oil companies, changed the face of Valdez when it was constructed in the mid-1970s as the terminus for the trans-Alaska oil pipeline. The pipeline stretches 800 miles from Prudhoe Bay on Alaska's North Slope over several mountain ranges to the Valdez terminal. Construction of the line began in 1974 and was completed in 1977. The pipeline is 48 inches in diameter and has a carrying capacity of 1.16 million barrels of oil a day. About 50 tankers are filled with crude oil monthly. Tours of the terminal cost $15 per person. 212 Tatitlek St, Valdez, AK 99686; 907/835-2686; operates every day May–mid-Oct.

VALDEZ MUSEUM / The museum, open year-round, has relics of Valdez past, starting with the gold-rush years. It features two restored fire engines, an 1896 hand pumper, a 1907 steam engine, and an exhibit on the history of oil. The new museum annex (436 S Hazelet Ave) is open only during summer and focuses on the 1964 earthquake. Nominal admission fee. 217 Egan St, PO Box 8, Valdez, AK 99686-0008; 907/835-2764; www.alaska.net/~vldzmuse/index.htm.

ALASKA CULTURAL CENTER / Prince William Sound Community College opened this museum in the summer of 1999 after it received a private collection of Eskimo art from Jesse and Maxine Whitney, who arrived in Alaska in 1946. They started their own collection and for about 15 years ran the Eskimo Museum near Fairbanks. The displays include an extensive collection of ivory, trophy mounted wildlife, full-size kayaks, and skin boats called *unimaks*. Drive north out of town about 3.5 miles and follow the signs to the airport. Valdez Airport, PO Box 97 Valdez, AK 99686; 907/834-1690.

ADVENTURES

BACKCOUNTRY SKIING / Skiing on **THOMPSON PASS** is booming. With miles of untracked powder on the slopes of the pass, local entrepreneurs have figured out ways to get skiers up and down the mountains. Air charters—both helicopter and fixed-wing planes on skis—can give you a lift to the top of a 1,000-foot run. This is steep terrain with tons of windblown snow. You need to be aware of avalanches. Be trained in assessing the dangers, know the precautions, and bring the appropriate gear. Try **ALASKA BACKCOUNTRY ADVENTURES** (907/835-5608, winter, or 907/283-9354, summer) or **GLACIER SNOWCAT** (907/373-3118). Also during the peak spring months for skiing, try **VALDEZ HELI-SKI GUIDES** (907/835-4528) or **VALDEZ H20 HELI-ADVENTURES** (800/578-4354). For guided backcountry skiing or touring, call Matt Kinney with **THOMPSON PASS CHALET** (907/835-4817).

HIKING TRAILS / For information, find the U.S. Forest Service Visitors Center on the edge of town. It's open only in summer (907/835-4680; in winter, call 907/424-7661). Two popular hiking trails are the **SOLOMAN GULCH TRAIL**, which leads up from the fish hatchery to Soloman Lake, and the **GOAT TRAIL**, which follows the original road through Keystone Canyon to Valdez. The Goat Trail trailhead is at **HORSETAIL FALLS**, about 13.5 miles out of Valdez. A new 10-mile trail starts in Valdez and goes out to **SHOUP BAY STATE MARINE PARK** in the Valdez Arm. There, three state park cabins are available to rent for overnight use through Alaska State Parks (3601 C St, Anchorage, AK 99503-5929; 907/269-8400; www.dnr.state.ak.us/parks/parks.htm).

SAIL TO COLUMBIA GLACIER / This is one of the most active tidewater glaciers in Alaska. It has been rapidly receding since 1978 and has lost about 6 miles of its once-spectacular face. The trip to Columbia takes you through the Valdez Narrows and out into the Sound heading west. On the way, you pass two marine parks popular for camping and fishing. **OUTFITTERS** who offer trips to the glacier include Prince William Sound Cruises and Tours (800/992-1297); Alaska Wilderness Sailing and Kayaking (907/835-5175); and Anadyr Sea Kayak Adventures (907/835-2814).

DRIVE THE RICHARDSON HIGHWAY / This road leads north out of Valdez toward the Alaska Interior. The road first winds up past Bridal Veil and Horsetail Falls through Keystone Canyon to Thompson Pass. About 30 miles from Valdez, Thompson Pass is spectacular and notable for holding most of the state's highest snowfall records. Near the top is the turnoff for **WORTHINGTON GLACIER STATE RECREATION AREA**. You can drive to the face of Worthington Glacier. All along the Richardson Highway to Glennallen, you will get glimpses of the trans-Alaska oil pipeline. The road cuts between the mountains of the **WRANGELL-ST. ELIAS NATIONAL PARK AND PRESERVE** (see The Roads North chapter). To the east are impressive Mounts Wrangell, Drum, Stanford, and Blackburn, some of Alaska's most picturesque summits. Just 30 miles shy of Glennallen is the community of **COPPER CENTER**. The tiny town, which sits on the banks of the Copper River, was founded during the gold-rush era of 1898. An old fish wheel still sits in the river. The **COPPER CENTER LODGE** (907/822-3245) was built in the early 1930s. Still in operation today, it houses a small museum containing Athabascan baskets, Russian artifacts, and mining memorabilia.

BEACHCOMBING

Spring is a great time for beachcombing along Prince William Sound—the time to see what the Gulf of Alaska has tossed out over the winter. Winter storms in the Gulf are notorious, at times producing waves impersonating major mountain ranges.

Occasionally, shipping containers tumble off barges, their contents spilling into the sea. Some of this stuff eventually makes it to shore, sometimes in mass quantities. As a result, Prince William Sound and Gulf Coast residents have found their shorelines littered with everything from rubber ducky tub toys to bundles of marijuana.

At Montague Island, driftwood piles alone tell the story of the power of nature, not to mention the remodeling job done by the Good Friday Earthquake in 1964. The kinds of souvenirs you'll find here include wrecked boats and airplane parts. In addition to unopened soda cans and plastic milk containers, beachcombers have found whale bones, Japanese glass floats, bottles with notes inside, and an abandoned World War II mine. The Forest Service has four public-use cabins on the outer coast of Montague, available by reservation for $35 per night. The Log Jam Lake Cabin is the best of the four. Decorated in a beachcombing motif, the cabin boasts a fine collection of strange trophies. For reservations, contact the U.S. Forest Service, Cordova Ranger District (907/424-7661).

Perhaps the best beachcombing of all can be found at Kayak Island, on the eastern edge of the Copper River Delta. Because the island sits perpendicular to the wind and currents, it acts like a giant catcher's mitt. Booty found here includes rubber turtle tub toys, life rings, and Japanese survival rations with this message written in Japanese and English: "Don't give up. But if all hope is lost, write down what you think should be in this kit." People have found everything from Skuffy the Tugboat, a toy with a warning not to use in water, to Nike shoes. (A huge shipment lost in the Gulf had people up and down the coast swapping shoes right and left in an effort to find pairs that fit.)

Chartered boats or planes, which can land on beaches at low tide, are your way out here. Fishing & Flying (907/424-3324), out of Cordova, has a great reputation, and its owners are avid beachcombers themselves. A group of three can charter a plane to either island for about $500, round-trip.

—Debra McKinney

GUIDES AND OUTFITTERS

ALASKA WILDERNESS SAILING AND KAYAKING / Formerly known as Alaska Wilderness Safaris, this company offers half-day and full-day kayaking trips from Growler Island across from Columbia Glacier. Owners Jim and Nancy Lethcoe, authors of two guidebooks to Prince William Sound, are very knowledgeable. First, you have to get to the island. Most folks go with Prince William Sound Cruises and Tours and stay at their tent camp on Growler Island. (The name "growler" means any iceberg that presents a navigational hazard.) "It's really great for people who don't want to camp in the rain," Jim Lethcoe says. The Lethcoes offer nine trips for paddlers, including overnight guided trips. They also rent windriders, for people who want to sail small crafts, and can arrange custom sailing trips early or late in the season. PO Box 1313, Valdez, AK 99686; 907/835-5175; MC, V: checks OK; www.alaskanwilderness.com.

ANADYR SEA KAYAK ADVENTURES / Anadyr offers an assortment of trips, from 3-hour paddles out of Valdez to daylong trips to Shoup and Columbia Glaciers to lodge-based or mothership-supported multiday tours. Owner Hedy Sarney will also help you plan a longer, custom-designed trip and will rent kayaks to experienced boaters. 217 N Harbor Dr, PO Box 1821, Valdez, AK 99686; 907/835-2814 or 800/TOK-AYAK; anadyr@alaska.net; www.alaska.net/~anadyr; AE DIS, MC, V; checks OK.

KEYSTONE RAFT AND KAYAK ADVENTURES / This outfit has one of the most popular river trips—a thrilling ride down the Lowe River through Keystone Canyon with Class III rapids, costing about $35 per person. Two other popular half-day and day trips are down the Tsina River and the Tonsina River. They also offer 10-day trips down the Copper River for about $2,000 per person. You can go by raft, or they will supply support for experienced kayakers. PO Box 1486, Valdez, AK 99686; 907/835-2606; www.alaskawhitewater.com; MC, V; checks OK.

SOMETHING FISHY CHARTERS / Owned by Rik VanStone, this is one of the most popular saltwater fish-guiding businesses in Valdez. Not only does Rik find fish, but he also neatly fillets them for you. PO Box 74, Valdez, AK 99686; 907/835-5732.

PRINCE WILLIAM SOUND CRUISES AND TOURS / Formerly known as Stan Stephens Cruises, this business has been around for nearly 20 years. They offer day trips to Columbia Glacier. They also run a tent camp on Growler Island, on the north side of Glacier Island, which faces Columbia Glacier. The trip to Columbia Glacier, with stopover at Growler Island for lunch, takes 9 hours and costs about $120. Stay overnight at their tent camp on Growler Island (adults, $200; children, $175) and spend the next day on a kayaking adventure with Alaska Wilderness

Sailing and Kayaking. PO Box 1297, Valdez, AK 99686; 800/992-1297; www.princewilliamsound.com; AE, DIS, MC, V; checks OK.

FESTIVALS AND EVENTS

THE LAST FRONTIER THEATER CONFERENCE / Sponsored by Prince William Sound Community College, the theater conference draws hundreds of playwrights and theater buffs from around the country. The "godfather" of the event is Edward Albee—triple Pulitzer Prize winner. It's a wonderful chance for Alaska's own community theater organizers to rub elbows with New York City's finest. Held in mid-June at the Valdez Civic Center, the conference features workshops, critiques, and readings. Cost is about $100 for the 5-day event. For more information, contact Prince William Sound Community College, PO Box 97, Valdez, AK 99686; 800/478-8800; www.uaa.alaska.edu/pwscc.

WORLD EXTREME SKIING CHAMPIONSHIPS / Draws the world's most daring skiers to Valdez every year. The competition is at the end of March or beginning of April. Held at Thompson Pass, the event requires thrillseekers to pick the steepest and most dangerous run down death-defying slopes, around exposed rocks, and over cliffs. A helicopter ferries competitors to the top. Judges award points for aggressiveness, form, fluidity, and control. Some consider the World Extremes a death-wish derby. Bring your binoculars. For information, call 907/835-2108.

RESTAURANTS

Alaska Halibut House

208 MEALS AVE, VALDEZ; 907/835-2788

This place is a favorite for locals because it's cheap fast food, but not McDonald's. The restaurant features fresh Alaska halibut, a salad bar, and a variety of hamburgers. *$; MC, V; local checks only; lunch, dinner every day; no alcohol; PO Box 1562, Valdez, AK 99686.* &

Mike's Palace Ristorante / ★★

201 N HARBOR DR, VALDEZ; 907/835-2365

Owner Mike Panagis' menu runs the gamut from steak and seafood to lasagne, pizza, and enchiladas. While the pizzas are alluring and come with thin, thick, or really thick crusts, many diners swear by the lasagne. It's a cozy restaurant with a view of the harbor. The walls, covered with old newspapers, tell the history of Valdez. *$$; MC, V; local checks only; lunch, dinner every day; closed Jan; beer and wine; directly across from the harbor.* &

Oscar's on the Waterfront / ★

141 N HARBOR DR, VALDEZ; 907/835-4700

While Oscar's serves three meals a day, it's breakfast that draws the crowd. The food is greasy, but the locals love it—and the eggs Benedict are the best in town. Another favorite is the Klondike potatoes, which are home fries grilled with onions and blanketed with Cheddar cheese. Grab a caffe latte at the Klondike Coffee Shop 2 blocks away. Also serves all-you-can-eat barbecue. *$$; MC, V; local checks only; breakfast, lunch, dinner every day in summer; beer and wine; 2 blocks west of the harbormaster's office.* &

Pipeline Club Restaurant

112 EGAN DR, VALDEZ; 907/835-4891

This is where the tanker crews and fishermen head for steak and seafood dinners. The restaurant's specialty is "Pipeline Pu Pu," created by a chef from the Hawaiian Islands. In Valdez, the dish is made with sliced steak sautéed with onion, bell pepper, soy sauce, tomato, and seasoning, then served on a bed of rice. Stick your head into the bar next door, where Captain Hazelwood had that famous Scotch on the rocks. Or was it two? *$$$; DC, MC, V; local checks only; dinner every day; full bar; in the town center, sandwiched between the Valdez Motel and the Westmark Inn.* &

LODGINGS

Best of All Bed and Breakfast / ★★

1104 MINERAL CREEK, VALDEZ, AK 99686; 907/835-4524

In business for nearly 15 years, this place has a reputation for good, hearty breakfasts. Really early risers get continental breakfast with fresh fruit and bagels. But those who can stick around until 8am get treated to Sue Kennedy's crepes, fancy pancakes, or waffles. A native of Thailand, Sue has decorated her home with a blend of Alaska and Thai art. She has three guest rooms, one with a private bath. *$$; no credit cards; no checks (except with advance reservations); PO Box 1578, Valdez, AK 99686; from the ferry terminal, drive up Hazelet Ave, turnoff for Mineral Creek Dr is near the end.*

Blueberry Mary's Bed and Breakfast / ★★

810 SALMONBERRY WAY, BLUEBERRY HILL, VALDEZ, AK 99686; 907/835-5015

One of only three B&Bs located on the ocean. Two rooms available, each has private entrance and ocean views, feather beds, and private baths. The two rooms share a kitchenette and a sauna. Mary serves a full breakfast, which most often includes blueberry pancakes since blueberries in season grow all over the hillside. Nonsmoking. *$; no credit cards; checks*

OK; open Memorial Day–Oct; www.alaska.net/~bmary; PO Box 1244, Valdez, AK 99686; about 1 mile from downtown.

The Lake House Bed and Breakfast / ★

MILE 6, RICHARDSON HWY, VALDEZ, AK 99686; 907/835-4752
Like a country inn, far from the hustle of town, this home perches on a bluff and has wide decks overlooking Robe Lake. The setting is remote, yet only 10 minutes from downtown Valdez. Mountains can be seen from every window. Most rooms have private baths. Prices include a continental breakfast. *$$; MC, V; checks OK; closed Nov–May; PO Box 1499, Valdez, AK 99686.*

Thompson Pass Mountain Chalet

MILE 19, RICHARDSON HWY, VALDEZ, AK 99686; 907/835-4817
This mountain chalet is north of town at Thompson Pass. Owner Matt Kinney guides backcountry telemark skiing, randonee skiing, and snowboarding trips. In the summer, he leads hikes. The chalet accommodates up to four people. Rates are roughly $100 to $130 a night for the chalet (plus $10 for each extra person) and include continental breakfast. *$; no credit cards; checks OK; PO Box 1540, Valdez, AK 99686; drive Mile 19 on the Richardson Hwy; from there it is a half-mile drive on a dirt road in summer or short ski or snowmachine ride in winter.*

Wild Rose's by the Sea B&B Retreat / ★

629 FIDDLEHEAD LN, VALDEZ, AK 99686; 907/835-2930
This deluxe bed-and-breakfast has a spectacular view of Valdez Narrows and surrounding mountains. It's close to the new hiking trail that goes out to Shoup Bay. Rose has three guest rooms. The Guesthouse Room has its own living room and dining area and is quite private. One room also has a Jacuzzi. She does the full-breakfast routine, featuring fresh baked goods, fruit, and a hot dish, usually a soufflé. *$$; MC, V; no checks; rbm@alaska.net; www.alaska.net/~rbm/index.html; PO Box 3396, Valdez, AK 99686; about 1½ miles from town.*

Cordova

Isolated and quaint, this fishing community is the hidden gem of Prince William Sound. The docks are lined with weathered canneries. The harbor brims with a fat fleet of mom-and-pop commercial fishing boats. The streets and hillsides are dotted with sun-worn bungalows. It's the kind of place where stray mutts wander down Main Street and everybody knows them by name. You won't need a car; everything is within walking distance.

Out Cordova's back door is the Copper River Delta, an immensely lush and diverse ecosystem fed by six glacial rivers. The town's history is rich with stories of trade and conflict between Natives, Russians, copper miners, and oil explorers. Cordova is strategically situated amid enormous runs of salmon and a bounty of shellfish. It was fish that reeled in the first Americans, who came to build a cannery here in 1889.

Michael J. Heney, a brilliant engineer, showed up a few years later to direct the building of the Copper River and Northwestern Railway, which winds alongside the Copper River 200 miles to McCarthy and Kennicott, towns built on the fortunes of copper and nestled in the Wrangell Mountains. Until the 1930s, Cordova thrived as a supply depot for the copper mines there and for the oil fields at Katalla, about 45 miles southeast of Cordova on the Gulf of Alaska.

About 2,500 people live here year-round, but the town nearly doubles when fishing starts in spring. It's an eclectic group of commercial fishermen, artists, intellectuals, Eyak Natives, and plain end-of-the-roaders. They live in bungalows clinging to steep slopes overlooking Orca Inlet or in old boathouses along Odiak Slough. The town has a reputation for making room for just about anybody, but at the same time it can become fiercely divided over any political issue. Everyone has an opinion. Just mention "the road." You'll get an earful.

Once upon a time, there were plans to build the Copper River Highway on top of the old railroad tracks that run up the Copper River to Chitina, where the road would link with the rest of Alaska. Construction began in the 1960s, but the 1964 earthquake buckled the Million Dollar Bridge, bringing the project to a halt. In recent years, there has been talk of renewing the project. Those who like the isolation of the surrounding mountains and the sea don't want the road. Those who want it say it will bring new blood and a more reasonable cost of living.

In late April and early May, the town bustles with birdwatchers. They are followed by a wave of commercial fishermen who fish 24-hour openings, then return to Cordova, where you'll see them down in the harbor mending their nets and gearing up for the next opening. The season ends in late August, and the town is pretty quiet until spring rolls around again. It's mild but wet here, with an average of 15 feet of rain a year. If the sun shines, don't expect the shops to stay open.

ACCESS AND INFORMATION

There are only two ways into Cordova, which is one of its beauties. You can fly in from Anchorage, Juneau, or Seattle on Alaska Airlines (800/426-0333), or you can take the **ALASKA MARINE HIGHWAY** (800/642-0066) ferry from Whittier or Valdez. From Whittier, it's about a 7-hour ferry ride. If you fly, the **MUDHOLE SMITH AIRPORT** (907/424-7151), named for an early bush pilot, is located about 12 miles out of town and has a shuttle service.

On weekdays, the **CORDOVA CHAMBER OF COMMERCE'S VISI-TORS CENTER** (PO Box 99, Cordova, AK 99574; 907/424-7260) offers a wealth of information. It's on First Avenue in downtown Cordova, right next to **ORCA BOOK & SOUND CO.**, also a good place for books, maps, and information.

EXPLORING

PRINCE WILLIAM SOUND SCIENCE CENTER / This independent, nonprofit research facility, housed down on the docks, is funded in part with settlement money from the 1989 *Exxon Valdez* oil spill. The work of the center focuses on the complex ecosystem of the Sound. Tours are available during business hours upon request. PO Box 705, Cordova, AK 99574; 907/424-5800; www.pwssc.gen.ak.us.

MOUNT EYAK SKI AREA / If the skies are clear and you can round up a group of six or so, the folks here will fire up the vintage chairlift to take you to the top of Mount Eyak. You'll have a spectacular view of Orca Inlet and miles beyond. Plus, you'll get to sit where Clark Gable and Marilyn Monroe once sat. This very same chairlift hoisted famous authors and movie stars such as Ernest Hemingway, Groucho Marx, Ingrid Bergman, Lucille Ball, and John Wayne to the top of the mountains in Sun Valley, Idaho, from 1936 to 1969. Alaska has it now. It's been in Cordova since 1974, and "you can't beat the view from here," says David Bradshaw, local chairlift historian. For more information, call 907/424-7766.

ADVENTURES

MOUNTAIN BIKES AND KAYAKS / For rentals and information on where to go, try **CORDOVA COASTAL OUTFITTERS** for just about any outdoor gear you can think of, ranging from kayaks and canoes to camping gear and fishing equipment. PO Box 1834, Cordova, AK 99574; 907/424-7424.

CHILDS GLACIER AND THE MILLION DOLLAR BRIDGE / The bridge and glacier are 52 miles out of town, on the old Copper River Road. Impressive and close, the 300-foot wall of ice sits across the Copper River. Thunderous calving of ice off the glacier echoes from the steel beams of the bent bridge, which buckled during the 1964 earthquake. You can still walk across the bridge. To get there, call **COPPER RIVER NORTHWEST TOURS** (907/424-5356), hitch a ride, take a taxi, or rent a car.

COPPER RIVER DELTA / A rich, diverse ecosystem and breeding ground for all sorts of waterfowl, the Copper River flows 250 miles through the Chugach Mountains to the Sound. It is a strong, turbulent river that produces highly prized red salmon. Because of the firm, meaty flesh and layer of belly fat, Copper River salmon rank as the state's most delicious wild salmon. The best way to see the delta, the glacier, and the bridge is to call Becky Chapek at **COPPER RIVER NORTHWEST TOURS** (907/424-5356). She runs bus tours to the delta three or four times a week, and offers a narrative on the area's history and wildlife with a snack thrown in. Hardy bike riders also can jump on for a one-way ride to the glacier, pedaling back at their own pace.

The Cordova Ranger District of the Forest Service maintains about 37 miles of **TRAILS** on the Copper River Delta and a dozen wilderness **PUBLIC-USE CABINS.** For information and reservations, contact U.S. Forest Service, Cordova Ranger District (PO Box 280, Cordova, AK 99574; 907/424-7661).

GUIDES AND OUTFITTERS

ALASKA WILDERNESS OUTFITTING COMPANY / Offers fly-in fishing, adventure trips, hiking, kayaking, and wildlife viewing. They have floating cabins in Simpson and Sheep Bays, cabins on shore, guided trips, and do-it-yourself trips where they'll set you up in a fully stocked cabin with a motorboat, then leave you on your own. You bring only sleeping bags and fishing gear. Before dropping you off, they will fly you over the best fishing streams in the area. (They do leave you with a radio, in case of emergency.) You can even opt for a combo trip—3 days of saltwater fishing, then off to a remote camp in the Wrangell Mountains for freshwater rainbow- and lake-trout fishing. Costs for 5-day trips run $1,200 to $3,000. PO Box 1516, Cordova, AK 99574; 907/424-5552; www.alaskaoutdoors.com/AWOC/; MC, V; checks OK; operates June–Sept.

FISHING AND FLYING / Offers flight-seeing or drop-offs to the area's many remote Forest Service and state park cabins or their own fishing camps on the Katalla and the Tsiu Rivers. If you really want a bird's-eye view of the Sound, take their mail plane. They're "the postman" in Prince William Sound. It's a cheap way to fly over the area's glaciers and set down in some of the Sound's remote villages, such as Chenega. They don't fly every day, and there is room for only three passengers, so call ahead. They also offer day flight-seeing trips to McCarthy. PO Box 2349, Cordova, AK 99574; 907/424-3324; AE, MC, V; local checks only.

SAGE CHARTERS / They will take you out fishing, birdwatching, or to watch sea otters. Rates depend on numbers of people and individual desires. The boat holds six people and costs $350 to $550 for a day charter. Scientists doing field work in the Sound often use this service. PO Box 723, Cordova, AK 99574; 907/424-3475.

FESTIVALS AND EVENTS

COPPER RIVER DELTA SHOREBIRD FESTIVAL / This festival draws hundreds of curious birdwatchers to Cordova every spring around the first of May to watch millions of migrating birds. In past years, the local chapter of the Audubon Society (907/424-7260) has sponsored a cruise with naturalists from Valdez to Cordova (see "Shorebird Festival" in this chapter).

ICE WORM FESTIVAL / Held the first week of February, the festival is a weeklong celebration and features a parade led by the guest of honor, a 100-foot ice worm. Some say the ice worm is only a mythological character. But what do they know? The true story is ice worms really do exist. As fanciful homework for the festival, read Robert Service's poem *Ballad of the Ice Worm Cocktail*. All over Alaska, you'll find these midwinter carnivals and celebrations to dispel "cabin fever" and break up the long, cold winter. Tap into them. They are great for local color. For more information, contact Cordova's Ice Worm Festival, PO Box 819, Cordova, AK 99574; 907/424-7260.

RESTAURANTS

Baja Taco / ★

NICHOLOFF ST AT THE HARBOR, CORDOVA; 907/424-5599
This funky red school bus serves a mean burrito and scrumptious fish tacos. Its menu, featured on a surfboard, stands next to the bus. The owners spend enough time in Mexico each winter to know how to keep the food spicy. *$; no credit cards; local checks only; lunch, dinner every day; closed Oct–April; no alcohol; PO Box 1748, Cordova, AK 99574.*

Cookhouse Cafe / ★★

I CANNERY RD, BLDG 7, CORDOVA; 907/424-5920
All the charm that is Cordova can be found at this little cafe, nestled on the dock between weathered warehouses looking out over Orca Inlet. Once the mess hall of the old cannery, Cookhouse Cafe has been restored to wood beams, white walls, and the gray-and-red trim of the traditional cannery colors. In the old days, when the steam whistle blew, cannery workers gathered for "mug ups"—coffee and pastries. The cafe has revived the tradition. Mainly geared to breakfast and lunch, the cafe also has special events. *$$; MC, V; checks OK; breakfast, lunch every day; closed Oct–May; no alcohol; PO Box 120, Cordova, AK 99574; head north along 1st Ave until you spot the old canneries.*

Killer Whale Cafe / ★

507 1ST AVE, CORDOVA; 907/424-7733
This little deli and coffee shop in the back of Orca Book & Sound Co. is right in the center of town and a favorite espresso stop. It also serves hearty soups and bulky sandwiches. The cheesecake is a killer. The bookstore makes nice browsing, with its eclectic collection of fine literature and local art. *$; no credit cards; checks OK; breakfast, lunch Mon–Sat; no alcohol; downtown.*

Reluctant Fisherman Cafe

401 RAILROAD AVE, CORDOVA; 907/424-7446
A great place to drink up a view of the harbor while sipping wine and lingering over halibut. Oscar, a friendly sea otter, swims nearby. The restaurant specializes in fresh Alaska seafood. Over the bar are brass plates listing all the local men and women lost at sea. *$$$; AE, DC, MC, V; checks OK; breakfast every day, lunch, dinner Mon–Sat; closed mid-Nov–Jan; full bar; near downtown, follow Council St to Railroad Ave.* &

LODGINGS

The Blue Heron Inn / ★★

ORCA RD, CORDOVA, AK 99574; 907/424-3554
Another old cannery turned quaint bed-and-breakfast. You get the entire downstairs of this cannery, complete with kitchen, private entrance, wood-fired sauna, and waterfall out back. It's a short walk across the road to Fleming Spit and first-class salmon fishing. *$$; MC, V; checks OK; PO Box 958, Cordova, AK 99574; located north of the ferry terminal, 1½ miles north of downtown on Orca Rd.*

Cannery Row Bunkhouse / ★★

1 CANNERY RD, BLDG 7, CORDOVA, AK 99574; 907/424-5920
Located above the Cookhouse Cafe, the old cannery bunkhouse has nine bed-and-breakfast rooms, austere and whitewashed. Showers are down the hall. Owner Silvia Lang has tried to preserve the simple bunkhouse flavor. In addition to the bunkhouse, there is Cannery Cottage, a beachside, two-bedroom cottage, which sleeps up to six people and is available year-round. An added attraction is Cordova's massage therapist, who has an office here. *$; MC, V; checks OK; closed Oct–May; PO Box 120, Cordova, AK 99574; a little north of downtown.*

Cordova Rose Lodge / ★★

1315 WHITSHED RD, CORDOVA, AK 99574; 907/424-7673
Permanently dry-docked in Odiak Slough next to an operating lighthouse, the old barge (now lodge) is filled with nautical artifacts. Stay in

the Captain's Quarters, the Officer's Quarters, or the Chief's Quarters. However, if you chose the Stowaway Room, the smallest and simplest, you're not allowed to complain. The joke is they follow the rules of the sea here. And you know what happens to stowaways. Because the barge is on the slough, it is popular with birdwatchers. *$$; MC, V; checks OK; PO Box 1494, Cordova, AK 99574; a quarter mile from downtown, go east on 1st, turn right on Whitshed.*

Reluctant Fisherman Inn

401 RAILROAD AVE, CORDOVA, AK 99574; 907/424-3272 OR 800/770-3272

If it's predictability and the conveniences of a standard hotel you are looking for, stay here. Ask for a room facing the harbor. You will pay about $20 more, but it's worth it. *$$$; AE, DC, MC, V; checks OK; PO Box 150, Cordova, AK 99574; 1 block from downtown.* &

KENAI PENINSULA

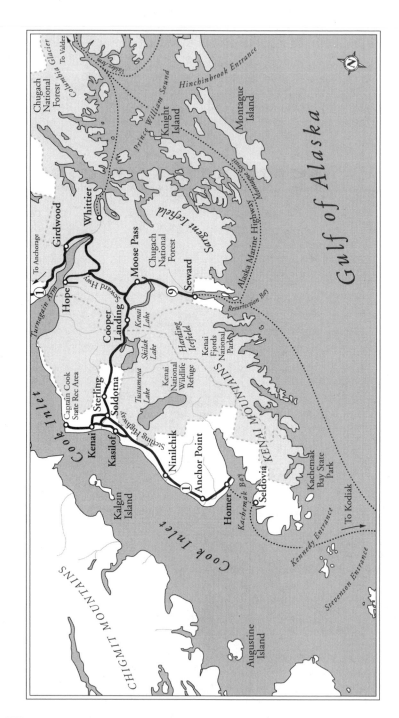

KENAI PENINSULA

Two hundred years ago, when the famous British navigator Captain James Cook sailed into the waters that today bear his name (Cook Inlet), he explored down Turnagain Arm in his search for the elusive route to the fabled Northwest Passage. Alas, he had to turn again. Hence the name of one of the most dramatic bodies of water in all of Alaska. The road down Turnagain Arm from Anchorage is your entry to Alaska's greatest playground—the Kenai Peninsula.

The original Kenaitze people gave the land their name. Then Russian fur hunters arrived. Their influence is reflected today by other names—the little town of Ninilchik with its onion-domed church, Kasilof near the mouth of the Kenai River, Seldovia across Kachemak Bay. Little gold rushes sprang up. The promise of a brighter day is laced into the names of all those diggings, from the Resurrection Trail and Sunrise to the little town of Hope itself.

After World War II, a whole new wave of adventurers arrived—the homesteaders. The road didn't go very far then. So they picked a likely spot on the map, then hiked, rafted, or flew into the wilderness to stake their claims and live off the land. They built log cabins, planted vegetables, hunted moose, and raised their families in the woods, near the ocean, or by the rivers.

"In the beginning, we had just enough for a little grubstake," remembers Marge Mullen, one of the original homesteaders in Soldotna. "I found out what that meant—a few cartons of groceries and a trusty rifle." The Mullens were the first homesteading family on Soldotna Creek in 1947, and around them grew up the town of Soldotna—today a popular fishing destination for Kenai River salmon fishermen.

Today, throngs of Alaskans and visitors (you'll recognize them from the baseball caps pulled low over their brows and the crazed look in their eyes) barrel down the highway to the peninsula in summer for one big reason: fish. Not just any fish, but *big* fish—like king salmon and halibut. (The world-record king salmon was pulled out of this river in 1985, weighing 97 pounds.) Never mind that our poor finned friends have eluded the nets of many foreign countries in their journey of thousands of miles through the ocean back to their home rivers to spawn, or that they've also swum out of the jaws of larger fish and past the claws of hungry brown bears. No, for now they face the final test: combat fishing on the Kenai. Things get so chummy on the banks of the rivers here that all those flying hooks don't necessarily nail your dinner; some nail your neighbor's nose or rear end instead. The hospital in Soldotna has a pinup of a fisherman on their wall. Every painful hook pulled out from every body gets hooked up here in the same place it got yanked out. Just in case you're wondering, no place has been left unhooked.

Fishing folk have every right to be wild about the Kenai River. It's truly extraordinary. Not only is it gorgeous, but it's also home to the largest race of salmon (size-wise) to swim up any river in the world. It is phenomenally productive. No river in the world, crossed by bridges, with two cities on either side of it, has sustained such a run. That's the challenge. Today, the river's health is a hot topic and has all government agencies in the state pondering its growing problems: maintenance of clean habitat, integrity of streambanks, and control of waste water. If you fish and you love the Kenai, it is vital to educate yourself and do your part.

Lest you think fishing is the last word here, the Kenai Peninsula has a glorious spectrum of all that is wonderful about Alaska: sheer beauty, massive icefields, crystal blue glaciers, dramatic fjords, dozens of hiking trails, and huge glacial green lakes. The exquisite emerald waters of Kenai Lake tumble into the Kenai River, which then cascades through the canyon into Skilak Lake ("Lake of the Sky") and around Caribou and Frying Pan Islands. The lake waters flow back into the river again and on in grandeur down to Cook Inlet. A national park, a national forest, a lovely state park, and a huge wildlife refuge cover most of this peninsula. In between are a few towns and a handful of hamlets. With so much accessible beauty, you could happily spend an entire summer here and never come close to doing it all.

ACCESS AND INFORMATION

Most people get to the Kenai Peninsula by car. If you are in a hurry, you can fly there from the Anchorage airport via smaller commuter airlines. Others come by ship, ferry, or fishing boat into the ports of Seward or Homer.

The **SEWARD HIGHWAY** (Alaska Route 1 to Route 9 on your map) runs from Anchorage to Seward. Along the way is the **HOPE TURNOFF**, which you'll reach after about an hour and a half of driving. The road to Hope is about 17 miles long and makes for a nice round-trip bike ride from the highway into the little town of Hope. Two hours or so into your journey, the highway splits. If you bear left, you will continue on the Seward Highway through Moose Pass to road's end at **SEWARD** on Resurrection Bay. That takes about a half hour. Many of the cruise ships dock in Seward.

If you bear right (west), you're now on the **STERLING HIGHWAY**, which will take you to Cooper Landing, past Kenai Lake, alongside the Kenai River, through the mountains to the flats, and into **SOLDOTNA** (about an hour's drive). From Soldotna, the road continues south for about 2 hours to **HOMER** and Kachemak Bay. At the highway's "Y" in

Soldotna, if you turn right onto the **KENAI SPUR HIGHWAY**, you will pass the town of Kenai and end 35 miles later at Captain Cook State Recreation Area on the shores of Cook Inlet.

During tourist season (mid-May through mid-September), the **ALASKA RAILROAD** runs one round-trip train a day, called *The Coastal Classic*, between Anchorage and Seward, stopping in Portage en route. The journey takes about 4½ hours and costs $90 round-trip.

In downtown Anchorage, **ALASKA PUBLIC LANDS INFORMATION CENTER** (605 W 4th Ave; 907/271-2737) has reams of information on trails, forests, refuges, and parks and will help you plot your journey. You can research available **PUBLIC-USE CABINS** on federal lands ($25 to $40 per night), then call the national toll-free line for reservations (877/444-6777). To reserve cabins on state lands ($35 per night), call the Department of Natural Resources Public Information Center (907/269-8400). There are also visitor centers in every town along the way, as well as park, forest, and refuge headquarters.

Portage Glacier and the Seward Highway

The drive from Anchorage to Seward takes approximately 3 hours. You cruise along **TURNAGAIN ARM**, through Chugach State Park into Chugach National Forest, past the state's most popular glacier, into the mountains, and end up in Seward, headquarters for Kenai Fjords National Park.

PORTAGE GLACIER and its iceberg-filled lake, an hour into your journey, is one of Alaska's treasures. With such proximity to the big city, it draws more tourists than any other attraction in the state. It even beats visitation to our highest mountain, Mount McKinley, in Denali National Park, by about 100,000 people a year. You can gaze from shore or take the **PORTAGE GLACIER CRUISES** (907/783-2983) from May through September (weather and ice conditions permitting). They run five 1-hour tours daily. The cost is $25 for adults, half-price for children. If you have time, be sure to watch the short film, *Voices From the Ice*, inside the theater at the **BEGICH, BOGGS VISITORS CENTER** (907/783-2326). The visitors center is open daily in summer and for long weekends in winter. In winter, the glacier takes on a severe and even eerie quality. Icebergs freeze into the lake, forming giant blue sculptures.

From here, you wind into the mountains and cross **TURNAGAIN PASS**, a popular skiing and snowmobiling area in winter. The cutoff to **HOPE** is a nice 34-mile round trip and is not heavily traveled. Hope is a sweet little collection of wood buildings at the edge of Turnagain Arm (see also Access and Information, above).

DRIVING TIPS

The drive down the Seward and Sterling Highways is spectacular in all seasons. But be aware that the word "highway" in Alaska really means "road" anywhere else. En route you will travel through park, forest, and refuge lands, and along glacially fed lakes and rivers. You'll curve around large bodies of salt water, through mountains and lowlands. Remember, too, that if you break down, you may be miles from any help. This is particularly important in the winter. Carry emergency survival gear with you in the car. This means flares, flashlight, warm clothes, warm shoes, a sleeping bag, extra food, and water. Double-check that you have tools for changing your own tires. Good footgear cannot be overemphasized. Pumps and hose won't get you very far if you have to walk for gas in the middle of winter. Winter or summer, day or night, drive with your headlights on. And watch for animals. Every year people slam into moose and bears, especially at night. If you see moose on the side of the road, slow down quietly. They are apt to bolt over the road right in front of you, then get transfixed by your headlights.

—Nan Elliot

Farther on, after the road splits, you'll pass through **MOOSE PASS**, named for an ornery moose who wouldn't budge off the old dog team trail that ran through here. If you have any knives, bring them and look for the water wheel on the right side of the road. A handwritten note says: "Moose Pass is a peaceful little town. If you have an ax to grind, DO IT HERE!" At least one four-star restaurateur we know from Anchorage sharpens his kitchen knives here on his way to go fishing in Seward.

Seward

While the Kenai Peninsula is famous for fish, it's also a great place to see glaciers. Seward is the easiest and best place to do both. The year-round population is about 2,000, but beware that it can swell to about 30,000 around the popular Fourth of July weekend festivities.

The town was named after William Seward, secretary of state under President Andrew Johnson, who engineered the purchase of Alaska from Russia in 1867. His critics around the country were appalled. The United States had spent $7.2 million, they cried, for icebergs and polar bears. Cartoonists showed Seward amid glaciers and walruses. They claimed the new territory should more aptly be called "Walrussia" or "Seward's Folly." Asked at the end of his long and distinguished career about his single greatest achievement, Seward responded, "The purchase of

Alaska! But it will take Congress and the American people a generation to find it out."

That original purchase price has been paid back thousands of times over in fur, gold, fish, timber, and oil. Ironically, now tourists come (and pay) to see icebergs, walruses, polar bears, and glaciers. While you'll see plenty of ice in Seward, you won't see walruses or polar bears this far south, unless you come for a strange event the third week of January, known as the Seward Polar Bear Jumpoff Festival. When everyone else is wearing parkas and wool hats, strange characters in costumes and capes—all for charity and the theater of the absurd—plunge into the frigid waters of Resurrection Bay and come flying back out. It's their entry fee to an elite and wacky club, the Polar Bear Club.

Resurrection Bay is the best of Seward, an inviting front yard, attracting boaters, birders, kayakers, fishermen, sailors, and whale watchers. Full of glaciers and incredible wildlife, all the western coast of the bay is in KENAI FJORDS NATIONAL PARK. Seward is the beginning of the railroad to Fairbanks and Mile 0 on the old historic Seward to Nome gold rush/mail route, today more familiarly known as the Iditarod Trail.

ACCESS AND INFORMATION

The SEWARD VISITORS INFORMATION CENTER (907/224-8051, fax 907/224-5353; chamber@seward.net) is located at the Seward Chamber of Commerce, Mile 2, at the north end of town and is open year-round. The visitors center for KENAI FJORDS NATIONAL PARK (PO Box 1727, Seward, AK 99664; 907/224-3175) is headquartered at the Seward small-boat harbor, close to the harbormaster. (See also Access and Information, above).

EXPLORING

Cruise the BOARDWALK filled with fishing charters and fjord tours. This is a great jumping-off place for both. Stroll the docks and look at the boats. Stop in at BARDARSON STUDIOS (800/478-7848), a fun store filled with books, art, and interesting Alaska stuff. In the heart of downtown, espresso, scones, and delicious pastries await at THE RANTING RAVEN BAKERY (228 4th Ave; 907/224-2228). The specialties of the house are upside-down cakes (don't miss the one with raspberries) and all kinds of fanciful scones (the banana white chocolate scone is a killer). In a big A-frame building, directly across the street from the harbormaster, is THE MILLER'S DAUGHTER (1215 4th Ave; 907/224-6091), a tasty and hopping place for breakfast or lunch, with freshly baked organic breads, sweet cream pastries, scones, bagels, homemade vegetarian soups, and a variety of sandwiches. SMOKE'N ALASKA SEAFOODS (1401 N Harbor Rd; 907/224-5190) in Seward's small boat harbor is a good place for a quick and light lunch of fried halibut and chips or a seafood pita wrap if you're going hiking and forgot lunch. While in town, visit a sweet little renovated church for the best espresso and interesting art, cleverly named **RESURRECT ART** (320 3rd Ave; 907/224-7161); two coffee tables are tucked up in the choir loft "closer to God" along with the office of the local environmentalist. A charming old-time Alaskan, Margaret Branson, runs **RESURRECTION BAY GALERIE** (500 4th Ave; 907/224-3212, fax 907/224-5990) downtown in a historic home, featuring all original works of art. She also offers a fun room with private bath tucked upstairs as a B&B, which will make you burst out laughing—it is truly an artist's creation—bright red walls, even the ceiling, and yellow floral bedspread, with a glimpse of the bay.

ALASKA SEALIFE CENTER / Opened to great fanfare in 1998, this marine wildlife research center is an elegant architectural bridge from the edge of the land in downtown Seward out into the sea. Located on Resurrection Bay, it gives scientists, students, and visitors "a window to the sea." You can watch Steller sea lions and harbor seals basking on the rocks or frolicking beneath the water and actually get close enough to learn the difference between tufted and horned puffins, those funny little clownlike birds that "fly" underwater. The sea otter exhibit is scheduled to open in the summer of 2000. Compared to aquariums Outside, it is not nearly so extensive, but it is extraordinary for its location and its mission. After the oil spill in Alaska waters from the *Exxon Valdez* in 1989, there was a movement of great urgency to fund a world-class facility in this northern climate for research, rehabilitation, and public education. It is the only cold-water marine research facility in the western hemisphere. The cost is $12.50 for adults; $10 for children up to age 16. Mile 0, Seward Hwy, PO Box 1329, Seward, AK 99664; 907/224-6300, fax 907/224-6320; every day May–mid-Oct, Wed–Sun in winter.

CHUGACH NATIVE HERITAGE CENTER / Right next to the Alaska SeaLife Center, co-anchoring the edge of the bay, the Native Heritage Center is also a treat, housed in the original old railroad depot built in the bungalow style of the early 1900s. Alaska's architectural history is very young and most has crumbled into the forest (such as old miner and trapper cabins, never built to last the centuries) or been bulldozed to make way for a lot of glitzy, poorly constructed buildings when the oil boom came. The charm of the old is preserved here. The depot was built in 1917 and was used by the Alaska Railroad until the Great Alaska Earthquake of 1964. After the earthquake, Seward lost sea frontage and rails. So, it became the terminal for the state ferry system. But today the ferries come in next to the cruise ship dock and near the current railroad depot. Chugach Native Corporation leases the building and has put more than $1 million into the renovation and restoration. The building is the

A GOOSE-TONGUE ADVENTURE

Some years ago, an old-timer friend in Seward took me to her favorite tidal goose-tongue patch on Resurrection Bay. The wind was blowing so hard we could not stand or talk. So we got down on hands and knees and went picking the salty greens. The wind was quite cold. Suddenly, Lila started crawling toward her car. I picked even faster, thinking we'd have to leave. Continuing to pick, I looked back and saw her crawling back in my direction dragging two large quilts. Struggling wildly, she got one over me while holding the other one down. Then she crawled under it and together we crawled along the beach, filling our big basket with thousands of goose tongues, a delicious tidal plantain. At last, we crawled back to the car. I powered the door open and we squeezed in with all our gear. We were almost blown away. Sitting there for a moment, Lila, who was about 80 then, said, "Kid, we got 'em."

—Joan Daniels

original green of the old depot, and the railroad theme is continued inside, which has been made into a beautiful art gallery of Native art with most everything for sale. Every hour in the summer, a half-hour play, *So They Say* (written and directed by Jane Lind), about the story of creation and the circle of life from the perspective of the Chugach and Aleut people, is featured. With wonderful costumes, it's a delight to see. 501 Railroad Ave; 800/947-5065 or 907/224-5065.

LOWELL POINT / Lowell Point is only about 3 miles south of downtown Seward, but it is a whole other way of life—many quaint, graying, weather-beaten homemade cabins mix among stands of dead trees, killed when the land sank into salt water during the 1964 earthquake, making good perches for eagles. Electricity came only within the last five years. As one resident said, "Architecture here takes a defensive stand against the ocean." The one road in and out, known as Lowell Point Loop Road by the residents there, is framed by the ocean on one side and steep mountains on the other. Sometimes waves wash over the road. However, on a beautiful day, it's a wonderful place to be and a good place for spotting whales, sea lions, and sea otters. There are a few quaint and funky B&Bs to stay in. Lowell Point also offers access to Caines Head State Recreation Area; see Adventures in this section.

ADVENTURES

MOUNT MARATHON / The mountain was named for the marathon races up to its summit (4,603 feet). The first "mountain marathon" was in 1915, and the tradition continues every Fourth of July. You can recognize competitors by the mud and blood. Try climbing this conical mountain any clear day in summer for a grand view over ice, snow, glaciers, and fjords. You'll discover that for part of the climb you're reduced to all fours. Then try to run down the mountain in as much time as it takes the winners to go both up and down (about 50 minutes total). The descent is half airborne, flying and sliding down snowfields and scree slopes. Good luck. Mortal folk take about 3 to 4 hours round-trip.

CRUISE KENAI FJORDS NATIONAL PARK / The immense Harding Icefield dominates the landscape of this park, the reservoir for a myriad of spectacular glaciers rumbling down the mountains to plunge into deepwater fjords. The best way to see the park is to take a flight-seeing tour or—even more popular—to take a day cruise from Seward down Resurrection Bay. You'll see calving ice, puffins, seals, whales, and great mountain and sea vistas. On cloudy days, the glaciers reflect deeper blues and the mists from the sea make the whole adventure that much more dramatic. Birdwatchers should take the tour that goes out to the Chiswell Islands, which rise out of the sea like floating honeycombs and swarm with life, from Steller sea lions to colonies of puffins. Every ledge, at every altitude on the rock face, seems to hold a different species. Down near tideline are the graceful kittiwakes and funny oystercatchers. Up high, the clown-faced puffins hang glide off their nesting sites. Several different operations will take you out for scenic cruises in the park; you'll find their offices at or near the small boat harbor. One of the oldest, established in 1974, is **KENAI FJORDS TOURS** (800/478-8068 or 907/276-6249; www.kenaifjords.com) in Anchorage. **MARIAH TOURS AND CHARTERS** (907/224-8623), operating since 1981, has smaller boats for perhaps a more intimate view. **ALASKA RENOWN CHARTERS** (907/224-3806) takes passengers summer and winter. **MAJOR MARINE TOURS** (800/764-7300 or 907/274-7300; www.majormarine.com) has a national park ranger on board every cruise to serve as naturalist. **ALASKA CATAMARAN CRUISES** (907/276-5959 or 888/305-2515; www.wildlifequest.com) has high-speed catamarans for whale watching and wildlife viewing; cost for the 6-hour cruise is $105.

VISIT EXIT GLACIER / Drive to Exit Glacier, also part of the Kenai Fjords National Park, and walk up to the face of a glacier. Not too close, though: calving ice is dangerous. A tourist was killed here a few years ago, while standing under overhanging ice that broke off at precisely the wrong moment. Remember, glaciers are rivers of moving ice. There's a comfortable nature loop trail for easy walking, and a steep 3-mile scramble up the rock at the side of the glacier to an overlook of the **HARDING ICEFIELD** for more energetic hikers. Watch for bears. The road to Exit Glacier turns off the Seward Highway at Mile 3.7 and leads 9 miles to the ranger station and parking lot for the glacier. The road is closed in winter. Access to the glacier then is by cross-country skis or snowmobile.

There is a public-use cabin available in winter. For more information, stop in at the headquarters to the Kenai Fjords National Park near the harbormaster's at the Seward marina (907/224-3175).

GO DOG MUSHING / If you are an Iditarod Trail Sled Dog Race fan, love dogs, or are intrigued by one of the great romantic pursuits of Alaskans, you'll enjoy meeting Iditarod musher Mitch Seavey and his family. They'll introduce you to the real heroes of the race, like Joe Joe (named after Joe Redington, Sr., "The Father of the Iditarod"), Dophin, Elvis, Blue, Rambler, Iceman, Badger, Barracuda, and a host of other Alaska sled dogs who train with Mitch every year for the one of the greatest races in the world, running across Alaska from Anchorage to Nome on the Bering Sea coast. In 1998, his best race ever, Mitch and his team came in fourth over the 1,049-mile trail. His father, Dan Seavey, mushed in the original race in 1973, when he came in third, and then in the silver anniversary of the Iditarod in 1997. The family conducts **IDI-TARIDE SLED DOG TOURS** (800/478-3139 or 907/224-8607) starting from their dog kennel. They have more than 70 sled dogs. You get to pet the puppies while they talk about the race, the sleds, clothing, and gear. Then they hook up two teams and take you on a wilderness run on trails via carts. Tours run 1½ hours, daily, May through September; winter tours by arrangement. PO Box 2906, Seward, AK 99664, summer; PO Box 735, Sterling, AK 99672, winter.

GO FISHING / There are dozens of charters for halibut and salmon fishing with little offices on the boardwalk or near the small boat harbor. If you're on a peanut-butter-and-jelly budget, fish from shore. You won't be alone. It seems nearly every mom-and-pop rig on the highway stops in at Seward to set up lawn chairs by the edge of the sea and wet a line. The second week of August is the **SEWARD SILVER SALMON DERBY**, the granddaddy fishing derby of them all on the peninsula. You might not only catch dinner, but also win a bundle of dough ($10,000) if you catch the biggest salmon, or even more dough if you hook the right salmon (some of them are specially tagged with coded tags worth anywhere from $25,000 to $50,000). For more information, call the Seward Chamber of Commerce (907/224-8051).

GO SEA KAYAKING / **SUNNY COVE KAYAKING COMPANY** (907/345-5339; www.sunnycove.com) can take you on 3- to 5-day kayaking adventures in Resurrection Bay and Kenai Fjords National Park, starting at $600 per person. In conjunction with Kenai Fjords Tours (800/770-9119), they also offer a half-day paddle around Fox Island combined with the wildlife cruise and salmon bake for $139 per person. Smaller, but more personalized, **ALASKA KAYAK CAMPING COMPANY** (PO Box 1101, Seward 99664; 907/224-6056 for multiday trips; 907/224-2323 for day trips; kayakcamp@hotmail.com; www.seward.net/kayakcamp), run by an enthusiastic retired Navy man, Bob Ceelen, conducts day trips with lessons or overnight trips. He has about a half a dozen doubles. His day trips are $98 per person and his evening trips are about $50 per person. He offers three trips: day trips to Caines Head and Tonsina Creek to see sea otters and sea lions; an overnight at Thumb's Cove across the bay where four major rivers converge and you can see three glaciers; and Bear Glacier Lagoon, 12 miles out across from Fox Island. He even does guided fishing from a kayak. His motto: "Catch a Coho in a Kayak!" **KAYAK AND CUSTOM ADVENTURES** (414 K St; 907/258-3866 in Anchorage; 907/224-3960 in Seward; 800/288-3134 outside Alaska) also offers day trips ($95 per person) out of Seward all summer long. They are experienced outfitters located in downtown Anchorage.

WALK THE COASTAL TRAIL / Caines Head State Recreation Area has a 4½-mile cliff and beach hike from Lowell Point to North Beach. Be aware that a portion of this trail can be walked only at low tide. Pick up a tide table and directions from the Seward Visitors Information Center. The trail begins at the Lowell Point parking lot, a mile from downtown Seward, on the western side of Resurrection Bay.

GO HIKING / There are some wonderful trails near Seward for hiking, mountain biking, and skiing, oftentimes with a public-use cabin for rent nearby. Many of the trails are located in the Chugach National Forest. Stop by the **SEWARD RANGER DISTRICT** (334 4th Ave; 907/224-3374) for a free handout of trails with maps and descriptions and to check on the latest trail conditions. Some of the beautiful trails are (round-trip) the 16-mile **PRIMROSE TRAIL**, 14-mile **LOST LAKE TRAIL**, 15-mile **PTARMIGAN CREEK TRAIL**, 7-mile **CARTER LAKE TRAIL**, and the 32-mile **RESURRECTION RIVER TRAIL**. If you wanted to hike all the way from Seward to Hope—72 miles—via trails with access to cabins, you'd go from the Resurrection River Trail to the Russian Lakes Trail and then the Resurrection Pass Trail. Wherever you go, practice "leave no trace" camping and pack out all garbage.

STAY IN A PUBLIC-USE CABIN / Many of the 18 cabins in the Seward Ranger District of the **CHUGACH NATIONAL FOREST** are quite remote—you cannot hike to them but must fly in, which ups the ante of the very reasonable, indeed, very cheap cost of staying, about $25 to $40 per night. Cabins near Seward include one on the Lost Lake Trail; Upper Paradise Lake Cabin and Lower Paradise Lake Cabin (both fly-in cabins); Resurrection River Cabin on Resurrection River Trail; and Crescent Lake Cabin and Crescent Saddle Cabin on Crescent Creek Trail. Cabins may be reserved by calling the National Reservation System (877/444-6777). Out in Resurrection Bay, there are several state park cabins for rent at $50 per night. Four of them are "great," say locals: one at Pony Cove; two at Thumb's Cove; and one at Calisto Canyon. Call Caines Head State Recreation Area (907/269-8400) for reservations.

RUN TO LOST LAKE / If you happen to be around Seward the third week of August and love running through wilderness, there is a 16-mile cross-country race through beautiful country from Primrose Campground at the end of Kenai Lake at Mile 18.8 on the Seward Highway to 6 miles north of Seward—**THE LOST LAKE BREATH OF LIFE RUN** (www.lostlakerun.org), a benefit to raise money for the Cystic Fibrosis Foundation. Since its first year in 1992, it has become popular with serious runners, fun runners, dog walkers, and even Olympic skiers. It has a reputation for being well organized and fun, with beer and a barbecue at the finish.

RESTAURANTS

Apollo Restaurant / ★

229 4TH AVE, SEWARD; 907/224-3092

The pizza is great. The Greek salad is tasty. The waiters are spicy. And the decor is one of ruins and gods and goddesses with a mixed menu of Greek and Italian specialties. *$$; AE, MC, V; local checks only; lunch, dinner every day; beer and wine; downtown Seward.*

Harbor Dinner Club / ★

220 5TH AVE, SEWARD; 907/224-3012

This is old-time Seward, tucked into a quiet corner of downtown. If things are too swinging at the small boat harbor, you can find a peaceful evening here sipping wine and eating beer-batter-fried halibut, seafood fettuccine, a croissant turkey sandwich, or fish and chips. They also do well with steak and prime rib. *$$; AE, DC, DIS, MC, V; local checks only; lunch, dinner every day; full bar; downtown.*

Le Barn Appetit Restaurant & Bakery / ★★

MILE 3.5, SEWARD HWY AT RESURRECTION RD, SEWARD; 907/224-8706, FAX 907/224-8461

This is a warm, hilarious, all-around family dining experience rolled into one. In addition, the food is delicious. Yvon, head chef and baker, was raised in Belgium. He's probably the most experienced chef in Seward, and a character to boot. His quiche is awesome, eclairs are wonderful, and he makes an excellent apple pie. He has also sailed with Jacques Cousteau and has a few wild stories from that era. (Ask about the shark skeleton in his bone museum on the second floor.) If that isn't enough, Le Barn is also a health-food store and a bed-and-breakfast. It's quite a menagerie out here and many lost children have found a home in its midst. Things get so busy that it's hard to run the business like a business all the time. But that's part of the experience. It's definitely worth the trip. *$$; MC, V; checks OK; breakfast, lunch, dinner every day (it can be hit-or-miss, but always worth the effort); no alcohol.*

Ray's Waterfront / ★★★

1316 4TH AVE, SEWARD; 907/224-5606
If you want gourmet and continental, go to Ray's—good appetizers, good seafood dishes, good wine list, good views, and good crowds. It's packed all summer. Some of their specialties and favorites are the pan-seared Thai scallops, Halibut Andaman roasted in macadamia nuts and sweet lime chili sauce, and cedar-planked salmon. If you're vegetarian (and even if you are not) don't miss a particular favorite—the Torta Rustica, a slice of pie baked in crust with a delicious blend of ricotta cheese, spinach, red peppers, and eggplant, accompanied by a lovely light dinner salad of onions, feta cheese, and black currants or cranberries for a sweet-tart flavor. While you wait, warm sourdough bread comes with a plate of olive oil mixed with pesto for dipping. If you don't want to wait for a table, go to the bar for drinks and appetizers like the roasted elephant garlic or mussels sauteed with fresh ginger, lime, and cilantro—and that's just for starters. *$$–$$$; AE, DC, MC, V; local checks only; lunch, dinner every day; closed Nov–Mar; full bar; overlooking the Seward Small Boat Harbor.*

LODGINGS

Connections

VARIOUS ADDRESSES THROUGHOUT TOWN, SEWARD, AK 99664;
907/224-5695 OR 907/224-2323
Connections is a personalized B&B booking and referral service run by a warm-spirited resident of Seward—Deborah Hafemeister. There are more than 100 B&Bs from Moose Pass to Seward, ranging from a room tucked up in the attic of an art gallery to more standard rooms in modern houses to cabins by the water or in the forest. Very few are true inns as most people from Outside are accustomed to expect. So B&Bs go in and out of business with some regularity in Alaska. One of the best ways to book is to go through Deborah's referral service so you get exactly what you're looking for. *www.alaskasview.com; PO Box 312, Seward, AK 99664.*

Hotel Edgewater

200 5TH AVE, SEWARD, AK 99664; 907/224-2700 OR 888/793-6800,
FAX 907/224-2701
Newly opened in 1999 in downtown Seward, this three-story hotel has 76 rooms and suites, dressed up in autumn colors of burgundies and reds.

There are 10 room types with different prices each season, beginning with the standard queen, which goes for $165 in summer and drops to $75 from October through April. The "Bayview Queen," with sliding doors onto a balcony overlooking Resurrection Bay, goes for $225 in summer. Six rooms have nice views of the bay. For the most part, though, the hotel did not take advantage of the great views from its location. The rooms are motel-like and uninspired. *$$$; DIS, MC, V; no checks; no restaurant/bar; edgewater@seward.net; www.hoteledgewater.com; PO Box 1570, Seward, AK 99664; downtown.* &

Sauerdough Lodging / ★★★

225 4TH AVE, SEWARD, AK 99664; 907/224-8946 OR 877/224-8946, FAX 907/224-8980

If you're into history, characters, downtown living, a hilarious and charming host, personalized service, and yummy wholesome and fun breakfasts, this is the hotel for you. Europeans especially love it, but we love it too! Book early: it fills fast. Your host, Gordon Turner, who once ran the old ice cream parlor downstairs, is known as "Duck Man Del Norte" and you'll understand why when he gives you the tour. The building itself is very historic, built in the early days of Seward's history by a German fellow named Sauer (thus, you see, the play on words in the name of the B&B). It was a warehouse and trading post, and upstairs where you'll be staying was originally where the young men who were building the railroad bunked. Mrs. Sauer was French. And she had a French friend, known only to history now as "The Lady in White" or "Madame" (the name was more than honorific). So Gordon refers to her as Madame LeBlanc, and it is her suite of rooms in the front looking over the street that is the most grand. There were French doors into her private quarters and men came here to dance with the other girls who lived in the adjoining rooms. Miss Ivy and Miss Barbara's suites of rooms are the two smallest, accommodating three people each, at $140 a night; Annie and Danielle's rooms can accommodate five each at $165 a night. And Madame LeBlanc's is $225 a night (tucking in seven folks and sometimes a ghost). Gordon serves wonderful fresh fruit breakfasts with Belgian waffles, cinnamon rolls, scones, or coffee cake and yogurt with granola. On the newly renovated main floor, there are four rooms ($79 each), a dining room with breakfast buffet, and a small museum. Nonsmoking environment. *$–$$; AE, DC, DIS, MC, V; checks OK; breakfast May–Sept; suites@ptialaska.net; downtown Seward.*

BED-AND-BREAKFASTS

DOWNTOWN / If you're looking for historical, **BALLAINE HOUSE LODGING** (437 3rd Ave, PO Box 2051, Seward, AK 99664; 907/224-2362), a two-story white house with red-and-blue trim, is the oldest building in town, home of one of the early settlers of Seward. Five rooms share one bathroom ($50 for a single; $75 for a double in summer; no smoking), but the hospitality is wonderful and they serve a huge breakfast. **ANNIE'S B&B** (531 3rd Ave, PO Box 1213, Seward, AK 99664; 907/224-8905) is another historic landmark located on "Millionaire's Row," and Annie does a nice job as hostess. **FALLS INN** (1103 2nd Ave, PO Box 2064, Seward, AK 99664; 907/224-5790), hosted by Louis and Diane Bencardino, opened its doors in 1997 and has been a popular spot. Stay here if you are not running from the law, as Mr. Bencardino is the former mayor and chief of police in Seward. And don't forget the little red room with private bath tucked above the art gallery, available May through September at **RESURRECTION BAY GALLERIE B&B** (500 4th Ave, PO Box 271, Seward, AK 99664; 907/224-3212, fax 907/224-5990), "for fine art lovers."

LOWELL POINT / ALASKA SALTWATER LODGE (PO Box 695, Seward, AK 99664; 907/224-5271) sits right on the ocean with a beautiful view from the large windows of the common room. The bedrooms are simple, bathrooms small—it's a bit like living on a boat. It's probably best if you have a bunch of buddies—like fishing or hiking pals—and rent the whole house. But if not, the cost is $85 for a double. Your hosts are Jim and Kathleen Barkley. **OCEAN FRONT BED & BREAKFAST** (PO Box 3322, Seward, AK 99664; 907/224-5699 or 907/362-1698) offers a charming room with a separate deck ($85 for a double) in a big wood house overlooking the water, the home of Butch and Gloria Sears.

CABINS OR ALASKA-STYLE / For many, the romance of being in Alaska is being tucked into your own little cabin or being in a log home surrounded by Alaska decor. **ALASKA STONEY CREEK INN B&B** (PO Box 1352, Seward, AK 99664; 907/224-3940, fax 907/224-2683) offers "Alaska country comfort." To get there, turn onto Lake Drive at Mile 6.5 of the Seward Highway and watch for signs. **ALASKA TREEHOUSE** (Mile 7, Seward Hwy, PO Box 861, Seward, AK 99664; 907/224-3867, fax 907/224-3978; treehouse@seward.net) is situated, not surprisingly, in the trees, with hiking trails at your doorstep and a wood-fired sauna and hot tub. They offer a huge breakfast of sourdough pancakes or waffles smothered in warm homemade berry jams. **BOX CANYON CABINS** (HCR Box 3509, Seward, AK 99664; 907/224-5046, fax 907/224-7651; cabin@ptialaska.net; www. Alaskan.com/sewardcabins) are tucked into the woods off the road to Exit Glacier—four log cabins (one historic and three new ones) with fully equipped kitchens are available. Your hosts are Shawn, Karie, and Halie VanDeusen. **CREEKSIDE CABINS** (on Old Exit Glacier Rd, PO Box 1514, Seward AK 99664; 907/224-3834) are handmade and quite sweet, sitting beside a stream where you can see salmon running in season. They'll fire up the sauna for you, too, if you wish. **RENFRO'S LAKESIDE RETREAT** (HC 64, Box 459, Seward, AK 99664; 907/288-5059 or 877/288-5059) sits on the edge of Kenai Lake about 8 miles from Moose Pass and 20 miles from Seward. Kenai Lake is one of the most beautiful lakes in the world. The log cabins are tucked on the edge of the forest with a view over the lake. Each has a loft, bath, and kitchen. Your hosts are Sharon and Mike Renfro.

WILDERNESS LODGES

Kenai Fjords Wilderness Lodge

PO BOX 1889, DEPT. SEW, SEWARD, AK 99664; 907/224-8068 OR 800/478-8068, FAX 907/224-8934
Accessible only by boat, the lodge is on Fox Island, 14 miles south of Seward in scenic Resurrection Bay. There are special overnight packages, where you stay in peaceful, private cabins, enjoy hiking with a naturalist, and kayak. Delicious, hearty meals with all-you-can-eat salmon complete the package. The next day climb aboard the return boat home for a half-day Kenai Fjords glacier and wildlife cruise en route. Owned and operated by Kenai Fjords Tours, the lodges cater to both day and overnight guests. There are two lodges—the larger, which can accommodate up to 300 people, is where the day tours out of Seward to the national park come for an afternoon or evening meal. The smaller, cozier lodge belongs to the overnight guests, who all live in small cabins in Halibut Cove with the ocean at their front doorstep. There is running water and hot showers, but no electricity, and phone contact is minimal. So leave your worries at home. This is a lovely experience if you have the money. It's sold as part of package, which includes your hourlong boat ride to the island, 2-person cabin accommodations, all meals, and a half-day cruise for $299 per person. *AE, DC, DIS, MC, V; no checks; open early May–mid-Sept; all meals provided; alcohol available.*

The Sterling Highway

Presuming you took the right-hand turn rather than continuing straight to Seward, you are now on the Sterling Highway, which will take you all the way to Homer.

The first part of the highway winds along a sparkling river to **KENAI LAKE**. If it's a sunny day, pause at the lake and breathe in its beauty, reflecting like a turquoise-and-emerald jewel in the summer and pure gold in fall. The road soon hugs the mountains, with the **KENAI RIVER** tumbling on the other side. You'll quickly pass through the hamlet of **COOPER LANDING**, which is the best place to put in for floating or fishing the Upper

WILD THINGS TO EAT

When foraging for wild foods, you'll need multiple containers for gathering. The easiest to use, I find, are a basket and some clear plastic bags. They're lightweight and you can identify your harvest instantly while keeping everything moist (unless the day gets too warm). A damp cloth or large cool leaves dipped in water laid over all will work. A small sharp knife and a little garden clipper are helpful. A few paper towels are good too. Woven-basket backpacks are great for carrying all your tools and treasures. Remember this: on the most casual walk, have a plastic bag or two in your pocket. Expect the unexpected. Keep different plants separate—they'll sometimes want separate treatment.

If you look on the nutrient chart, you'll find that dandelions make everything else you eat look like a major waste of chewing time. In picking dandelions, take as much of the root as possible. Wash it well and chop it along with the greens, or dry it in a basket for winter tea. It has enormous quantities of minerals. Many brave and vibrant greens grow in moist places near streams and in the mist of waterfalls. This is the water ouzel's garden. Beautiful little cress plants can be plucked, roots and all. The scallop-leaf saxifrage and the sourgrass (actually a sorrel with tender-tart leaves) can be easily cut by the clump. Violet leaves are tiny, but plentiful, and found along streams where moose forage when willow leaves first emerge. You'll find they are sweet and tender, with oodles of vitamin C.

If you're terrified of trying wild mushrooms, halt that pronto. It spoils a lot of fun. Get a good book on Alaska mushrooms and get going. By following the rules and very simple tests, you'll find several indisputable varieties that are delicious. When you collect different types, keep them separate. Apparently they can be perfectly innocent and safe until they kiss another species. Then their little enzymes begin some devilish dance and can become very wicked.

Wherever you are, the smallest strip of unpaved ground will be growing something you can eat. Look at the surroundings and decide whether to pluck it. Go looking. If you garden, you'll be meeting all the relatives of your vegetables and herbs. Also, seek out people known for eating wild foods. They're your best resource.

—Joan Daniels

Kenai River (far more peaceful and beautiful than the Lower Kenai). Great hiking abounds all around you.

Farther on, there's a road to **SKILAK LAKE,** another great adventure and beautiful lake. (A word of warning to all paddlers on large lakes on the peninsula such as the Kenai, Skilak, and Tustumena: Pay attention. Winds can pick up, in the afternoons especially, and can fill these lakes with waves and turbulence as fierce as those of the ocean. Many unsuspecting boaters have drowned. Whatever you do, save the beer drinking for shore.)

Shortly, you will descend out of the mountains onto the flats of muskeg and swamp spruce. From here, it's a long, straight shot into **SOL-DOTNA**. Beyond Soldotna, the drive is through rolling hills alongside steep bluffs overlooking Cook Inlet, with some gorgeous views of the mountains and volcanos (**MOUNTS REDOUBT AND ILIAMNA**) across the inlet. Visit the picturesque little Russian church sitting up on the bluff at the village of **NINILCHIK**; then continue on past **ANCHOR POINT**, another great fishing destination for saltwater fishermen, and on into **HOMER**.

Cooper Landing

A tiny hamlet on the edge of the crystal blue-green waters of Kenai Lake and the Kenai River, Cooper Landing was named after an old gold prospector and Civil War veteran named Joseph Cooper who came here in 1884 looking for paydirt. He found traces of it in Cooper Creek, but more than that, he found extraordinary beauty. Originally, the place was known as Cooper's Landing. Only a handful of folks live here year-round, about 425. As you can see from the setting, it's a beautiful spot to take off into the mountains on hiking, biking, and skiing adventures. Trails abound. Pick up a copy of *Kenai Pathways: A Guide To Outstanding Wildland Trails of Alaska's Kenai Peninsula*, published by the Alaska Natural History Association and available in parks and visitors centers in Alaska. In the winter the local ski club, known informally as "The Moose-ski-teers," has all kinds of club activities you can join in such as the Full Moon Ski and Bonfire. Talk to David Rhode (907/595-1314; hylocichla@aol.com), a delightful character who grew up here and one of the local activists and movers-and-shakers.

ADVENTURES

GO HIKING / Lots of good hiking takes off in this area. The start or finish of the **RESURRECTION TRAIL**, depending on your direction, traverses the mountains from Cooper Landing to Hope, about 35 miles of walking with public-use cabins for rent along the way. A madhouse in salmon season, the trail along the Russian River to **LOWER AND UPPER RUSSIAN LAKES** is a lovely walk, once you get past all the fishermen. There are also cabins. At the **RUSSIAN RIVER FALLS**, in the right season, you can see those extraordinary salmon leaping up the falls. **COOPER LAKE** is also a nice walk. Pick up a copy of *55 Ways to the Wilderness in South-central Alaska* by Helen Nienhueser and John Wolfe, Jr. It's a marvelous guide to trails all over the Kenai Peninsula, around Anchorage, and in the Matanuska Valley, complete with detailed descriptions and directions.

RESTAURANTS

Eagles Crest / ★★

KENAI PRINCESS LODGE, COOPER LANDING; 800/426-0500, RESERVATIONS; 907/595-1425, HOTEL
A huge fire crackles in the fireplace in the dining room and the windows look out to spectacular mountains, covered with snow in winter and ablaze with colors in fall. The warm, lovely setting couldn't be more conducive for enjoying good company, a glass of nice wine, and a tasty plate of hors d'oeuvres, or a delicious bowl of tomato soup with garlic and basil. The entrees are filling but not overly memorable. Stick with the lighter fare for taste sensations. *$$–$$$; AE, DC, DIS, MC, V; local checks only; breakfast, lunch, dinner every day; full bar; in the main lodge.* &

Gwin's Lodge / ★

MILE 52, STERLING HWY, COOPER LANDING; 907/595-1266
This hand-built log lodge first opened for business in the 1950s and still has the old charm and '50s roadhouse atmosphere. "When Helen Gwin was cooking, you could arguably get the best hamburger in America here," says a local old-timer. There's a lot of grease flying around back there in the kitchen, but it's still friendly, fun, and a good homespun place to eat. After a day's fishing or floating, a beer and Gwin's Macho Nachos will leave you totally contented. A whole range of hearty appetizers (none slimming, but definitely yummy) and a wide variety of omelets, fish, steak, and burgers are also available. *$$; DIS, MC, V; local checks only; lunch, dinner in winter; open 24 hours a day in summer; full bar; gwin's@arctic.net; across the road from the Kenai River in Cooper Landing, past the bridge at Mile 52.*

LODGINGS

Kenai Princess Lodge / ★★★

MILE 47.7, STERLING HWY, COOPER LANDING, AK 99572; 800/426-0500, RESERVATIONS; 907/595-1425, HOTEL
Perched on the mountainside above the blue-green tumbling waters of the Kenai River, this is a grand wilderness lodge that caters to your romantic image of Alaska—rustic wood bungalows with woodstoves, a grand stone fireplace in the lobby, and outdoor decks with snowcapped mountains above and salmon-filled river below. The outdoor hot tubs are particularly fun on a star-filled winter evening after cross-country skiing. Princess Tours owns the operation, so the lodge (with 70 rooms and

suites) is hopping with tourists in the summer. If you want a more peaceful time, try winter, or fall when the peninsula is ablaze with colors. *$$$; AE, DC, MC, V, DISC; checks OK; PO Box 676, Cooper Landing, AK 99572; at the intersection of Bean Creek Rd.* &

Soldotna and Kenai

Folks come to Soldotna in droves to fish the Lower Kenai River. The community has no real "downtown," but the "Y" in the highway is often considered the center. The town grew up around the homesteaders, a special breed of folks who have plenty of stories to tell about the early days, which for this town were not so long ago. They started arriving after World War II, around 1947. If you're looking for an upscale or humorous Alaska gift, stop in at **NORTHCOUNTRY FAIR** (35082 Kenai Spur Hwy; 907/262-7715), which is a short distance after you turn right at the "Y" toward Kenai. Or if you're in the mood for really good coffee and a friendly atmosphere, stop in at **KALADI BROTHERS COFFEE** (315 S Kobuk St; 907/262-5980), located in the big turquoise building in Soldotna.

The "Y" is where you turn right to the oil town of **KENAI** and the **CAPTAIN COOK STATE RECREATION AREA** at the end of the road, about 35 miles. *Kenai,* loosely translated from the original peoples who settled here, the Dena'ina Athabascan Indians, means "two big flats and river cut-back." The town takes its name from the Kenaitze Indians, a branch of the Dena'inas. The history of Kenai (at 7,000 the largest town on the peninsula) is a mix of cultures from Dena'ina Athabascan to Russian fur traders to homesteaders to the most recent arrivals—oil workers.

ACCESS AND INFORMATION

The **SOLDOTNA VISITOR INFORMATION CENTER** (907/262-1337), open daily in summer (Mon–Fri the rest of the year), is located just south of the Kenai River Bridge on the Sterling Highway with a wooden stairway down to the Kenai River for an up-close view. The **KENAI NATIONAL WILDLIFE REFUGE** (907/262-7021) has headquarters in Soldotna, and the **KENAI VISITORS & CULTURAL CENTER** (11471 Kenai Spur Hwy; 907/283-1991; kvcb@alaska.net) is full of exhibits and information. See also the Access and Information section at the beginning of this chapter.

EXPLORING

RIVER CITY BOOKS & ESPRESSO CAFÉ / For the last 50 years, the Mullen family has been making a difference—whether it's preserving homestead history, protecting rivers, forests, and streambanks, adopting parks, starting a recycling movement or gourmet restaurant or bookstore, or sitting on the city council. They were the first homesteading family to settle here, and the town of Soldotna literally grew up around them. The latest venture of Peggy Mullen, the eldest daughter of homesteader Marge Mullen, is a lovely little bookstore on another corner of the homestead property. Opened in the summer of 1999, it is the only bookstore in Soldotna and, as with everything the Mullens do, it's tastefully and respectfully done. The little cafe uses fresh lettuce and vegetables from the garden in back for its salads and sandwiches, they serve a wicked espresso, and the desserts are decadent too. Books range from best-sellers to a large selection of books on Alaska and quite a delightful array of children's books. It's very charming, full of cheerful colors and soft chairs and a secret sunny patio and garden in back. Located at the "Y"—instead of turning right to Kenai at the light, turn left into the parking lot of the little melon-colored building with blue doors and natural spruce gateway. River City Books and Café is in the back. 43977 Sterling Hwy, Ste A, Soldotna, AK 99669; 907/260-7722, fax 907/260-7447; peggym@alaska.net.

WALK THE OLD TOWN OF KENAI / Twelve miles from Soldotna, the old town of Kenai is situated high on the bluff overlooking the mouth of the Kenai River and all of Cook Inlet and the Alaska Range. Originally the Kenaitze Indians hunted, trapped, and fished here. In the 1700s, Russian fur traders came to this part of the New World, then called Russian America, primarily to hunt sea otters. The sea otter's dense, luxuriant pelt was known as "soft gold." Russian Orthodox missionaries followed, and you can see where the distinctive bright blue onion domes and gold crosses of the **HOLY ASSUMPTION OF THE VIRGIN MARY ORTHODOX CHURCH** still stands, beautifully preserved. Walk to the little memorial chapel, built with rough-hewn squared logs and crested with a tiny cupola, blue and white with gold stars. From its vantage point on the edge of the bluff you have a spectacular view west across Cook Inlet to the snowy mountains and recently active volcanoes of the Alaska Range. Wander the paths and look at a few old homestead cabins. Then stop in at **VERONICA'S COFFEE HOUSE** (907/283-2725), a sweet little cafe, picturesque and weatherbeaten gray, to warm up with gourmet coffee, tea, scones, or soup. Open daily; on Thursday and Friday evenings, there's live music.

ADVENTURES

FISH THE KENAI / Wherever you fish in Alaska, it is wise to come with respect. What seems like an abundance of fish today is fragile and easily damaged by streambank erosion, development, overfishing, and pollution. You have only to think of the great rivers of the world to understand how unique the Kenai is. No river running through any city in the world has ever sustained the world-class run of fish that the Kenai does. But fishing on the Kenai in summer is intense. There are 300 to 400 fishing guides on this one river alone. Some are more ethical and conservation-minded than others. We encourage you to choose wisely. It has been suggested that, not far off in the future, the Kenai king salmon will be strictly a catch-and-release fishery (see Wilderness Guides below). The most productive area for king salmon is the **LOWER KENAI RIVER** below Soldotna. It's also the combat fishing zone. Parties of anglers drift here in small and medium-size boats, running up the river and drifting down. As one fisherman said, "King salmon are like cars on the freeway, moving in predictable patterns. They don't change lanes very often." But the human scene is like Coney Island. The first run of kings begins in late May, and each one averages more than 30 pounds. The second run usually arrives in late June or early July, with salmon averaging more than 40 pounds each. July is the most popular month for king salmon fishing on the Kenai. Regulations currently say anglers are allowed to keep two king salmon a season, although that could change in the near future.

For a different experience on the Kenai, fish the **UPPER KENAI RIVER**. It's more peaceful and far more scenic, with blue-green glacial water sweeping through ice-streaked mountains. Here you can fish for salmon but also rainbow trout and Dolly Varden. Plus, you fish from drift boats, with no motors, which are rowed by guides down the river. Several companies offer the scenic combo, both rafting (including some whitewater) and fishing on the upper Kenai. By far the best is Alaska Wildland Adventures (800/478-4100). If you are looking to enjoy fishing and combine it with natural history, this is the team to go with.

FLOAT THE KENAI RIVER / A great day outing is to float the Kenai River from Cooper Landing to Skilak Lake with **ALASKA WILDLAND ADVENTURES** (16520 Sterling Hwy; 907/595-1279 or 800/478-4100; www.alaskarivertrips.com) based in Cooper Landing, Mile 51 on the Sterling Highway. They have a shorter trip, but you don't get the thrill of the rapids going through the canyon and then the grandeur of coming out into Skilak Lake. You may see moose, coyotes, wolves, and bears, if you're lucky. It's a beautiful trip, rain or shine. These guys do a great job. Trips depart daily in summer.

CAPTAIN COOK STATE RECREATION AREA / Turn right at the "Y" in Soldotna and go to Mile 36 on the North Kenai Road. This state park is splendid for camping and picnicking right on the edge of the ocean bluff; you'll have the whole Alaska Range spread before you on a clear day. Walk the beach looking for agates, barbecue salmon high on the bluff while watching for beluga whales, and go to the campfire talks. Some of the old homesteaders are often there to tell their stories. It's a grand place. Call Alaska State Parks (907/262-5581) in Soldotna for more information.

VISIT THE KENAI NATIONAL WILDLIFE REFUGE / The visitors center is in Soldotna and has lots of information and an interpretive trail that takes you, "with new eyes," down the trail to the lake and through the forest. (It's called "The Keen-Eye Trail.") The wildlife refuge itself covers about half of the Kenai Peninsula, and a multitude of outdoor recreational activities are available, from hiking and canoeing to hunting and fishing. For more details, call the visitors center (907/262-7021).

LEARN ABOUT VOLCANOES / En route to Homer from Soldotna, on 80 scenic acres south of the little town of Ninilchik, is the proposed site for the **NORTH PACIFIC VOLCANO LEARNING CENTER**, which may indeed be completed by the year 2001. The center will have a view of four Cook Inlet volcanoes and hands-on exhibits, as well as interpretive nature trails on the surrounding grounds. Geologically, Alaska is very young. Volcanoes still erupt along the 1,000 mile-coastline known as the northern link in the "Pacific Ring of Fire." Cone-shaped Mount Redoubt, the most impressive statement on the horizon here, erupted in 1968 and again in 1989–1990, lighting up the skies with smoke, fire and ash. Mount Iliamna, south of Redoubt, has more than 10 glaciers flowing off its peak and has not been active recently. But Mount Augustine, which is most visible from Homer, has erupted three times in the last 40 years. Call the Alaska Volcano Observatory (907/474-7320) in Fairbanks for updated information on this project.

DIG FOR CLAMS / At **CLAM GULCH STATE RECREATION AREA**, about 40 minutes south of Soldotna, you can either watch locals digging for razor clams on the low tides or get in on the action yourself. Consult the tide books and purchase a $10 license wherever fishing licenses are sold. You'll need a bucket, a shovel, and a fast eye.

SEND YOUR KIDS TO CAMP KUSHTAKA / In a glorious setting on the edge of Kenai Lake, this camp is a great place for kids to spend a week in summer (while parents attend to business or pleasure elsewhere in Alaska). Kids live in cabins, paddle the lake, hike mountains, and take wilderness camping trips. The philosophy here is "It all happens on the trail"—new friendships, new songs, new adventures, new muscles—and while sitting around campfires laughing and toasting s'mores. The camp is run by the Alaska Council of Camp Fire Boys and Girls (3745 Community Park Loop, Ste #104, Anchorage, AK 99508; 907/279-3551).

GUIDES AND OUTFITTERS

There are more than 300 **FISHING GUIDES** on the Kenai, but we are recommending only a few of the top guides—although this list is by no

A MOOSE FOR WINTER

In this age of packaged foods, many people look questioningly at the hunter who attempts the grueling task of pulling down a wild creature in the interest of feeding his or her family. Admire it or not, it falls into the realm of the romantic and the practical—eating foods native to your surroundings. For the homesteader or Bush family, hunting provides.

Actually, hunting a moose is not so difficult. It's the work of skinning, butchering, and packing the beastly thing out that is not so easy. He's big. He's really big. For instance, his liver overflows a dishpan. By a lot. A girlfriend of mine suggested we make an all-female hunting expedition. I said that would be fine if we didn't get anything. But, if we were successful, women's lib would have to go on the back burner. I want Conan and King Kong to help march moose haunches out of the woods. I've been flat on my face in the mud with a moose quarter on my back. You don't forget that!

After the kill, you must be sure the fellow is deadly asleep before opening him up to cool. Then begin the surgery. But first get a fire going; it's practical and a cheerful addition to the big job ahead. You can heat water, help ward off vampire bugs, and toast choice tidbits of fresh meat on a stick. You can also melt down some fat in a pot or coffee can and chew on some cracklings. (This is when you forget about things like fashion and eyeliner. Only two things count: food and warmth.)

Among the "specialty pieces," I like the brains, so I always go after those enthusiastically. This is hard on some people. Gives them the creeps. Sometimes I make head cheese. It's rather a grisly business but the result will make you famous with old-timers who grew up eating it. It is very good. Later, on a stormy day before Thanksgiving, the whole cabin is in an uproar with apples, sour cherries, cider, raisins, citrus peels, spices, and brandy in a hot and burbling mincemeat made from flavorful shoulder or neck meat. What a pie this makes!

Here's the part I don't like. The men never want to pack out the hide. It's so heavy. By the time all the meat is packed out, everyone is out of steam. I always try for the hide. I say it's good cut in little strips and deep-fried. They look at me with disgust. I tell them it's rainproof and I'll make them a gun case with it. They say, "Right." I try everything. We usually leave the hide. A tanned moose hide is a prize—strong and beautiful, with many uses.

Here's the part I love. When you eat a mooseburger, you know what real food tastes like. You don't wolf it down. You relish it. This is the hearty food that allows you to skate by the meat counter; pass up all those questionable additives and distorted hormones; and head home with some garlic, peppercorns, and a good red wine for your moose bourguignon.

—Joan Daniels

means complete—who have demonstrated through their guiding operations a concern for the health of the river and salmon, as well as the enjoyment of their customers. Before you hire someone, you might ask your potential fishing guides if they are members of the guides' association and what they do to help protect fish habitat. If you're looking for a **FLY FISHING/DRIFT BOAT GUIDE**, try Andrew Szcaesny of Alaska Fish and Float (907/262-9439) in Soldotna. Other Drift Boat Guides in Soldotna include Valarie Early of Early Fishing (907/262-6132), Randa's Guide Service (907/262-9494), and Nick's Guide Service (907/262-3979). **DRIFT BOAT/POWER BOAT GUIDES** are available in Cooper Landing through Alaska Rivers Company (907/595-1226) and Alaska Wildland Adventures (907/595-1279). In Soldotna, try Laine Lahndt (907/262-3234), Dan Meyers of Alaska Clearwater Sportfishing (907/262-3797), Larry Carlson of Larry's Guide Service (907/262-1815), and Fred Pentt of Big Boys, Inc. (907/262-2521). **POWER BOAT GUIDES** include Angler's Lodge and Fish Camp (907/262-1747) in Sterling, and Jeff King's Budget Charters (907/262-4564), Alaska Flaggs Kenai Charters (907/262-5426), and Sourdough Charters (907/262-5300), all three in Soldotna.

ALASKA WILDLAND ADVENTURES / This outfit rates at the top of the list. It's an impressive operation with an unusual focus on the Kenai River. They do natural history, sportfishing, rafting, and scenic overland trips. The staff is enthusiastic, skilled, and knowledgeable. Headquartered in a cluster of cabins on the banks of the Kenai River at Cooper Landing, they offer river floats, drift fishing, "soft" adventures, and "senior safaris" (where you stay in a comfortable lodge at night). They also operate **KENAI BACKCOUNTRY LODGE**, located on Skilak Lake, for hiking, kayaking, and naturalist adventures (4-day/3-night packages). The retreat is small and charming, on the edge of a spectacular blue-green lake, and caters to intimate wilderness experiences in comfort with four Yukon tent cabins and two small log cabins. The outfit offers sportfishing packages on the Kenai and Kasilof Rivers with accommodations at their Kenai Riverside Cabins. Wildland also manages Denali Backcountry Lodge in Kantishna, on the edge of Denali National Park, so you can combine experiences on the Kenai Peninsula and in Denali National Park. 16520 Sterling Hwy, Cooper Landing, AK 99572; 800/478-4100 or 907/783-2928, fax 907/783-2130; wildland@alaska.net; www.alaskawildland.com.

RESTAURANTS

Charlotte's Bakery, Café, Espresso / ★★

115 S WILLOW, STE 102, KENAI; 907/283-2777

Charlotte Legg, a former cook at Through The Seasons restaurant, runs her own cafe now, with little wooden tables and red roses and desserts that are seriously rich and dangerous. One of the first five women hired by the Teamsters during the building of the trans-Alaska oil pipeline, Charlotte used to drive trucks from Valdez to Fairbanks. But in January 1975, on an icy road, her truck jackknifed. The cab hung over a steep precipice. At this critical moment (she grins as she tells this story), she decided, "It was time to go back to the kitchen"—a refrain some of the not-so-liberated, disgruntled men had been singing to these first women

all along. Charlotte cut a wide swath for women and excellence then, and she's still doing it in her little cafe. Her raspberry almond torte with white chocolate–cream cheese frosting and the sour cream raisin meringue pie make a valiant race for your taste buds' top choice. Everything here is homemade and delicious, and not only for sweet tooths. Popular breakfasts include sourdough pancakes and hearty omelets. Choose tasty, spicy soups for lunch, like Jambalaya Red Pepper or vegetarian chili. The Cobb salad with bacon, blue cheese, and eggs is visually pretty and filling. Favorite sandwiches are the Caesar chicken, grilled with Parmesan cheese and stuffed into a hoagie bun, and the Hawaiian Wannabe, teriyaki-marinated grilled chicken with ham, pineapple, and provolone cheese tucked into a warm homemade croissant. *$; MC, V; checks OK; breakfast, lunch, early dinner Mon–Sat in summer; breakfast, lunch Mon–Sat in winter; in downtown Kenai.* &

LODGINGS

Harborside Cottages Bed & Breakfast / ★★

813 RIVERVIEW DR, KENAI, AK 99611; 907/283-6162 OR 888/283-6162

Situated on a green lawn with lovely flowers right at the edge of the bluff overlooking the mouth of the Kenai River, all of Cook Inlet, and the magnificent Alaska Range, these small, white cottages are the perfect place to be on a sunny summer evening. In salmon season, you can watch the fishing fleet heading out the river to catch the openings and watch dozens of beluga whales heading upriver to feed. The bank here is gradually eroding due to the wind and weather coming in from the open ocean and the action of the river, but it'll be a few years before they have to pull these cottages back from the edge. In the meantime, enjoy. *$$; AE, DIS, MC, V; checks OK; open May–Sept; cottages@ptialaska.net; PO Box 942, Kenai, AK 99611; on the bluff in Kenai, near Old Town.*

Soldotna Bed and Breakfast Lodge / ★★★

399 LOVERS LANE, SOLDOTNA, AK 99669; 907/262-4779, FAX 907/262-3201

With the charm of a Swiss chalet—carved window boxes filled with flowers at every window and the attention to detail that has made Swiss innkeepers so famous—this wonderful B&B with 16 rooms sits on the banks of the Kenai River and has a lovely green garden out front and a gazebo down by the river's edge. In the summer of 1999, the original hosts from Bern, Switzerland, passed the baton to a young, multilingual couple, Monika Leiber and Steven Anderson, who are keeping up the fine European tradition here (in addition to English and German, they also speak Japanese). This is a top-notch establishment. Six rooms have a river view. And if you're there from May to September for fishing, you can even have a full, hearty, hot breakfast beginning at 4:30am. Rates vary from $110 to $180 for a double in summer; lower in winter. Nonsmoking. $$–$$$; AE, MC, V; *checks OK; monika@soldotnalodge. com; www.soldotnalodge.com; off the Sterling Hwy, on the banks of the Kenai River.*

Homer

Remember those friends from college who took off for Alaska in the Volkswagen van with their guitars and dogs? Don't be surprised if you find them in Homer, a little town at the end of the road that has long been a haven for artists, writers, and counterculturalists. If you drive here, stop at the overlook point on the highway just before you descend into town and you'll see what all the fuss is about: a shimmering bay ringed by snowcapped mountains and glacier-carved valleys. The **HOMER SPIT**, an impossibly skinny wisp of land, stretches 4.5 miles into the bay. Never mind that on summer weekends the end of the spit looks like one giant RV park. Keep looking out over the bay—the view is exquisite.

The community is named for Homer Pennock, a turn-of-the-century adventurer who expected to make a fortune in gold and never did. Coal, woven through the bluffs, was king in the early years. Now this town of 4,000 relies on commercial fishing and, increasingly, sportfishing and tourism for its livelihood.

Known by one local sage as "Our Cosmic Hamlet by the Sea," Homer gets its batteries charged every year by an influx of young people who travel here for summer jobs in the fishing industry. Traditionally they camp on the Spit, and thus are known as "Spit rats," which is not an entirely pejorative term. Every fall, some of them are so enchanted they stay the winter. Eventually they become residents, mixing with the descendants of homesteaders and lending Homer a flavor of Bohemian hipness. In fact, Homer is the beloved hometown of pop sensation Jewel, whose grandfather, the late Yule Kilcher, homesteaded here. She returns rarely, but her relatives abound.

The Spit is the main draw here, and in summer the area is a crowded hodgepodge of businesses catering to both visitors and the commercial fishing fleet. Halibut charter offices, knickknack shops, and restaurants crowd the end of the Spit, and some complain that the place looks more and more like Tijuana with each passing year. Still, there's no better place than the Spit for taking the pulse of the Kachemak Bay economy. A stroll through the harbor will give you a good feel for it, or stop in at the **SALTY DAWG** (907/235-9990), a dark little bar in a historic building with sawdust on the floor. Commercial fishermen sit cheek-by-jowl with visitors, and the place is so cramped that you'll have no difficulty striking up a conversation.

ACCESS AND INFORMATION

Homer is quite spread out, so you'll probably need a car, although one entrepreneur has a trolleylike bus that makes the rounds, and hitchhiking around town is acceptable. Most people drive down from Anchorage, but flights are reasonable and **NATIONAL CAR RENTAL** has a few cars available at the airport, if booked in advance.

The **HOMER CHAMBER OF COMMERCE** (907/235-7740) can send you maps and brochures. Also, you might want to contact **CENTRAL CHARTER** (4241 Homer Spit Rd; 800/478-7847 or 907/235-7847). It's a booking agency that can make reservations for your adventures on charter boats and ferries and with many B&Bs in town.

EXPLORING

PRATT MUSEUM / Art, history, and marine life exhibits are nicely done. Kids, bird-nerds, and, well, just about anybody will love the bird cam, which uses a feat of engineering to bring the wonders of nature to the great indoors. The bird cam is a remote-control video camera situated on Gull Island, a rookery in the middle of Kachemak Bay. The camera beams its footage back to the Pratt. Museum patrons operate the controls to zoom in on kittiwakes or puffins. Also, "Darkened Waters," a former Smithsonian exhibit about the *Exxon Valdez* oil spill, is not to be missed. It does a good job of conveying the enormity of the 1989 spill in Prince William Sound in easily understood terms. You can hear a recording of Captain Joseph Hazelwood's first report to the Coast Guard that he'd run "hard aground." Admission is $5. 3779 Bartlett St; 907/235-8635.

PTARMIGAN ARTS / This gallery features top-notch local artists and craftspeople. It carries everything from jewelry to photographs, handmade clothes to hand-painted silk. 471 E Pioneer Ave; 907/235-5345.

BUNNELL STREET GALLERY / Bold exhibits of paintings done with oils and watercolors, as well as wearable art, glass, steel, or group shows of mixed media—you never know what kind of cutting-edge art you might find at this nonprofit co-op. The Bunnell also offers special-event evenings of performance art. 106 W Bunnell St; 907/235-2662.

WALKS AND DRIVES / Homer has some nice walks. **BISHOP'S BEACH** is one good example near downtown. A drive out **EAST END ROAD** or **SKYLINE DRIVE** will be rewarded with spectacular views and perhaps a moose or two. Birdwatching is also very popular. Some 100,000 shorebirds migrate through Homer in the first two weeks of May. Homer has responded with the annual **KACHEMAK BAY SHOREBIRD FESTIVAL**, an early-May event that includes identification workshops, guided bird tours, and art activities.

ADVENTURES

KACHEMAK BAY is the best thing about Homer. It's teeming with marine life and provides an opportunity to see sea otters, harbor seals, porpoises, maybe even a whale. Unless it's stormy, some good ways to enjoy the bay are listed below. And if you want to interact with the water without actually floating on it, consider fishing for salmon at the fishing hole on the Spit. It's combat fishing at peak season, but hey, it's a pretty cheap and easy way to bag a wild salmon of your own.

HALIBUT CHARTER / This is probably the most popular activity. There are dozens of outfits, many of which can be booked through Central Charter (800/478-7847 or 907/235-7847). A word of caution: you really need to have the fishing bug to do this. Trips usually start early in the morning and go all day, often in rough water. Skippers won't turn around just because one of the party is horribly seasick. Still, many people gladly brave all this for the chance to reel in a 200-pound lunker.

KAYAKING / Sea kayaking offers an excellent way to get intimate with the sea. **TRUE NORTH KAYAK ADVENTURES** (907/235-0708) runs day trips for beginners from an island across from Homer, as well as multi-day trips. Owners Alison O'Hara and Kevin Bell provide water-taxi service to the island, lessons, lunch, and a guide to give natural-history tours. Or try **ST. AUGUSTINE'S CHARTERS**—the affable owners, Scott Burbank and Susan Aramovich, offer guided day trips and also rent kayaks. Book through Inlet Charters (907/235-6126).

BOAT TOURS / Homer has an embarrassment of riches here, but a few stand out. The **DANNY J**, also known as the Kachemak Bay ferry, is a brightly painted former fishing boat that makes two trips a day to Halibut Cove. The early departure, at noon, stops by **GULL ISLAND**, a bird sanctuary crammed with all manner of winged things. For reservations call Central Charter (800/478-7847 or 907/235-7847). **ST. AUGUS-TINE'S CHARTERS** makes seeing wildlife the top priority. They offer marine wildlife tours as well as ferry service to **KACHEMAK BAY STATE PARK**. They cater to backpackers, serious birders, and photographers. Book through Inlet Charters (907/235-6126). A large tour boat, the **RAINBOW CONNECTION** (907/235-7272), offers narrated day cruises to Seldovia, via Gull Island.

RESTAURANTS

Boardwalk Fish & Chips

HOMER SPIT RD, HOMER; 907/235-7749
Best known for its deep-fried halibut-on-a-stick, the Boardwalk also serves salmon, clams, shrimp, scallops, charbroiled hamburgers, and chicken. There are a few items that are not deep-fried, but most everything is, and most everything tastes darn good. French fries are the standard frozen variety, but the coleslaw is good. The view is worth knocking over a few tourists to secure a table near the enormous windows. *$; MC, V; local checks only; lunch, dinner every day; closed Oct–March; beer and wine; on the Spit, across the road from the Salty Dawg.* &

Cafe Cups / ★★★★

162 W PIONEER AVE, HOMER; 907/235-8330
When Cups opened in 1991, Homer's era of artsy chic arrived. The front of this whimsical building is overrun by giant tea cups and an assortment of gilded treasures. Inside, big colorful paintings compete with zany objets d'art. The place would be cool even if the food were only average. But it's not. The menu is eclectic, part California with Pacific Rim influences and a twist of Alaska. Consider, for example, the Thai steak salad—grilled flank steak, with cucumber, fresh mint, and basil, tossed in tangy lime chile dressing. They have an extensive selection of wines by the glass. Good breakfasts, too. *$$$; MC, V; checks OK; breakfast, lunch, dinner every day; open April–Oct (shorter hours in winter); beer and wine; downtown Homer, across the main drag from the library.* &

The Fresh Sourdough Express Bakery & Cafe / ★

1316 OCEAN DR, HOMER; 907/235-7571
A longtime Homer restaurant, Sourdough Express was great, then became a tourist trap, and is now back in the hands of its original owner, on its way back to greatness. It sells bread and other baked goodies. Locals sometimes complain that service in the restaurant is tediously slow, but you'll find hearty breakfasts ranging from pancakes and eggs to biscuits and gravy. The Sourdough Joe scramble, made of three eggs and no-nitrate reindeer sausage, hits the spot. Lunch offerings range from

"stuffs" (dough filled with stuff) to reindeer grill to a free-range buffalo burger. Food is reasonably priced and tasty, and, if you're on vacation, you probably can justify a wait. The Sourdough also makes brown-bag lunches well suited for a day on the bay. *$; MC, V; local checks only; breakfast, lunch, dinner every day in summer; breakfast, lunch every day in winter; beer and wine; heading toward the Spit from downtown on Ocean Dr, it's on the left.* &

The Homestead / ★★★★

MILE 8.2, EAST END RD, HOMER; 907/235-8723
Chef Sean Maryott was also the founding chef of Cups, so if you dine at both you really get a sense of his genius. The Homestead, an old log-cabin restaurant that used to be a basic steak-and-potatoes joint, retains its traditional feel, but has new verve. Top-quality Alaska seafood is served with ginger, chipotle, cilantro pesto, or a variety of other tastes. For the carnivorous, there's filet mignon and other tender steaks. The Caesar salads, made at your table, are especially good. The service is very professional. *$$$; AE, MC, V; checks OK; dinner every day; closed Jan–March; full bar.* &

Land's End Chart Room

4786 HOMER SPIT RD, HOMER; 907/235-0406
With the best view in town, the food here doesn't really have to be great, and sometimes it isn't. But this restaurant is right at the tip of the Spit, and from a window table you'll have a panoramic view over the bay, yet be close enough to watch sea otters playing near the beach. The dinner fare, which ranges from local fresh seafood to burgers and steaks, doesn't always add to the experience, although it doesn't usually detract. An appetizer might be oversalty, an entree underspiced, and another dish just right. The clam chowder is excellent, and desserts are fresh and made on premises. If you're after the best food in town, go to the Homestead. But if you want to splurge, as well as have a view to die for, head to Land's End. *$$$; AE, DC, MC, V; local checks only; breakfast, lunch, dinner every day; full bar; at the very end of the Spit.* &

The Saltry / ★★★

ACROSS THE WATER FROM HOMER, HALIBUT COVE; 907/296-2223
This is more an experience than a restaurant. Take the *Danny J* ferry over to Halibut Cove, a wildly cute community of artists and fishermen. No roads or parking lots here, just boardwalks, trails, and docks. Houses are built on pilings and perched on rocks. The boat docks at the Saltry, which serves—what else?—seafood. The restaurant concentrates on fresh everything, and many of the vegetables are grown out back. On a sunny day, the deck is nice, but cooler than you might expect. The *Danny J* schedule leaves enough time for a meal and a little stroll to the art gallery

along the one boardwalk open to the public. Reservations are crucial, particularly in summer; make them through Central Charter (800/478-7847 or 907/235-7847). *$$$; MC, V; local checks only; lunch, dinner every day; open Memorial Day–Labor Day; full bar; if you're in Halibut Cove, you can't miss it.*

Two Sisters / ★★

106 W BUNNELL, HOMER; 907/235-2280

A bakery and coffee shop not to be missed. You'll find terrific pastries, both sweet and savory, as well as Greek-style pizza and focaccia bread. The "Sisters" whip up a mean espresso and nice biscuits and gravy, making this the best place in town for a spot of breakfast. The atmosphere matches the food: bright and homemade. It's tiny and very popular with the locals, so have patience if it's jammed. *$; no credit cards; checks OK; breakfast, lunch, early dinner Mon–Sat; no alcohol; in the same building as the Bunnell Street Gallery, near Bishop's Beach.*

LODGINGS

Bay View Inn

2851 STERLING HWY, HOMER, AK 99603; 800/478-8485 OR 907/235-8485

OK, so this is more motel than inn, but it's cute. More important, check out the view. The Bay View is next to the overlook park on the big descent into Homer, so if you were mesmerized at the overlook, this is the place for you. The 12 nonsmoking rooms all have a great view and private entrances. Some have kitchenettes, and there's a honeymoon cottage. Owner Dennis Novak makes the most of the location with lawn, Adirondack chairs, and picnic tables. *$$; AE, DIS, MC, V; no checks; bayview@ alaska.net; www.bayviewalaska.com; PO Box 804, Homer, AK 99603; just off the highway, below the overlook.*

Brigitte's Bavarian Bed and Breakfast / ★★

ON STELLER'S JAY, HOMER, AK 99603; 907/235-6620

Hosts Brigitte and Willie Suter do things just so. Each of the three hand-crafted cottages has its own private entry and bath. These two—one is German, the other Swiss—pride themselves on breakfast, which is served in the main house, all guests around the table, lively conversation encouraged. The Suters serve homemade sourdough bread, smoked salmon, and blueberry waffles. They grow their own herbs, make their own jams, and raise the chickens that lay your eggs. *$$; no credit cards; checks OK; bbbb@xyz.net; PO Box 2391, Homer, AK 99603; go 3 miles out East End Rd, turn left on Bear Creek Loop, take Steller's Jay to the right. Continue up the hill through 4 switchbacks to the very last house.*

Chocolate Drop Inn / B&B / ★★★

57745 CLOVER AVE, HOMER, AK 99603; 907/235-3668 OR 800/530-6015
This large, log building feels like a lodge and is nicely situated on a hill overlooking Kachemak Bay. Named for the shape of a mountain across the bay, the Chocolate Drop has six rooms, each with private bath. There's a honeymoon suite with a private indoor Jacuzzi and a family suite with its own kitchen and living room. An outdoor hot tub sits on the deck. *$$; AE, MC, V; checks OK; Chocdrop@xyz.net; ChocolateDropInn. com; PO Box 70, Homer, AK 99603; drive 7 miles out East End Rd, turn left on Portlock, then left on Clover.*

The Driftwood Inn & RV Park

135 W BUNNELL AVE, HOMER, AK 99603; 800/478-8019 OR 907/235-8019
There are prettier places, but this homey 21-room hotel has some nice conveniences. Canine guests are allowed in some of the rooms, and there are coin-operated washers and dryers on site. About half the rooms have private bathrooms. Some of the rooms have a double bed with a single bunk above, which may remind you of a romantic boat ride or of the time you were locked in a closet. The location is great for one-car groups that want to go their separate ways. While mom and dad sleep in, gramps can walk to Bishop's Beach, and the teens can have breakfast across the street at Two Sisters. *$$; AE, DIS, MC, V; checks OK; driftinn@xyz.net; www. netalaska.com/driftwood; from the Homer Bypass, turn downhill onto Main St, then left on Bunnell.*

Halcyon Heights B&B / ★★★

61850 MISSION RD, HOMER, AK 99603; 907/235-2148
This is a big, luxurious B&B, with six rooms, each with private bath. Bob and Gail Ammerman have been in business for a decade, so they know what they're doing. Of course, there's a great view, but the best part is the outdoor Jacuzzi, up on a deck away from the house with a crow's-nest view of the bay and the mountains. It's available to guests, day and night. *$$; AE, DIS, MC, V; checks OK; halcyon@xyz.net; www.akms. com/halcyon; PO Box 3552, Homer AK 99603; head 1 mile out East End Rd, then 2 miles up East Hill Rd to Mission Rd.*

Island Watch Bed and Breakfast / ★★★

IN THE HILLS ABOVE HOMER, HOMER, AK 99603; 907/235-2265
If you want a taste of the real Alaska, stay in one of two beautiful, hand-crafted cabins in the hills of Homer. The view is expansive across the horse paddock and down to the water and mountains beyond. A handsome woman with a merry laugh, Eileen Mullen grew up on a homestead on the banks of the Kenai River. She's a woman of impressive achievements—fisherwoman, captain, horsewoman, and cabin builder.

Her robust breakfasts will get you to the top of any mountain. The little cabins ($140 per night) are a classic experience, but she also has a very warm and comfortable suite with private bath in the house ($110 per night), and rooms go for $90, double occupancy. Call for special winter rates. *$$; MC, V; checks OK; island@xyz.net; www.xyz.net/~island/; PO Box 1394, Homer, AK 99603; 5 minutes from downtown, call for directions.* &

Land's End Resort / ★

4786 HOMER SPIT RD, HOMER, AK 99603; 800/478-0400 WITHIN ALASKA OR 907/235-0400

If it weren't for its location, Land's End would be just a modern, charmless hotel trying for a nautical theme. But, perched as it is at the very tip of the Spit, it has appeal. If your room faces the bay, the beach begins practically at your bedside. Rooms facing the parking lot are slightly cheaper, but why bother? The Port Wing rooms on the bay side are a fair deal. They're basically small doubles, but with twin trundle and folddown single, they'll sleep a tight-knit family. The two-story suites in the Midship Wing seem poorly designed, with a window and deck too small to take advantage of the view. The restaurant is inconsistent, but the deck's the best place in town to have a drink and watch boat traffic in the harbor. *$$$; AE, DC, MC, V; checks OK; landsend@alaska.net; www.alaskan.com/landsendresort/; end of the Spit.* &

Old Town B&B / ★★

106 W BUNNELL, HOMER, AK 99603; 907/235-7558

All three rooms in this romantic bed-and-breakfast above an art gallery have beautiful views of the bay. Stay here long enough and you'll be overcome by an urge to write poetry or paint watercolors. Owners Kurt Marquardt and Asia Freeman have a finely tuned sense of beauty, resulting in a space that is spare and windswept. The location, in what was once central Homer, is a short walk to the shops of downtown, and even closer to Bishop's Beach. Monday through Saturday, breakfast is downstairs at the fabulous Two Sisters bakery. *$; MC, V; checks OK; oldtown@xyz.net; www.xyz.net/~oldtown; at the corner of Bunnell and Main St.*

Quiet Place / ★★★

ACROSS THE WATER FROM HOMER, HALIBUT COVE, AK 99603; 907/296-2212

This is across the bay from Homer and, for land-lubbing city slickers, it will feel like another world. The buildings of this secluded community, connected by waterways and boardwalks, are largely built on pilings over the water. There are no roads. Quiet Place has five cabins, each sleeping two to four people. They also rent kayaks to guests. Staying here offers a wonderful chance to paddle, eat at the Saltry, and hike in the state park. $$$; MC, V; checks OK; closed in winter; www.quietplace.com; PO Box 6474; Halibut Cove, AK 99603.

The Shorebird Guest House / ★★

4774 KACHEMAK DR, HOMER, AK 99603; 907/235-2107
Staying at the Shorebird is like having a complete little house of your own on a bluff with a great view of the bay. It has all the modern amenities. With two queen beds and a set of bunk beds, it will sleep an extended family and is a good place for kids since there are no other guests to disturb. A fully furnished kitchen will please those who want to fend for themselves. Stairs down the bluff lead to the beach. $$; no credit cards; checks OK; open May–Sept; peeps@alaska.net; www.alaska.net/ ~peeps; PO Box 204, Homer, AK 99603; drive to the base of the Spit and turn left on Kachemak Dr, then go 3 miles and look for the sign.

Wild Rose / ★★★

5010 EAST HILL RD, HOMER, AK 99603; 907/235-8780
These four well-built cabins sitting high on a hill have a lovely view and, with log construction and lots of natural wood, a very rustic feel. Some of the cabins have full kitchens, all have private baths, and one has two bedrooms. Because breakfast is brought to the cabin the night before, guests can keep their own hours and their privacy. $$; DIS, MC, V; no checks; wildrose@xyz.net; www.AlaskaOne.com/wildrose; PO Box 665, Homer, AK 99603; drive 1 mile east on East End Rd, turn left up East Hill Rd for another mile, turn right at the sign.

Kachemak Bay State Park

The sheltered coves, spruce-tufted islands, and glacier-covered mountains of this park go on forever—actually, for 300,000 acres, along 200 miles of wild coastline, making this one of the largest coastal parks in the country.

Kachemak Bay itself is teeming with life, mammal as well as lower forms. Get out on the water and you might see sea otters, harbor seals, porpoises, or even whales. Hundreds of species of birds thrive in this coastal habitat, including bald eagles, loons, and mergansers. And the seabirds—well, just visit Gull Island, a rookery that's on the route for most of the tour boats and ferries out of Homer. Some 12,000 birds vie for space on this rock, including tufted puffins, cormorants, kittiwakes, and marbled murrelets.

The land is home to black bears, moose, coyotes, and, on the rocky peaks, mountain goats. With all this, the park is heaven for humans of the outdoorsy variety who might like to kayak, hike, pick berries, or photograph wildlife.

ACCESS AND INFORMATION

Since this park can't be reached by road, getting here requires coordinating with one of the **WATER TAXIS OR FERRIES** in Homer. Try Central Charter (800/478-7847 or 907/235-7847) in Homer for reservations; or for more information, call the park office in Homer (907/235-7024). In summer, you can reach the ranger station in Halibut Cove (907/235-6999). See also Adventures in the Homer section, above.

ADVENTURES

HIKING / POOT PEAK, the chocolate-drop-shaped mountain prominent from Homer, can be climbed in a day, but it makes a much better overnight trip. Have a boat drop you off at the head of **HALIBUT COVE LAGOON**. If you reserve well enough in advance, you might be able to stay at the public-use cabin nearby. If not, hike to the lake and camp there. You can leave your pack behind and tackle the peak the next day. There are about 14 developed trails in the park, ranging from 1 mile to 6.5 miles. Get a copy of the park's hiking trails by calling the State Parks office in Homer (907/235-7024).

NATURAL HISTORY TOURS / Knowledgeable naturalists lead excellent day programs at the **CENTER FOR ALASKAN COASTAL STUDIES** field station on the south side of Kachemak Bay. You go over in the morning on the *Rainbow Connection* and spend all day studying tide pools, rain forest flora and fauna, or geology. The program varies, depending on the interests of the group. This nonprofit organization is great for inspiring interest in marine science in children and adults. The full-day tour costs $55 for adults, $48 for seniors, and $43 for children up to 12. Bring lunch, waterproof boots or shoes, camera, and binoculars. PO Box 2225 Homer, AK 99603; 907/235-6667 or 907/235-7272, reservations.

ALASKA COASTAL JOURNEYS / If hands-on marine science education is your thing and you want a longer trip, opt for Alaska Coastal Journeys (907/235-2228). They run 3- to 5-day programs from May through September from a base camp on the south side of Kachemak Bay. They have programs for families and adults, but they specialize in children's camps. The programs include boating, birdwatching, kayaking, and tide pool exploration. Sally Oberstein is director and co-owner with internationally renowned naturalists Conrad and Carmen Field. www.alaskacoastaljourneys.com.

WILDERNESS LODGES

Kachemak Bay Wilderness Lodge

PO BOX 956, HOMER, AK 99603; 907/235-8910, FAX 907/235-8910

This is the most achingly beautiful place on the Kenai Peninsula. The hosts, Diane and Mike McBride, have been perfecting their lodge for nearly 30 years, and the result is total luxury in a rustic setting. Each of the guest cabins has all the comforts of electricity and a full bathroom, but the ambience is rugged Alaska. The materials for the lodge, the dock, and many of the buildings were salvaged from wrecked ships. The sauna sprouts wildflowers and berries from its sod roof. The dining room chandelier is made of a boat hull that was grounded on a nearby beach. The decorations are old floats and other treasures the McBrides found while beachcombing over the years. Here and there are finds from far away: a claw-foot bathtub, an antique concertina, and, in the solarium, a 1915 cherry piano, a gift from a grateful guest. The McBrides are expert naturalists and dyed-in-the-wool conservationists, with a walk-soft philosophy they live by but don't lay too heavily on the guests. The early-morning yoga sessions Mike leads in the solarium are entirely optional. A soak in the hot tub, outdoors but shielded from the view of other guests, is, however, a must. The staff will take you by Boston Whaler for fishing or wildlife viewing on China Poot Bay or beyond. Kayaks are also available. There are plenty of hiking opportunities right from the lodge. There is a 5-day minimum stay, and it'll cost you. Guests arrive on Monday and stay until Friday for a cost of $2,500 per person. Ten guests a week are the maximum. *No credit cards; checks OK; open May–mid-Sept; on China Poot Bay (the McBrides will reserve your seats on the MV Rainbow Connection).*

Tutka Bay Lodge

PO BOX 960, HOMER, AK 99603; 800/606-3909 OR 907/235-3905

This is a place of big, handsome cabins, on an isthmus between Tutka and Little Tutka Bays. It's high on comfort—the cabins have private bathrooms and massage showerheads—and low on the funkiness factor. Everything is sturdy and well built, starting with the helipad just up from the boat dock. The cuisine relies on a whole medley of Alaska seafood fresh from Kachemak Bay—salmon, mussels, halibut, clams, and oysters. The owners, Jon and Nelda Osgood, are as gracious as can be. Jon, a helicopter pilot, quit his federal career years ago and Nelda left her school district job so they could live here full time. They've been taking in guests for nearly 20 years now. They'll take you on a wildlife boat tour of Tutka Bay or to Seldovia. You can also hike or ride mountain bikes. For an extra charge, they'll arrange fishing charters, sea kayaking, or helicopter tours. They have a 2-night minimum stay, costing $325 per person per night.

Special expeditions such as charter fishing are at an extra cost. They can accommodate 12 to 14 guests at a time. *AE, MC, V; checks OK; open mid-May–mid-Sept; www.tutkabaylodge.com; 9 water miles south of Homer in Tutka Bay.*

Seldovia

Before the road connected Homer to the rest of the world, Seldovia was the economic hub of the Lower Kenai Peninsula. It was served by two steamship lines from Seattle, and the early Homer settlers told of rowing or sailing to the big city of Seldovia for mail and supplies. Now the roles are reversed, and it's Seldovia that's the sleepy little village.

Much of the town was built on boardwalks, but the land sank some 4 feet during the 1964 Good Friday Earthquake, and a somewhat less quaint Seldovia was rebuilt. Still, a small portion of the old boardwalk, running along the Seldovia Slough, is enough to give you a feel for the town that was.

Although tiny by comparison to Homer, Seldovia has in some ways more recreational opportunities for visitors. For hunter-gatherer types, the August crop of blueberries, salmonberries, and raspberries makes for easy picking. And the pebbly beaches on this side of Kachemak Bay are rife with butter and steamer clams, there for the taking if you have a sportfishing license. There are several nice hikes and one terrific mountain-bike adventure.

Everything about this town is small-scale. You will not need a car; a van service, the Jakolof Bay Express, will take you anywhere you need to go. Street addresses are, for the most part, fairly useless, as many streets aren't posted, and the locals may not agree on the name anyway.

ACCESS AND INFORMATION

Several boats serve Seldovia daily in summer, provided by **RAINBOW TOURS** (907/235-7272), such as the MV *Rainbow Connection* and the MV *Sizzler*, departing from the Homer Spit. It's also just a short hop (15 minutes) from Homer to Seldovia by Smokey Bay Air (2100 Kachemak Dr, Homer; 907/235-1511). The center of Seldovia is an easy stroll from the landing strip. The cost to go by sea or air is about $50 round-trip. The Jakolof Bay Express (907/234-7660) will give you a ride around Seldovia or to good hiking, biking, kayaking, berry picking, or wherever in their "smoke-free vehicle." An Alaska state ferry, the MV *Tustemena* (907/235-8449), operates between Seldovia, Homer, and Kodiak; call for schedule information.

For more information, call the **SELDOVIA CHAMBER OF COMMERCE** (907/234-7612). Seldovia is legendary for its berries. If you are going to pick berries, you will need to call the **SELDOVIA NATIVE ASSO-CIATION** (907/234-7625) for a free berry-picking permit. They will also buy surplus berries from you for their own berry kitchens.

EXPLORING

A hip coffeehouse on the waterfront, **THE BUZZ** (907/234-7479) is the place to get your espresso, as well as quiche, muffins, pastries, and aromatherapy. The Buzz also rents mountain bikes and fishing gear and is the depot for the **JAKOLOF BAY EXPRESS** van, which will take you to the Jakolof Dock or anywhere else in town you need to go.

After you've copped your buzz, head over to **HERRING BAY MER-CANTILE** (907/234-7410). Open daily, this gift store is a cute boutique of unusual Alaska-made treats with a few imports. Owner Susan Springer makes her own hand-rubbed, block-print cards right in the shop.

For lunch or dinner, look for the wildly colorful and languorous fish, home of the **MAD FISH RESTAURANT** (907/234-7676; madfish@alaska.net). Open daily in summer, they serve what else but fresh seafood, along with homemade soups, sandwiches, and luscious desserts. You can find them across from the boat ramp in the heart of Seldovia.

If you want to take home a sweet selection from Seldovia, visit the berry kitchens at **ALASKA TRIBAL CACHE** (907/234-7898 or 800/270-7810), located on Main Street, for homemade jams, jellies, and syrups made from local berries by members of the Seldovia Village Tribe.

ADVENTURES

KAYAKING / Guided day trips (and orientation) with Kirby and Lynn Corwin are available through **KAYAK'ATAK** (907/234-7425). Owner Kirby has a delightfully zany sense of humor. If you know your stuff and want to paddle on your own, Kirby is also the guy to see. He has a desk inside the Herring Bay Mercantile. They're often out, but leave a message and they'll get back to you.

BOAT TOUR / You may have taken a boat to get here, but if you want more, try the **JAKOLOF FERRY** noon passage to Halibut Cove. You'll get a total of 2 hours on the water and 2 hours in delightful Halibut Cove, and you'll be back at the Jakolof Dock by 4pm.

MOUNTAIN BIKING / The premier mountain biking adventure in the area is the **JAKOLOF-ROCKY RIVER ROAD**, 15 miles of an old logging road that cuts across the very tip of the Kenai Peninsula. You can bring your bike on the Jakolof Ferry. From the Jakolof Dock, turn left and start pedaling. Strong cyclists can make it a day trip, but it's better as an overnighter. You can also rent bikes in Seldovia at the Buzz.

WALKING AND HIKING / Hike the delightful **OTTERBAHN** from the edge of town about a mile through the woods to the beach. The trail was built with interpretive signs by the kids at school and named by them— a tribute to the otters, land and sea, and a spoof on the German speedway known as the Autobahn. From town, you can also see the top of **GRADUATION PEAK**, so named because it's a fun day hike and done as a celebration every year by graduating high school seniors in their caps and gowns. **OUTSIDE BEACH** is another peaceful and lovely destination a mile from town.

LODGINGS

Across the Bay Tent & Breakfast Adventure Company / ★

**JAKOLOF BAY RD AT KASITSNA BAY, SELDOVIA, AK 99663;
907/235-3633, SUMMER; 907/345-2571, WINTER**
Reminiscent of summer camp, this outfit is right on the beach and serves budget travelers who are willing to skimp on accommodations. As the name implies, guests stay in tents, but they're wall tents on raised platforms with beds and mattresses. Bring your own sleeping bags. The place is on Kasitsna Bay, an 8-mile taxi ride from Seldovia, but probably best reached directly by boat from Homer. Hot showers and a large wood-fired sauna are always available. Hosts Mary Jane and Tony Lastufka offer mountain bike rental and kayak tours for an extra charge. With beach fires and salmon bakes, this is a busy, convivial kind of place with miles of beach. Breakfast is served in the main house; lunch and dinner are extra. A propane burner and a covered cooking area are available for those who want to do for themselves. Tent and breakfast costs $48 per person; tent and all meals costs $75 per person; guided kayak tours cost $95 per person; and mountain bikes rent for $25 a day. *$; MC, V; checks OK; closed Oct 1–May 1; ecotour@ptialaska.net; www.tentandbreakfastalaska.com; PO Box 112054, Anchorage, AK 99511; 8 miles outside of Seldovia.*

Dancing Eagles / ★★

**CORNER OF MAIN AND WATER STS, SELDOVIA, AK 99663;
907/234-7627 SUMMER, 907/278-0288 WINTER**
Quintessential Seldovia. This laid-back B&B is at the end of the old boardwalk, built on pilings over the water The four-bedroom (shared-bath) house faces east, guarding the entrance to the slough, and the roomy cabin looks west over the harbor. The two are connected by a large deck, on which sits a wood-fired hot tub that's cranked up every night. The cabin is perfect for a family with kids, sleeping six. Gourmet breakfast baskets are delivered to the door. Single rate is $55 a night; double is $85 a night; cabin is $125 for two. The Lethin family has run this

operation for 20 years. *$$; no credit cards; checks OK; open May–Aug; dancingeagles@pobox.alaska.net; www.dancingeagles.com; PO Box 264, Seldovia, AK 99663; walk the boardwalk to the end at the corner of Main and Water Sts, although you won't find any street signs.*

Seldovia's Boardwalk Hotel

DOWNTOWN, JUST ABOVE THE HARBOR, SELDOVIA, AK 99663; 800/238-7862 OR 907/234-7816
Formerly Annie McKenzie's, this hotel is not on the old boardwalk, but it does have a good view of the harbor. The rooms are standard but it's a good bet for visitors who want a basic hotel, no frills. *$$; DIS, MC, V; checks OK; PO Box 72, Seldovia, AK 99663.*

Seldovia Rowing Club / ★★

ON THE OLD BOARDWALK, SELDOVIA, AK 99663; 907/234-7614
This is the oldest B&B on the Kenai Peninsula, in operation for 20 years. Its flamboyant proprietor, artist-actress Susan Mumma, taught school in Seldovia for 23 years and now devotes her time to her art and to welcoming guests to her homey B&B, which has a "Victorian-nautical" flavor. Two suites accommodate guests with outside decks and sitting rooms. One has a kitchen. Located on the historic Seldovia Boardwalk, at the edge of the Seldovia Slough, the Rowing Club has never been a rowing club, although there is an old dinghy tied up for those who get a hankering to test their prowess. Rather, it was once a fisherman's net house and then a boat house. How did it get its name? It's a long story. Ask Susan. It won't be a big surprise that she taught drama as well as art. Get ready for breakfast! Not only is it delicious— it's also performance art! Rates per suite: $85 to $95 per night in summer and $75 to $85 per night in off-season. Nonsmoking. *$$; MC, V; checks OK; rowing@ptialaska.net; www.roomsplus.com/bb/ak/s/rowing/rowing.htm; PO Box 41, Seldovia, AK 99663; on the old boardwalk, a short walk to town.*

Swan House South Bed and Breakfast / ★★

175 AUGUSTINE AVE N, SELDOVIA, AK 99663; 800/921-1900, OUTSIDE ALASKA; 907/234-8888, SUMMER; 907/346-3033, ALL YEAR
Judy and Jerry Swanson's B&B feels more like a modern little inn than somebody's home. It's sleek, adult, and not the least bit funky. All five rooms have private baths. The large, open living room with white pine trimmings gives the place a lodgelike touch, and there's a nice view of the historic boardwalk. (The Swansons also own a B&B in Anchorage.) *$$; AE, DIS, MC, V; checks OK; open May–Sept; swan/@alaska.net; www.alaska.net/~swan; 6840 Crooked Tree Dr, Anchorage, AK 99516; from town, cross the bridge over the slough and make the first right.*

KODIAK ISLAND

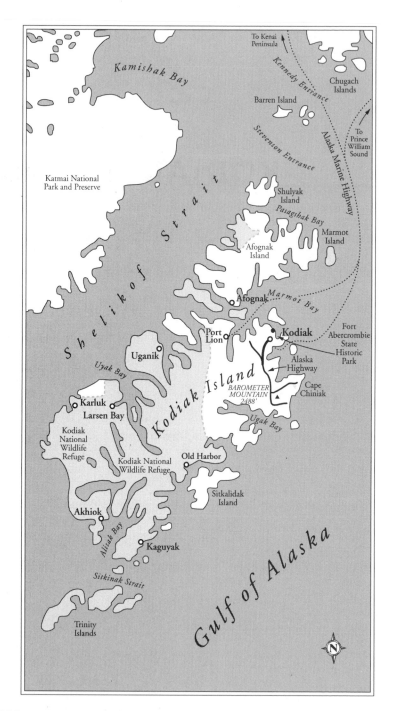

KODIAK ISLAND

Kodiak Island is often one of the last places discovered by visitors to Alaska. Unlike places on the state highway system or Southeast Alaska's extensive network of ferries, Kodiak isn't on the way to somewhere else. Few people just wander through. A trip to "The Rock" is a commitment, but one that can bring many rewards.

Whether you arrive by boat or by plane, you're bound to be surprised by the town of Kodiak's metropolitan appearance. Opulent homes line the cliffs and beaches that surround the city on three sides, and downtown Kodiak is a compact, bustling commercial center adjacent to one of the city's two harbors. Despite the island's isolation, residents enjoy a cosmopolitan lifestyle with access to uncrowded beaches, extensive wilderness trails, and easy mountain hikes.

Kodiak is the second-largest island in the United States after the island of Hawaii. Situated in the northern Gulf of Alaska, just east of the Alaska Peninsula, the Kodiak Island Archipelago is home to about 15,000 people, less than 100 miles of mostly unpaved roads, and 3,000 of the world's largest brown bears. About two-thirds of Kodiak Island is devoted to the Kodiak National Wildlife Refuge, with more than 200 species of birds, 6 species of salmon, and a multitude of marine mammals and other wildlife.

Salmon has remained an important source of income for the past 100 years, while other fish, such as crab, halibut, shrimp, pollack, and shellfish, have shown fluctuating abundance. Halibut is currently the biggest moneymaker, although it has not matched the heady days of the rich king crab industry that financed some of the fancy homes in this wilderness outpost. Kodiak consistently rates as one of the country's most productive fishing ports.

ACCESS AND INFORMATION

For **AIR TRAVELERS**, Alaska Airlines (800/426-0333) and ERA Aviation (800/866/88394) fly several times daily from Anchorage. Kodiak is an elongated city, 5 miles from end to end. Although city bus service is available, most visitors will enjoy the freedom a **RENTAL CAR** will afford; Avis (9007/487-2264), Budget (907/487-2220), and Rent-A-Heap (907/487-4001) are all located at the airport. If you want to bring your own car or motor home to the island, this requires some planning. Contact the Alaska Marine Highway (800/642-0066; www.dot.state.ak.us/external/amhs/home.html) at least a month in advance for reservations. Aboard the **FERRY** MV *Tustumena*, the journey takes 9 hours to sail from Homer to Kodiak or 12 hours from Seward to Kodiak.

SUMMERS in Kodiak are cool, with temperatures most often between 50°F and 65°F. A thermometer reading of 75°F will tempt pale, sun-starved locals to don bathing suits for a dip in the frigid ocean. Inner-tubing on the Buskin River is a favorite sunny-day sport for local youngsters. In the WINTER, Kodiak is one of the warmest cities in Alaska. Islanders often take delight in calling their relatives in Dubuque, Iowa, or Charleston, W. Va., who are shivering with subzero temperatures, and informing them that the high temperature that day is 45°F and sunny. Winters are not all fun, however. Sometimes the temperature drops to −20°F, and the island's famous windstorms can pass the 70mph mark, literally soaking low-lying areas with seawater. The winter freeze-thaw cycle is hard on local roads, which are often rife with potholes.

A good source of information is the KODIAK ISLAND CONVENTION AND VISITORS BUREAU (100 Marine Wy, Kodiak, AK 99615; 907/486-4782 or 800/789-4782; kicvb@ptialaska.net; www.webcom.com/kodiak/welcome.html). A visitors center is located at the ferry terminal and open year-round.

EXPLORING

In 1964, an earthquake centered in Prince William Sound created a huge wave that sucked most of downtown Kodiak out to sea. As the city began to recover, planners redesigned the downtown into a series of closely spaced office buildings, known as "The Mall." Most of the city's shops are located in THE MALL or less than a block away. The two main drags, Mill Bay Road and Rezanof Drive, parallel one another the length of Kodiak, and most other businesses are located on these two streets.

THE TREASURY (907/486-5001), formerly known as The Shire, is located on The Mall and is a good source for books about Kodiak. A block away, NORTHERN EXPOSURE GALLERY AND FRAME LOFT (122 W Rezanof; 907/486-4956), features a broad selection of prints and photographs by Alaska's leading artists. Other sources for books, artwork, and sheer knowledge of Kodiak are the community's two museums. THE BARANOF MUSEUM (101 Marine Way; 907/486-5920), is located in one of the oldest remaining Russian buildings in Alaska. The museum is friendly, homey, and packed with history. Its collections span Alutiiq prehistory, Russian occupation, and World War II. The gift shop offers some Native artwork, but is best known for Russian lacquerware, icons, and samovars, as well as books. Nearby, the ALUTIIQ MUSEUM AND ARCHAEOLOGICAL REPOSITORY (215 Mission Rd; 907/486-7004; alutiiq2@ptialaska.net) focuses on the seagoing Alutiiq people and their more than 7,500 years in the Kodiak region. The museum often hosts visiting exhibits that highlight the culture of other Alaska Natives. Its small gift shop features artwork, jewelry, and books.

KODIAK BROWN BEARS

Kodiak Island is roughly the size of Connecticut, although two-thirds of the island is a national wildlife refuge and not accessible by road. The refuge is the domain of the Kodiak brown bear, the coastal relative of the grizzly and arguably the world's largest carnivore. In early summer, bears congregate along streams to fish for salmon. Most locals advise hikers not to explore trails outside town without carrying a firearm. But if it is not second nature for you to operate a gun, carrying one will cause you more trouble than not. Better opt for Mace or cayenne pepper spray, which also have been effective in discouraging bears.

Bear attacks are very rare. Only one person this century has been killed by a bear on Kodiak. If you spot a bear on the trail, do not turn and run. Do not run at all. The bear will think you're prey. A bear can outrun you easily. Band together with your hiking companions, make some noise, and back up slowly.   —Mark Gillespie

If all that culture makes your throat dry, or if you need to settle down in a quiet spot to soak in your newfound knowledge, there are plenty of options. During its boom years in the early '80s, Kodiak was famous for its ubiquitous bars and liquor stores, but that scene has greatly changed as espresso bars go head-to-head with saloons. **HARBORSIDE COFFEE AND GOODS** (216 Shelikof St; 907/486-5862) could pass for a caffeine cache anywhere in Washington or California, except for the fishing fleet clustered at its doorstep. **SWEETS 'N' MORE** (117 Lower Mill Bay Rd; 907/481-1630), at the downtown Y intersection, is Kodiak's first cyber-cafe, supplementing its coffee and tea menu with candies and computer access. On the opposite side of the Y, **MONK'S ROCK** (202 E Rezanof; 907/486-0905) offers a unique window into Kodiak's Russian Orthodox community. The coffeehouse is staffed by students from St. Innocent's Academy, and you can pick up icons or peruse classical and religious books while waiting for your latte. **MILL BAY COFFEE** (3833 E Rezanof; 907/486-4411) offers delectable fresh-baked pastries and an occasional art display. It is a short walk from Mill Bay Beach, a popular destination for joggers and bicyclists, which is accessible on an extensive paved trail that circles the east end of town.

There are not many roads to explore in Kodiak, but the landscape these roads take you to is unparalleled in Alaska. Sheer cliffs emerge from the ocean, giving way to lush green hillsides that Irish tourists swear look just like home to them. Puffins skim the water along wide sandy beaches, while eagles circle overhead. For that first overview of Kodiak itself, wind your way through the streets of **ALEUTIAN HOMES**, the city's first sub-division, and take a drive to the top of **PILLAR MOUNTAIN**. This is where the locals come to watch Fourth of July fireworks and take photos of the city and surrounding islands. The road is closed in winter, and you may need 4-wheel-drive after a long stretch of rain, but the view is worth it. Within walking distance of downtown Kodiak, and across the Near Island Bridge, is **NORTHEND PARK**. An easy hike, ideal for families, winds through dense spruce and past tide pools to beautiful beaches with views of downtown Kodiak. Nearby is **ST. HERMAN'S HARBOR**, one of two local boat harbors. The other, **ST. PAUL'S HARBOR**, is right off The Mall downtown. Both allow an interesting opportunity to view a working harbor with fishermen busy offloading tons of fish or mending nets. Watch the sea lions and eagles scavenging scraps or strike up a conversation with a fishermen or two. Most are happy to explain what they do. Fishing is the passion and lifeblood of this town.

Five miles north of town **FORT ABERCROMBIE STATE HISTORIC PARK**, with its rugged coastline and lovely woods, displays a cannon once mounted on a high bluff overlooking miles of open sea. The park also holds summer tours of the **MILLER POINT BUNKER**, a former underground concrete residence for watchmen who patrolled the horizon for signs of enemy ships during World War II. Elsewhere in the park are small concrete pillboxes, which are mere turrets with slits facing seaward. When one stands inside, it's impossible to imagine the amount of concentration servicemen had to have to be alert and watchful in the cold, windy weather of the North Pacific.

Four roads branch off from Rezanof Drive, Kodiak's primary boulevard. To the north, Rezanof becomes **MONASHKA BAY ROAD** and ends 11 miles later, at one of the island's few white sand beaches. (Most of Kodiak's beaches are composed of black slate sand.) A system of trails leads for several miles into a majestic Sitka spruce forest. Hikers will appreciate the spongy texture of the mossy forest floor. This area is called **TERMINATION POINT**.

To the south, Rezanof Drive becomes the **CHINIAK HIGHWAY**. You quickly pass the western edge of the island's spruce forest. The hills are now covered with alpine grasses and flowers. You'll see jagged mountain ridges, windy seaside cliffs, and river valleys, which provide pasture for horses, cattle, and domestic buffalo. At the end of the road is **CHINIAK**, populated mostly by people who think even Kodiak is getting too big for comfort. Drop in at the **RAVEN'S NEST** for a look at Jane Van Atta's whimsical artwork of wire, beads, and driftwood. Then stop by **ROAD'S END RESTAURANT AND LOUNGE** (907/486-2885), a popular greasy spoon famous for its huge hamburgers (served on French bread), deep-fried halibut sandwiches, and homemade pies. Road's End usually closes in February and opens in March at the first sighting of the gray whales' migration, so call ahead during the winter months to make sure that it's open. There's no bank in Chiniak, and Road's End doesn't take credit cards, so plan ahead.

Branch right on the Chiniak Highway to travel along **ANTON LARSEN BAY ROAD**, which snakes up between Barometer and Pyramid Mountains and down to a long shallow inlet. In the summer, Anton Larsen Bay is so thick with salmon you can see one jump just about every 5 seconds. The trip is short (about 11 miles) but quite spectacular. If your tastes run more to "birdies" than salmon, the U. S. Coast Guard's nine-hole **BEAR VALLEY GOLF COURSE** 907/486-7561 or 907/487-5108 is open May through October and has all the rental gear you need.

PASAGSHAK ROAD forks to the right from the Chiniak Highway, 30 miles to the south of Kodiak, and leads to Pasagshak River and Pasagshak Bay. The area beaches can be deeply peaceful on a calm day, but when the surf is up, watch out. Cowabunga! Kodiak is home to a tiny but hard-core band of wave riders. Die-hard surfers come from around the world to glory in these waves, too. (Wet suits, yes. Bikinis, no.)

For even greater contrast, a few miles past Pasagshak is the **KODIAK LAUNCH COMPLEX**. Operated by the Alaska Aerospace Development Corp., this is the first nonmilitary satellite launch complex in the United States. Designed to capture the market for moving small payloads into space, the complex is sending up satellites with polar orbits for Lockheed Martin Astronautics. In a twist of irony, the drive past the space-age launch complex ends at ancient **FOSSIL BEACH**, a dream for rock hounds.

All of Kodiak's **OUTLYING ROADS ARE UNPAVED** and often in poor condition. Most of the land on either side of the roads is privately owned. From Middle Bay to Cape Chiniak, the principal landholder is Leisnoi Inc. (3248 Mill Bay Rd; 907/486-8191), the Kodiak Native corporation. Leisnoi requests anyone hiking or camping on its land to carry a free permit, available at the corporation office and other locations around town.

ADVENTURES

Kodiak may have its share of creature comforts, but many of the island's visitors do not arrive to nibble cinnamon rolls and look at artifacts. It's the vast wilderness that draws them—the island beyond the city.

The mountains on Kodiak lie fairly low compared to others in Alaska. **BAROMETER MOUNTAIN**, a three-sided triangle that bookends a long ridge, stands only 2,488 feet high, while the island's tallest mountains barely exceed 4,000 feet. (Barometer Mountain is so named because you can tell if the weather is worsening or improving by watching the cloud ceiling move along Barometer's sides.) The peaks of Kodiak's mountains are easily climbed in an afternoon. On a warm day, hikers can be spotted against the bare, grassy mountainside making their way to the top for a view of the Pacific or the mainland's snowcapped peaks across Shelikof Strait. Summer is time for the best **SPORTFISHING** in the world. Many people prefer Kodiak's relatively unspoiled streams to the crowded, combative atmosphere on the mainland's Kenai River. Kodiak salmon can be just as large as their Kenai Peninsula cousins, with king salmon sometimes weighing in at more than 100 pounds. The prize fish of the region is halibut, a flatfish that feeds on the bottom of the ocean until it reaches sizes in excess of 300 pounds. Several **CHARTER BOAT OPERATIONS** offer excursions for halibut, salmon, and rockfish, such as Eric Stirrup's MV *Ten Bears* (907/486-2200), or Chris Fiala's Kodiak Island Charters (907/486-5380 or 800/575-5380; urascal@ptialaska.net; www.ptialaska. net/~urascal). As Kodiak seeks to expand its tourist attractions, new charter operators pop up each year. The Kodiak Charter Association (907/486-6363 or 888/972-6363), located in the lobby of the Best Western Kodiak Inn, maintains a list of available boats. Charter operations usually offer day tours and supply gear and assistance for hauling in the big ones. If you plan to keep your catch, make sure your charter will butcher and wrap the fish for you—most do.

Several air-taxi operators (contact the visitors bureau) provide flights over the stomping grounds of the famous Kodiak brown bear, in the **KODIAK NATIONAL WILDLIFE REFUGE** and **KATMAI NATIONAL PARK**. Some operators actually guarantee that you'll see a bear on your flight. If you'd like a closer, longer look, visits to **BEAR-VIEWING** lodges such as Rohrer's Bear Camp (PO Box 2219, Kodiak AK 99615-2219; 907/486-5835), located within the refuge, provide guided viewing for several days.

If you'd rather be asea than ashore, **KAYAKING** offers the quietest, most up-close exploration of the coast. Kodiak Kayak Tours (907/486-2722; fish2live@aol.com) and Mythos Expeditions (907/486-5536; mythosdk@ptialaska.net; www.mythos-expeditions.com) offer guided kayak tours near Kodiak. No experience is necessary, and you're almost sure to spot land and sea creatures including whales, sea lions, sea otters, puffins, elk, fox, and bears. Mythos also will transport you and all the gear you need to distant bays for your own guided or unguided kayak tour.

WINTER KAYAKING is actually a popular pastime on the island. When the wind isn't blowing and the moon is out, one may paddle through luminescent algae and reflections of stars. The ambient air temperature on these days is usually right around freezing. Mythos Expeditions (see above) especially recommends trips in March and April, when migrations of gray whales skirt Kodiak's coast. Charter boats also carry

THE CRAB FESTIVAL

This festival was quite bawdy in its early years; now, the emphasis is on family fun, complete with a carnival, vendors, races, and barbecues. Today's Crab Festival is not without strange events, however. Watch for swimmers in bright red neoprene suits lining up for the annual **Survival Suit Races**.

Survival suits, also known as "full-immersion suits," insulate stranded mariners from the frigid waters of the North Pacific Ocean. Without such protection, a person can die within minutes from hypothermia. In the race, a team of four swimmers dashes 100 yards to the water's edge, correctly zips themselves into survival suits, and plunges into the water for a 300-yard swim to a life boat anchored in the harbor. The race is meant to simulate a real-life emergency and gives nonfishermen a taste of what the fishing fleet must be prepared to handle.

On the last day at the main event, **The Fishermen's Memorial Service** is held in front of Fishermen's Hall on Marine Way at a monument bearing the names of Kodiak fishermen lost at sea. The names of each man or woman who has perished that year are read as a bell tolls from the Holy Resurrection Orthodox Church. Kodiak awaits the year when the bell will be silent.

The Crab Festival (907/486-5557) lasts from the Thursday before Memorial Day until the following Monday.   —Mark Gillespie

WHALE-WATCHERS to prime viewing points around the island. The community marks the season with a 10-day "Whale Fest" in April, featuring movies, lectures, artwork, and other whale-related events. Even the local paper posts daily reports of whale sightings.

One of Kodiak's most unusual tourist opportunities is the chance to take part in an **ARCHAEOLOGICAL DIG**. Dig Afognak (907/486-6014; dig@afognak.com; www.afognak.com/dig) places you at a working field camp in weeklong sessions. No archaeological experience is necessary, and the work includes breaks for fishing, exploring, and informal learning sessions. Dormitory-style tents, family-style meals, and friendly hosts give Dig Afognak the aura of a summer camp for grown-ups. Day trips are also possible, depending on availability.

Although the snowpack may not amount to much in downtown Kodiak, the surrounding mountains provide some excellent cross-country and telemark **SKIING**, as well as snowboarding. Weather conditions vary from year to year, and access may be challenging, but the folks at Orion's Boards & Cords (103 Center Ave; 907/486-8380) will have all the latest information.

NIGHTLIFE

As an old saying goes, "In Kodiak, Alaska, there are more bars than churches." But this might not be the case anymore since the Salvation Army bought a notorious strip joint called the Beachcomber's Bar and converted it into a place of worship. Another bar conversion happened to the Ship's Bar downtown, when a hairstylist moved in and cleverly renamed the establishment "The Ship's Barber."

It would be a mistake to say all of Kodiak's bars have gone the way of the now-scarce king crab, though. Billing itself as "Alaska's Largest Navigational Hazard," **TONY'S** (907/486-9489), on The Mall, is the headquarters for community stunts such as the **PILLAR MOUNTAIN GOLF CLASSIC**, a late-March, cross-country golf event that has been featured nationally on ABC Sports and in *Sports Illustrated*. The course is one hole at par 70. Golfers use bright orange balls for better visibility in the alpine snow. The rules specifically forbid the use of dogs to find lost balls or power tools to remove brush from the fairway. **THE VILLAGE BAR** (907/486-3412), also on The Mall, regularly brings live comedy acts to town.

RESTAURANTS

Beryl's Sweet Shop

202 CENTER ST, KODIAK; 907/486-3323

A short-order grill and candy shop tucked away in The Mall, Beryl's (rhymes with "curls") serves cold-cut sandwiches, hamburgers, delicious homemade soups, and ice cream treats. Fresh pies and cakes are also available, as well as a good selection of espresso drinks. The co-owners make frequent trips to Russia, and you can buy souvenirs such as lavishly decorated tea services, hand-painted Ukrainian Easter eggs, and colorful nesting dolls. *$; MC, V; checks OK; breakfast, lunch every day; no alcohol.*

The Captain's / ★★

202 E REZANOF DR, KODIAK; 907/486-4144

Once the site of a Chinese restaurant, the Captain's slowly is changing decor from Oriental to nautical, but don't let that stop you from diving into the menu. Selections include soups, salads, and sandwiches, but locals head straight for the Captain's hefty potato skillets—new potatoes sauteed in garlic and onion and topped with goodies such as black beans and salsa or feta cheese and fresh tomatoes. Home-baked bread, biscuits, and sweets fill in any empty corners. The man behind the stove is often Father Jonas Worsham, a Russian Orthodox priest, and your wait staff may be seminarians from St. Innocent's Academy. *$; no credit cards; local checks only; breakfast, lunch Tues–Sat; no alcohol; located upstairs over Monk's Rock coffeehouse.* &

El Chicano / ★★

103 CENTER ST, KODIAK; 907/486-6116
"El Cheez," as some locals call it, offers heaping helpings of familiar Mexican dishes. Don't let your eyes be bigger than your stomach. The "License-Plate Burrito" really is as big as a license plate. Pace yourself through the generous entrees so you'll have room afterward for traditional flan or fried ice cream, which arrives crisp and smothered with chocolate. (If you're strong-willed, there's also a Weight Watchers menu.) El Chicano often features a live mariachi band or salsa dancing during Mexican holidays such as Cinco de Mayo. *$$; AE, DIS, MC, V; checks OK; lunch, dinner Mon–Sat; full bar.* &

Henry's Great Alaskan Restaurant / ★

512 MARINE WAY, KODIAK; 907/486-3533
It can be dim and smoky, but Henry's is where many Kodiak residents head for a good, reasonably priced meal. Steaks, gourmet hamburgers, sandwiches, pastas, and salads anchor the menu, along with daily all-you-can-eat specials such as prime rib or chicken-fried steak. The local favorite is Wednesday's crawfish pie special. *$$; AE, DIS, MC, V; local checks only; lunch, dinner every day; full bar; on The Mall.* &

Mongolian Barbecue / ★

1247 MILL BAY RD, KODIAK; 907/486-2900
This typical Chinese-American restaurant has something special. The all-you-can eat Mongolian barbecue buffet allows each diner to fill bowls with fresh ingredients such as meat, seafood, noodles, vegetables, and a variety of sauces. The brimming bowl is then tossed onto a giant grill and cooked as you watch. The result is fast, tasty, and healthy, too—no oil or MSG is added. If you have small children with small appetites, they'll usually get a discount. Traditional Asian foods are also on the menu, but most locals opt for the barbecue or for the lunch buffet. *$$; MC, V; local checks only; lunch, dinner every day; beer and wine.* &

Second Floor Restaurant / ★★★

116 W REZANOF DR, KODIAK; 907/486-8555
Many Kodiak Islanders believe the community's civilization quotient increased several points when the Second Floor Restaurant opened downtown, serving traditional Japanese cuisine. Second Floor serves excellent tempura dishes. Don't pass up the homegrown Kodiak Roll, sushi made from locally caught seafood. The restaurant offers a good selection of imported beers, including Japanese brands. There's also a children's menu. *$$$; MC, V; local checks only; lunch Mon–Fri, dinner every day; beer and wine; located upstairs, over the Peking Restaurant—look for the side door.*

LODGINGS

There are few bargains on this remote island. An alternative—typically less expensive and sometimes more luxurious—is one of Kodiak's **BED-AND-BREAKFASTS**. Most are in private homes, some with spectacular views of the water. The Kodiak Convention and Visitors Bureau (100 Marine Wy, Kodiak, AK 99615; 907/486-4782 or 800/789-4782; kicvb@ptialaska.net; www.webcom.com/kodiak/welcome.html), in the ferry terminal, maintains lists of bed-and-breakfasts and remote wilderness lodges.

Best Western Kodiak Inn / ★

236 W REZANOF DR, KODIAK, AK 99615; 907/486-5712, 888/KODIAK-4, OR 888/563-4254

Formerly known as the Westmark Hotel, the Kodiak Inn overlooks St. Paul Harbor. Because it's convenient to downtown, it's where most local civic groups meet and visiting business types stay for overnights. Tours and charters may be booked in the lobby. The Chart Room Restaurant is one of the best spots in town, for its killer view and wonderful steaks and seafood. Outside the restaurant, check out the photos depicting the aftermath of the 1964 tidal wave. *$$; AE, DC, DIS, MC, V; local checks only; kodiakin@ptialaska.net; www.ak-biz.com/kodiakinn/.* ᕽ

Buskin River Inn / ★

1395 AIRPORT WY, KODIAK, AK 99615; 907/487-2700 OR 800/544-2202

The Buskin, as it's known locally, is an easy walk from the state airport. If you're just passing through on your way to a fishing or hunting camp or if you have a car, it's a convenient location. Otherwise, you might prefer something closer to town. The on-site travel agency is a plus, and the Eagle's Nest restaurant is a worthy stop, especially during king crab season. *$$; AE, V, MC, DC, DIS; local checks only; info@ kodiakadventure.com.* ᕽ

DENALI NATIONAL PARK AND THE PARKS HIGHWAY

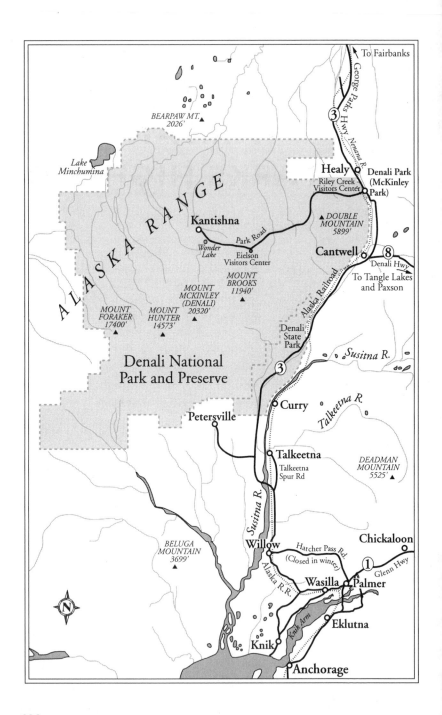

DENALI NATIONAL PARK
AND THE PARKS HIGHWAY

While you may think the Parks Highway was named for the parklands that surround the extraordinary massif of Mount McKinley (Denali National Park and Denali State Park), it was actually named for George Parks, one of the territorial governors of Alaska in the early 1900s. Officially it's known as the George Parks Highway, but everyone refers to it simply as the Parks Highway. It runs from the Matanuska Valley just south of Palmer north to Fairbanks, a journey of 324 miles. Paralleling the Susitna and Chulitna Rivers and the Alaska Railroad, the route wends its way up a broad glacial valley. The land here is dotted with swamp spruce, lakes, old homesteads, cabins, a multitude of bars, little roadhouses, and a small assortment of whistlestops and towns, all framed by incredible mountain ranges in the distance.

Wasilla

Thirty years ago, the town was little more than an airstrip and a charming grocery near the old railroad section house (now on the Register of National Historic Sites). But it boomed with strip malls during the pipeline construction years of the late 1970s, and big money was liberally laced with questionable taste. The wild feel of the place is gone. But never fear. It lives on in the woods and foothills a stone's throw away. The **MATANUSKA-SUSITNA CONVENTION AND VISITORS BUREAU** (907/746-5000; www.alaskavisit.com) is located in a log cabin near the juncture of the Parks and Glenn Highways at Mile 35.5 on the Parks Highway. Open daily, mid-May through mid-September.

ADVENTURES

SNOWMOBILING / Alaska Snow Safaris (907/783-7669 or 888/414-7669; www.akadventures.com) offers half-day and daylong expeditions, complete with gear.

SKY TREKKING ALASKA / Owner and chief pilot Lori Egge offers custom-designed itineraries covering all regions of Alaska for those who like to do their trekking from the air, setting down by remote wilderness streams for fishing, kayaking, or a gourmet picnic. Egge also offers package air tours, such as "winter treks" that fly the route of the Iditarod Trail Sled Dog Race in March, from checkpoint to checkpoint, for 12 days. That trip costs about $5,200 per person. But because Egge's trips are custom-designed, the costs vary widely. You can find her at Fiskehauk

Airways, 485 Pioneer Dr, Wasilla, AK 99564; 907/373-4966 or 800/770-4966; skytrek@alaska.net; www.skytrekkingalaska.com.

PADDLE OR SKI TO REMOTE CABINS / The NANCY LAKE STATE RECREATION AREA (907/745-3975) offers canoeing through an 8-mile chain of lakes in the Lynx Lake Loop, good for a mellow weekend expedition. There are also 12 rustic cabins, insulated for winter use, which may be rented on a daily basis; they're good for cross-country ski weekends. If you want to be more pampered with hearty German cuisine waiting for you at the end of the trail, but still ski through some great country with beautiful views of Mount McKinley, reserve a weekend at DENALI VIEW CHALET (907/333-9104), more popularly and fondly known as "Sepp's Cabin," as it belongs to a wonderful longtime Alaska character, Sepp Weber.

FESTIVALS AND EVENTS

IDITAROD TRAIL SLED DOG RACE / The best of Wasilla happens in March during "Iditarod time" at the official re-start, which has its ceremonial beginnings on Fourth Avenue in Anchorage the first Saturday of every March. After racing from Fourth Avenue to Eagle River, mushers and handlers truck their teams to Wasilla for the "re-start" the next day. This is as festive as the first day of the race. For spectators, there's more room to get a really good view of this extraordinary event. And mushers and dogs are just darned glad to get out of the booby traps of civilization and on the real trail to Nome. For more information, call Iditarod Headquarters (907/376-5155).

IDITASPORT EXTREME / Held in the early part of February, the Iditasport was originally inspired by the late, great Joe Redington, Sr., founder of the Iditarod Trail Sled Dog Race. This event was once a series of individual races. First came the Iditaski, a long-distance ski covering 210 miles of the historic gold-rush trail. Then came the Iditashoe, a mere 105-mile dash on snowshoes, followed by the Iditabike, with contestants bumping down more than 200 miles of the winter trail on mountain bikes. Today all these races happen at the same time under one umbrella event—the Iditasport. Prepare for the cold. This is not an event for the faint of heart. Call 907/345-4505 for more information.

DANCING BEARS DANCE CAMP / Another one of the best annual events in the region occurs at King's Lake Fine Arts Camp off Fishhook Road in Wasilla every Memorial Day weekend at Dancing Bears Dance Camp. The motto of this fun-loving group is "Dance 'til you drop"—three days of nonstop clogging, squares, contras, swing, old-time fiddling, and calling with guest callers and musicians from all over Alaska and the United States. Dance workshops start early in the morning, run all day, and are followed by dancing and music all night. It's a joyful rite of spring. Except for summer, dances and workshops are held monthly in Anchorage. For a schedule, contact Dancing Bears, PO Box 200366, Anchorage, AK 99520-0366; call the "Bear Phone" at 907/566-2327; or check www.alaska.net/~seb/dbears.

Knik

This is a journey into Iditarod country. Or at least a glimpse into the modern-day lore of the Iditarod Trail Sled Dog Race. The historic Iditarod Trail runs out of Knik. A lot of dog mushers live down here, and it's also the site of the big log cabin **IDITAROD TRAIL SLED DOG RACE HEADQUARTERS AND VISITORS CENTER** (907/376-5155), at Mile 2.2 on the Knik Road, open daily in summer. Stop in and steep yourself in characters and stories. If you want to volunteer on the next race or bid for a seat in the sled bag of one of the starting mushers for a $500 to $3,000 ride down Fourth Avenue come race day, this is where you can do it. If you want to go **DOG MUSHING,** they can put you in touch with mushers currently offering daylong or multiday trips, winter or summer.

RESTAURANTS

Legends / ★★

SETTLERS BAY, MILE 8, KNIK-GOOSE BAY RD, KNIK; 907/376-5298 OR 888/560-5298
Steak, salad, seafood, pasta, and wild game grace the menu of this lovely location in the valley, surrounded by spectacular views of the Chugach and Talkeetna Mountain Ranges. It is a delight that Settlers Bay once again has a fine restaurant, with its sweeping panorama and pleasant, airy, exposed-beam wood interior. Definitely worth the hour drive from Anchorage, Legends is a treat for valley residents. *$$$; AE, DIS, MC, V; checks OK; lunch, dinner every day, brunch Sun; beer and wine; 8 miles along the Knik-Goose Bay Rd from the Parks Hwy turnoff in Wasilla.* &

Hatcher Pass

Hatcher Pass is beautiful, with alpine meadows and streams; a narrow, winding dirt road; ruins of old gold mines; and looming mountains with names like Microdot, Skyscraper, and Government Peaks. **HATCHER PASS ROAD** from the Palmer side to the Willow side is a fun trip in summer, but closed to the Willow side in winter. The easiest way to get to Hatcher Pass is to drive past Palmer on the Glenn Highway, turn left on

Fishhook Road, and follow it all the way to Hatcher Pass. In winter, Hatcher Pass gets generous amounts of snow, making it a great destination for early and late cross-country skiing.

THE ALASKA RAILROAD

Heading north out of Anchorage on the Alaska Railroad toward the majestic peaks of the Alaska Range and its crown jewel, Mount McKinley, you'll travel along the broad Susitna River Valley and through the old railroad stops that motorists never see. Most were named by old gold prospectors. Their names alone reflect hope, nostalgia, and a hankering for home and warmer climes: Gold Creek, Sunshine, Colorado, and Honolulu. The view is especially dramatic in spring during breakup, when huge chunks of ice float down the Susitna River. Chances are good for seeing bald eagles, moose, and caribou, so keep a lookout.

The railroad, which extends from the ice-free port of Seward to the Interior gold-rush town of Fairbanks, was built in the 1920s to open up the rich Interior for development. Today, the railroad carries coal, gravel, logs, petroleum products, and half a million passengers every year. It is North America's last full-service railroad, offering both freight and passenger service.

In summer, the train runs daily between Anchorage and Fairbanks with a stop at Denali National Park. The Anchorage-to-Fairbanks run takes 12 hours; Anchorage to Denali takes 8. Package deals are available through the railroad (800/544-0552).

In winter, the railroad provides a special service called "The Hurricane Turn," mainly for Alaska homesteaders, cabin dwellers, and wilderness folks. The name comes from Hurricane Gulch, 170 miles north of Anchorage, where a dramatic bridge spans an even more dramatic canyon. The northbound train from Anchorage turns around there and heads south again.

This is the last "flag-stop" service in the United States. Officially, waiting passengers along the tracks are supposed to wave a white flag, but the train crew usually slows to a halt at the wave of a hand. Other trains will not stop in the summertime. The Hurricane Turn uses special, self-propelled silver "Budd" cars that have their own engines so they don't need a locomotive to pull them.

Regularly scheduled passenger trains stop only at Wasilla, Talkeetna, and Denali. In the winter, weekend passenger trains can be flagged down. Passengers generally include Alaskans traveling to their remote cabins or homesteads for a weekend or adventurers beginning multiday wilderness cross-country ski trips. Many enjoy a long weekend by riding the Hurricane Turn out of Anchorage on Thursday, then catching the southbound train back to Anchorage on Sunday.

—Kris Capps

ADVENTURES

EXPLORE INDEPENDENCE MINE STATE HISTORICAL PARK / One of the best things to do in summer at Hatcher Pass is to explore the old mine buildings and the main building, which are preserved today as a historical park. This hardrock gold mining operation was one of Alaska's greatest gold producers in the 1930s. Call 907/745-2827.

ALPINE HIKING / Located above tree line, this is a wonderful area for alpine hiking in all directions. Pick your ridge and go for it, or follow one of the established trails. The trail to **REED LAKES** is a popular day hike.

RENT A LLAMA / One of the most unusual ways to journey to Hatcher Pass is to rent llamas and an artist for a day with **LLAMA BUDDIES EXPEDITIONS** (907/376-8472). The llamas carry your paint, palette, and gourmet lunch, while you hike from one beautiful spot to the next with an Alaska artist who helps stir your imagination to translate it all onto paper and canvas. They cater to non-artists, too. Cost is $150 per person.

BACKCOUNTRY SKIING / In winter, Hatcher Pass is a backcountry ski haven. It usually has skiable snow long before and long after many other places near Anchorage. Folks come here to cross-country ski on set tracks (there is a $5 charge for use of groomed trails) or to forge their own trails up the mountains with cross-country, or telemark skis or snowboards.

AVALANCHE EDUCATION / Do not trip lightly into these mountains. Avalanches have buried several backcountry travelers here in past years. If your skills and knowledge are thin in this area, you're in luck, because Hatcher Pass is the teaching arena for the best avalanche education/training program in the country, provided by the internationally renowned **ALASKA MOUNTAIN SAFETY CENTER**, run by Doug Fesler and Jill Fredston. Their team of experts conducts weekend avalanche and mountaineering workshops during the winter and launches people into summer with a sea kayaking workshop out of Seward in Resurrection Bay. For a schedule of classes, contact 9140 Brewsters Dr, Anchorage, AK 99516; 907/345-3566 or 907/345-4345.

LODGINGS

Hatcher Pass Lodge / ★★

TALKEETNA MOUNTAINS, NORTH OF PALMER, 18 MILES FROM THE GLENN HWY, PALMER, AK 99645; 907/745-5897, FAX 907/745-1200
At 3,000 feet above timberline in the Talkeetna Mountains, Hatcher Pass Lodge sits in a bowl of jagged mountains amid miles of groomed cross-country ski trails and backcountry skiing. In summer, the scenery is one of alpine flowers and great ridges to hike. After an exhilarating day outside, stay overnight in one of the nine cozy little A-frames and private

cabins run by Hatcher Pass Lodge. Rooms in the lodge are $70; cabins are $115 a night for two; and pets are $15 extra. Situated on a 10-acre private inholding in the Independence Mine State Historical Park, the lodge, while small, is also a festive place to eat. The food is quite tasty— Swiss cheese fondue, gourmet pizzas, and a variety of soups, salads, and sandwiches. You can get hot liqueur and espresso drinks from the bar. *$–$$; AE, DIS, MC, V; local checks only; breakfast, lunch, dinner every day; full bar; www.hatcherpasslodge.com; PO Box 763, Palmer, AK 99645; to drive to Hatcher Pass and the lodge, take the Glenn Hwy from Anchorage past the town of Palmer (about a 45-minute drive); turn left on Palmer-Fishhook Rd, continue until it merges with Hatcher Pass Rd, and follow that all the way up to the lodge and Independence Mine. Depending on snow conditions, this may take you another 45 minutes. You will want to have 4-wheel drive in winter.*

Talkeetna

If you're looking for "an end-of-the-road experience" or you want to take a flight around Mount McKinley on a clear day, turn off on the Talkeetna Spur Road just past Mile 98 on the Parks Highway. It's 14 miles to the little village with Alaska's most famous mountain rising as its backdrop. Nowhere else on earth does a massif rise so dramatically from nearly sea level as McKinley. If measured from base to summit, it is the tallest mountain in the world. In 50 miles, the land rises from 350 feet (Talkeetna) to 20,320 feet (the summit of McKinley).

The history of Talkeetna (pop. 260) has spanned old bachelor gold miners, feisty dames, daring bush pilots, back-to-the-earth flower children, dog mushers, hippies, wild mountain guides, and every year an international onslaught of climbers bound for the summit of Mount McKinley. With such a diverse mix of locals comes an eclectic mix of architecture. As renegade English professor Ed Craver, who lived here for many years along the banks of the river, once wrote: "One of the first things a traveler notices in Talkeetna is the bazaar of construction. There are A-frames and timber frames, domes and teepees, log cabins and plywood shacks . . . enough turrets and towers for a medieval village and even a shoe-shaped home for the old woman."

ACCESS AND INFORMATION

The **TALKEETNA HISTORICAL SOCIETY** (907/733-2487) runs a Visitor Information Center in an old cabin in the heart of town, as well as a fun little museum—partly housed in the original one-room schoolhouse— covering Talkeetna's unusual mining, mountaineering, and bush flying history. There is also a new **NATIONAL PARK SERVICE RANGER**

STATION (907/733-2231) in Talkeetna, open daily with displays, literature, history, and information on climbing the mountain.

ADVENTURES

FLY AROUND MOUNT MCKINLEY / On a clear day, take a flight around Mount McKinley, soar over the summit, or land on one of its glaciers. The pilots here are some of the best in the world. They routinely fly hundreds of climbers to the mountain in late spring and early summer, landing most of them at Kahiltna Glacier base camp, at around a 7,000-foot elevation. It's a spectacular flight. For flight tours, call **HUDSON AIR SERVICE** (907/733-2321), the oldest air service in Talkeetna; **DOUG GEETING AVIATION'S** McKinley Flight Tours & Glacier Landings (800/770-2366 or 907/733-2366); **K2 AVIATION** (800/764-2291 or 907/733-2291); or **TALKEETNA AIR TAXI** (800/533-2219 or 907/733-2218).

CLIMB THE MOUNTAIN / If you're looking for a more intimate view of Mount McKinley or one of the other mountains in the Alaska Range, perhaps even a summit bid, you could hire no finer guides than **ALASKA DENALI GUIDING** (PO Box 566, Talkeetna, AK 99676; 907/733-2649, fax 907/733-1362). Brian and Diane Okonek have been guiding on Denali for years and are highly respected for their wilderness savvy and attention to safety and detail. They're wonderful human beings to boot! **MOUNTAIN TRIP** (PO Box 111809, Anchorage, AK 99511; 907/345-6499; mttrip@aol.com; www.mountaintrip.com) is another highly respected guiding outfit in the high mountains.

FESTIVALS AND EVENTS

TALKEETNA MOOSE DROPPING FESTIVAL / In Alaska, any excuse is a party. So beat feet to Talkeetna for the famous moose dropping throwing competition and legendary Mountain Mother contest. In addition there's a parade, arts and crafts booths, a 5-kilometer run and walk, great music, and a barbecue. Held on the second weekend in July in Talkeetna. Mile 14.5, Talkeetna Spur Rd; www.moosedrop.com.

BACHELOR AUCTION–WILDERNESS WOMAN CONTEST / For more than a decade, the Talkeetna Bachelor Society has invited all single ladies to participate in their Wilderness Woman Contest the first weekend in December. In the spirit of good fun, women have responded by demonstrating their formidable finesse in "firewood-hauling, water-fetching, snow-machining, fish-catching, moose-dispatching, beverage-opening, and other vital skills for daily living on the Last Frontier." In the evening, bachelors are auctioned off to the highest bidder. A sense of humor is highly recommended. Call 907/733-2323 or 907/733-2262 for more information.

LODGINGS

Talkeetna Lodge / ★★

MILE 12.5, TALKEETNA SPUR RD, TALKEETNA, AK 99676;
907/265-4500 OR 877/258-6877
Newly opened in the summer of 1999, the magical part of this lodge is
its deck; on a clear day it offers breathtaking views of Mounts McKinley
and Foraker and a sweep of the Susitna Valley. Its small photo gallery is
the beginning of a tribute to mountaineering history and some of the legendary characters who have climbed in the Alaska Range. Owned by a
Native corporation, Cook Inlet Region Inc. (CIRI), the lodge, 2 miles
from the center of Talkeetna, has nearly 50 rooms with four outer guest
buildings accommodating 12 each. The high season is June through
August (rates vary winter to summer, from $79 to $179 for a double).
$$; AE, DIS, MC, V; checks OK; dining room; www.talkeetnalodge.
com; shuttle to town and railroad station; PO Box 93330, Anchorage,
AK 99509-3330. ⅃

Denali State Park

Denali State Park is one of Alaska's best-kept secrets because most trav-
elers continue north to the more popular (and populous) Denali National
Park. With a little effort, hikers can easily climb out of the thick vegeta-
tion and emerge onto beautiful alpine tundra ridges. The park is about
half the size of Rhode Island and runs on both sides of the Parks High-
way. On the east side, two ridges—**CURRY AND KESUGI**—provide the
backbone of the park and run 35 miles north and south. They offer stu-
pendous views of Mount McKinley and surrounding peaks. Hiking here
is also a sure way to avoid crowds.

ACCESS AND INFORMATION

The **ALASKA PUBLIC LANDS INFORMATION CENTERS** in downtown
Anchorage, Fairbanks, and Ketchikan are the best places for information
on Denali State Park as well as a wealth of information on other parks
and refuges throughout Alaska (in Anchorage: 605 W 4th Ave; 907/271-
2737; in Fairbanks: 250 Cushman St, Ste 1A; 907/456-0527; and in
Ketchikan: 50 Main St; 907/228-6220). Or you can call the **ALASKA
STATE PARKS INFORMATION CENTER** in Wasilla (907/745-3975). To
reserve state park cabins you can prepay at any one of the aforemen-
tioned information centers around Alaska or, in the summer, at the
DENALI STATE PARK VISITOR CONTACT STATION, which is located at
the Alaska Veterans Memorial at Mile 147.2, George Parks Highway.

The Alaska Natural History Association has a small bookstore here, which also sells maps.

ADVENTURES

BACKPACKING / LITTLE COAL CREEK TRAIL is a short day hike or first stop for an overnight backpacking trip. It is also the quickest access to get above tree line in this section of mountains. Two miles into the hike on a clear day, enjoy a "forever" view of mountains and glaciers on the other side of the Chulitna River. If you're a strong hiker, you can get there in less than an hour. The trail is not particularly steep. Vegetation is thick en route, so make lots of noise to let bears know you're in the area. Black bears are common.

FISHING AND CAR CAMPING / BYERS LAKE is a great stop for car camping, especially for those folks with fishing poles in hand. Fish for grayling, burbot, rainbow trout, lake trout, and whitefish. The state campground has 66 sites and charges $12 a night. If you want to get a little farther away from civilization, pack your tent and hike or canoe to a more remote campground about 2 miles away.

RENT A CABIN / There are two cabins available for rent every day at **BYERS LAKE**. One is road accessible; the other is a half-mile walk or canoe to the other side of the lake and has a fantastic view of Denali. The $35-per-night fee must be prepaid (see above).

LODGINGS

Mount McKinley Princess Wilderness Lodge / ★★

MILE 133.1, PARKS HWY, DENALI PARK, AK 99755; 907/733-2900 OR 800/426-0500, FAX 907/733-2922
Sister to the Denali Park Lodge right outside the national park entrance, this new $20 million hotel is the first major hotel built along the south side of the park, which is still virtually inaccessible by road. Just 3 miles from the park border, overlooking the Chulitna River, this hotel boasts a spectacular view of Mount McKinley on a clear day, from the deck or from the floor-to-ceiling windows in the impressive Grand Room. A variety of activities are available here, from flight-seeing and river rafting to hiking on state park trails. Rooms run $179 to $199 in peak season; shoulder season rates are cheaper. $$$; AE, DC, MC, V; local checks OK; closed Oct–May; full bar; mailing address: 2815 2nd Ave, Ste 400, Seattle, WA 98121. ᕗ

MCKINLEY "FIRSTS"

"To the summit!" was the rallying cry of Mount McKinley's first and most colorful guide. A boisterous Swiss American, Ray Genet made mountaineering history in Alaska. He was part of the first successful winter expedition on McKinley in 1967. Three members—Dave Johnston of Talkeetna, Art Davidson of Rainbow, and Ray—reached the summit. But the next day on descent, winter storms scoured the slopes and hurricane-force winds dropped the temperature, with windchill to −148°F. They were trapped for five days in a snow cave near the top. In the 11th hour, it was Genet who struggled painfully out into the winter gale to find a cache with cooking gas so they could melt snow for water. Davidson wrote a gripping account of that journey in his book *Minus 148°*.

In the fall of 1979, Genet climbed to the top of Mount Everest in Nepal, the highest mountain in the world. Beneath the summit, while on descent, he froze to death on a bivouac. But his legend lives on: Genet's son, Taras, at age 12, became the youngest person to summit Mount McKinley in 1991.

McKinley is an arena of "firsts." Appropriately, the first to set foot on the top of the highest mountain in North America was a young Athabascan-Irish lad, Walter Harper, part of the Hudson Stuck expedition in 1912. Barbara Washburn, in 1947, was the first woman to climb McKinley and still holds the record for climbing both the North and South Peaks in a single expedition. In 1970, the famous Japanese world adventurer Naomi Uemura made the first successful solo ascent. In February 1984, Uemura returned to the mountain for the first solo winter summit bid. Tragically, he died upon descent. Following in Uemura's footsteps, mountain guide Vern Tejas in 1988 became the first to reach the summit alone in the winter and return alive.

—Nan Elliot

Denali National Park and Preserve

Ah, the magic of Denali! It's no surprise thousands of people travel here every year. A wilderness area roughly the size of Massachusetts, this is home to some of the most magnificent creatures on earth. It is all framed by a range of breathtaking icy peaks leading up to the highest mountain on the North American continent—Mount McKinley. Memories here are not soon forgotten: the sight of a moose calf wobbling behind its mother, a wolf relentlessly digging for a ground squirrel, or a blond grizzly bear loping over the tundra. While most visitors will see bears and some will see caribou or a wolf, this is not a zoo. Sighting animals takes patience, persistence, and constant looking, looking, looking. Denali is home to 163 species of birds, 37 species of mammals, and 450 species of plants.

If weather cooperates during your visit, you may even see the top of Mount McKinley, rising 20,320 feet above sea level. During summer months, this imposing peak creates its own weather system and may be clearly visible only a third of the time. When the mountain is "out," there is no mistaking which peak is McKinley. It looms dramatically over every other mountain on the horizon.

A prospector dubbed the mountain "McKinley" in 1896, in honor of William McKinley of Ohio, who became the 25th president of the United States. Long ago, Athabascan Indians called it Denali, which means "the high one." Debate continues today over whether the name should be officially changed to Denali. Meanwhile, most Alaskans call it simply "The Mountain." More than 1,000 climbers attempt to scale McKinley every year. Only half succeed. To date, nearly 100 have died trying to reach the summit. Climbing McKinley is serious business and often can take 20 to 30 days. The mountain not only is high, but can be bitterly cold. Severe storms may hit without warning, and winds can gust to 150mph.

In 1922, only 22 tourists came to admire the wonders of this newly created park. By 1939, there were 2,200 visitors. In 1971, visitors numbered 44,528. In 1994, numbers soared to 490,311 visitors. The best season to come is May, when snow is still melting, through September, when the tundra turns red and gold. In between, the flowers bloom in June, mosquitoes attack voraciously in July, and rains often hit in August. Snow may fall at any time. Each season holds its own charm. One road leads into this magnificent wilderness, and private vehicle traffic is restricted.

ACCESS AND INFORMATION

Whether you're coming from Anchorage or Fairbanks, there are economical ways to get to Denali National Park if you're not driving your own vehicle. The **PARKS HIGHWAY EXPRESS** (907/479-3065 or 888/600-6001; Info@alaskashuttle.com) is a shuttle bus that runs daily between Fairbanks and Anchorage. The trip takes 9 hours, but the bus will drop you off anywhere in between. One-way costs $55; round-trip $99. **ALASKA BACKPACKER SHUTTLE** (800/266-8625 or 907/344-8775, fax 907/522-7382; abst@juno.com; www.alaska.net/~backpack), either vans or buses, drives to Denali daily from Anchorage, leaving early in the morning, $40 one-way.

THE RILEY CREEK VISITOR CENTER (907/683-1266, summer; 907/683-2294, winter) is located at Mile 1 on the park road, just after turning off the George Parks Highway. Here you can buy tickets for the bus into the park, get backcountry camping permits, or learn about easily reached hiking trails. Video programs cover everything from bear safety to how to safely ford a river. Rangers give programs twice daily and lead moderate-to-strenuous hikes through backcountry wilderness. There is also a visitor center near the end of the park road at Eielson.

In addition to campground fees and shuttle-bus fees to ride into the park, each visitor must pay an **ENTRANCE FEE**: a 7-day pass for an individual is $5 and for a family, $10.

The park is divided into 43 units, and **BACKCOUNTRY PERMITS** are required for wilderness trips. To preserve the wilderness experience for backpackers, the number of people allowed into any given unit is limited. Sometimes units close due to wildlife activity, such as a curious grizzly bear. During the peak summer rush, they may be booked for days. Be flexible. Permits are issued 1 day in advance. (Reservations are not accepted.)

As far as **WHEN TO VISIT**, July is the busiest time at Denali. Recreational vehicles that have driven north from the Lower 48 arrive in force by then, and campgrounds and hotels are usually booked. The "shoulder" seasons—May and September—are some of the best times to visit if you want to avoid crowds. Park workers begin plowing the park road in March and, in an average year, the road is open to the public as far as Savage River Bridge (Mile 15) in early April and as far as the Teklanika River rest stop and overlook (Mile 30.3) in early May. This is a great time to load up the bicycle, drive to either one of these spots, and enjoy a traffic-free bike ride on the park road. Expect cool temperatures—often below freezing—and be aware that the road could close again at any time due to snow.

A good general source of information is the national park service Web site: **WWW.NPS.GOV/DENA**.

CAMPING / Permits are required to camp at any of the park's seven campgrounds except Morino campground, near the entrance to the park. In addition to the campground fee, add the park entrance fee and a $4 reservation fee per site. The only campgrounds you can drive to are Riley Creek, Savage River, and Teklanika River. All others are reached by bus. **RILEY CREEK** is the first campground past the park entrance, open year-round. **MORINO BACKPACKER CAMPGROUND**, Mile 1.9, is for backpackers only. **SAVAGE RIVER** is at Mile 13. **SANCTUARY RIVER**, Mile 23, is for tents only. **TEKLANIKA RIVER**, Mile 29, has a number of sites for both tents and RVs. **IGLOO CREEK**, Mile 34, is for tents only. And **WONDER LAKE**, Mile 85, is for tents only. Sanctuary River and Igloo Campgrounds are available by walk-in at the visitor center. Riley Creek, Savage River, Teklanika River, and Wonder Lake can all be reserved in advance.

TRAVEL AND TOURS WITHIN THE PARK / You can drive the park road in your own vehicle as far as Teklanika, before the buses start running on

Memorial Day weekend and after buses stop running at the end of the season, if weather permits and the road is open. During summer months, private-vehicle use is restricted beyond Savage River (Mile 14.8); only "inholders," those who own property inside the park at Kantishna, can travel beyond that point.

Once you are in the Denali National Park area, you can use the free **"FRONT COUNTRY" SHUTTLE BUS** to get from hotels to places inside and outside the park. Bus stops are clearly marked with schedules. Check with your hotel.

The primary way to experience the park is via the **PARK'S SHUTTLE BUS**. A trip into the park along the park road costs between $13 and $32, depending on how far you travel. You will need to reserve a seat at the Riley Creek Visitor Center; be aware that you may have to wait up to 3 days. The buses leave from the visitor center every half hour, from early morning to late afternoon. They begin operating the Saturday before Memorial Day and end the second Thursday after Labor Day. Reserve seats in advance through the national park service (800/622-7275; 907/272-7275 in Anchorage or outside the United States).

Denali Park Resorts (800/276-7234) offers two narrated tours. The **WILDLIFE TOUR** goes to Toklat at Mile 53 or, if the mountain is "out," to Stony Hill at Mile 62. A box lunch is provided for the 7-hour trip; the cost is $65 in peak season, $48 in shoulder season. The **NATURAL HISTORY TOUR** travels to Primrose Ridge at Mile 17, making interpretive stops along the way to places such as the Savage Cabin, a historic patrol cabin. It's a 3-hour trip, with a snack provided. The cost is $40.

Travel the length of the park road with an experienced naturalist guide and eat a buffet lunch at the Kantishna Lodge before returning the same day on a **KANTISHNA TOUR**. The special Kantishna bus leaves from park-entrance hotels at 7am. It arrives at Kantishna at noon, and you are allowed enough time for lunch, gold panning, relaxing, or exploring. Leave Kantishna at 3pm to return to the park entrance in time for dinner. Cost is $109 per person. To make reservations, contact PO Box 81670, Fairbanks, AK 99708; 800/942-7420.

A special **CAMPER BUS** carries travelers, their backpacks, and camping gear to campgrounds inside the park, particularly Sanctuary, Igloo Creek, and Wonder Lake Campgrounds, which do not allow vehicles. Backpackers with backcountry permits generally travel on this bus and stay in a campground their first night. Be sure to reserve and pay for a seat when you pick up your backcountry permit. Call 800/622-7275, or 907/272-7275 in Anchorage or outside the United States.

For 4 days each fall, beginning the second Friday after Labor Day, the park allows 400 vehicles per day to drive the length of the park road. Permits are distributed through a **ROAD LOTTERY** and are contingent on weather and road conditions. To earn this privilege, mail a self-addressed, stamped envelope to the park headquarters (PO Box 9, Denali National Park, AK 99755) between July 1 and July 31. List your choice of dates in order of preference. Permits are assigned by a drawing held in early August. Only one application per person.

EXPLORING

VISIT AN ART GALLERY / Fine art by Alaskans is on display and for sale at **GOOSE LAKE STUDIO**, run by one of Alaska's best-known artists, Donna Gates King, wife of Iditarod champion Jeff King. The log-cabin gallery offers one-of-a-kind artwork including pottery, quilts, silk scarves, and paintings, as well as parkas with traditional fur ruffs. Mile 239, Parks Hwy; 907-683-2570, winter; 907/683-2904, mid-May–Sept.

VISIT A CHAMPION WORKING KENNEL / Three-time Iditarod champion Jeff King opens his Goose Lake Kennel to visitors three times a day during summer for **HUSKY HOMESTEAD TOURS**. Meet the real champs—the dogs—and learn how they train. Half of the 1½-hour narrated tour is spent outdoors meeting the adult dogs and puppies, and learning about training and equipment. The other half is indoors, amid a display of mushing paraphernalia, art, and souvenirs. Although Iditarod commitments require Jeff King to travel regularly, he is often there in person. He or other Iditarod race veterans present the program about their Alaska lifestyle, the homestead, and the race itself. Cost is $30. At the end of a winding gravel road off Mile 230, Parks Hwy; 907/683-2904, summer; 907/683-2570, winter; www.huskyhomestead.com.

ADVENTURES

TRAVEL THE PARK ROAD / A journey into Denali National Park is a journey into the heart of wilderness. From the time you board the bus at the visitor center until you reach Wonder Lake 5 hours later, you'll pass through forest and tundra and, if you're fortunate, see some of the animals that live here.

Most of the park is above timberline, which in Denali starts at 2,700 to 3,000 feet; you get above timberline about 10 miles into the trip. The trees on the tundra include dwarf birch, willow, and alder. The first 15 miles of road are home to many of Denali's **MOOSE**. By early fall, the bulls are showing off their massive antlers and butting heads to vie for the affections of cow moose waiting nearby. They can be spotted either in the forest along the road or as the trees give way to open tundra.

The first glimpse of the mountain comes just about 8 miles into the park as you pass from the forest into tundra. At that point, it looms large even 72 miles away. As the road dips and turns, you'll lose sight of it periodically. It will disappear when you drop into the **SAVAGE RIVER** drainage and come into view again 8 miles later at the top of a hill called **PRIMROSE RIDGE**, then again at Sable Pass. The first place you can see the full mountain, including its base, is at **STONY HILL OVERLOOK** at Mile 62. Here, the mountain is 37 miles away.

CARIBOU can be seen almost anywhere along the park road. They are usually moving or grazing on sedges and grasses. Sometimes they can be seen on snowfields, where they flee in order to escape harassing insects, particularly warble flies and nose flies. The easiest animals to find are **DALL SHEEP**, bright white spots on the mountain slopes. **IGLOO CANYON** is a good place for sheep viewing.

SABLE PASS, at Mile 39, is home to the Toklat **GRIZZLY BEAR**, and this area has been closed to hiking and camping since 1955. But grizzly bears can be seen anywhere along the park road, digging for roots, strolling through the tundra, or snoozing on a sunny hillside. Many are blond in color, easily blending in with fall's golden and red tundra.

The grandeur of the park is evident at the top of **POLYCHROME PASS**, Mile 45.9. There, you can revel in the spectacular view of a broad valley, lined with tendrils of glacial streams flowing from distant mountains. On the other side of Polychrome, you'll pass over the **TOKLAT RIVER**. Early conservationist Charles Sheldon lived on the Toklat River during the winter of 1907–1908. His stay inspired him to campaign to preserve the area as a national park.

The road continues to undulate through valleys and over hills. At Mile 58.3 is **HIGHWAY PASS**, the highest point on the park road, at 3,980 feet. Just a little farther is Stony Hill Overlook. From **EIELSON VISITORS CENTER**, at Mile 66, visitors can ogle the mountain from the warmth of the glass-enclosed building. This is also where you can change buses and continue on to Wonder Lake, if seats are available. Naturalists offer tundra walks here at different times each day. Eielson is named in honor of pioneer Alaska bush pilot Carl Ben Eielson. Just past Eielson, weather permitting, you can see the 1-mile-wide **MULDROW GLACIER**, the longest glacier on the north side of the Alaska Range. As the road heads west, it drops onto rolling tundra and the land becomes flatter and wetter.

You're getting closer to the mountain, and at Wonder Lake Campground the mountain is only 27 miles away. **WONDER LAKE** is 4 miles long and about 280 feet deep. It is home to lake trout, burbot, arctic char, and lingcod. Beaver cruise along near shore, caribou wander by, and moose commonly wade in for an aquatic lunch. Beyond Wonder Lake lies **KANTISHNA**, once an active mining district, now home to four luxury resorts, open only to guests who make arrangements in advance.

FLOAT OR PADDLE THE NENANA RIVER / Located outside the entrance to Denali National Park, at Mile 238.5 on the Parks Highway, the **DENALI OUTDOOR CENTER** offers inflatable-kayak trips for full or half days, whitewater instruction in hardshell kayaks, and raft trips down the nearby Nenana River. This is the only company offering inflatable-kayak trips, which even beginners can safely enjoy. Participants need to bring warm clothes, preferably polypropylene or wool (no cotton), and their enthusiasm. The center provides full dry suit and paddling gear, including helmet, wet suit booties, gloves, lifejacket, and paddle. The dry suit has latex gaskets at the ankles, wrists, and neck to keep water out and keep paddlers dry. The water is very cold—in the 40°F range—so it is important to dress appropriately. An experienced guide takes paddlers down the river, usually through Class II and III rapids. The inflatable kayaks are stable and maneuverable. They also are self-bailing, so water that sloshes in flows back out on its own. If you tip over, you just flip the kayak right side up again and crawl back in. Custom, multiday trips on the Nenana River and other rivers are also available. If you are a paddler new to the area and looking for either a paddling partner or information on Nenana River rapids, check in here. This has become *the* center for whitewater paddlers. Mountain bike rentals are also available. PO Box 170, Denali National Park, AK 99755; 907/683-1925 or 888/303-1925; docadventure@hotmail.com; www.outdoorcenter.com; open May–Sept.

DENALI RAFT ADVENTURES / This outfit has been running the Nenana River for more than 20 years and offers a variety of trips. You'll be outfitted in either rain gear or flotation suits on chilly days. The suits are like snowmobile suits with flotation and can be cinched tight at the wrists, feet, and neck to protect from water. Trips range from the scenic 2-hour Mount McKinley Float to a thrilling 2-hour trip down Wild Canyon Run, 11 miles of big waves and vertical canyon walls through rapids with names like Coffee Grinder and the Narrows. The 4-hour Healy Express Run is a combination trip. Drawer 190, Denali National Park, AK 99755; 907/683-2234; denraft@mtaonline.net; www.denaliraft.com.

FESTIVALS AND EVENTS

NENANA RIVER WILDWATER RACES / This 23-year-old festival of whitewater rodeos and slaloms down the Nenana River is usually held on the second weekend following the Fourth of July. This is a great spectator event. Contact the Denali Outdoor Center (see above) for information.

RESTAURANTS

Alaska Cabin Nite Dinner Theater / ★

 MILE 238.9, PARKS HWY, DENALI PARK; 907/683-2215, SUMMER, 800/276-7234 OR 907/276-7234, WINTER

Definitely for tourists, but folks love it. The cast members have lovely singing voices, and the 40-minute performance tells the story of Kantishna, an early mining town at the west end of the park road, through the lives of real-life pioneer Fannie Quigley and a cast of other characters. Dinner is delicious—Alaska salmon, barbecued ribs, side dishes, rolls, and dessert, all chuck-wagon style. The servers are also the performers. Performances nightly at 5:30pm and 8:30pm; cost is $39. *$$; MC, V; checks OK; dinner every day; closed Oct–May; beer and wine; down the hill from the McKinley Park Chalets, at Mile 238.9, Parks Hwy (follow the signs).* &

The Perch

MILE 224, PARKS HWY, DENALI PARK; 907/683-2523 OR 888/322-2523

This quiet restaurant on Carlo Creek is the place to get away from the busy hubbub of Glitter Gulch, the tourist strip more than 10 miles north. Locals come here to enjoy a peaceful meal with a lovely view. There's a good reason it's called The Perch—it sits atop a hillside, surrounded by mountains. Known for its bread—often baked for other eateries in the area—the Perch offers everything from halibut and salmon when they're in season to hamburger night once a week. While the food is not exceptional, the atmosphere is nice and locals especially like that it's open on weekends during winter months. They say Sunday brunch is the Perch's best meal. Available for private parties anytime. *$$; AE, DIS, MC, V; checks OK; breakfast, lunch, dinner every day in summer; dinner Fri–Sat, brunch Sun in winter; full bar; theperch@yahoo.com; www. alaskaone.com/perchhrest.* &

LODGINGS

Denali Grizzly Bear Cabins & Campground / ★

MILE 231, PARKS HWY, DENALI PARK, AK 99755; 907/683-2696

Jack and Ede Reisland homesteaded this chunk of land along the banks of the Nenana River back in 1958 and now welcome summer visitors. Cabins nestle in a birch and spruce grove; each one is unique. Fisherman Cabin has a pair of hip waders and a net nailed above the door. The Sourdough Cabin has a handpainted scene of the northern lights. Some of the cabins date back to the early 1900s and are from Fairbanks. Jack dismantled them, then reassembled them at the campground. You also can stay in your own tent near the river, in surprisingly secluded settings. Recreational vehicles park on the other side of the campground, near the highway. Coin-operated hot showers are available. *$; DIS, MC, V; no checks; closed mid-Sept–mid-May; summer address: PO Box 7, Denali Park, AK 99755; winter address: 910 Senate Loop, Fairbanks, AK 99712; across the highway from McKinley Village Lodge.* &

Denali Princess Lodge / ★★

MILE 238.5, PARKS HWY, DENALI PARK, AK 99755; 800/426-0500
The lodge has everything, including outdoor hot tubs overlooking the Nenana River. Rooms are clean and comfortable, and employees are friendly. Many people staying here are on package tours with Princess Cruise Tours (800/426-0442), but the hotel offers reasonable prices during the "shoulder" seasons. A large deck also overlooks the river, and landscaped walkways line the bluff, a good spot for an evening stroll. If it's windy or too chilly, just move inside and enjoy the same view from the comfort of the lounge. *$$$; AE, DC, DIS, MC, V; checks OK; fine dining room and cafe; closed Oct–early March; full bar.* &

WILDERNESS LODGES

Camp Denali

DENALI OUTDOOR WILDERNESS CENTERS, BOX 67, DENALI NATIONAL PARK, AK 99755; 907/683-2290, FAX 907/683-1568
The first wilderness camp at Denali National Park was founded by Celia Hunter and Ginny Wood. Both were World War II pilots who first flew north in order to ferry military planes to Alaska. Originally outside park boundaries, Camp Denali became an island of private land when the park expanded in 1980. The tent camp has grown every year, with a lodge and permanent chalets eventually built to replace the tents. Today, it accommodates up to 40 guests in log or frame cabins, each with a view of Mount McKinley. Cabins sleep from two to six and come with small wood-burning stoves for heat and propane lights. A gas hot plate for heating water is available in each building. Guests may use outhouses or a central bathhouse that is a short walk from each cabin. Resident naturalists lead guests on hikes and teach natural history. The hikes range from short interpretive walks to 12-mile hikes. Two or three of these are offered every day. Camp Denali is allowed day use of the park road, so guests can spend a long time observing wildlife. Evening programs and special workshops featuring visiting experts focus on all aspects of Denali, such as birds, the aurora borealis, nature photography, or tundra ecology. There is no extra cost for the sessions. Minimum stay is 3 nights: $325 per adult per day; $245 for children under 12 (per person, double occupancy, plus tax). Families get a 10 percent discount if three or more occupy the same cabin. Prices include round-trip transportation from the park rail station, lodging, all meals, guided activities, natural-history

interpretation, evening programs, use of recreational equipment such as bicycles or canoes, and park entrance fee. *No credit cards; checks OK; closed mid-Sept–early June; no bar, but you may bring your own alcohol; dnpwild@alaska.net; www.gorp.com/dnpwild.*

Denali Wilderness Lodge

PO BOX 50, DENALI NATIONAL PARK, AK 99755; (800) 541-9779
This lodge is not actually in Denali National Park, but rather lies a short flight east of the park in the Wood River Valley. Once owned by a well-known Alaska hunting guide, Lynn Castle, the lodge has been transformed into a haven for tourists who want to shoot wildlife with a camera instead of a gun. Located on the shore of the scenic Wood River, the lodge features gourmet meals, charming cabins with private baths, and an impressive wildlife museum. You won't see Mount McKinley from here, but the country is spectacular. Visiting experts present special evening programs. It is possible to fly out just for the day. $290 per person per night, double occupancy, includes accommodations, meals, and activities such as horseback riding, naturalist-guided hikes, and evening programs. Flights to and from the lodge (about $100 round-trip from Denali Park) are additional. Flight-seeing and river rafting are also available. *AE, DIS, MC, V; local checks only; closed mid-Sept–mid-May; full bar; www.denaliwildernesslodge.com.* ຊ

Kantishna Roadhouse

WESTERN EDGE OF DENALI NATIONAL PARK, AK 99755; 800/942-7420 OR 907/683-1475, SUMMER; FAX 907/479-2611
The historic Kantishna Roadhouse once provided comfort to miners and travelers in the early 1900s. When gold was discovered in the Kantishna Hills, so many miners flocked to the area that whole towns grew. They had names such as Glacier City, Diamond, Roosevelt, and Square Deal. Kantishna was once called Eureka and had a population of 2,000 people in 1905. In the mid-1920s, gold fever ebbed. Today, Doyon Native Corporation owns the roadhouse and mines tourism, not gold. The lodge provides resident naturalists for guided hikes, natural-history programs, or activities such as panning for gold or mountain biking. Approximately $300 per person per night, double occupancy; cost includes round-trip transportation from the park entrance area, all meals, activities, and horse-drawn wagon rides. Ten percent discount if three or more people occupy the same cabin. Singles add $100 per night. *AE, DIS, MC, V; checks OK; closed mid-Sept–early June; full bar; kantshna@polarnet. com; www.alaskaone.com/krhouse; PO Box 81670, Fairbanks, AK 99708.*

North Face Lodge

DENALI OUTDOOR WILDERNESS CENTERS, BOX 67, DENALI NATIONAL PARK, AK 99755; 907/683-2290, FAX 907/683-1568
A sister lodge to Camp Denali, this wilderness outpost rests near the remains of an old log cabin. Grant Pearson, an early superintendent of the park and the original owner of the lodge, staked out the property in 1957. Located a mile away from Camp Denali, the lodge has 15 guest rooms, private baths, and, of course, a view of Mount McKinley. Minimum stay of 2 nights: $325 per adult, $245 for children under 12 (per person per night double occupancy, plus tax). Families get a 10 percent discount if three or more occupy the same cabin. Prices include round-trip transportation from the park rail station, lodging, all meals, guided activities, natural-history interpretation, evening programs, use of recreational equipment such as bicycles or canoes, and park entrance fee. *No credit cards; checks OK; closed mid-Sept–early June; no bar, but you may bring your own alcohol; dnpwild@alaska.net; www.gorp. com/dnpwild.*

The Denali Highway

(Note: Mile markers on the Denali Highway read east to west and west to east. We have chosen to take you from east to west.)
The Denali Highway offers one of the most scenic drives in Alaska. From Paxson on the Richardson Highway it is 135 miles to Cantwell on the Parks Highway. The road is primarily gravel, except for the first 21 miles out of Paxson. The ride can be rough, dusty, and hazardous to your tires. Be sure to bring mounted spares. Potholes and other rough spots in the road require you to keep your speed well below 50mph and actually closer to 30mph. Four hours is a quick trip. Take your time and you will be rewarded with fabulous vistas and maybe wildlife sightings.

When the Denali Highway opened in 1957, it provided a route from the Richardson Highway to what was then Mount McKinley National Park, today Denali National Park. Before that, visitors could reach the park only by train, plane, or dogsled. The road that led from the entrance of the park to Wonder Lake was already in use, so visitors often sent their vehicles to the park via rail. After the Parks Highway was built, more than a decade later, the Denali Highway became a destination in itself.

ACCESS AND INFORMATION

In the summer, there are a few inns along the way that offer some amenities, but you should come prepared with extra water and food for emergencies. Also be prepared for changes in weather. The day may start out sunny and warm and change dramatically to cold, rain, wind, and even snow, any month of the year. The road is not plowed in the wintertime.

You can camp anywhere along the highway. There are many beautiful spots. However, if you want a few amenities, there are three Bureau of Land Management (BLM) campgrounds along the highway, with a total of 46 campsites (note: mile markers are calculated from Paxson). **TANGLE LAKES CAMPGROUND**, Mile 21.5, water pump, toilets, boat launch, picnic area. This is the starting point for a 3-day river trip (see below). **TANGLE RIVER CAMPGROUND**, Mile 21.7, water pump, toilets, boat launch. You can launch a boat here for an extended wilderness canoe trip on the upper Tangle Lakes. **BRUSHKANA RIVER CAMPGROUND**, Mile 104, fire pits, water pump, toilets, tables, trails, and 17 campsites.

ADVENTURES

TANGLE LAKES / On both sides of the highway, a series of beautiful lakes—Tangle Lakes—connected by the Tangle River are a popular destination. **ROUND TANGLE, LONG TANGLE, AND LOWER TANGLE LAKES** are on the north side of the road, and **UPPER TANGLE LAKE** is on the south side of the road. The name Tangle comes from the maze of lakes and streams in this drainage system. The lakes offer good **FISHING**, even from shore. Catch trout, grayling, or burbot. Be sure to check state fishing regulations and have a fishing license in hand before you wet a line. The Tangle Lakes are also terrific for **BIRDING**. With a little luck you might see arctic warblers, Smith's longspurs, gyrfalcons, or ptarmigan. **CANOEISTS** can paddle across any of the lakes and instantly find themselves in remote Alaska wilderness with tundra hiking in any direction. Be sure to wear rubber boots, though, because some of that hiking is wet. You can rent a canoe for $3 an hour from Tangle River Inn, Mile 20, and also from Tangle Lakes Lodge, Mile 22 (see Lodgings, below).

RIVER TRIP / Experienced paddlers looking for a longer trip can paddle across Round Tangle and Long Tangle Lakes to reach the **DELTA RIVER**, designated as a Wild and Scenic River. This 30-mile trip is best done in a leisurely 3 days. At the end of Long Tangle Lake, you'll have to portage a half mile around a waterfall. The 1½-mile section of river just below the falls is notorious for demolishing canoes, since the water moves swiftly and the river is very rocky. To paddle this section, you should know how to maneuver through rapids rated Class III. Generally, this trip is done in a raft or a canoe. Takeout is at Mile 212 on the Richardson Highway.

ON THE HIGHWAY / As you drive west on the Denali Highway, on a clear day you'll have spectacular views the whole way. Keep a sharp eye on ponds and lakes. Swans and other migratory waterfowl nest in these areas and can be easy to spot.

Between Mile 17 and Mile 37, there are more than 400 archaeological sites. Designated the **TANGLE LAKES NATIONAL REGISTER ARCHAEOLOGICAL DISTRICT**, this area contains some of the earliest evidence of human occupation in North America.

The second-highest point on Alaska's road system is **MACLAREN SUMMIT** (4,086 feet). (The highest is 4,800-foot Atigun Pass on the Dalton Highway.) Just before Maclaren Summit, catch a panoramic view of the Alaska Range, including **MOUNT HAYES** (13,832 feet) and **MACLAREN GLACIER**. A short trail to Maclaren Summit takes off across the tundra at Mile 37. This is alpine tundra, home to ground squirrels and arctic rodents called pikas.

At Mile 43.5, you might want to mountain bike or hike the **MACLAREN RIVER ROAD** as it follows along on the west side of the Maclaren River for 12 miles to Maclaren Glacier. After 4 miles, you must ford the west fork of the Maclaren River, a glacial stream that can be dangerously high after heavy rains. That is followed by 5 miles of good trail, a half mile of willow thicket, and another 3 miles of good trail.

Continuing on your route, you'll drive over the **SUSITNA RIVER**, a major drainage in this area. Eventually, the Susitna turns west, flows through the Talkeetna Mountains, and empties into Cook Inlet. Caribou routinely migrate through the area past the Susitna River, so keep an eye peeled for bands of them. At Mile 93.8, a 5-mile trail leads to **BUTTE LAKE**, a popular local fishing hole. Trout, grayling, and burbot are in the lake. The beauty of the Denali Highway is that you can take off hiking in any direction.

CLASSIC RIVER TRIP / Floating the **UPPER NENANA RIVER** is a beautiful wilderness canoe trip beginning at Mile 117 (or Mile 18 coming from Cantwell), where the Nenana River flows right next to the Denali Highway. Launch a canoe or raft here and spend the day floating swift but flat water through the Reindeer Hills. The river leaves the road and cuts through the mountains, making its way about 20 miles to the Parks Highway. Takeout is at the Nenana River Bridge north of Cantwell, at Mile 215.7 on the Parks Highway. The access road to the bridge is just south of there, at Mile 213.9 on the Parks Highway. The only disruptions to the peacefulness of the trip are the jet boats, or worse, air boats, which take visitors to the Brushkasna River. Boat pilots are generally courteous, however, and slow down when approaching canoes. The trip takes 4 to 6 hours, but may be faster at higher water.

LODGINGS

Gracious House

MILE 82, DENALI HWY, CANTWELL, AK 99729; 907/333-3148,
WINTER; 907/822-7307, SUMMER (A RADIOPHONE, SO LET IT RING)
Gracious House has been serving travelers along the Denali Highway for
41 years. The name comes from the owner's last name, Butch Gratias.
For a break from the dusty road in summer, check into a motel room
here. The restaurant primarily serves short orders. Drivers can buy gas
here, get flat tires repaired, or find a tow for disabled vehicles. If you're
looking for a little adventure, Gracious House Flying Service offers scenic flights. Butch is also a registered guide and offers guided hunts. *$;
MC, V; no checks; closed late Sept–May, but open for up to 40 self-sufficient winter visitors with 2-week advance notice and at least 6 people; full bar; winter address: PO Box 212549, Anchorage, AK
99521-2549.*

Maclaren River Lodge / ★

MILE 42, DENALI HWY, PAXSON, AK 99737; 907/822-7105
This is the only lodge open year-round on the Denali Highway. Snow-
mobilers and dog mushers visit regularly during winter months. Competitors in the Iditarod Trail Sled Dog Race in March will stop here for
lunch while doing training runs in the area. The lodge has seven rooms,
two cabins, plus a bunkhouse, all of which can house a total of about 40
people. Summer rates are $65 for a room, $25 for a bunk; winter rates
are $80 for a room, $30 for a bunk; and cabin rentals are $150 and $180.
*$; MC, V; local checks only; breakfast, lunch, dinner every day; no alco-
hol; PO Box 3018, Paxson, AK 99737.* ᕋ *(main lodge only)*

Tangle Lakes Lodge / ★

MILE 22, DENALI HWY, PAXSON, AK 99737; 907/822-4202, SUMMER;
907/688-9173, WINTER
Originally known as Butcher's Hunting Camp, this lodge, built in 1952,
is now owned by Rich and Linda Holmstrom. It burned down in May
1998 and was completely rebuilt the following summer. Rich is a fal-
coner, and you can see him working his falcon in the fall hunting season.
The area is tundra with low bushes, so there are lots of ptarmigan and
spruce hens, which makes it a good area for falcons. "My wife calls it my
$1.4 million ptarmigan camp," says Rich. The lodge has log cabins that
sleep three people for $65 per night and new log cabin duplexes, about
10 units total. You can rent canoes for the Tangle Lakes ($5 an hour, $10
for 3 hours, or $25 all day). Rich also can guide you to good fishing or
hiking. Cabins with woodstove heat are available for rent in the wintertime. *$; MC, V; checks OK; breakfast, lunch, dinner, every day; closed
Oct–May; full bar; tanglelakeslodge@corecom.net; www.alaskan.com/*

tanglelakes; winter address: PO Box 670386, Chugiak, AK 99567; 1 mile past the end of the pavement.

Tangle River Inn / ★

MILE 20, DENALI HWY, DELTA JUNCTION, AK 99737; 907/822-7304 OR 907/822-3970; 907/895-4022, WINTER

Overlooking Tangle Lakes, this inn features home-style cooking and boasts the only karaoke bar along the Denali Highway. For about $65 per person, you can stay in one of the motel rooms or cabins. For $25 per person, stay in a log bunkhouse. The bunkhouse sleeps 10 and is good for family reunions or parties who plan to float the Delta River the next day. The inn advertises the cheapest gas in 100 miles and guarantees that its lodgings are less expensive than any in the nearest towns—Delta Junction and Glennallen on the Richardson Highway. *$; MC, V; local checks only; breakfast, lunch, dinner every day; closed Oct–April; full bar; tangle@alaska.net; www.alaska.net/~tangle; Box 783, Delta Junction, AK 99737.* &

FAIRBANKS AND THE INTERIOR

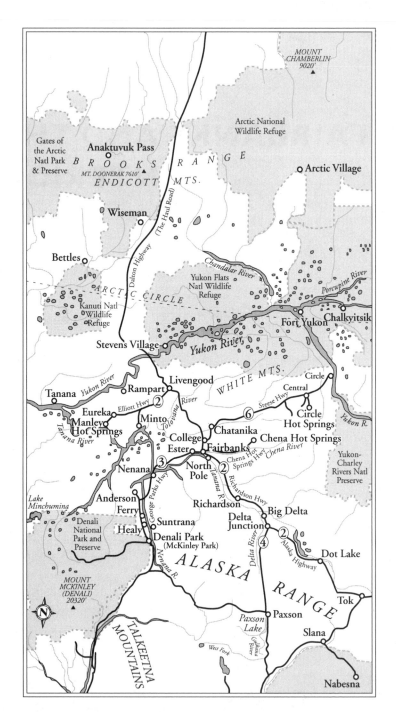

FAIRBANKS AND THE INTERIOR

Think of the Interior as the "outback" of Alaska, where asphalt is rare and locals still fight to keep roads unpaved. The few roads that do exist are rebellious. They buck and squirm in an effort to remain untamed. Their resistance (or freeze-thaw action) creates vehicle-launching waves in the pavement called "frost heaves." If you're at all prone to motion sickness, look out.

In the Interior, the major "highways" are the rivers. The smaller ones, like the Chena running through Fairbanks, are the side streets. The larger ones—the Tanana, the Koyukuk, the Yukon—are the freeways. Native people have depended on these waterways for food and transportation for centuries. Today, these rivers still feed the people and connect their villages by boat in summer and by snowmobile and dog team in winter.

Lured first by gold in the 1890s, then by the opportunity for self-reliance, the "sourdoughs" of the Interior tend to be seasoned souls who'd rather take their chances carving a living out of the land than punching a time clock in exchange for a pension. They love elbow room. They hate regulations. They are miners, trappers, hermits, socialites, teachers, artists, scientists, climbers, dog mushers, and general wilderness junkies. You'll find condo dwellers whose idea of "the great outdoors" is the space between the front door and the carport. You'll find cabin dwellers whose idea of "the big city" is any place with a gas pump. People of the Interior are as diverse as the weather. They grow some of the most impressive gardens in some of the most unlikely places. They seem to possess more household goods held together by duct tape than any other demographic group in America.

It's the land that encourages them to do things differently. Something about it says follow your heart. Be wide open, daring, and wild. There are rolling boreal forests as far as the eye can see, great meandering rivers, ponds and lakes reflecting overcast skies like beads of scattered mercury. This is land with no fences.

In the fall, the land shakes its subtle beauty and gets outright loud. Stoplight reds. Emergency yellows. Golds more gold than nuggets. There's nothing more stunning than tundra the color of spawned-out salmon.

Well, there is one thing: a clear winter night when the northern lights shimmer across the sky like curtains of light fluttering in a breeze. Entire barrooms have been known to empty out on nights like these, their patrons pouring onto the streets to hoot and howl at the heavens.

The sky here makes such great theater in part because it's so darn big. The Interior comprises about a third of the state, with the Brooks Range at its northern border, the Alaska Range at its southern, and the city of Fairbanks right about in the middle. More than 99,000 people live within the boundaries of this 192,660-square-mile region; 12 percent are Indian and Eskimo. That amounts to almost 2 square miles per man, woman, and child.

In summer, the midnight sun is like an elixir. People get rejuvenated. Vegetables grow Godzilla-size. It's not uncommon to forget to go to bed.

The opposite problem occurs in winter. People forget to get up—or at least they'd like to. With less than 4 hours of daylight in Fairbanks, the body tends to slide into hibernation. Add weather inversions, dead car batteries, and freezing-cold outhouse seats, and you'll see why Interior winters aren't for everyone.

The highest temperature ever recorded in Alaska was in the Interior: 100°F in Fort Yukon on June 27, 1915. So was the lowest. It plummeted to −80°F at Prospect Creek, up the Dalton Highway, on January 23, 1971. The thing about the weather here is that you can get both extremes in the course of a day. Warm winter winds called "chinooks" can raise the temperature from −25°F to 25°F in a few hours.

The point is, when you visit the Interior, dress in layers and be prepared for all of the region's various moods. Because when it's good, it's very, very good, and when it's bad, it's horrid.

Fairbanks

We may as well get this right out in the open. Fairbanks was a mistake. Much to the delight of the state's largest city (Anchorage), the state's second-largest city (Fairbanks) exists only due to one man's error in judgment and somebody else's subsequent stroke of luck.

Before we launch into that tale, you should know that rivalry between Alaska's two biggest cities is rather animated. Fairbanks may call itself "the golden heart" of Alaska, but to "Los Anchorage" residents it is, and always will be, "Squarebanks." While Fairbanks is the "city on the edge of nowhere," Anchorage is the "city on the edge of good taste." Now, back to that mistake known as Fairbanks. Athabascans were here first—living, hunting, and fishing up and down the shores of the Chena and Tanana Rivers. Then, in August 1901, a trader from Ohio, one E. T. Barnette, found himself marooned on the banks of the Chena River with $20,000 worth of goods, about 200 miles short of his destination. The sternwheeler captain that Barnette had hired to get to Tanacross got fed up and gave the boot to him, his distraught wife, and his mountain of goods on what is now the corner of First Avenue and Cushman Street.

Fortunately for Barnette, along came an Italian immigrant named Felix Pedro, who hit gold in the hills above his cache in 1902. In the right place at the right time, Barnette set up shop in time for the ensuing gold rush, eventually becoming the town banker. He led the campaign to name the town after Charles W. Fairbanks, a U.S. senator from Indiana who became vice president under President Theodore Roosevelt. At one point, Barnette was reportedly worth millions.

By 1910, Fairbanks was Alaska's most cosmopolitan city, while Anchorage was still muskeg and swamp. The U.S. Census counted 3,542 residents that year, with another 7,000 others, mostly miners, in camps nearby.

During Fairbanks' formative years, Barnette ruled—until word got out that he'd served 18 months in an Oregon prison 20 years earlier for grand larceny. In 1911, when his bank went bankrupt, the locals were convinced he'd cheated them out of their life savings and ran him out of town. For years, no one knew what had happened to him. There were rumors of his squandering away the town's money, living in style in Mexico. There were rumors he'd died. Well, he did die, but not until 1933. Fairbanks' founding father fell down a flight of stairs in Los Angeles, cracked his skull, and died at the age of 70.

Fairbanks has drawn every kind of personality imaginable, as well as some unimaginable—from hard-driving entrepreneurs to free spirits who followed the Grateful Dead to Alaska in 1980, fell in love with the state, moved north, and never left. Its history is peppered with people such as the late Hulda Ford, who slept on the street and died of malnutrition in 1957 while holding title to something like a half-million dollars in real estate.

Fairbanks is the birthplace of the Alaskan Independence Party, which has called for secession from the Union. It's also the location of the main campus of the University of Alaska and home to the supercomputer and Alaska's Geophysical Institute. Housed in the Arctic Regions Supercomputing Center, the supercomputer is actually two machines—Denali and Yukon—that are among the most highly advanced computers in the world, developed primarily for the military. They're used to simulate complex events, from oil reservoir flow to nuclear explosions. Scientists come here from all over the world to study everything from the center of the earth to the center of the sun.

While Anchorage may have better packaging, Fairbanks is the type of place that challenges visitors to look beyond the obvious. Fairbanks sits on the banks of the Chena River and is surrounded by rolling hills that turn practically fluorescent in the fall. In summer, the Interior is where other Alaskans come for sun. Sure, it can get to –40° in the winter, but it can also get to 90°F in the summer (the average in July is 63°F).

Just a few miles outside Fairbanks, you can be alone in the wilderness hiking, fishing for grayling, panning for gold, or pondering the trans-Alaska oil pipeline with its 1.8 million barrels of oil a day gushing their way to oil tankers in Valdez.

ACCESS AND INFORMATION

You can get to Fairbanks by driving the Alaska Highway, the Richardson highway, or the Parks Highway. Or you can take the Alaska Railroad from Anchorage. Or even quicker, you can fly. There are several scheduled FLIGHTS a day, starting with Alaska Airlines (800/426-0333). Seasonal bargain transportation between Anchorage and Fairbanks, with stops in Denali National Park, makes travel between Alaska's two largest cities a bit kinder on the budget. Try ALASKA BACK-PACKER SHUTTLE (907/344-8775, fax 907/522-7382; www.alaska.net/~backpack) or PARKS HIGHWAY EXPRESS (888/600-6001, fax 907/479-3065; Info@AlaskaShuttle.com).

Once you get to town, there's a public bus system (MACS, Metropolitan Area Commuter System; 907/459-1011) to transport you. G.O. SHUTTLE & TOURS (800/478-3847 or 907/474-3847, fax 907/474-4366; Goshuttl@polarnet.com) will haul you around to the major tourist attractions. If you prefer to travel through town via river, ALASKAN PEOPLE PLEASERS (907/451-8602; biteme@mosquitonet.com; www.mosquitonet.com/~biteme) offers "boat limo" service for $25 per person per hour aboard the *Quantum Leap*, a 24-foot inboard jet boat.

Stop first at the FAIRBANKS VISITORS INFORMATION CENTER (550 1st Ave; 800/327-5774 or 907/456-5774; info@explorefairbanks.com; www.explorefairbanks.com). In addition to the usual, you'll find menus, the nightlife column from the local newspaper, and a board for posting messages such as "Looking for hitchhiker to split gas, costs to Prudhoe Bay." Open daily in summer, and weekdays in winter.

At the ALASKA PUBLIC LANDS INFORMATION CENTER 250 Cushman St; 907/456-0527; www.nps.gov/aplic/center, located in the basement of the old Fairbanks Courthouse, you'll find maps, brochures, articles, and log books on hiking, rafting, canoeing, skiing, camping, photography, hunting, fishing, gold panning, scenic drives, and more. Parks, refuges, Wild and Scenic Rivers—all are featured here. During summer months, there's a naturalist program covering songbirds, bear mythology, and edible plants in the forest. The center is open daily in summer and Tuesday to Saturday in winter.

Call THE WEATHER LINE (800/472-0391) for Interior forecasts; for local information, call 907/452-3553. For Interior weather via the Internet, try www.faiwsfo.org. For even more detail, from aviation

SKINNY DICK'S HALFWAY INN

You already know about the stuff flowing through the trans-Alaska oil pipeline. This place specializes in the other kind of Alaska crude. Notorious for its sleazy name, copulating bears logo, and raunchy jukebox tunes, Skinny Dick's is probably not the kind of place a Sunday-school teacher would appreciate. For starters, the joint is a bar, not an inn at all. Dick, however, *is* skinny and the place *is* about halfway between Nenana and Fairbanks. Decor includes dollar bills stuck to the walls and bikini undies and boxer shorts emblazoned with those infamous mating bears. Skinny Dick is especially known for his Bloody Marys. "B.S. is my other good point," he says. Mile 328, Parks Hwy; 907/452-0304.

—Debra McKinney

forecasts to hourly reports from every corner of the state, visit: www. alaska.net/~nwsar.

Our advice on bug dope: don't leave your room without it, June through August. The **MOSQUITOES** can be wicked. Hooded jackets made of mosquito netting, soaked overnight in repellent, are the ticket for serious bug territory. Available at most sporting goods stores.

Another tip: many private homes and bed-and-breakfasts will ask you to leave your shoes at the door. Don't take it personally. It's an Alaska thing.

EXPLORING

So you want to get the most Alaskan experience out of this little expedition to Fairbanks as possible? And in the shortest amount of time? You want to take in history, Native culture, wilderness, and dogs? You want to experience the thrill of a gold strike, the chill of a harsh winter, the spasm of innards as you come nose to nose with a perturbed bear as big as your house? But you want to do it from the safety and comfort of a bar stool? No problem. Fairbanks has got you covered. Read on.

ALASKALAND / This 44-acre pioneer theme park was built to commemorate the 100th anniversary of the purchase of Alaska from Russia. While entrance to the park is free, some attractions come with a fee. Alaskaland is home to some of the state's best relics. Among them is the SS *Nenana*, the largest wooden-hulled stern-wheel river steamer ever built west of the Mississippi. You'll find a replica of a gold-rush town, historical cabins, art, aviation and history museums, a famous and posh railroad car, the Palace Theatre & Saloon, the Alaska Salmon Bake, two playgrounds, a historical carousel, train rides, picnic areas and more. 2300 Airport Wy, Fairbanks, AK 99707; 907/459-1087;

open year-round, many attractions closed in winter; intersection of Airport Wy and Peger Rd.

ALASKA SALMON BAKE–PALACE THEATRE & SALOON / The best way to fully appreciate this musical journey down gold-rush lane is to go to the Alaska Salmon Bake first so there'll be no stomach growling to interrupt the show. Rick Winther owns both attractions, so the two were meant for each other. They're both at Alaskaland. The evening salmon bake offers steak with all the trimmings or all the salmon, halibut, and barbecued ribs you can stomach for $20. The musical revues at the Palace feature turn-of-the-century costumed performers telling tall tales laced with 20th-century humor. A rowdy one is for adults only; the other, "Golden Heart Revue," is for the whole family. The Alaska fashion show is a hoot. Greasy Carhartts. Breakup boots. Parkas adorned with glow-in-the-dark duct tape. Both shows are $12. Show time is 8:15pm. 2300 Airport Wy, Fairbanks, AK 99709; 800/354-7274 or 907/452-7274, Salmon Bake; 800/354-7274 or 907/456-5960, Palace; intrasea@polar-net.com; www.alaskasbest.com/salmon; beer and wine (Salmon Bake); full bar (Palace); open mid-May–late Sept; intersection of Airport Wy and Peger Rd. &

RIVERBOAT DISCOVERY / The moment you board this stern-wheeler, you begin an adventure into the history of the Interior, the lives of Native people, the Chena and Tanana Rivers, and all the creatures and person-alities along the riverbanks. You'll float past a fish wheel, a Native fish camp, and the home of four-time Iditarod champion Susan Butcher and her husband, Dave Monson, winner of the Yukon Quest Sled Dog Race. Either they or their handlers give a sled-dog demonstration. Step ashore at a replica of an Athabascan Indian village. Captain Jim Binkley, whose father was one of the original riverboat pilots during the gold-rush era, began the excursion business in 1950 with a 40-foot motor launch. Binkley now has three stern-wheelers, the largest being the *Discovery III*, a triple-decker capable of carrying more than 900 pas-sengers. Cost is $40 for adults, $30 for ages 12 and under, with twice-daily departures. 1975 Discovery Dr, Fairbanks, AK 99709; 907/479-6673, fax 907/479-4613; reservations@riverboatdiscovery.com; www.riverboatdiscovery.com; mid-May–mid-Sept; turn west off Airport Wy onto Dale Rd, follow signs. &

ALASKAN TAILS OF THE TRAIL WITH MARY SHIELDS / Mary Shields may be a wonderful and gentle storyteller, but her sled dogs are the stars of the show: Kid-O, Big Boy, Little Girl, Flopsy, Uproar, Captain, Rita, Sunny Girl, and Solo. "They upstage me constantly," she says. The first woman to finish the Iditarod Trail Sled Dog Race, Shields is the author of five books, including *Sled Dog Trails*, and is the subject of the PBS film

Season of the Sled Dog, which has aired in 17 countries. In this tour, she opens her home to visitors interested in taking a peek at how Alaskans live. After introducing her dogs and talking about training, racing, breeding, and the like, she turns her dogs loose and they race around, frolic, and get their social hierarchies all straightened out; then she calls for order again. Only she's made a game of it. The dogs know they can sleep in any doghouse they want. So when she hollers, they dash for their favorites. Visitors howl as two or three dogs play king of the mountain on the roof of the most coveted accommodations. Afterward, there's time up at Mary's home, a log house with a sod roof, for refreshments, stories, and photos. The tour is 2 hours and children need to be 8 or older. Cost is $25 for adults, $20 for children 12 and under. PO Box 80961-W, Fairbanks, AK 99708; 907/455-6469 (phone and fax); mshields@mosquitonet.com; www.maryshields.com; checks OK; mid-May–mid-Sept; 12 miles northwest of downtown Fairbanks, call for directions. &

GOLD DREDGE NO. 8 / This is the best opportunity in Alaska to see a historic, five-deck gold dredge—or giant mechanical gold pan—in all its former glory. Between 1928 and 1959, this iron monstrosity gobbled up millions of ounces of gold from Goldstream and Engineer Creeks near Fairbanks. In addition to mining equipment and tailings galore, you'll see a collection of mammoth tusks and other prehistoric bones found in the area. Registered as a National Historical Site, Gold Dredge No. 8 is actually three museums constructed from the original miners' bunkhouse, bath house, and office. You can spend the whole day panning for gold if you like. Tour with goldpanning and lunch is $28 for adults, $21 for children, or you can purchase a tour or goldpanning separately at a lower cost. Tours begin every 45 minutes. 1755 Old Steese Hwy (Mile 9), Fairbanks, AK 99712; 907/457-6058; gidg@alaska.net; open every day, mid-May–mid-Sept; take the Steese Expressway north, left onto Goldstream Rd, left onto Old Steese, after about 1 mile watch for sign. &

EL DORADO GOLD MINE / Nobody gets away without gold, the owners promise. They make sure you get at least a few specks by keeping their panning area stocked with pay dirt. But first, this 2-hour tour takes you on a narrow-gauge train ride into a permafrost tunnel, where you learn about underground mining techniques and see prehistoric bones up to 30,000 years old. Though the tunnel smells a bit like a pair of 30,000-year-old socks, it gives you not only a sense of being deep underground but also a knowledge of how gold is formed and how it gets to where miners find it. Back out in the daylight, Dexter Clark and "Yukon Yonda" explain how placer mining works and demonstrate what it's like to be stricken with gold fever. (Check out Yonda's Fort Knox accessories—but don't try anything funny; she could probably bench-press a musk ox.) After a crash course in gold panning, visitors grab bundles of dirt and are herded to a panning shed. This is another Binkley family venture (Riverboat Discovery). It's also a working mine. Train tours depart morning and afternoon; cost is $25 for adults, $20 for children 12 and under. 1975 Discovery Dr, Fairbanks, AK 99709; 907/479-7613, fax 907/479-4613; reservations@eldoradogoldmine.com; www.eldoradogoldmine.com; open mid-May–mid-Sept; Mile 1.3, Elliott Hwy, just past the community of Fox. &

CREAMER'S FIELD MIGRATORY WATERFOWL REFUGE / This is a gold-rush-era dairy farm. The buildings are historic, and the land now belongs to the birds. Each spring, snow buntings blaze the migration trail as early as mid-March, followed by Canada geese, tundra swans, pintails, golden plovers, sandhill cranes, peregrine falcons, and others. Some of the more rare sightings include snow geese and the Eurasian wigeon. The refuge has observation platforms, a 2-mile trail, and guided nature walks. Bring binoculars and bug dope. Early mornings and late evenings are best for spying moose. In winter, there are 40 miles of groomed ski trails. Trail guides are available at the **FARMHOUSE VISITORS CENTER**. 1300 College Rd, Fairbanks, AK 99701; 907/459-7307 or 907/452-5162); www.state.ak.us/adfg/wildlife/region3/refuge3/creamers.htm; open Tues–Sat in summer, Sat only in winter.

LARGE ANIMAL RESEARCH STATION / This is more popularly known as the Musk Ox Farm. Once extinct in Alaska, musk oxen are stout, pre-historic-looking creatures resembling wool-bearing refrigerators on hooves. Yet beneath that shaggy exterior lies the softest and finest fiber produced by an animal. The underhairs, or qiviut, are warmer and softer than cashmere. Operated by the University of Alaska Fairbanks' Institute of Arctic Biology, this is home to the largest group of captive musk oxen and caribou in the world and draws researchers from all over. During summer months, viewing is best in early morning or late evening, after temperatures have cooled and the animals aren't hiding in shade. Bring binoculars. You'll find displays and a viewing platform there. Guided tours are offered on select days June through September, $5 for adults and $2 for students; call for times. PO Box 757000, Fairbanks, AK 99775-7000; 907/474-7207; from the university, head north on Farmers Loop, left on Ballaine, left on Yankovich; farm is on the right.

UNIVERSITY OF ALASKA MUSEUM / Perched atop a ridge overlooking the Tanana Valley, this museum is considered one of the best in the state. Its most famous exhibit is **BLUE BABE**, a restored 36,000-year-old, Ice Age bison, found in the permafrost by local miners. She was so well preserved that she even had most of her hide. The museum features exhibits on the natural history and cultural heritage of the Interior, Native arts and crafts, and the state's largest display of gold nuggets, some fist-sized; $5 for adults, $3 for students. The Northern Inua program runs twice daily June through August, with athletes demonstrating skills from the World Eskimo-Indian Olympics, as well as traditional games, songs, and dances; $6 for adults, $4 for youth, $2 for children. Dynamic Aurora, also twice daily, tells the secrets of the northern lights through slides, video, and demonstration; $4 for adults, $2 for youth, $1 for children (discounts available for the works). PO Box 756960, Fairbanks, AK 99775-6960; 907/474-7505. &

GEORGESON BOTANICAL GARDENS / Do not leave town without visiting the veggies. Under the spell of the midnight sun, they grow into giants. While you're at it, check out all the other marvels of Alaska agriculture, including the brilliant, jumbo-size flowers. Since this is an experimental farm, there are new things in the garden every year. Free tours are available; call for times. Otherwise, just walk on through. PO Box 757200, Fairbanks, AK 99775; 907/474-1944, fax 907/474-1841; open June–Sept; Tanana Loop, 1 mile southwest of the lower University of Alaska Fairbanks campus. &

SANTA CLAUS HOUSE / Don't be alarmed if you mysteriously find yourself humming "Jingle Bells" as you pull off the Richardson Highway here. This is a town with a serious Santa fixation. Each holiday season, **NORTH POLE** (pop. 1,600) gets deluged with children's letters to Santa, as well as grown-ups' letters requesting North Pole postmarks on their Christmas cards. Everywhere you look, there are establishments such as Santa's World Travel and Santa's Senior Citizens. Light poles resemble giant candy canes, and streets have names like Kris Kringle Drive and Rudolph Lane. The name of this city was no accident. Back in the early 1950s, when it was being incorporated, the townsfolk considered names like Moose Crossing and Mosquito Junction, but voted for North Pole instead. That sealed its fate as a theme town. The 30-foot Santa out front of the Santa Claus House gift shop/tourist trap is a clue you've arrived at Santa central. 101 St. Nicholas Dr, North Pole, AK 99705; 907/488-2200; off Richardson Hwy, 14 miles south of Fairbanks. &

YELLOW EAGLE GOLD MINING TOURS / This one's referred to as "the real thing." Yellow Eagle is the third-largest working placer gold mine in the United States. No other road-accessible, working gold mine of this caliber is open to visitors in the state. These tours are for those interested in learning about modern-day gold-mining techniques, so you won't find actors in turn-of-the-century miners' costumes sloshing gold pans around. Instead, you'll see enormous earth-moving trucks and thousands of gallons of water per minute separating gold from gravel in industrial-strength sluice boxes. There's an old gold dredge on the property for historical comparison. You'll learn to do it the old-fashioned way with a pan spiked with paydirt. (You're guaranteed to see some color in the bottom of your pan, which you keep.) Tickets are $25 for adults, $15 for children 12 and younger. For $10 more, you can have your picture taken holding a pan full of thousands of dollars worth of gold dust and nuggets. Tours cater to small groups of 25 or fewer, and are about 2 hours. PO Box 449, Ester, AK 99725; 907/479-0470, fax 907/479-0492; ccven@ptialaska.net; www.yegoldminingtours.com; open May 15–Sept 15; 6 miles south of Fairbanks on the Parks Hwy. &

SHOPPING / You'll find everything from gold nugget jewelry to moose nugget swizzle sticks within a few blocks' radius of the Fairbanks Visitors Center. Within the souvenir genre, the downtown favorite is the **ARCTIC TRAVELERS GIFT SHOP** (201 Cushman St; 907/456-7080). If you're in the market for smoked salmon, stop by **SANTA'S SMOKEHOUSE** (2400 Davis Rd; 907/456-3885), home of the original salmon sausage and salmon hot dog, offering a variety of gift boxes. **BEADS AND THINGS** (537 2nd Ave; 907/456-2323) sells beads and things, but also some Native crafts on consignment—mukluks, porcupine quill earrings, ivory, soapstone carvings, birch-bark baskets, and more. **ALASKA RAG CO.** (552 2nd Ave; 907/451-4401) specializes in custom, hand-woven rag rugs made of 100 percent recycled materials and discarded clothes. In addition, you'll find the creations of 65 Alaskan artists. (At the Fairbanks Visitors Center, pick up a free copy of the "Fairbanks Arts Directory," which lists everything from artists' studios to arts festivals.)

At the **GREAT ALASKAN BOWL CO.** (4630 Old Airport Rd; 907/474-9663), you can watch craftspeople at work and create your own gift bowls, choosing from a variety of Alaska-made products, or you can bring in your own. The **TANANA VALLEY FARMERS MARKET** (1800 College Rd; 907/479-5525 or 907/459-8420), located next to the Tanana Valley Fairgrounds, is an Alaska-grown and Alaska-made seasonal market, offering everything from veggies to quilts, every Saturday from May to September. The midweek market is usually on Wednesday, but changes from year to year.

With more than 40,000 titles of new and used books to paw through, including a healthy Alaskana section, you and your traveling companion are likely to become separated for days in **GULLIVER'S BOOKS** (3525 College Rd; 907/474-9574). Before filling out a missing-person report, check upstairs, which is loaded with used books, like a literary garage sale. Also upstairs you'll find the **SECOND STORY CAFE**, where you can order coffee drinks, soup, wraps, bagels, and goodies, and they offer free Internet connection.

ADVENTURES

RENTALS / Several businesses rent outdoor toys, such as camping equipment, bikes, rafts, canoes, and car racks, including **INDEPENDENT RENTAL** (2020 S Cushman St; 907/456-6595). **ARCTIC 7 RENTALS** (4312 Birch Ln; 907/479-0751, fax 907/479-2229; gables7@alaska.net; www.alaska.net/~gables7/7bridges.htm) rents bikes, kayaks, and canoes, as well as motors that can be attached to the transom. **BEAVER SPORTS** (3480 College Rd; 907/479-2494; www.beaversports.net) rentals run the gamut and include camping gear, boats, bikes, skis, snowshoes, and in-line skates. Some of these outfits can also arrange shuttles.

VIEWS / For the best view of the city, head to Hagelbarger Turnout on Hagelbarger Road, off the Steese Highway. The best view of Denali (also known as Mount McKinley) can be seen from the west ridge of the University of Alaska Fairbanks campus. For the best view—period—give a call to one of the **HOT-AIR BALLOON** companies and take in the sights from about 1,000 feet up. Midnight Sun Balloon Tours (907/456-3028) or Advanced Balloon Adventures (907/455-7433) offer rides that run about $180 for adults.

HIKING / For a short hike, try **ANGEL ROCKS TRAIL**. This 3.5-mile round trip takes you along the North Fork of the Chena River, through the forest, and up into a maze of granite pinnacles that could pass as castle ruins. The highest point is 1,750 feet, atop a rock overlook. These outcroppings, called "tors," were formed millions of years ago when molten rock pushed upward but cooled and solidified before breaking ground. The trail begins at Mile 48.9 of the Chena Hot Springs Road.

For a long hike, try **WHITE MOUNTAINS SUMMIT TRAIL**. On a clear day, panoramic views of the Alaska Range, Minto Flats, and the White Mountains may find you bursting into a Julie Andrews impersonation. From the trailhead at Mile 28 on the Elliott Highway, the 20-mile trail climbs just under Wickersham Dome 7 miles in, follows ridges, drops into forest, and climbs to the highest point, 10 miles in, at 3,100 feet. The trail ends at Beaver Creek, where there's good fishing, camping, and even a cabin to rent. Call for reservations (907/474-2251).

BIKING / For getting around town, grab a copy of the free Fairbanks-area bike map at the visitor center. Or, pick up a copy of Jon Underwood's *Fairbanks Mountain Bike Trail Guide* for $3.95 at **BEAVER SPORTS** (see above). The staff at **ALL WEATHER SPORTS** (4001 Geist Rd; 907/474-8184) has good information, too.

Our favorite mountain bike ride is **FERRY TRAIL**. This ride begins in Ferry, a small mining town about 100 miles south of Fairbanks, and goes through the historic Liberty Bell Mining District for as many miles and side trips as you can pedal. Go at least 9 miles, as far as **BOOT HILL**. For years, local miners have tossed their worn-out shoes and boots upon this mound, creating a footwear graveyard that's a hoot to see. There's no sign for Ferry. Turn east off the Parks Highway at Mile 259.4. You'll come to a parking lot, then walk along the railroad tracks and over the Tanana River via footbridge. Ask locals where to pick up the trail.

BOATING / The Alaska Public Lands Information Center (250 Cushman St; 907/456-0527) is an oasis of information for river travelers. In addition, there are river logs containing the comments of boaters who've made various trips. Ask for a copy of the BLM's *Alaska River Adventures*, which has descriptions of rivers, including Beaver Creek, Birch Creek, the Delta River, Fortymile River, Gulkana River, Squirrel River, and Unalakleet River. The National Weather Service's River Information Program (907/266-5160) provides information on river conditions and water-level updates, from breakup to freeze-up, May through October. **CANOEALASKA** (907/479-5183, fax 907/479-5383; canoeak@ mosquitonet.com; www.mosquitonet.com/~canoeak) will take you paddle-rafting down the Chena River for $99 per person (four-person minimum), including gear. This company also offers 2- to 10-day trips on the Delta, Gulkana, and Fortymile Rivers, and Birch and Beaver Creeks. In addition to day and overnight floats on the Chena, Chatinika, and Gulkana Rivers, **INTERIOR AK ADVENTURES** (800/890-3229 or 907/388-4193; aktours@compuserve.com) offers "Midnight Sun Floats," from 6pm to midnight for $85 per person. If you are interested in floating the Fortymile River or the Yukon River between Dawson City, Yukon Territory, and Circle, Alaska, **EAGLE CANOE RENTALS** (PO Box 4, Eagle, AK 99738; phone/fax 907/547-2203) can set you up. Rental between Dawson and Circle is $270 per canoe; between Eagle and Circle, $165.

FISHING / Rivers and lakes of the Interior are a fisherman's dream. You'll find Dolly Varden, arctic char, pike, sheefish, arctic grayling, rainbow trout, five different species of salmon, and more. You don't even have to go very far. The **CHENA RIVER**, which runs through downtown Fairbanks, offers salmon fishing and catch-and-release for grayling, which is usually good upriver, off Chena Hot Springs Road. For a recorded fishing report, call or stop by the Alaska Department of Fish and Game (1300 College Rd; 907/459-7385). Fish and Game stocks more than 70 lakes and sloughs within an hour or two of town, so ask about those too. **TWO RIVERS DRIFTERS** (PO Box 16229, Two Rivers, AK 99716; 907/488-8269) uses a drift boat, no motor, for a peaceful fly-fishing experience on the Chena for $140 per person, two-person maximum, including fishing gear and lunch. **CHILDS CHARTERS** (2091 Yellow Snow Rd, Fairbanks, AK 99709-6349; 907/455-6028) will help you catch everything from northern pike to king salmon via motorboat with a full canopy for $250 per boat for a half day, and $400 for a full day, fishing gear, bait, and rain gear provided.

BUSH FLIGHTS / Federally subsidized mail runs make regular flights to villages throughout the Interior and the Arctic coastal plain. This means savings for travelers on flexible schedules. Rather than the package mail-run "tours," ask about drop-off and back-haul rates. Two Fairbanks-based flying services offering these flights are **WARBELOW'S AIR VENTURES INC.** (907/474-0518; wav@polarnet.com) and **FRONTIER FLYING SERVICE** (907/474-0014; info@frontierflying.com; www. frontierflying.com).

GUIDES AND OUTFITTERS

BACKCOUNTRY LOGISTICAL SERVICES / For those who'd prefer to lead their own remote trip, but need help with logistics and gear like foldable Ally Pak canoes, this outfitter offers a self-guided, 10-day raft trip on Beaver Creek with all gear (rafts, tents, cookstoves, etc., but not food or sleeping bags) and an emergency locator transmitter for around $500 per person, including fly-out. For information, contact PO Box 82265, Fairbanks, AK 99708; 907/457-7606.

NATIVE TOURS

Several tour companies offer culturally sensitive, quality trips to remote Native villages. Many of the tour leaders are village people themselves. Remember always that villages and fish camps are people's homes, not a theme park. Listen. Be respectful. Ask before you take photographs. You are in somebody else's home.

YUKON STARR ENTERPRISES / Yukon Starr offers scenic tours of the Yukon River out of the village of Tanana for up to six passengers. Lifelong Alaskan Paul Starr is an Athabascan and a certified master river pilot who will show you firsthand the land he loves, stopping at friends' fish camps along the way. The cost is $150 per person for a full day, not including airfare to Tanana (around $130 round-trip), plus $75 per couple for an optional overnight. PO Box 126, Tanana, AK 99777; 907/366-7251, fax 907/366-7103; no credit cards; checks OK; mid-June–mid-Aug.

ATHABASCA CULTURAL JOURNEYS / Fly to the village of Huslia, home to about 250 Athabascans living in the Koyukuk National Wildlife Refuge. Members of local families greet guests and serve as their guides. Experience life in a fish camp, taste Native foods, and go boating and hiking. You'll learn traditional crafts such as beadwork and sewing skins. You'll also learn to read animal signs and how to pick a fish net, and you'll hear stories, myths, and folklore. Guests stay in tents in a fish camp during their 3-day, 3-night visit; call for current prices. PO Box 72,

Huslia, AK 99746; 800/937-0899 or 907/829-2261; no credit cards; checks OK; June–Sept; in fall, villagers lead hunting trips.

ARCTIC VILLAGE TOURS / The Venetie Tribal Government invites visitors to Arctic Village in the heart of the Brooks Range, as well as to Venetie on the Chandalar River in the Yukon Flats. When you step off the bush plane in either village, it's like entering a different nation. If you feel strongly about oil drilling in the Arctic National Wildlife Refuge, the Arctic Village is the tour for you. Whether you're pro or con, you'll get the chance to hear how the Gwich'in people, who depend on the Porcupine Caribou Herd, feel about the subject. Canoe trips, hikes, and fishing trips can be arranged with local Indian guides. Overnight trips to Arctic Village and Venetie in the summer are $430 and $390, respectively, which includes round-trip airfare from Fairbanks, food, lodging, equipment, and guide service. (For day trips, it's $300.) Overnight winter trips, with sled-dog and snowmobile excursions, are available too. PO Box 82896, Fairbanks, AK 99708; 907/479-4648; no credit cards; no checks.

YUKON RIVER TOURS / The Athabascan people of Stevens Village, on the banks of the Yukon River, invite people to visit one of their fish camps. Guests take a bus up the Dalton Highway to the Yukon River Bridge, where they board a boat and head upriver to a working fish camp in the Yukon Flats Wildlife Refuge. At camp, where men once cut wood to fuel the old stern-wheelers, you'll see villagers fishing with nets and fish wheels and cutting salmon for drying or smoking, as they have done for generations. Guests also visit a cultural center, put together by the village elders, to learn about life on the Yukon and the Native people's annual subsistence cycles. The center includes artifacts, old photographs, and a display of traditional subsistence tools. The tour lasts about 1½ hours, although visitors can arrange to spend the night in one of the wall tents at the fish camp for an extra $10, if they like. You'll need to bring your own sleeping bag and some food, though chances of being offered a chunk of salmon are good. The village itself is about 20 more miles upstream, and special tours can be arranged, as well as tours of the Rampart Canyon. Shuttles for private river trips are also available. 214 2nd Ave, Fairbanks, AK 99701-4811; 907/452-7162, fax 907/452-5063; dlacey@mosquitonet.com; MC, V; checks OK; tours June 1–Sept 1.

ALEXANDER'S RIVER ADVENTURE / Wes Alexander, an Athabascan and certified master river pilot, picks you up in a heated, 28-foot jet boat in downtown Fairbanks and takes you 25 miles downriver to his family's fish camp. His wife, Mary, makes a hearty lunch of whatever is in season—fresh salmon, moose stew. You'll see the family's fish wheel and learn traditional ways of putting up food. You'll meet Alexander's mother, a delightful woman who makes moccasins and does lovely beadwork. Day and overnight trips are available. The cost is $99 per person for the day, and $225 for an overnight in a wall tent at camp. PO Box 62, Nenana, AK 99760; 907/474-3924, cell 907/322-4247, fax 907/474-3926; no credit cards; checks OK; operates June–Sept.

NIGHTLIFE

There's a species of wildlife here in Fairbanks that the tourist brochures fail to mention. It's a nocturnal creature known for its voracious thirst and tendency to dance with wild abandon with or without a partner. Those who wish to see this phenomenon, but who don't have a clue where to go, can try **AURORA LIMOUSINE SERVICE** (1477 Shypoke Dr; 907/451-3525, fax 907/479-8876), with designated drivers well versed in everything from honky-tonk to heavy metal. Rates are usually by the hour, but for a nightlife tour there's a flat rate of $175 for 3 hours of sampling the city's most popular nightlife haunts.

BLUE LOON SALOON / Like to dance? Here's where you do it. In addition to local bands, the Loon brings in such names as Bo Diddley, Laura Love, Leo Kottke—to name a few. It throws disco parties, swing nights, techno bashes, folk fests. Eclectic, that's all there is to it. Don't like to dance? That's OK, too. The Loon shows movies most nights—pull up a couch. 2999 Parks Hwy; V; local checks only; full bar; 3 miles south of town.

HOWLING DOG SALOON / "Doing my part to [tick off] the Religious Right," says a bumper sticker above the bar. That about sums up the place. This Alaska classic is legendary. One step inside the rustic saloon and you'll see why. Decor by committee hangs from the ceiling—everything from moose antlers to hundreds of hats from the heads of people all over the world, as well as a few sets of bras and undies. The Dog is also known for its animated, all-night volleyball games out back. If all this recreating finds you low on oats, drag yourself over to the Dawghouse Performance Pizza counter for some of the best pizza in Fairbanks, "made by real Italians from New York." The bar features 17 microbrews on tap. There's often live music, but never a cover charge. 2160 Old Steese Hwy, Fox; 907/457-8780; AE, DIS, MC, V; local checks only; open April–Nov; full bar; about 11 miles north of Fairbanks, intersection of Steese Expressway and Old Steese Hwy in Fox.

THE MARLIN / This is a cross between a cozy college bar and a basement jazz club, though you'll also hear about every other species of music here live most nights, including open mike on Tuesdays. The Marlin serves Guinness on tap and rotates nine microbrews. There's a nonsmoking section and yummy pizza to soak up the beer. 3412 College Rd; 907/479-4646; MC, V; local checks only; Mon–Sat; full bar; near the university on College Rd.

FESTIVALS AND EVENTS

MIDNIGHT SUN BASEBALL GAME / They say people do strange things on account of the moon. Here, it's the sun that messes with your mind. This annual baseball game, played on the Friday night closest to summer solstice (June 21), begins at 10:30pm and lasts until 2am, with no lights. The game, which features the local semi-pro baseball team, the Alaska Goldpanners, dates back to 1906, when it was originally played between "The Drinks" and "The Smokes," so called because the local newspaper refused to identify their sponsors and give them free publicity. Incidentally, The Drinks won after 10 innings. For more information on the game, call 907/451-0095.

MIDNIGHT SUN RUN / This 10K fund-raiser run brings characters out of the woodwork. In the costume category, entrants have run dressed as mosquitoes, cows, fish, and cans of insect repellent. One hardcore ran in a suit of armor. The audience gets a little crazy, too. Residents have been known to drag out couches, recliners, and floor lamps to the street to watch. The run begins at 10pm, but the party lasts well into the night— such as it is on the longest day of the year. For more information, call 907/452-7211.

GOLDEN DAYS / This 2-week festival in mid-July is not only Fairbanks' biggest bash, but it's an opportunity to end up in jail. In addition to all the normal stuff like races, contests, and parades, you can buy a warrant for $5 and give the sheriff and his band of thugs a name and address, and off they'll go, guns a-blazing, with their roving slammer—a set of bars pulled around town by a 1-ton truck. Your victim's sentence could be 5 minutes or 25 minutes. It all depends on how good a sport you are.

Golden Days commemorates the discovery of gold near Fairbanks in 1902. There's a Felix Pedro look-alike contest (Pedro being the prospector who started all this), a hairy legs contest, a beard and mustache contest, and the Rubber Ducky Race, in which 6,000 rubber duckies are tossed into the Chena River. The first ducks to reach the finish line downriver earn prize money for their ticket holders. For information, call 907/452-1105.

FAIRBANKS SUMMER ARTS FESTIVAL / This is the art community's gift to the people of Fairbanks. The annual event is a study-performance festival, with up to 65 guest artists from around the world sharing their talents in theater, music, opera, dance, ice-skating theater, and visual arts. There are workshops and free performances. The festival is held on campus at the University of Alaska Fairbanks at the end of July and beginning of August. For information, call 907/474-8869.

WORLD ESKIMO-INDIAN OLYMPICS / You've never seen anything like it. For four days in mid-July, Native athletes, dancers, and artisans from around the state gather here to play traditional games, perform dances, and test their strength and skills in a variety of events, including high kick, knuckle hop, ear-pull, and white man versus Native women tug-of-war. With the exception of the latter (which Native women always win), all the games originate from a lifestyle that demanded (and still demands) extraordinary skill and agility to survive. In addition, beautiful Native artwork is for sale. For information, call 907/452-6646.

ATHABASCAN OLD TIME FIDDLERS FESTIVAL / That's right: Athabascan fiddles, as in violins, played with an attitude. Along the Yukon River, 19th-century French, Canadian, and Scottish fur traders left behind a taste for old-time fiddle tunes and the dances they inspire. This November festival of performances and dances is one of the biggest winter gatherings in the Interior. For information, call 907/452-1825.

FESTIVAL OF NATIVE ARTS / Native people from all over Alaska gather in Fairbanks in late February or early March to sing, dance, and hold drumming circles at the University of Alaska. Arts and crafts tables fill the Great Hall. Native artists and craftspeople sell everything from ivory carvings to dance fans and beaded mukluks. For information, call 907/474-7181.

YUKON QUEST INTERNATIONAL SLED DOG RACE / This is the epic of all sled-dog races. Blasting off in mid-February, competitors say this 1,000-mile, international race over gold-rush and mail routes is colder and tougher than the more well-known Iditarod Trail Sled Dog Race between Anchorage and Nome. Starting points alternate each year between Fairbanks and Whitehorse, Yukon Territory. For information, call 907/452-7954.

WORLD ICE ART CHAMPIONSHIPS / During this annual festival in March, carvers take huge blocks of clear blue ice and create a frozen art gallery, with some pieces so delicate you'd hate to sneeze. This international ice-sculpting competition draws sculptors from all over the world. Eighty to 100 teams participate. For information, call 907/451-8250.

CHATANIKA DAYS / Witness cabin people unwinding after a long, dark winter the second weekend of March. In addition to a pool tournament, a band, and general merrymaking, this celebration of spring includes an outhouse race from the Chatanika Gold Camp to the Chatanika Lodge. Mile 28, Steese Hwy; 907/389-2164.

RESTAURANTS

Bun on the Run / ★★

3400 BLOCK, COLLEGE RD, FAIRBANKS
You walk up to the window of this food wagon; order a sandwich, a snack, or a cinnamon bun; and away you go. Bun on the Run. Get it? The business is the brainstorm of sisters Gretchen Petersen and Ingrid Herreid, who spent much of their childhood in the Bush and learned to bake from their mom. There's nothing else like it in Fairbanks, not only because no one could come up with a catchier name, but because no one could deliver the goodies the way these two do. Their pastry lineup includes a variety of scones, sour-cream cakes, coconut bars, crème de menthe brownies, muffins, cinnamon rolls to die for, and "The Ultimate Decadence," a fudge brownie with cream cheese layers. Sandwiches ($5) feature turkey, cheeses, and locally grown veggies slathered with home-made pesto on freshly baked buns. On a warm summer day, outdoor seating is available, so you don't have to take your bun and run. *$; no credit cards; checks OK; breakfast, lunch Mon–Sat; open May–Sept, depending on weather; no alcohol; in the parking lot between Beaver Sports and the Marlin.* &

Gambardella's Pasta Bella / ★★

706 2ND AVE, FAIRBANKS; 907/456-3417, FAX 907/456-3425
This downtown Italian eatery has a surprisingly warm, urban atmosphere for a city full of establishments sporting moose antlers and other decorative body parts. Highly recommended for its aromatherapy value alone—it's filled with the smell of freshly baked bread and Italian spices. They make their own sausages here, too. Don't miss the focaccia, an Italian flat bread made with virgin olive oil, fresh garlic, olives, and fresh rosemary. They have wicked good lasagne with four Italian cheeses, the best pizza and calzones in the Interior, and homemade cheesecake. Chicken Balsamic—chicken breast sautéed in balsamic vinegar, with fresh tomatoes and black olives—is quite tangy and addictive. The

murals and artwork on the walls are by the owner/general manager sister team, Lisa and Laurie Gambardella. *$$; AE, MC, V; local checks only; lunch Mon–Sat, dinner every day; beer and wine; downtown.* &

Pike's Landing / ★★★

4438 AIRPORT WAY, FAIRBANKS; 907/479-6500, FAX 907/479-6513
On a warm, sunny day, there's no finer place for lunch than on Pike's deck overlooking the Chena River, as water-skiers, canoeists, and families of ducks pass by. Pike's elegant dining room overlooks the river, so reserve a table by the window. You'll find such entrees as Alaska king salmon, sauteed garlic prawns, and seafood baked en croute—crab, scallops, shrimp, and cheeses served in a puff pastry. The crab bisque with aged Kentucky whiskey is excellent. After the main courses, you may find yourself seduced by the decadent dessert tray. Succumb. *$$; AE, DC, DIS, JCB, MC, V; checks OK; lunch, dinner every day, brunch Sun; full bar; 4⅕ miles up Airport Way W, watch for sign.* &

The Pump House Restaurant & Saloon / ★★★

796 CHENA PUMP RD, FAIRBANKS; 907/479-8452, FAX 907/479-8432
The exterior of this restaurant looks like a tin workshed because it once was one. The original Chena pump house, on the banks of the Chena River, was part of a vast system of pumps, sluiceways, ditches, and flumes built by the Fairbanks Exploration Co. to support its gold dredging operations. Reconstructed as a restaurant and bar in the late 1970s, today the Pump House has the most colorful atmosphere of any restaurant in the city, with a solid mahogany bar and a pressed-tin ceiling. The inside is full of antiques, old photographs, and relics. An enormous, 1,100-pound Kodiak bear greets you at the door, but don't fret; he's what you'll soon be—stuffed. Belly up to the oyster bar or hunker down to a game of backgammon in the bar. *$$; AE, DIS, MC, V; local checks only; lunch, dinner every day in summer; dinner every day in winter; brunch Sun; full bar; pumphse@polarnet.com; www.pumphouse.com; up Chena Pump Rd, on the left, watch for sign.* &

River City Bagels & Deli and Coffee Roasters / ★★

364 OLD CHENA PUMP RD, FAIRBANKS; 907/451-8648,
FAX 907/451-8646
This bright, lively eatery has the largest selection of freshly baked bagels in the Interior, with flavors from cinnamon raisin to sun-dried tomato. European-style pastries are baked on the spot. In fact, everything here is fresh, made with local produce and products whenever possible. Even the house-roasted deli sandwich meats are the real thing, right off the bone. Soups rule here, and Reubens are huge and hearty. And there are at least a dozen salads to choose from. The horseshoe-shaped coffee and pastry bar was salvaged from the old Woolworth's lunch counter and features

the full-service espresso bar and custom roasting corner. This is serious coffee. Watch the master roaster on weekdays at 4pm; he'll custom-roast your order. *$; MC, V; local checks only; breakfast, lunch every day, early dinner Mon–Sat; no alcohol; in the Chena Pump Plaza off Chena Pump Rd, intersection of Parks Hwy and Geist Rd.* &

The Thai House / ★★★

526 5TH AVE, FAIRBANKS; 907/452-6123
This place practically has a cult following among the Fairbanks dinner crowd, particularly those who travel and know a good pad thai when they see one. Among local favorites are the red, green, and yellow curries; the leg of lamb marinated in a special blend of spices; and the Pa Ram Gai. All the important stuff is there: friendly service, consistently tasty food, and an assortment of hot oils and spices for turning up the heat when there's a request for "blistering hot." *$$; MC, V; local checks only; lunch, dinner Mon–Sat; beer and wine; downtown.* &

Two Rivers Lodge / ★★

4968 CHENA HOT SPRING RD, FAIRBANKS; 907/488-6815,
FAX 907/488-9761
In true Alaska fashion, much as if a taxidermist had been the interior decorator, antlers, pelts, bearskin rugs, and rusty old traps fill this lodge built of burnished logs and rough-cut lumber. Two Rivers features a menu of game dishes such as pheasant and quail, steaks, and some surprises, including alligator tail flown in fresh from Louisiana. Grapefruit pie, a light cream pie made of ruby red grapefruit, was named Grand Champion at the Alaska State Fair. In addition to fine dining, Two Rivers also offers fine drinking in the Trapline Lounge. *$$$; AE DC, DIS, MC, V; checks OK; dinner every day; full bar; www.alaskaone.com/2rvslodge; mile 16.9, Chena Hot Springs Rd.* &

LODGINGS

The Fairbanks Visitors Information Center (800/327-5774 or 907/456-5774) keeps an entire forest worth of brochures on local **BED-AND-BREAKFASTS**, as well as a two-volume binder with descriptions and photographs of the homes, owners, and rooms. Or try the Fairbanks Association of Bed & Breakfasts (PO Box 73334, Fairbanks, AK 99707-3334; 907/452-7386, fax 907/456-7060; FABB@polarnet.com; www.ptialaska.net/~fabb).

Captain Bartlett Inn / ★★

1411 AIRPORT WAY, FAIRBANKS, AK 99701; 800/544-7528,
800/478-7900, OR 907/452-1888
If you want a hotel that's truly Alaskan, look no further. The main lobby of this cozy hotel is made of logs and decked with old photographs and

rustic doodads. The hotel restaurant, Slough Foot Sue's, has an old-road-house atmosphere, including a huge stone fireplace. All 197 guest rooms and suites have a turn-of-the-century feel with four-poster beds, hard-wood furniture, and warm-colored wallpaper throughout. Outside, there's a large patio and brilliant flowerbeds. Fairbanks' beloved Wanda Burroughs plays ragtime and honky-tonk tunes on the piano Monday through Friday from 4:30 to 7:30pm in the Dog Sled Saloon. You'll also find a free appetizer bar there. Double occupancy rates start at $140 in the summer and $99 in winter. *$$; AE, DC, DIS, MC, V; checks OK; breakfast, lunch, dinner every day; full bar; cbi@polar.net.com; accessible from frontage road off Airport Way.* &

Cloudberry Lookout B & B / ★★★

310 YANA CT, FAIRBANKS, AK 99708; 907/479-7334, FAX 907/479-7134
It took Suzi Lozo and Sean McGuire eight years to build their post-and-beam, three-story home on 40 acres. On a knoll overlooking a lake, surrounded by boreal forest, the Lookout is stunning. This log-frame home is loaded with glass and topped by an aurora borealis–viewing tower. To get there, you climb spiral steps notched into a 198-year-old spruce log. Partway up is an aerial library stocked with natural-history and Alaska books. You then keep going another floor to the aurorium. The Lookout also has a third-story outdoor walkway, a solarium on the south side of the house, and a music room with a grand piano (Suzi is a piano teacher). Skiing and nature trails are nearby, and dog-mushing tours can be arranged. Rates run $85–$105, double occupancy; children over 13 welcome. Nonsmoking. *$$; AE, MC, V; checks OK; open March–Oct; cloudbry@mosquitonet.com; www.mosquitonet.com/~cloudbry; off Goldhill Rd, call for directions.*

Fairbanks Princess Hotel / ★★★

4477 PIKES LANDING RD, FAIRBANKS, AK 99709; 800/426-0500 OR 907/455-4477, FAX 907/455- 5094
Without a doubt, this is Fairbanks' finest hotel. This tastefully decorated, 200-room hotel sits on the banks of the Chena River. A large, terraced riverside deck and lovely flowerbeds make it worth staying put on a warm, sunny day, watching canoeists and ducks paddle by. The deluxe rooms are elegantly decorated, with light wicker furniture and goose-down comforters on the beds. During summer, a boat shuttle stops at the dock and will take you sightseeing or drop you off at one of the riverside restaurants. Amenities include a health club and free airport shuttle. Double occupancy rates begin at $199 in summer and $129 in winter. Dining lounges range from formal to casual. *$$$; AE, DC, MC, V; checks OK; breakfast, lunch, dinner every day; full bar; off Airport Way W, turn south at Pike's Landing, follow signs.* &

Forget-Me-Not Lodge–Aurora Express / ★★★

**1540 CHENA RIDGE, FAIRBANKS, AK 99708; 907/474-0949
OR 800/221-0073, FAX 907/474-8173**

The *Aurora Express* is the name of a train sitting in Sue and Mike Wilson's front yard. A real train. The Wilsons started their bed-and-breakfast business in their fabulous custom-built home on 15 acres with a view of the city and the Tanana Valley. Then, in a dream, Sue's dearly departed Irish grandmother told her to get a caboose. No fooling. So she did. "When my grandmother speaks to me, I listen," she explains. The *Golden Nellie*, formerly Caboose 1068, has a golden ceiling, heavy velvet drapes, and original chairs re-covered in brocade. The caboose looked so lonely in the front yard, Sue added two Pullman sleeper cars and a water tanker, then two more cars and a locomotive, all on several hundred feet of winding track. The cars have been renovated with queen-size beds, private baths, and themes ranging from the Bordello to the Immaculate Conception, a room with an angel-and-cherub motif and an arched ceiling painted as a blue sky full of fluffy clouds. Double occupancy rates start at $85. The Wilsons' 5,000-square-foot home, the Forget-Me-Not Lodge, has several lovely guest rooms as well if you'd prefer something more traditional, although nothing about the Wilson place is traditional. Exceptional is more like it. The Lilac Room, $135 for two, is deluxe, with a small dormer sitting area with a great view. *$$; MC, V; checks OK; www.aurora-express.com; 6.5 miles up Chena Pump Rd, watch for sign on the right.* ᕃ

Grandma Shirley's Hostel / ★★

510 DUNBAR, FAIRBANKS, AK 99707; 907/451-9816

Now here's a hostel with character, including a surrogate grandma. And no curfew! For $16.25 per person, guests sleep in nice, clean bunkrooms with made-up beds and pine plank floors. Showers come equipped with towels, soap, and shampoo. Grandma Shirley provides coffee, tea, and hot chocolate. Guests can also use her kitchen, her spices, her oil—whatever you need for cooking your own food—and can pick fresh goodies from her garden and greenhouse. She will do your laundry and deliver it to your bunk for $4 a load. You never know who you'll meet here; Grandma Shirley has had guests from 7 months old to 82 years old. *$; no credit cards; checks OK; by bus, take the purple route, get off at F and Dunbar, walk 1 block, watch for sign; by car, off Trainer Gate Rd, turn left on E, then right on Dunbar.*

North Woods Lodge / ★

CHENA HILLS DR, FAIRBANKS, AK 99708; 800/478-5305
OR 907/479-5300, FAX 907/479-6888

In the budget category, this place on the edge of town runs the gamut, from rooms to campsites. The woodsy, laid-back atmosphere is what makes it stand out. Avoid the more expensive rooms downstairs, unless you don't mind sleeping in a basement and cooking in a garage. Suggested for families is the log house for $130, but be sure to ask for the entire main floor and loft or you could end up sharing the place with others. In a separate facility, the sleeping loft, or hostel, is about as basic as it gets, with two small rooms of side-by-side mattresses for $15 a head. Cooking, laundry, and shower facilities are available. There's an outdoor hot tub and a grill to use. On holidays and other special occasions, owner Tom Ridner may toss on a fresh salmon or halibut. Small, zero-frills cabins without bathrooms start at $45 for two, and campsites are $12 for one person, $15 for two. Showers are free. Free pickup from airport, bus, and train. *$; MC, V; checks OK; www.AlaskaOne.com/northlodge; PO Box 83615, Fairbanks, AK 99708; up Chena Pump Rd, past the Chena Pump House Restaurant turn right on Roland Rd, after 1½ miles turn right on Chena Hill Dr, watch for wooden sign on the right.*

A Taste of Alaska Lodge / ★★★

551 EBERHARDT RD, FAIRBANKS, AK 99712; 907/488-7855
OR 907/488-3838, FAX 907/488-3772

This wonderful log home, full of antiques and Alaska artifacts, is situated on a 280-acre family homestead, most of which was once an old potato and wheat farm staked in 1946. The lodge overlooks the city and the Alaska Range, and in the winter offers great aurora viewing. The 10-acre field out front draws an occasional moose and sandhill cranes that stick around all spring and summer. The owners, Debbie and Dave Eberhardt, rent cabins on their property and rooms in a 7,000-square-foot lodge, which also can be rented for weddings and other special events. Bed-and-breakfast rates run $125–$250, double occupancy. Gold panning, hiking, and hot-tubbing are available. Buffet breakfasts include quiche, crepes, bacon, sausage, yogurt, fresh fruit, muffins, Danishes, granola, and more. The Eberhardts can arrange sled-dog rides and other adventures. *$$$; AE, MC, V; checks OK; tasteak@mosquitonet.com; www.mosquitonet.com/~tasteak; 5 miles up Chena Hot Springs Rd, turn right on Eberhardt Rd.* &

WILDERNESS LODGES

Denali West Lodge

PO BOX 40 #ABP, LAKE MINCHUMINA, AK 97757; 907/674-3112
One hundred miles from the nearest highway, this stunning hand-hewn log lodge on the shore of Lake Minchumina is a visit to another world. It's not a seasonal outpost for Jack and Sherri Hayden; it's their home. They're located on the western border of Denali National Park and Preserve, and Mount McKinley is practically in their laps. Guests stay in cozy log cabins with sod roofs, woodstoves, and birch log beds, and have access to custom guide service 8 hours a day. The list of options includes fly-in fishing at the base of Mount Foraker, hiking, canoeing, wildlife photography, and birding excursions. You can fish for northern pike in front of the lodge. During winter season, the Haydens offer sled-dog expeditions on historic trapline, mail, and gold-mining trails, followed by a stint in the sauna back at the lodge, if you so desire. Dinner features fresh salmon or game, barbecued or cooked on a woodstove. The lodge accommodates 6 to 10 guests. *DIS, MC, V; checks OK; open Feb–mid-April and late May–mid-Sept; minchumina@aol. com; www.denaliwest.com; no road access.* &

Alaska Tolovana Adventures–Tolovana Lodge

PO BOX 281, NENANA, AK 99760; 907/832-5569
The restored Tolovana Roadhouse, on the National Register of Historic Places, is one of the last of the original roadhouses in Alaska. Located on the Tolovana and Tanana Rivers, the lodge serves as a base camp for guided fishing and canoeing trips in summer, hikes and waterfowl hunts in fall, and accommodations for winter travelers and outfitters. Its location next to the Minto Flats State Game Refuge makes this a prime spot for birders. In summer, a day trip via river is $110 per person if there's a full boat (six people), which includes fishing, meals, and a pickup in Nenana. Add $75 for an overnight. In winter, a half-hour sled-dog ride is $35, an overnight with all gear is $500. There are also extended trips to the roadhouse. *MC, V; US checks OK; open late May–Sept and Feb–Mar; tolovana@ptialaska.net; www.AlaskaOne.com/tolovana; about 55 miles west of Nenana.*

Nenana

At the confluence of the Nenana and Tanana Rivers, this village of less than 500 folks was originally an Athabascan fish camp before its conversion to a transportation center. Now it's home port to a tug and barge fleet that supplies villages along the Tanana and Yukon Rivers.

The town's name comes from a Native word meaning "good place to camp between two rivers." These days, it's a good place to stop for gas, a bite to eat, and a stroll back in time. Look for fish wheels in action and their catches drying in the sun during salmon run season. The white crosses across the river mark graves at a Native cemetery. It was here in Nenana that President Warren G. Harding, the first U.S. president ever to visit Alaska, drove in "the golden spike," symbolizing the completion of the Alaska Railroad between the ice-free port of Seward and the Interior city of Fairbanks. The old **NENANA RAILROAD DEPOT** is on the National Register of Historic Places. There's a new cultural center on the bank of the Tanana River, with a salmon bake next door.

Housed in a quaint log cabin with a sod roof is the **NENANA VISITORS CENTER** (907/832-9953) on the Parks Highway at the Nenana turnoff. You can buy tickets there for the Nenana Ice Classic at $2 a guess (see below). The center is open daily from Memorial Day through Labor Day.

FESTIVALS AND EVENTS

NENANA ICE CLASSIC / The main attraction in town is the Nenana Ice Classic. A tripod is set up in the middle of the river after freeze-up, and participants guess the exact day, hour, and minute the river ice will start breaking up in the spring. The first stirring dislodges the tripod, which sets off a siren, which tips a meat cleaver, which cuts a rope, which pulls a cotter pin, which stops a clock, which determines the winner or winners. This annual event goes back to 1917, when Alaska Railroad surveyors pooled $800 in prize money to bet among themselves. Since then, the jackpot has grown to more than $330,000, divided among winners, the town till, and tax collectors. The earliest breakup was April 20, 1940, at 3:27pm; the latest was May 20, 1964, at 11:41am. 907/832-5446; tripod@ptialaska.net; www/ptialaska.net/~tripod.

THE ANNIHILATOR / Nenana is also the home of one of Alaska's toughest 10-kilometer runs: The Annihilator. Held in June, this potentially bloody run starts at the railroad tracks and basically goes straight uphill for 1½ miles. That's the easy part. The descent is so steep, runners start coming down off the mountainside on a fixed rope.

RESTAURANTS

The Monderosa / ★

MILE 309, PARKS HWY, NENANA; 907/832-5243
This roadside bar and grill has a reputation with locals for having the biggest and best hamburgers in the Interior. Guess that's why they call

'em Mondo Burgers. *$; no credit cards; checks OK; lunch, dinner every day; full bar; PO Box 385, Nenana, AK 99760; 4 miles north of Nenana.*

Ester

With two gold booms under its belt, Ester was quite the boisterous little miners' mecca in its day. The first boom came with the discovery of gold on Ester, Cripple, and Eva Creeks around the turn of the century, which drew prospectors by the hundreds. The second came in 1936, when the Fairbanks Exploration Company built Ester Gold Camp to support its nearby dredge operation. The camp shut down in the 1950s, and most of the miners moved on. Today, about 250 people live in houses and cabins scattered throughout the woods. It may be the peace and quiet that attracts residents now, but it's the town's former wild ways that lure tourists. The old gold camp has become one of the most popular tourist attractions in the Interior; be sure and visit one of the restaurant-saloons noted below for a bit of fun and a taste of history.

NIGHTLIFE

GOLDEN EAGLE SALOON / Just up the road from the Ester Gold Camp is where the locals hang out. Until recently, an assortment of local dogs hung out there too, in spite of the sign saying "No Animals Allowed." As the story goes, one Friday night, two of them got into a fight. Then their owners started going at each other. (Yeah, there was beer involved.) The four of them made such a ruckus, the bartender got fed up and laid down the law. "That's it! No more dogs!" A hush went over the crowd. "What? No more dogs?" "No more dogs," he hollered, "on Friday nights." Saturday through Thursday were still OK—at least for a while. But times are a-changin'. Now the "No Animals" sign applies to dogs, too. Besides good stories, the Golden Eagle offers food, with a choice of—a hamburger. The bartender will hand you a paper plate with a slab of ground beef, a bun, and some trimmings, and point you toward the gas-fired grill. So the appeal of this place isn't obvious the moment you walk in the door. Still, you're bound to meet some colorful folks. Like the guy who lives across the road, as the bartender tells it, who leaves his window open year-round. Not for health reasons, either. If someone rings the bell, indicating a free round, he wants to be able to hear it, dash over, and slip in the back door. *General Delivery, Ester, AK 99725; 907/479-0809; no credit cards; local checks only; every day; full bar; from Ester turnoff, turn right on Main St, and right again at the T.*

RESTAURANTS AND LODGINGS

Ester Gold Camp Dining Hall & Hotel / ★★

3175 COLLEGE RD #1, FAIRBANKS, AK 99709; 800/676-6925 OR 907/479-2500

The gold camp, on the National Register of Historic Places, draws more than 20,000 visitors a season. Entertainment revolves around the restaurant and the Malemute Saloon, after which you can sleep it off in the rustic charm of an old hotel room. Rates are $65 for double occupancy, shared bath. The camp's hefty feed trough includes halibut fillets baked in a light wine sauce, reindeer stew, and country chicken for $15 per adult. Add crab for $22 per adult; children's prices vary. Locals say it's the best all-you-can-eat crab buffet in the Interior. If you can still move, waddle on over to the Malemute Saloon, complete with swinging doors, an antique mahogany bar, a player piano, beer-barrel tables, and a sawdust floor that spills out the front door. The bar specializes in drinks with names like Moose Milk, Iceworm Cocktail, and Dog Bite. *Service With a Smile,* a musical revue heavy on Robert Service, features costumes, songs, and stories from the gold-rush era. The camp offers free shuttle service from most major hotels and campgrounds in Fairbanks. *$$; MC, V; checks OK; dinner every day; late May–early Sept; full bar; intrasea@polarnet.com; www.alaskasbest.com/ester; from the Parks Hwy just south of Fairbanks, follow signs at the Ester turnoff.* &

Chena Hot Springs Road

EXPLORING

TACKS' GENERAL STORE, MILE 23.5 / If you get a sweet-tooth cramp about halfway up the road, stop in here for a slab of killer pie. Try the strawberry-rhubarb with apple-crisp crust. It's big enough to share, but why would you want to do that?

CHENA RIVER STATE RECREATION AREA, MILE 26 TO MILE 53 / Chena Hot Springs Road bisects a 254,080-acre playground of marshes, sloughs, rolling boreal forest, alpine tundra, and turretlike granite pinnacles. Within its boundaries are some of the region's best hikes, as well as opportunities for rock climbing, horseback riding, river running, fishing, and wildlife viewing in summer months, and ski touring, dog mushing, snowmobiling, and snowshoeing in winter months. ANGEL ROCKS TRAIL, at Mile 48.9, is a pretty excursion and a favorite hike among locals. GRANITE TORS TRAIL, Mile 39, is Angel Rocks squared, with large pinnacles of quartz, diorite, and granite poking out of the ground.

THE NORTHERN LIGHTS

The mystery of the night—the aurora borealis—may be the Interior's most alluring quality. Some nights there is only a single streak of green; other nights, the sky explodes with streamers of light like colorful confetti. They shimmer, spiral, and pulsate. They do the hula. They play crack-the-whip. The Interior is the ultimate domed theater, with the ideal latitude, enormous skies, and long, dark winters. Of all the skies Alaska has to offer, scientists from the University of Alaska's Geophysical Institute chose to set up shop here in the Interior, 30 miles north of Fairbanks at Poker Flats, where they shoot rockets into the atmosphere to learn more about the aurora.

This polar phenomenon occurs when solar winds slam into the earth's magnetic field, causing electrons to react with atmospheric gases. The impact sends them into a major uproar, lighting them up like neon signs. This all happens 50 to 200 miles overhead. Color depends on the height of the interaction, due to the varying composition of atmospheric gas. Green, the most common color, comes when the impact is low, around 60 miles above the earth's surface. Reds occur around the highest impact zone. In the winter of 1958, the reds were so intense in the Fairbanks area that residents thought the surrounding hills were on fire.

Too bad there's a logical explanation. The legends are far more fun. One Eskimo tale says the lights are the pathway to heaven, lit by departed souls holding torches to the world beyond. In another, spirits are playing ball in the sky, kicking up colorful cosmic dust.

No matter how many times you may have seen this chorus line of lights, it never gets old. People will rouse each other from deep sleep without a hint of apology. The best time to see the aurora is on a clear dark night around 2am. The lights make dashing to the outhouse at 40 below a little more thrilling.

—Debra McKinney

The 15-mile loop, with a high point of 3,300 feet, offers access to alpine tundra and "The Tors," a favorite local rock-climbing haunt. The trail begins at the Tors Trail Campground, near Mile 39 of Chena Hot Springs Road. Seven miles in, the trail is less developed. Keep an eye on the weather; fog makes it tricky to keep track of the trail markers. **CHENA DOME TRAIL**, at Mile 50.5, is a 29-mile, 3-day loop that circles the Angel Creek drainage area and is mostly on tundra ridgetops. The highest point is Chena Dome, a flat-topped ridge at 4,421 feet. On a clear day, the views are awesome, as is the tundra in July, when it's covered in wildflowers, and in late August and early September, when it's aglow with autumn colors. You'll find the trailhead on the left side of the road, at Mile 50.5 of Chena Hot Springs Road. **ANGEL CREEK CABIN** is a public-use cabin, accessible by a 1.5-mile side trail (22.5 miles in). It's available for rent, but you must make reservations well in advance through the Alaska Division of Parks & Recreation (907/451-2695). As a day hike, it's 3 miles to timberline, and another 6.2 miles from there to Chena Dome. There are a total of six cabins available in the recreation area; call ahead.

LODGINGS

The Resort at Chena Hot Springs

MILE 56.5, CHENA HOT SPRINGS RD, FAIRBANKS, AK 99707; 800/478-4681 OR 907/452-7867, FAX 907/456-3122

Your muscles will be thanking you profusely long after you've dried and gone back to Fairbanks (an hour and 15 minutes away). The spring-fed, indoor swimming pool is kept around 98°F in a building with floor-to-ceiling windows and three hot, hotter, and hottest tubs. The very hottest is a tub kept at 104°F, which sits outside on a 2,800-square-foot redwood deck. The dining room, with log walls and a stone fireplace, specializes in beef, seafood, and pasta. During winter, the resort offers cross-country skiing, dog-sled tours, guided snowmobile rides, horse-drawn sleigh rides, ice skating, and aurora borealis watching. In summer, there's horseback riding, hiking, and mountain bike rentals. The resort can arrange transportation; so can a number of local tour companies, which you can find through the Fairbanks Visitors Information Center. The resort has three seasonal rate structures: the highest is December 21 through April 15, the lowest September 16 through December 20. In summer, hotel rooms start at $105 for a double; cabins with no running water are $65. $$; AE, DC, DIS, JCB, MC, V; checks OK; full bar; chenahs@polarnet.com; www.chenahotsprings.com; PO Box 73440, Fairbanks, AK 99707; at the end of Chena Hot Springs Rd.

The Steese Highway

Built in 1927 to connect Fairbanks with Circle on the Yukon River, this mostly gravel road has been open year-round since 1984, though some maps won't tell you that. The first 44 miles are paved, with some nasty frost heaves. The gravel stretch is in better shape, although it can get a little muddy around Twelvemile and Eagle Summits. (Call 907/451-5204 for a road report.) There's fishing, gold panning, rustic lodges, and great hikes, as well as a motley mix of roadside attractions, such as the TRANS-ALASKA OIL PIPELINE VISITORS CENTER.

Opportunities for fishing abound between Mile 29 and Mile 40 on the Chatanika River. At Mile 86, you'll reach TWELVEMILE SUMMIT, elevation 2,980 feet. Then on to EAGLE SUMMIT, 3,624 feet, 20 miles up the road. Winds can be strong enough here to rip up road signs, so watch your hat. Down the other side, the mountains give way to hills, which give way to the **YUKON FLATS**. When you hit a slab of pavement, you'll know you've reached the town of **CENTRAL**, hub of the Circle Mining District, one of the oldest and most active in the state. This hardworking, no-sniveling type of town is home to miners, homesteaders, and others with little use for city ways.

A hard right takes you to **CIRCLE HOT SPRINGS**. The lodge there was renamed Arctic Circle Hot Springs in 1999. If you continue straight, the road narrows, gets windier, and finally dead-ends at the **YUKON RIVER** in **CIRCLE** (pop. approx. 95), which began as a mining supply town in 1887 and was so dubbed because it was thought to be on the Arctic Circle. (To check winter road conditions, call 907/451-5204.)

EXPLORING

TOM'S USED BOOKSTORE TENT, MILE 127.5 / Proprietor Tom Lavender runs his little shop in Central out of a large wall tent with a dirt floor, a woodstove in the corner, and a plywood office tacked on front. Books here start at one thin dime. If Tom's not there, go in and browse. If you find a book you'd like to buy, just leave the money in the drawer in the office. Central may be the last holdout for that sorely missed business virtue known as "trust." Near the Central Motor Inn; open during summer season; hours are whenever to whenever, just ask around for Tom.

ADVENTURES

PINNELL MOUNTAIN NATIONAL RECREATION TRAIL / This trail offers stunning views of the Alaska Range to the south and the Crazy Mountains and Yukon Flats to the north. The entire trail follows treeless, tundra-clad ridgelines for 27.3 miles, starting and ending on the Steese Highway at Eagle Summit (Mile 107.3) and Twelvemile Summit (Mile 85.6). The trail is defined by wooden posts and cairns. Allow at least 3 days and be prepared for summer temperatures that can range from 20°F to 80°F and high winds that can whip up anytime. Keep your eyes open for caribou and the occasional moose or bear. Wildflowers are jamming from mid-June to mid-July. The terrain is a little kinder if you begin at the Eagle Summit trailhead. Water can be a problem on this trail, especially later in the season. **ALASKA PUBLIC LANDS INFORMATION CENTER** (907/456-0527) can give you an update. Call for a recorded trail-condition update (907/474-2372); two small **CABINS**, 10 miles from each trailhead, are available on a first-come, first-served basis.

LODGINGS

Arctic Circle Hot Springs / ★★

MILE 8.3, CIRCLE HOT SPRINGS RD, CENTRAL, AK 99730;
907/520-5113, FAX 907/520-5116
At this hot springs, there's nothing between you and the stars but your bathing suit. As the story goes, the hot springs were "discovered" in 1893 by a hunter tracking a moose. When the hotel first opened in 1930, miners could get a bed, three square meals, and a hot bath for $3 a day. The dining area is so homey you could wander in for breakfast in your robe and slippers and not feel awkward. In the winter, there's a network of trails for cross-country skiing and snowmobiling; sled-dog rides can be arranged. Summer attractions include fishing, gold panning, hiking, and mountain biking on old mining trails. There is also an Olympic-size pool, massage therapy, and a cozy library. Be sure to ask about the ghost. If you want to check up on any local history, Harrie Hughes lives in one of the old miner's cabins there and is more than 100 years old. The resort has 24 rooms in the old hotel and 14 cabins for rent; hotel rates are $100 for a double; suites are $125. Cabins run $110 for the first two occupants, $15 each additional person, and dogs are allowed. Hostel space is $20. *$$; MC, V; checks OK; breakfast, lunch, dinner every day; full bar; Box 30069, Central, AK 99730.* &

Chatanika Gold Camp / ★

MILE 27.9 STEESE HWY, CHATANIKA, AK 99712; 907/389-2414,
FAX 907/389-2748
Built in 1921, the old gold camp is on the National Register of Historic Places. For 30 years, the complex provided room and board to miners. Now it does the same for travelers and Fairbanksians escaping the city. The camp itself is like an old ghost town. There's a bunkhouse, cabins, a bar, and an Alaskana restaurant with an enormous antique woodstove. The breakfast buffet on Sundays features sourdough pancakes and fluffy sourdough biscuits, all you can eat for $10 per adult. The camp is seriously into winter sports and offers bus service to Cleary Summit Ski Area, as well as cross-country skiing, snowmobiling, sled-dog rides, and aurora borealis watching. One winter special features dinner for two, breakfast, and a room with a Jacuzzi for $90. There's live music on weekends and most Sundays, and free spaghetti on Wednesday nights. Rooms are $55 for a double, cabins $50 to $65. *$; no credit cards; checks OK; full bar; 5550 Steese Hwy, Fairbanks, AK 99712.* &

ROAD TRIPS NORTH

One company making the trip up the Dalton Highway from Fairbanks is **Trans-Arctic Circle Treks** (907/479-5451, fax 800/479-8908; arctictk@ptialaska.net; www.ArcticTreks.com), which takes you to Prudhoe Bay on a 3-day tour for $579, including accommodations. Also offered is the 2-day Arctic Blast from Fairbanks to Prudhoe Bay, with a night at Barrow's Top of the World Hotel and a cultural tour of the northernmost city for $899. **Van Go Tours & Alaska Places** (907/235-5431; akplaces@alaska.net) offers off-the-beaten-path, custom itineraries and tour-guide services all over the state.

—Debra McKinney

Chatanika Lodge

MILE 28.5, OLD STEESE HWY N, CHATANIKA, AK 99712; 907/389-2164, FAX 907/389-2166

You'll find this rustic log lodge decked to the teeth with quintessential Alaskana—diamond willow, moose antlers, totem poles, and a satellite dish. You'll find all kinds of things inside to gawk at, too, including a shrine to the owner's Harley Davidson, the best salt and pepper shaker collection in all of Alaska, and donated dollar bills coating the walls. Rooms are $60 for a double. On Friday and Saturday nights, an all-you-can-eat halibut and catfish dinner is $17 for adults, $7.50 for children. On Sundays, it's all-you-can-eat deep-fried chicken for $12.50 adults, $6.50 children. *$; MC, V; local checks only; breakfast, lunch, dinner; full bar; 5760 Old Steese Hwy N, Fairbanks, AK 99712.* ♿

The Elliott Highway

It may seem like all roads out of Fairbanks lead to hot water, and it's almost true. This former gold trail dead-ends at Mile 152 (mileage begins in Fox) at the community of **MANLEY HOT SPRINGS** (pop. about 100). Alas, though, the hot springs resort has closed. This tidy old trading-post town is what you're likely to envision when you think of Bush Alaska. It has log cabins surrounded by great gardens, houses made of salvaged building materials huddled among the trees, and a historic roadhouse serving as the town's community center. You'll meet mushers, miners, trappers, fishermen, and other folks carving a living out of the land. There's fishing for northern pike in the Manley Hot Springs Slough and for salmon in the Tanana River. Built in 1906, **THE MANLEY ROAD-HOUSE** (907/672-3611) is a National Historic Site and offers room and board and a lot of antiquities, including some of the bar's regulars. Before heading out on the Elliott, stop about a quarter mile out of Fox and fill your water bottles at **FOX SPRINGS**, which has pure artesian springwater that runs year-round. This is where many locals living without running water come to fill their jugs. For the hugest heap of breakfast in the Interior, stop at **HILLTOP TRUCKSTOP** at Mile 5.5; it's famous for pies, too. The first 28 miles of the highway are paved; the remaining 124 are not. Watch for moose and other wildlife, including spruce hens attempting self-sacrifice in the middle of the road. The road is wide and hardpacked up to its rendezvous with the Dalton Highway, west of Livengood. From then on, it narrows and gets into a little roller coaster action.

In addition to hot springs, the Elliott offers access to fishing spots, hikes in the **WHITE MOUNTAINS NATIONAL RECREATION AREA**, a local rock-climbing spot called **GRAPEFRUIT ROCKS** at Mile 38.5, and a side trip at Mile 110 to the Athabascan village of **MINTO**, at the edge of **MINTO FLATS STATE GAME REFUGE**.

EXPLORING AND ADVENTURES

BLIXT PUBLIC-USE CABIN / This is a 12-by-20-foot log cabin with a loft that sits on a hillside overlooking the Tolovana River Valley, on the east side of the Elliott Highway, near mile 62. The cabin is accessible year-round, due to its close proximity to the road. There's a woodstove, bunkbed, and an outhouse. Spring water is available nearby, but you'll need to treat it. You'll also need all your camping gear. Use of the cabin is through reservation only ($20 per night). To reserve, contact the Bureau of Land Management, 1150 University Ave, Fairbanks, AK 99709; 907/474-2250.

TOLOVANA HOT SPRINGS / At Tolovana Hot Springs, you'll be hauling drinking water and using an outhouse, but the payoff is soaking your bones in outdoor hot tubs 100 miles from the nearest traffic light. Getting there isn't easy. The 11-mile trail can be nasty in summer since it passes through a swamp. Flying is the way to go. Travel is much easier in the winter by snowmobile, dog team, or skis. But you must be prepared for what the operators refer to as "extreme weather," otherwise known as wicked, bone-numbing cold. That said, imagine lying back in a hot tub in the middle of nowhere and watching the northern lights with your hair frozen solid. In an effort to keep the setting serene, use of the natural hot springs is by reservation only, even if you are camping. Cabins are rustic but comfortable. Fully guided trips are available, including travel by dog team. Rates, which double during holidays, range from $25 to $120, depending on which cabin you get and whether you come during the week or on the weekend. Cancellations must be made two weeks in advance for a full refund. A map is provided once reservations are made. Mile 93, Elliott Hwy, PO Box 83058, Fairbanks, AK 99708; 907/455-6706; www.mosquitonet.com/~tolovana. &

HUTLINANA WARM SPRINGS / About 500 yards east of the Hutlinana Creek Bridge, Mile 129.3 on the Elliott Highway, you'll find a well-defined trail running north along the creek for 8 miles to the warm springs, an undeveloped pool about 3 feet deep and lined with rocks. There's room for tents nearby.

THE ARCTIC

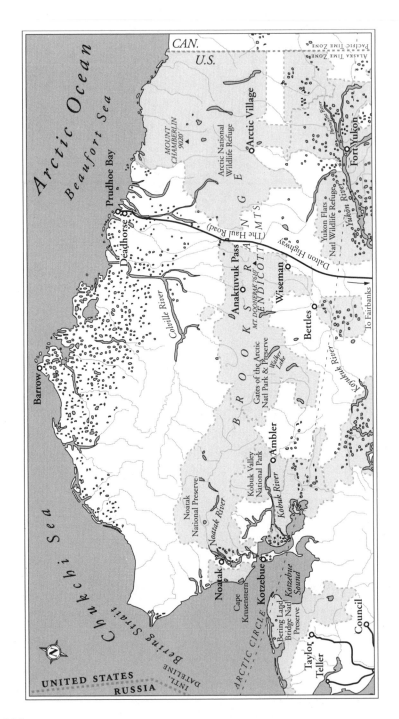

Arctic Ocean

Beaufort Sea

Chukchi Sea

Bering Strait

CAN.

U.S.

Pacific Time Zone

Alaska Time Zone

Mount Chamberlin 9020'

Arctic National Wildlife Refuge

Arctic Village

Fort Yukon

Porcupine River

Yukon River

Yukon Flats Nat'l Wildlife Refuge

Prudhoe Bay

Deadhorse

The Haul Road

Dalton Highway

Anaktuvuk Pass

MT. DOONERAK 7610'

ENDICOTT

BROOKS RANGE MTS.

Wiseman

To Fairbanks

Colville River

Bettles

Koyukuk River

Barrow

Gates of the Arctic Nat'l Park & Preserve

Walker Lake

Noatak National Preserve

Noatak River

Kobuk Valley National Park

Ambler

Kobuk River

Noatak

Cape Krusenstern

Kotzebue

Kotzebue Sound

ARCTIC CIRCLE

Bering Land Bridge Nat'l Preserve

Council

Taylor

Teller

UNITED STATES

RUSSIA

INTL. DATELINE

N

294

THE ARCTIC

Stretching north of the Arctic Circle (66° 33' north latitude) is a wilderness of spare taiga ("land of little sticks") and tundra ("a flat or rolling, treeless plain"). The Brooks Range, that "range of blue light" described by early explorer Robert Marshall, sweeps across the Arctic, separating the forests from the 80,000 square miles of tundra known as the North Slope. Rivers south of the mountains flow into the Yukon River, which empties into the Bering Sea; northern rivers flow into the Arctic Ocean.

The Arctic is a frigid zone, with cold winters and short, cool summers. With less than 10 inches of precipitation per year, it is really a cold desert. Temperatures range from 80°F in summer to –60°F and colder in winter. Permafrost underlies much of the region, in places to a depth of up to 3,000 feet. These frozen soils account for the countless lakes and ponds that dot the coastal plain. Thirty percent of its surface is covered by fresh water. Pingos, steep-sided mounds with ice cores, and polygons, patterned ground caused by ice wedges, are distinctive surface features related to permafrost.

Arctic, from the Greek *arctos* for bear, refers to the two constellations—Ursa Major (Great Bear) and Ursa Minor (Little Bear)—that rotate around Polaris, the North Star, the one fixed point in the sky. These constellations contain the easily recognized Big and Little Dippers. As one travels north, the bears loom higher and higher in the night sky. The seasonal change in daylight, which limits available energy, is the single most important physical characteristic of the polar region.

On June 21, summer solstice, the day when the sun is at its greatest distance from the equator, the sun does not set at the Arctic Circle and, due to refraction, appears not to set for four days. In Barrow, the northernmost American city, the sun does not set for 84 days, from May 10 to August 2. On winter solstice, December 21, the sun does not rise at all at the Arctic Circle. In Barrow the sun remains below the horizon for 67 days, from November 18 to January 24.

No large cities and only a few large villages dot the region. Barrow is the largest community and a regional trade center. Prudhoe Bay is the industrial center, with its wealth and jobs flowing out statewide. Most communities are small and isolated, with subsistence-based economies. The 414-mile-long Dalton Highway, built as the trans-Alaska pipeline haul road, bisects the Arctic north to south and parallels the pipeline. All other access to the region is by aircraft.

Inupiat Eskimos predominate in the region. Nunamiut Eskimos— *The People*—live in Anaktuvuk Pass. Athabascans, both Gwich'in and Kutch'in, also live in the region. The Gwich'in live just north of the Arctic Circle in Arctic Village, the Kutch'in along the southern edge.

POLAR BEAR ALERT

While you rest in your hotel room, check out the message channel on the television (Channel 20). It displays local notices and advertisements while the radio station (KBRW, 680 AM) provides the audio. It never hurts to tune in before you go for a long walk on the beach, just in case there's a polar bear warning in effect. Roughly half the world's 20,000 polar bears pay an occasional visit along Alaska's Arctic coast. Spring and fall are their favorite seasons to drop in on Barrow, and the police always maintain a bear patrol on Halloween to protect little trick-or-treaters.

Speaking of bears, how would you like to join the Polar Bear Club? You don't have to stare down the Arctic's most fearsome critter at close range to qualify. No, just find an opening among the ice floes and dive in. Fran Tate, owner of Pepe's North of the Border Restaurant (see review), will arrange to verify your total submersion in the Arctic Ocean. She'll also call the paramedics if you don't rocket back to the beach. For your pain and suffering (and a small fee), you will earn a certificate, an embroidered patch, and a lifetime membership in one of the most exclusive clubs in America.

—David Harding

Seasonal abundance of wildlife is characteristic of a region marked by long, hard winters. Much of the region's wildlife is migratory and transient. Two large herds of caribou, the Western Arctic Caribou Herd and the Porcupine Caribou Herd, attract wildlife watchers from around the world. The smaller Central Arctic Caribou Herd sometimes frequents Prudhoe Bay.

The Arctic is the last great stretch of wilderness on the face of the earth. As Justice William O. Douglas said in 1960, "The Arctic has a call that is compelling. The distant mountains make one want to go on and on over the next ridge and over the one beyond. This last American wilderness must remain sacrosanct."

ACCESS AND INFORMATION

One road takes you from Fairbanks into the Arctic—**THE DALTON HIGHWAY**, also known as the old "Haul Road" (see below). Alaska Airlines (800/426-0333) has **JET SERVICE** to Barrow, Deadhorse/Prudhoe Bay, and Kotzebue. Cape Smythe Air (907/852-8333), in Barrow, can take you to coastal villages and other destinations. Frontier Flying Service (907/474-0014), in Fairbanks, regularly flies to Anaktuvuk Pass, Bettles, and Kaktovik. Larry's Flying Service (907/474-9169), in Fairbanks, flies to Anaktuvuk Pass and Arctic Village. Warbelow's Air Ventures (907/474-0518), in Fairbanks, goes to Ambler, Kobuk, and Shungnak and also flies charters and tours. Wright Air Service (907/474-0502), also in Fairbanks, flies to Anaktuvuk Pass, Arctic Village, and Bettles.

Those who fly strictly **AIR CHARTERS** are Arctic Air Alaska (907/488-6115), with Sandy Hamilton in Salcha, Alaska, but with charters to all Brooks Range destinations; 40-Mile Air (907/474-0018), at the Fairbanks International Terminal, with charters and North Slope tours; and Yukon Air Service (907/479-3792), in Fairbanks, with Don Ross, who has made the Arctic National Wildlife Refuge a specialty.

AMBLER AIR SERVICE (907/445-2157) is the very best small-town air service, especially if you are flying to Kobuk National Park. It is located in the small Inupiat village of Ambler. David Rue has been running this flight service since 1976. He knows the area along the Kobuk River as well as anyone. His pilot, Scott Jones, is affable and unflappable—just the qualities that make for a good bush pilot. These folks fly on floats, wheels, and skis and do a lot of support work for river rafters, fishermen, and government agencies. They charter and also have limited scheduled service to Kobuk River villages and Fairbanks. They offer very competitive rates.

Note: Many Bush villages ban **ALCOHOL** importation and possession. Check with air carriers and your outfitter before transporting alcohol in any quantity. "Any quantity" means just that. Some villages are very diligent about enforcement.

The James Dalton Highway

If you want to drive to the Arctic, there's only one way. Head north along the old North Slope Haul Road, originally built in 1974 as part of the construction of the 800-mile-long trans-Alaska oil pipeline, running from Prudhoe Bay to the port of Valdez. Officially opened to the public in 1995, the route is now called the Dalton Highway, although most Alaskans still call it "The Haul Road."

The road begins in forested rolling hills at **MILE 73 ON THE ELLIOTT HIGHWAY**, crosses the inclined bridge over the Yukon, and runs 414 miles from the Yukon River over the Brooks Range to Prudhoe Bay on the Arctic coast. The highway was named for James William Dalton, an engineer involved in pioneer Arctic oil exploration. The only services and fuel stops between the Elliott Highway and Prudhoe Bay are **YUKON VENTURES ALASKA** (907/655-9001), located at the Yukon River Bridge, Mile 56, and **SOURDOUGH FUEL/SLATE CREEK INN** (907/678-5201), at Coldfoot, Mile 175, where you'll find the best truck stop—albeit the only truck stop—north of the Arctic Circle.

ROAD TRAVELERS should be well prepared for emergencies and carry food and survival gear, two *mounted* spare tires, extra gasoline, and spare parts. Mishaps or breakdowns can have painful financial consequences. Towing companies charge $5 per mile, figured both directions. The Dalton Highway alternates between mud and thick dust. Drive slowly and with headlights on at all times. Give way to large trucks. *Watch for flying rocks and tire blowouts!* Winter use is not advised for casual travelers.

The road north from Coldfoot traverses the Brooks Range and the North Slope tundra and has phenomenal vistas of mountains, tundra, and wildlife. Moose are commonly seen south of the mountains, Dall sheep in Atigun Pass, and caribou, grizzlies, musk oxen, waterfowl, and occasionally wolves in the north. Even though the road opened to the public in 1995, streams along the road have long been overfished. Fish in frigid Arctic waters grow slowly and are never in overabundance. One fish caught near Toolik was 46 years old, and it was a midget by Alaska standards. (Catch-and-release should be the byword here.)

Interesting stops north of Coldfoot are numerous and include **WISE-MAN**, turnoff at Mile 188.6, a historic mining town and a community of

MOSQUITOES

The Arctic from mid-June to early August is a good place to avoid if you fear mosquitoes. Mosquitoes are often thought of as tropical, but some of the densest concentrations are found in northern regions. Permafrost traps water on the surface, providing prime insect hatcheries. How bad are the mosquitoes? In July 1995, one scientist near Toolik slapped the back of another, killing 270 mosquitoes in a single blow!

A biologist estimated that the North Slope's summer mosquito population outweighs the biomass of all its other living creatures. At least 27 species of mosquito are found in Alaska, measuring from an eighth- to a quarter-inch long. Only female mosquitoes bite; males buzz around looking for mates. The constant humming of mosquitoes, beating their wings more than 300 times a second, disturbs some people more than actual bites. Mosquitoes are capable of flying 30mph but are fragile and easily grounded, even by a light breeze. Cold weather also grounds or kills them. Warm, still mornings and evenings are prime time for mosquitoes.

Female mosquitoes need blood protein to manufacture eggs. They home in on their prey by using their twin antennae to sense warm, moist air rising from the body. When they bite, they inject saliva that contains a chemical to prevent blood clotting and improve blood flow. It is the victim's allergic reaction to the saliva that makes mosquito bites itch. Once her abdomen is full, the female mosquito flies off—often before the victim can feel the bite. She then rests for several days, digesting the meal, before about 25 whose heyday was in 1910. Many log buildings from the 1920s are still in use, one of which is a museum of area history. (Excellent side-road access.) The sheer granite rock faces of the south side of **MOUNT SUKAPAK** are impressive, but a peaceful lakeside view of the more slanting north side is available from Mile 205. It is believed this mountain marks the traditional boundary between Eskimo and Athabascan territories. **CHANDALAR SHELF**, Mile 237.1, offers views of the Chandalar River headwaters and 6,425-foot Table Mountain. **ATIGUN PASS** (4,800 feet), Mile 244.7, is not a pass at all in the true sense, but a cut in the mountains through which the pipeline and road passes. A marvel of engineering, it also marks the Continental Divide and the break to the true North Slope of Alaska. Dall sheep are regularly seen here. From the first **ATIGUN RIVER** crossing at Mile 253.1, the road passes through gorgeous alpine tundra and mountain vistas. Tree line is far behind and the open country offers views of Galbraith Lake, the pipeline, caribou, grizzly bears, and even wolves. **SLOPE MOUNTAIN** (4,101 feet), just west of the road at Mile 305, is another excellent place to see Dall sheep. A

laying between 75 and 500 eggs. In summer, campers, hikers, floaters, and fishermen will have intimate contact with mosquitoes, but even those on tours to places such as Barrow, Kotzebue, and Prudhoe Bay will encounter at least some biting insects.

Mosquito sprays, lotions, and pumps containing the active ingredient DEET are the most effective and widely used repellents in Alaska. However, formulas containing 100 percent DEET (short for N,N'-Diethyl-m-toluamide) may pose some neurological risk to humans, especially children and infants. Experts are divided on the actual risk. Many health experts recommend using only repellents with formulations of less than 30 percent DEET. DEET-free repellents made from citronella are growing in use. Naturapel is a popular alternative. Some people swear by Avon's Skin-So-Soft bath oil, which contains pennyroyal. Mosquito coils made of pyrethrum, Buhach powders, and citronella candles are also widely used. "Bug jackets," or bug suits, are the choice of a few trekkers. Head nets, gloves, and long-sleeved shirts offer time-tested protection.

Casual travelers to larger villages or destinations need to take along nothing more than a small bottle of repellent or perhaps a lightweight head net. However, no one should venture cross-country without ample protection. Mosquitoes are capable of "hearing" and detecting motion as well as sensing warmth and moisture. Hot, sweaty backpackers staggering across uneven tundra or through brushy terrain are ideal targets. On one such trek, a friend took a picture of me in a "fur coat." The "coat" was made of bugs.

—Tom Walker

side road runs behind the Sag River Highway Camp and gives access to the river. Musk oxen are sometimes seen here. Watch for wildlife all the way to **PRUDHOE BAY**, Mile 414.

The last 90 miles into **DEADHORSE** are often very rocky and dusty and should be driven slowly. Deadhorse/Prudhoe Bay is the end of the line, where the road meets the ice of the sea. Access to the oil fields at Prudhoe Bay and Kuparuk is tightly controlled; check at the Prudhoe Bay Hotel (907/659-2449) for **OIL-FIELD TOURS**. Although in many Alaskans' opinions the pipeline paralleling the road is Alaska's greatest eyesore, marring an otherwise beautiful landscape, one has to admire the 800-mile-long, $8 billion project as an engineering marvel. On average, 1.8 million barrels of oil pass through the pipeline each day.

GUIDES AND OUTFITTERS

NORTHERN ALASKA TOUR CO. / Northern Alaska Tour Company offers several short Arctic Circle adventures. One tour takes you on a 1-day narrated drive in a small van along the old haul road to the Arctic Circle. This trip offers travelers with limited time a look at the sub-arctic forests and tundra, a visit to an Athabascan fish camp or trading post, and a ceremonial crossing of the Arctic Circle. Another tour offers a 1-day drive up the highway combined with a flight to the Nunamiut Eskimo village of Anaktuvuk Pass. Also offered are a 3 day/2 night drive/fly trip to Prudhoe Bay and other natural-history and cultural tours. PO Box 82991, Fairbanks, AK 99708; 907/474-8600; fax 907/474-4767; adventure@alaskasarctic.com; www.alaskasarctic.com; MC, V; checks OK.

Barrow

More than 300 miles above the Arctic Circle, this is the northernmost settlement in the United States, and it feels like it. Take a ride out to Point Barrow and you've gone as far north as dry land will allow. The 1,300 miles still separating you from the North Pole is ocean, clogged with ice and populated by polar bears, whales, walrus, seals, and other mythic critters. This is not just the end of the road, it's the absolute edge of the planet.

Visitors to Barrow encounter reminders of this marginal planetary location at every turn. Satellite dishes seem to point at the ground as they track communications satellites in orbit over the Lower 48. Tour companies issue parkas to arriving guests in mid-July. Even the concepts of "day" and "night" must be renegotiated out here on the edge. When you're sitting on top of the world, 84 days pass between a single sunrise in May and the next sunset in August.

Barrow (pop. 4,500) usually makes the national news when the sun sets in November, not to rise again until the end of January. But in 1998, *The Wall Street Journal* did a story on the town's penchant for America's number-one sport: baseball. Well, up here, softball. The story, "Batters Shiver, Bears Lurk," reported that, contrary to the hot-weather version the rest of the country recognizes, games here often are canceled on account of fog alerts, high-wind advisories, subzero temperatures (in summer!), or polar bears loping into town.

The Inupiat Eskimos have inhabited the Arctic coast for more than a millennium. Even with the advent of a cash economy, hunting remains an essential cultural activity. The most important hunt of all occurs in the spring and fall, when bowhead whales migrate along the coast. The **NALUKATAQ FESTIVAL** in June celebrates a successful spring whaling season. The Inupiat equivalent of Christmas, it attracts relatives from the outlying villages and can last for several days.

The Inupiat have pursued economic development with the same aggressive pride that keeps their traditional customs and language alive. In response to the discovery of America's largest oil field at Prudhoe Bay, the Inupiat formed a regional government, the North Slope Borough, to guarantee their voice in development decisions.

EXPLORING AND ADVENTURES

The new **INUPIAT HERITAGE CENTER**, a museum celebrating the past and present-day life of the Inupiat Eskimo peoples of the North Slope, opened in 1999. There is a major exhibit on the bowhead whale, hunting, and the importance of the whale in the life of the people. A gift shop of local art is in the planning stages. Call 907/852-4594 for more information.

ARCTIC MUSHING TOURS (907/852-6874) offers dogsled rides year-round. **BORDER VENTURES** (PO Box 214, Barrow, AK 99723; 907/852-2010, fax 907/852-2023) has bikes for rent, if cycling on gravel roads is your thing.

The North Slope Borough's Public Information Office (907/852-0215) can give you accurate information on the schedule of local events.

RESTAURANTS

Brower's Cafe

DOWNTOWN BARROW; 907/852-3435

For a good view and sense of history, stop in at Brower's Cafe, located in a historic building on the far side of town, an area called Browerville. It's the site of the whaling and trading station operated before the turn of the century by Charles Brower, a Yankee whaler who settled here in 1882, learned the language, married a local woman, and established what has become one of the largest Eskimo families in Barrow. Brower's Cafe has a nice ocean view, and after your meal you can photograph the arched whale jawbones and *umiak* (traditional seal-skin whaling boat) out front. The wonderful Polar Haven Coffee Co. is also located here. *$$; no credit cards; checks OK; breakfast, lunch, dinner every day; no alcohol; PO Box 457, Barrow, AK 99723.*

Pepe's North of the Border Restaurant / ★

1204 AGVIK ST, BARROW; 907/852-8200

A stop here is de rigueur. Mexican and American food are on the menu, but the real pizzazz at Pepe's is its owner, Fran Tate. Approaching the age when most folks retire, Fran is a dynamo in a mini-skirt. She's also a consummate promoter of Barrow, which landed her on the *Tonight Show* a few years back. During her 15 minutes of fame, she presented an *oosik* to Johnny Carson. "What's an oosik?" Johnny asked, as he beheld the 2-foot-long bone. Fran replied, "Let's just say every male walrus has one." *$$; MC, V; local checks only; breakfast, lunch, dinner every day; no alcohol; PO Box 403, Barrow, AK 99723; located in town.*

ESKIMO ETIQUETTE

Do's: If you can manage a few words of the Inupiaq language, you're assured a warm smile in return. Try these words for starters: **Maktak** (pronounced "muk-tuk") is the thick skin and a few inches of fat from the bowhead whale. It is a staple of the Inupiat diet. **Quyanak** (koy-ah-nuk) means "thank you." Or get fancy with **Quyanakpak** (koy-ah-nuk-puk), "thank you very much." **Uutukuu** (oo-tuh-koo) is a good word to know in case you are offered a helping of maktak dipped in seal oil. It means "just a little bit." **Aarigaa** (ah-dee-gah) means "that's good!"

Don'ts: It's not polite to be offended by the dead animal parts drying on racks or lying around people's yards. Depending on the time of year, you're liable to encounter slabs of whale or walrus meat, strips of caribou, whole seals, or strings of ducks. Keep in mind that animals represent much more than food here. If you're a die-hard animal rights activist, it's best to swallow your opinions. An elder once described her first visit to a zoo in the Lower 48. She was a child at the time, and she couldn't understand why all the animals were caged. "It's not right," she said. "Someone should take them home and eat them." She felt much more comfortable when she visited a farm. At least there the animals had a useful purpose.

—David Harding

LODGINGS

Top of the World Hotel / ★★

1200 AGVIK ST, BARROW, AK 99723; 800/882-8478, 907/852-3900,
OR 800/478-8520, IN ALASKA
It's not the only hotel in town, but it has the best location and serves as
the hub of visitor activity. Ask for a room in the new wing. Even better,
snag oceanside rooms, like 150, 248, or 250, for the best views. Walking
maps and lists of activities are available at the front desk. The hotel operates local sightseeing excursions year-round through TUNDRA TOURS
(907/852-3900), and in the summer months hosts a daily Inupiat cultural
presentation of song, dance, games, and crafts in a large tent on the
beach. Even if you're fairly independent, the hotel package is still the best
way to get oriented. There are different room rates for pleasure, business,
or government, ranging from $119 to $179. *$$; AE, DC, DIS, MC, V;
local checks only; tow@asrc.com; PO Box 189, Barrow, AK 99723.*

Kotzebue

A regional service hub, Kotzebue (pop. 3,000) is located on a 3-mile-long
spit jutting into Kotzebue Sound. This predominately Inupiat village
serves as the trade center for 10 northwestern villages. Summer visitors
see Eskimo blanket tosses and other cultural activities. The NANA
MUSEUM OF THE ARCTIC (907/442-3747) in Kotzebue is a highlight.
The best large museum anywhere north of the Arctic Circle, it features
Northwest Coast Inupiat cultural history, displays, dioramas, and live
performances unmatched statewide.

If time permits, walk out to Kotzebue's "NATIONAL FOREST"—one
black spruce growing on the treeless tundra of the Arctic, planted in 1958
as a seedling by fishing buddies stationed at the Kotzebue Air Force Base.
Withstanding the fierce winds of the coast, permafrost, and subzero tem-
peratures, it is now 11 feet tall.

Air charters and scheduled flights provide access to Kotzebue, sur-
rounding villages, the eastern Brooks Range, Kobuk Valley National
Park, Noatak National Preserve, Cape Krusenstern National Monu-
ment, and Selawik National Wildlife Refuge. The best tours are with
NANA TOUR ARCTIC (907/442-3301).

Best lodgings (and these are relative) are at the NULLAGVIK HOTEL
(Box 336, Kotzebue, AK 99752; 907/442-3331; *AE, M, V; local checks
only*)—which is also the only place in town.

The Brooks Range

Stretching from the Yukon border almost to the Chukchi Sea, these mountains separate the muskeg and forest of Interior Alaska from the treeless tundra expanses of the Arctic Coast. The peaks and valleys of this northern extension of the Rocky Mountains, with elevations from 4,000 to 9,000 feet, spawn numerous spectacular rivers and streams, flowing both north and south, and support fish and wildlife in, at times, astonishing numbers.

Impressive peaks include **MOUNT IGIKPAK** (8,510 feet), the highest point in the western Brooks Range; and **MOUNT CHAMBERLIN** (9,020 feet) and **MOUNT MICHELSON** (8,855 feet), the two tallest peaks, which are located in the eastern Brooks Range and within the Arctic National Wildlife Refuge. The **ARRIGETCH PEAKS**, along with **MOUNT DOONERAK** (7,610 feet), are impressive spires in the central range. **BOREAL MOUNTAIN** and **FRIGID CRAGS**, rising on either side of the North Fork of the Koyukuk River, are Robert Marshall's **"GATES OF THE ARCTIC."**

Temperatures vary from about 85°F in summer to –60°F in winter. Summer offers 24 hours of daylight, wind, and mosquitoes. Winter offers 24 hours of darkness, wind, and ice. This is real wilderness, with miles of great, uninhabited expanses. Bush travelers should be self-reliant and skillful. Those who come prepared can choose from a plethora of activities, ranging from river rafting to mountain climbing (see below).

There are far more parks and refuges in the Arctic and in the Brooks Range than listed here—and each is a gem. Whole books have been written about the parks, rivers, and refuges and the exquisite country that surrounds them. The following is a small sample of some of the most popular. Even then, it will be a rare day when you see anyone else of the human species.

ACCESS AND INFORMATION

The best places to obtain initial information on the Brooks Range and the Arctic's national parks and wildlife refuges are the **ALASKA PUBLIC LANDS INFORMATION CENTERS** in Anchorage (605 W 4th Ave, Ste 105; 907/271-2737) and in Fairbanks (250 Cushman St, Ste 1A, 907/456-0527). In summer, stop in or call the **U.S. DEPARTMENT OF INTERIOR VISITORS CENTER** in Coldfoot (907/678-5209).

The community of **BETTLES** on the south side of the range is a prime jumping-off point for travel into the central Brooks Range. It is served by charter and scheduled **FLIGHTS** from Fairbanks. Contacts in Bettles include Bettles Air Service (907/692-5655), Bettles Lodge (Bettles, AK 99726; 907/692-5111 or 800/770-5111), Sourdough Outfitters (907/692-5252),

Gates of the Arctic National Park (907/692-5494), and Kanuti National Wildlife Refuge (907/692-5555).

Gates of the Arctic National Park and Preserve

Astride 200 miles of the central Brooks Range, this park covers about 8.4 million acres of mountains, valleys, and rivers, an area four times the size of Yellowstone National Park. Access is via plane from Bettles, Fairbanks, or Kotzebue. Road access is via the Dalton Highway.

Unlike most parks, Gates of the Arctic, established in 1980, is completely undeveloped. There are no visitor facilities of any kind within the park. Visitors must seek their own trails and adventures. But those who do will enjoy pristine territory in which to camp, canoe, climb, fish, photograph, river raft, and view wildlife. Winter activities include cross-country skiing and dog mushing.

Hiking often is difficult. The tundra is covered with grass tussocks, knots of Arctic cottongrass that twist and turn under foot. River crossings can be dangerous and difficult. Frostbite in winter and hypothermia in summer are real threats. It is important to check in with park rangers in Bettles, Coldfoot, or Fairbanks before embarking. Consult with those who have local knowledge and file a trip plan—you'll be glad you did, should a search-and-rescue operation be necessary. For more **INFORMATION**, contact the Superintendent at the Gates of the Arctic National Park and Preserve (PO Box 74680, Fairbanks, AK 99707; 907/456-0281).

The best **RECOMMENDED HIKE** for this area runs from the North Fork of the Koyukuk River to the village of Anaktuvuk Pass via **ERNIE CREEK**. Ernie Creek was named by Robert Marshall for Ernie Johnson, a Finnish prospector and trapper who explored much of the region just after the turn of the century. This trek is for the hardy and capable who want to sample the essence of the Brooks Range. Novices are advised to hire a guide. The trip can begin at a fly-in drop-off point near Gates of the Arctic National Park and end in Anaktuvuk Pass or vice versa. The route traverses **ERNIE PASS** and **VALLEY OF THE PRECIPICES**. Expect to see Dall sheep and to encounter bears, perhaps even wolves. Contact the national park office listed above. Depending on your drop-off point, the hike is 25 to 35 miles. Because there is no developed hiking trail and some of the route is over muskeg and tussocks, good hikers can walk about 2 to 2.5 miles per hour. Due to the demands of part of the route, 4 to 5 hours of walking per day is enough.

AMONG THE PEOPLE

First-time travelers to the Bush are often surprised by conditions in rural communities. Dilapidated cabins stand next to modern houses; satellite dishes sprout next to racks groaning under the weight of walrus meat; yards seem full of junk snowmobiles and rusting barrels. But it is the lack of fresh, clean water and modern sanitation that most shocks tourists: "Honey Buckets? Gross!"

An Inupiat guide in Barrow once said that the hardest question she has to answer from tourists is "Why is this community here?" They see a lack of industry, agriculture, and trade. They notice the pockets of poverty and unemployment, and the incredibly high cost of goods and services. Born and raised in Barrow, the guide has no satisfactory answer for visitors.

Alaska Natives have a rich and varied cultural heritage tied to the land. Until a very short time ago (a few decades, really), the people lived in small family bands or tribal groups and moved seasonally from one choice subsistence site to another. Some followed caribou; others relied on marine mammals. They all collected and cured furs, fish, berries, roots, and plants. Starvation, privation, and hardship were facts of life.

Life began to change forever around the turn of the century when European adventurers, prospectors, whalers, and missionaries began arriving. Change was rapid and, in many cases, devastating. People began to settle near missions and whaling stations. Traders brought modern implements, a cash economy, religion, and science. Disease, alcohol, deceit, and prejudice were also part of the package.

The raison d'être for the existence of Barrow, as well as other villages in the "next-

WILDERNESS LODGES

Iniakuk Lake Wilderness Lodge

PO BOX 80424, FAIRBANKS, AK 99708; 907/479-6354

In its 27th year, this beautiful lodge on the shores of Iniakuk Lake is the best in all the Arctic. It is small, with 12 guests maximum. Guests enjoy fishing, hiking, canoeing, river rafting, wildlife watching, flight-seeing, birding, massage therapy, and photography, or simply relaxing in the handcrafted lodge. Longtime Alaskan and owner Pat Gaedeke offers gourmet meals and fresh-baked goods. One highlight is "whirlwind adventures"—spur-of-the-moment excursions that take advantage of the best the wilderness has to offer at each changing light. Another is "Dinner at the Continental Divide"—a flight-seeing trip into the Brooks Range that culminates in dinner and champagne at the divide. Pat also offers guided stays at two well-maintained cabins on the Alatna River within Gates of the Arctic National Park. River rafting is also available. This

to-nowhere," may elude some visitors, but in reality the same question can be asked of many towns and cities in decline in the rest of the country. Gone are the mills, factories, and trade routes that caused many such places to spring up. Perhaps only in the stark reality of the Arctic is the incongruity of location so obvious.

Permafrost and remoteness are major, almost insurmountable hurdles to sewage treatment, safe water distribution, and trash and garbage disposal. Everything costs much more in remote places. Unemployment is high, with poverty as the result. Nutrition, health care, and education suffer in isolation. A subsistence way of living may not mean life or death to the people now, but it renews cultural pride and adds immeasurably to the quality of life in places where a can of soup costs $6.

While many villages offer cultural performances for visitors, village life is not a tableau enacted for tourist season. Things seen are often not what they seem. One person's "yard full of junk" may be another's collection of spare parts. Hauling drinking water by hand is both a necessity and hard work, not a photo opportunity. The lined face of an aging Nunamiut woman may clearly convey wisdom and strength of character, but she isn't a photographer's model who can be rudely approached. No matter how humble, village homes and property should be respected by visitors and not stared at as if they were part of some Disney-ish "Arcticland." Poverty does not mean quaint. Uniqueness does not mean carte blanche for photographic intrusion. The people of the Arctic have survived in a cold land of darkness and hardship for centuries. They deserve respect.

—Tom Walker

lodge is fly-in only, accessible by a 30-minute flight from Bettles. Rates are $450 per day at the main lodge, $295 per day for guided cabin stays, and $195/day for unguided river cabin stays. Airfare is not included. *MC, V, checks OK; iniakuk@alaska.net; www.gofarnorth.com.*

Kobuk Valley National Park

The Kobuk River flows through a wide, forested valley between the Baird and Waring Mountains. The river meanders through spruce, birch, and aspen forests and past several Inupiat villages before emptying into Kotzebue Sound. The boundaries enclose 1.7 million acres of undeveloped parkland.

Just 75 miles east of Kotzebue, this park boasts two Wild and Scenic Rivers: the Kobuk and the Salmon. Villagers along the river are dependent on subsistence hunting and fishing for much of their livelihood, so visitors often are surprised to find that hunting continues within the boundaries of this park. Private property along the river should be respected. Sportfishing for grayling, pike, char, and sheefish is often outstanding. The vast Western Arctic Caribou Herd crosses the Kobuk in early September en route to southern wintering grounds. Floaters have found themselves amid large herds swimming the river.

THE GREAT KOBUK SAND DUNES, which cover 25 square miles, inland from the south bank of the river, are the park's most notable feature. These dunes, up to 125 feet high, would look more at home in an Edward Abbey novel than they do in Arctic Alaska. Travelers can hire local guides with boats, float down the Kobuk on their own, or be dropped off by plane. The dunes are accessible from the river by a short hike up Kavit Creek. Watch for bears. For INFORMATION, contact Superintendent, Kobuk Valley National Park (PO Box 1029, Kotzebue, AK 99752; 907/442-3890).

Arctic National Wildlife Refuge

Truly America's Ser-engeti, the most northern of all our national refuges has been much in the news lately. Essentially, there are those who are fighting fiercely to protect it and those who want to drill for oil in it. It is a priceless treasure. Rivers flow clear and pure and the land embraces musk oxen, moose, polar bears, black and brown bears, wolves, and the great Porcupine Caribou Herd. Part of the refuge is mountainous with limited tree cover, but much of it is tundra and marsh. Refuge winters are long and severe, summers short and intense. The brief summer growing season, with its attendant insect plague, supports minimal plant growth. A white spruce tree growing at the northern tree line may take 300 years to achieve a base diameter of 5 inches. Both Inupiats and Gwitch'in subsist off refuge lands. Visitors enjoy summer float trips, hiking, photography, climbing, fishing, and hunting. The main lure for many people is viewing the spectacular caribou migrations and post-calving aggregations. For INFORMATION, contact Refuge Manager, Arctic National Wildlife Refuge, Federal Building and Courthouse (Box 20, 101 12th Ave, Fairbanks, AK 99701; 907/456-0250).

ADVENTURES: RIVER FLOAT TRIPS

CENTRAL BROOKS RANGE / It is very difficult to pick one *best* float trip because Gates of the Arctic National Park offers so many great trips on wonderful rivers north and south of the divide. Perhaps the best choice is the Kobuk River float, from its headwaters at Walker Lake to Kobuk Village. Plan an overnight stay at the lake to enjoy the mountain setting before traveling between the Baird and Waring Mountains 125 miles to Kobuk. There are two sets of rapids to portage, but mostly the trip is a peaceful 6- or 7-day run that requires no extraordinary boat-manship, just common sense and camping experience.

EASTERN ARCTIC / Float trips in the Arctic National Wildlife Refuge have exploded in popularity over the last decade. Two outstanding trips are down the Kongakut and Hulahula Rivers. Both, depending on the timing of the trip, offer exceptional views and encounters with the 175,000-strong Porcupine Caribou Herd. Dall sheep, bears, golden eagles, waterfowl, and small mammals are commonly encountered. Musk oxen are also sometimes seen. Neither trip is particularly haz-ardous, but experience in wilderness travel is very important. Guided trips are recommended for novices and the inexperienced. Access is via air from Kaktovik and Arctic Village.

CENTRAL NORTH SLOPE / The Colville River flows north to the Arc-tic Ocean past cliff-nesting falcons, hawks, and eagles; fossilized remains of Pleistocene mammals visible in sloughing permafrost bluffs; and tun-dra mammals, large and small. The 428-mile-long Colville, seventh-longest river in the state, begins in the De Long Mountains of the Brooks Range and runs to the coast. It is slow-moving and easy to run but is extraordinarily remote. Umiat is about 230 miles from the headwaters. Travelers need to be prepared and experienced in wilderness trekking. Access is via Barrow, Bettles, Umiat, or Deadhorse.

WESTERN BROOKS RANGE / A float down the Wild and Scenic Noatak River through the Noatak National Preserve begins near Mount Igikpak and, if desired, can terminate almost 400 miles later in Kotzebue Sound. From the headwaters to the village of Noatak takes about 15 days or so, but shorter trips are possible, depending on pickup or drop-off points. The mountains around the headwaters are spectacular, as is the only slightly hyperbolic Grand Canyon of the Noatak. There are several Class II rapids along the river, but altogether it's a fairly easy float. Again, this is a remote wilderness river, and the inexperienced should consider a guide service. The river is becoming an ever more popular destination. Access is via Bet-tles for the headwaters and via Kotzebue for the lower river.

ADVENTURES: FLIGHT-SEEING TRIPS

CENTRAL BROOKS RANGE / Two trips to recommend: the Arrigetch Peaks, just west of the Alatna River, and through the Gates of the Arctic. The granitic, Teton-like spires of the Arrigetch are a favorite visitor attraction, but our personal favorite is a flight up the North Fork and by Frigid Crags and Boreal Mountain to Mount Doonerak. Inspiring coun-try at any season, but indescribable at the peak of fall colors. Bettles is the most economical place to begin a flight. Road travelers should check at Coldfoot to see if charter service is available there now.

EASTERN BROOKS RANGE / Circumnavigate Mounts Chamberlin and Michelson. These are some of the only glaciated peaks in the eastern Arctic, and on a summer "night" they glow with golden rays of the midnight sun. It's an expensive flight from almost all access points, notably Kaktovik and Arctic Village; therefore, it's best arranged as an adjunct to another trip.

WESTERN ARCTIC / Fly from Kotzebue, early or late in the day, along the coast 10 miles to Cape Krusenstern. From this altitude the traveler can best appreciate the starkness of the Chukchi Sea coast and this landscape that has supported people for 6,000 years. Flying services in Kotzebue offer flight-seeing here, as well as around Kotzebue Sound and to local villages.

GUIDES AND OUTFITTERS

Not all guides are appropriate for all clients. One client may swear by one guide, while another may swear *at* that same guide. Check references and clearly spell out desires and expectations. Some of these guides offer very similar trips but have different perspectives on the same areas and adventures. This list is not to be considered inclusive. Some great guides work for large organizations. Veteran Arctic guide and photographer Wilbur Mills, for example, sometimes guides for the Sierra Club.

Airfare from Fairbanks into the Bush is not always included in the price of a trip—be sure to ask about this in advance. Arctic air travel is not cheap. Because trips must be planned well ahead of time, provisions and supplies purchased, logistics secured and paid for in advance, most wilderness guides and outfitters often require large deposits at the time of booking. Expect to pay a deposit of anywhere from 30 to 50 percent. Final payment may be required as much as 90 days in advance of the trip. This is standard procedure, but individual arrangements can be worked out.

ALASKA WILDTREK / Alaska Wildtrek specializes in adventures especially suited for European travelers or anyone interested in wildlife viewing, rafting, hiking, and wilderness camping. One offering is called "The Arctic Parks," a **BACKPACK AND RAFTING ADVENTURE** to three parks: Gates of the Arctic, Kobuk Valley, and Noatak. The multilingual owner, Chlaus Lotscher, also leads climbing adventures to places like Mount Chamberlin and Mount Michelson in the Arctic Wildlife Refuge. An internationally published photojournalist, Lotscher will assist photographers in obtaining high-quality images. PO Box 1741, Homer, AK 99603; 907/235-6463; aktrek@xyz.net; www.alaskan.com/alaskawildtrek; no credit cards; checks OK.

WILDERNESS BIRDING ADVENTURES / Lisa Moorehead has been a wilderness guide for 19 years and holds a master's degree in cultural anthropology. Bob Dittrick, a biologist, has been guiding 13 years and birding for 30 years. Together, they offer **BIRDERS** the chance to explore via raft and to backpack wilderness areas missed by most serious birders. Two special offerings are a raft/hike in the Arctic National Wildlife Refuge during the caribou migration and a Nome beach birding trip suitable for both beginning and experienced birders. Also offered are trips designed to locate uncommon or rare species. An example: a 4-day backpack trip in the Arctic Refuge to see grey-headed chickadees. PO Box 10-3747, Anchorage, AK 99510-3747; 907/694-7442 (phone and fax); wildbird@alaska.net.

GOLDEN PLOVER AIR / The son of legendary bush pilot Bud Helmericks, Jim Helmericks lives on family property on the Colville River delta, just a few miles from the Arctic Ocean. The ponds and tundra around the Helmericks' modern home are a family wildlife refuge and an exciting place for birders to visit. Helmericks is an outstanding bush pilot and can **CUSTOM-TAILOR TRIPS** of all kinds for birders and adventurers. Standing in stark contrast to the tussock-covered coastal tundra, the Helmericks property is a true oasis for a select, limited number of guests. Lodging, family meals, and air and boat logistical support are provided by Jim and his wife, Teena. An excellent terminus for Colville River rafters, who then can be flown into Prudhoe Bay. Colville Village via Pouch 340109, Prudhoe Bay, AK 99734; 907/659-2625 or 907/659-2622; jwhgpa@corecom.net; www.alaskaone.com/goldenplover/; no credit cards; checks OK.

ALASKA PERIMETER EXPEDITIONS AND OUTFITTERS / Born and raised in Alaska, Henry D. "Te" Tiffany IV made his first successful hunt at age 10. One of the youngest licensed registered guides, Tiffany offers **TRADITIONAL FAIR-CHASE HUNTS** from comfortable tent camps established in the Brooks Range and on the Koyukuk River. Tiffany stresses quality over quantity and books only a small number of hunters. PO Box 329, Ester, AK 99725; 907/456-4868; apehunt@ptialaska.net; no credit cards; checks OK.

PEACE OF SELBY LODGE / Art and Damaris Mortvedt have 25 years of experience living in the upper Kobuk Valley. Their Peace of Selby (Lake) Lodge is a family-run, family-oriented business. The Mortvedts offer customized fishing, float trips, wilderness hikes, and peaceful getaways at lake and river cabins in the true wilderness of the Gates of the Arctic National Preserve. **FISHING**—for grayling, Dolly Varden, lake trout, northern pike, and sheefish, often called the "tarpon of the north" by many fishing writers—is prime with this outfitter. Lodge rates are $300 per day per person. Do-it-yourself cabins are $300 per day for four people. PO Box 86, Manley Hot Springs, AK 99756; 907/672-3206 (phone and fax); peaceofselby@compuserve.com; www.gorp.com/selby/.

ABEC'S ALASKA ADVENTURES / Ramona Finnoff has been guiding river travelers for more than 19 years and has extensive experience in whitewater kayaking, rock and ice climbing, skiing, dog mushing, and mountaineering. Three special offerings are a **RAFT AND BACKPACKING COMBINATION TRIP** during the caribou migration in the Arctic National Wildlife Refuge; a backpack in the pristine headwaters of the Nigu/Alatna Rivers; and Ramona's favorite, the Noatak River float and backpack. All three are good bets for folks who will make only one trip to the wilderness of Arctic Alaska. 1550 Alpine Vista Ct, Fairbanks, AK 99712; 907/457-8907, fax 90/457-6689; abec@abecalaska.com; www .abecalaska.com; no credit cards; checks OK.

WILDERNESS ALASKA / Macgill Adams' goal is to see and visit *all* of the Arctic National Wildlife Refuge; his guided treks, therefore, are not limited to "the same old routes." Each trip offers some portion that is unique as well as open to opportunity. The refuge's great glory lies in the ability to **OBSERVE WILDLIFE** in undisturbed settings. Adams, ably assisted by Dee Dee Van Vliet, works hard to ensure that Arctic novices learn to appreciate not only the smack-in-the-face beauty of the Brooks Range but also the glorious subtleties of the plain and coastal lagoons. Trips offered throughout the Brooks Range. PO Box 113063, Anchorage, AK 99511; 907/345-3567; macgill@alaska.net; www.gorp.com/ wildak; no credit cards; checks OK.

EQUINOX WILDERNESS EXPEDITIONS / Equinox offers floats and treks throughout the Arctic. Owner Karen Jettmar, a former park ranger, has 25 years of experience in wilderness Alaska, including kayaking, hiking, rafting, and a solo climb of Mount McKinley. Special offerings include **WOMEN-ONLY TRIPS**. Jettmar tailors her expeditions to the special sensitivities and experience levels of her participants. 618 W 14th Ave, Anchorage, AK 99501; 907/274-9087; equinox@alaska.net; www. equinoxexpeditions.com; no credit cards; checks OK.

NOME

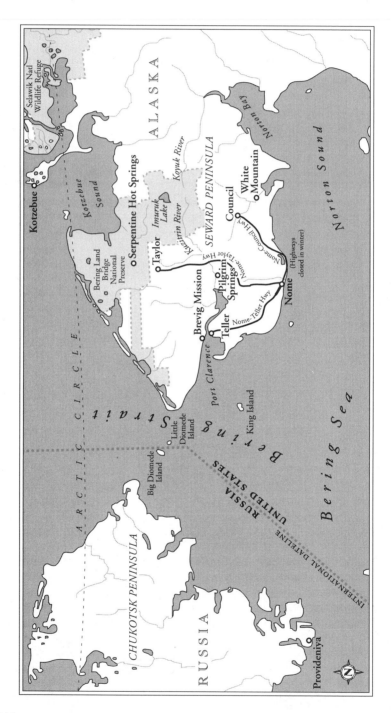

NOME

At first glance, Nome may seem a bit disheveled, even homely. But it gets cold here—like 50 below or colder. So it's best to think of Nome as unpretentious. Everything serves a purpose. Function rules. And although they inhabit one of the furthest reaches of the continent, people here do not feel isolated. As one bemused resident explained, "We are smug in the shared belief that Nome is really the center of the universe."

Nome is on the Seward Peninsula, 102 miles below the Arctic Circle, with its back to the hills and its face to the sea. People work hard here. The land demands it. They play hard, too. Rituals tend to be unusual. In spring, they dig out bathing suits and plunge into the icy Bering Sea. In fall, they race down Front Street in bathtubs on wheels.

Above all, the people of Nome know how to have a good time. They celebrate with wild abandon. Any excuse will do—anniversaries, divorces, their birthdays, their dogs' birthdays, the bars being open—it doesn't matter. As reported in *The Wall Street Journal*: "Every night is Friday night in Nome, Alaska. Except Friday night—which is New Year's Eve."

Today, the city is home to about 4,000 people and is the hub of Northwest Alaska. Once this town was only desolate, windswept tundra. Then, in 1898, gold was discovered on the black sands of Cape Nome and within months there sprang up a tent city of 20,000 hopeful goldseekers. It was known as the "poor man's gold rush," because gold lay all over the beaches just for the taking. Gamblers, con men, prostitutes, and other characters straight out of a B-movie flocked to the north. They entertained themselves in high style. The legendary lawman and gunslinger Wyatt Earp even owned a saloon here. At one time, Nome had a French lingerie shop and piano-moving businesses. Although fires and storms have wiped out nearly all remnants of this colorful era (a devastating blaze in 1934 destroyed 90 percent of the historic buildings), Nome still identifies heavily with its past.

There is no road *to* Nome. But there are about 300 miles of roads *around* Nome. The city is located 539 air miles north of Anchorage, and the only way to reach it is by air or sea or sled-dog team. Nome is most famous today in Alaska and around the world not for its gold but for being the end of "The Last Great Race," the 1,049-mile winter dash by sled dog team down the Iditarod Trail from Anchorage every March.

ACCESS AND INFORMATION

Regularly scheduled **FLIGHTS** to Nome are available from Anchorage on Alaska Airlines (800/426-0333) and Yute Air (888/359-9883), and from Fairbanks on Frontier Flying Service (907/474-0014). Nome also has van service to the Eskimo village of **TELLER** (72 miles northwest of Nome), taxicabs, and several businesses that rent vehicles (see Adventures, below).

Located on Front Street, the **NOME CONVENTION & VISITORS BUREAU** (PO Box 240, Nome, AK 99762; 907/443-5535; www.alaska. new/~nome) has historical photos and scrapbooks on Nome, bird lists, flyers on fishing and wildlife, and information on lodging and tours. The staff is knowledgeable and friendly and can help you get set up to do any of the activities highlighted below.

Nome's daytime summer **TEMPERATURES** range from the low 50s to the mid-70s, and in the winter, it can range from about 20°F to –50°F. If you plan to visit in summer, be prepared for rainy weather and sometimes chilly winds. If you can schedule a trip in September, you'll enjoy the best time of year, when the tundra changes to colors as vibrant as any New England hillside and the ubiquitous summer mosquitoes are gone.

EXPLORING

SHOPPING / There are a half-dozen gift shops on Front Street, selling Native ivory carvings and other Alaskana. Especially good are the **ARCTIC TRADING POST** (907/443-2686), **MARUSKIYA'S** (907/443-2955), and the ivory store run through the **SITNASUAK NATIVE CORPORATION** (179 Front St; 907/443-2632). Harder to find, but worth the effort is the **CHUKOTKA-ALASKA STORE** (185 W 1st Ave; 907/443-4128). Owner Victor Goldsberry packs this small shop with a multitude of mementos from the Chukotka region of Russia, directly across the Bering Strait from Nome. You'll see traditional Russian designs as well as Siberian Yup'ik handicrafts and furs. Goldsberry is a rich source of information about the people of the Chukotka Peninsula. Stay and chat awhile.

The "Grand Poobah" and former mayor of Nome is Leo Rasmussen, who owns **RASMUSSEN'S MUSIC MART** (77 Federal Wy; 907/443-2798). Rasmussen has had a hand in almost every unusual and silly summer event that has evolved in Nome over the last 30 years. Located just off Front Street, his store is a pleasant jumble of all those things you never thought you might need; Leo himself is a pleasant jumble of anecdotes and facts about this place. Expect him to try to sell you a plaque on a tripod mile marker of the Iditarod National Historic Trail, which enjoys the same federal status as the Appalachian Trail on the East Coast. Leo is president of a nonprofit corporation that manages fundraising and development for the historic trail.

ADVENTURES

GO ROAD TRIPPING / In the summer, what Nome really has to offer that no other place in Bush Alaska has is the rare chance to travel deep into the country by road. The Nome area has more than 300 miles of well-maintained **GRAVEL ROADS** to explore, with unique opportunities for hiking, mountain biking, fishing, skiing, boating, birding, wildlife viewing, and other adventuring. Birding is big, with more than 180 species found on the Seward Peninsula from late May through July, including Asiatic birds rarely seen in North America.

The roads are generally open May through October, depending on snowfall, and maintained during summer and fall. Cars may be rented from **STAMPEDE AUTO RENTALS** (907/443-3838) and **ALASKA CAB GARAGE** (907/443-2939). If you don't want to rent your own vehicle, **STROM CAB SERVICE** (907/642-2047) makes regular runs between Nome and Teller (evenings only). They also do custom tours and drop-offs all along the road system.

Three major roads, plus one short drive, lead out of Nome and are outlined below. There are no services—no gas, no food, no lemonade stands—once you leave the town. Keep your eyes open for reindeer, musk oxen, bears, and foxes, as well as abandoned gold dredges. Be prepared to do battle with mosquitoes.

Head out on the **NOME-TELLER ROAD,** and about 40 miles northwest of Nome you'll see another road (about 7 miles long) wandering off toward the sea to **CAPE WOOLLEY,** a fish camp formerly used by King Island Natives during summer months. The main road dead-ends 72 miles northwest of Nome in the Inupiat Eskimo village of **TELLER,** a community of 300 people located on the sea between Grantley Harbor and Port Clarence. Joe Garney, Iditarod musher, also lives in Teller—look for the yard with 40 or so dogs. During summer months, many Teller families head upriver, through Imuruk Basin and up the meandering Kuzitrin River, to fish camps at Mary's Igloo. **GRANTLEY HARBOR TOURS** (Box 586, Teller, AK 99778; 800/478-3682, in Alaska, or 907/642-3682), run by Kenneth and Emily Hughes, is custom-designed to help you get deeper into the country, whether you're on a photo safari, fishing, or meeting a local ivory carver.

The **NOME-TAYLOR HIGHWAY** is more popularly known as the **KOUGAROK ROAD.** This 85-mile road does lead to Taylor, but Taylor is a private mining operation and not open to the public. At the Kuzitrin River Bridge, where the road becomes more like a trail, it's time to turn around. About 8 miles out of Nome, there's good fishing in the **DEXTER VALLEY.** About 38 miles out, **SALMON LAKE** is a beautiful spot for fishing, camping, or a picnic. About 50 miles out, take the left-hand turn to **PILGRIM HOT SPRINGS,** 7 miles off the main road. Don't miss it. Pilgrim Hot Springs is an interesting historical site with a wooden hot tub for soaking (it's free). It was once a Catholic mission, boarding school, and orphanage. During the flu epidemic of 1918, the mission was overwhelmed by Native children who'd lost their families. The Jesuits ran the orphanage for 23 years, until it was closed in 1941. Now Pilgrim Hot Springs is owned by a New York family, and maintained and used as a summer camp by Nome's Green family. Before you explore the area or take a dip in the springs, find a caretaker and ask permission, or call Louie Green (907/443-5583).

The **NOME–COUNCIL ROAD** follows the coast for about 30 miles before wandering inland toward Council, 72 miles northeast of Nome. **CAPE NOME**, about 13 miles out, has a sweeping view of the Bering Sea. About 34 miles out is the ghost town of **SOLOMON**. Just before Solomon you'll see the old gold-rush train, "The Last Train to Nowhere." About 65 miles out, you'll see a rare sight for the Seward Peninsula—trees! Council is another former gold-rush town turned fishing camp with a summer population of 40.

The **ANVIL MOUNTAIN ROAD** is a short 5-mile jaunt out of Nome that takes you to the top of Anvil Mountain and offers a view of Nome and the Bering Sea. Take Bering Street north to the Nome-Beltz Highway. Once you pass Icy View, Nome's one and only suburb, you'll see a right-hand turn. Take it. About 2 miles up, turn left and continue until you reach the top where four giant antennae stand. This used to be part of the U.S. Air Force DEW Line system, a first line of defense against anticipated Soviet attack during the Cold War days.

MUSH DOGS / Aaron Burmeister is an Iditarod veteran. He or his brother Noah can take you on a half-hour sled-dog ride for $25 or arrange **LESSONS** and longer rides, even multiday trips, through their company Flat Dog Kennels (PO Box 1103, Nome, AK 99762; 907/443-2958). In the summer, the sled dogs pull you on wheels rather than runners. If you happen to be in town during the Iditarod, there is also an amateur **"BUSINESSMAN'S SLED DOG RACE,"** where local mushers give newcomers a brief training session and send them out on a 3-mile race. Pay a $50 entry fee to the Nome Kennel Club to get in on the action. Contact Nome Convention & Visitors Bureau, PO Box 240, Nome, AK 99762; 907/443-5535.

GO GOLD PANNING / Pick up a pan at one of the local stores and hit the beach. Gold panning is allowed on a 2-mile stretch east of Nome, between town and the Fort Davis Roadhouse. If you want to do it as part of a tour, contact the Nome Convention & Visitors Bureau, PO Box 240, Nome, AK 99762; 907/443-5535.

VISIT RUSSIA: TOURS TO PROVIDENIYA / A Bering Air Piper Navajo was the first American aircraft to fly through the "Ice Curtain" between the United States and Russia in May 1988. Now, hundreds of flights later, **CIRCUMPOLAR EXPEDITIONS** (907/272-9299, fax 907/278-6092;

wallack@alaska.net) offers a 3-day, 2-night whirlwind tour of Nome's sister city of Provideniya in the Russian Far East. It's advised that you check into the current political situation in the Chukotka region of Russia before you travel. The Siberian regions have been especially hard hit by the recent economic troubles in Russia, so plans must be made well in advance because of all the paperwork. You also will need a valid passport. Circumpolar Expeditions will help make arrangements for required invitations and visas. The cost is $999 per person. Circumpolar Expeditions also can arrange fishing and kayak tours in the Chukotka region.

NOME DISCOVERY TOURS / Former Broadway showman Richard Beneville gives a lively and well-informed tour of Nome and its environs. Beneville caters to independent groups, and his presentation is peppered with his trademark expression, "Hello, Central!" which was once used by party-line telephone operators. Ask him about his home in one of Nome's few surviving gold-rush landmarks, the former Discovery Saloon. 1st Ave and D St; 907/443-2814.

GUIDES AND OUTFITTERS

ARCTIC TOURS / This well-produced short tour of the area is part of Alaska Airlines' vacation package to Nome, but it's also open to the general public. The tour includes a visit to a working sled-dog camp operated by Howard Farley, who raced in the first Iditarod; a visit to a reindeer corral; and a gold-panning demonstration. Contact tour headquarters at the Nome Nugget Inn, PO Box 430, Nome, AK 99762; 907/443-2323.

INUA EXPEDITIONS / *Inua* means "spirit," and guide Keith Conger introduces his clients to that spirit of the land and the people whose lives are intertwined with it. His current special focus is arranging wilderness **MOUNTAIN BIKING TRIPS** for all abilities. A schoolteacher in Nome, Conger is an enthusiastic adventurer who has arranged marathon cross-country bike races and regularly skis in summer on mountain snowcaps, which he swears are the year's best skiing. He can tailor a bike expedition to your ability, whether you prefer easy trails or gnarly brambles in places no one else has ever been. Make sure you arrive with a tough bike. Keith also can set up wilderness trips for independent travelers, using his connections to arrange an unforgettable hiking or rafting trip. Call ahead for rates. Box 1333, Nome, AK 99762; 907/443-4994.

FESTIVALS AND EVENTS

IDITAROD TRAIL SLED DOG RACE / This world-famous 1,049-mile sled dog race begins in Anchorage the first Saturday of March and ends several days later here in Nome. The race commemorates the old mail

THE IDITAROD TRAIL SLED DOG RACE

The Iditarod Trail Sled Dog Race commemorates the old dog-team trail across Alaska from one gold rush to another. The town of Iditarod was once a booming inland empire of gold, built in an unbelievably mosquito-infested swamp (even by Alaska standards) halfway between Anchorage and Nome in the early 1900s. Today, it's a ghost town. The gold and mail trail, covered by dog team in the winters, ran from Seward on the coast to the fabled gold town of Nome, more than 1,000 miles away over two mountain ranges, up the frozen Yukon River, and across the frozen Bering Sea.

Nome's glory days were fading when gold was discovered in the country surrounding the Iditarod River. So a spur route from the Seward-to-Nome trail was cut to the new boomtown of Iditarod. Gradually, the whole route became known as the Iditarod Trail.

On the first Saturday of every March, men, women, and dogs test their mettle against the elements and mush down Fourth Avenue in Anchorage in a ceremonial start to the 1,049-mile Iditarod Trail Sled Dog Race, run from Anchorage to Nome. The race is the brainchild of the late Joe Redington, Sr., known affectionately in Alaska as the "Father of the Iditarod." Because of his love of dogs, challenge, and adventure, he struggled against enormous criticism to create the race, which today is famous around the world as "The Last Great Race."

—Nan Elliot

route–gold rush trail and the courageous diphtheria serum run between Nenana and Nome in 1925. The winning time for the first Iditarod, held in 1973, was 20 days. With improved breeding, training, equipment, and trail conditions, it is now run in a little more than 9 days. As the finish line for the race, Nome draws mushers, media, and groupies from all over the world. Iditarod time is something to behold, with everything from Native dancing and drumming to golfing on the frozen Bering Sea. You'll also find a whole ream of sports going on, from the 3-mile Businessman's Sled Dog Race (see Adventures, above) to Iditabasketball tournaments, drawing more than 50 teams from all over the state. The Iditarod Awards Banquet is usually held on the Sunday following the winner's arrival. Because of all this activity, March is the best time to visit Nome. Accommodations fill up quickly at Iditarod time, so book early. Once everything is full, a call goes out to the community for spare rooms; even floor space is for rent. Contact the Iditarod Trail Committee, PO Box 870800, Wasilla, AK 99687; 907/376-5155.

BERING SEA ICE GOLF CLASSIC / Held in mid-March at Iditarod time, this is a six-hole fund-raising tournament played on the frozen Bering Sea, with bright orange golf balls and coffee cans sunk into the ice as holes. Golfers tee off outside the back door of one of the bars after the prerequisite number of drinks. They ham it up for this one, wearing plus fours and outfitting their huskies as caddies. Contact the Bering Sea Lions Club, PO Box 326, Nome, AK 99762; 907/443-5278.

MIDNIGHT SUN FESTIVAL / Nome revels in the ancient tradition of celebrating the summer solstice, and with good reason. The longest day of the year here doesn't end in night. The sun never goes down. The Midnight Sun Festival is a hodgepodge of small-town parades, races, and contests. At high noon, a half-dozen residents stage a mock robbery at the National Bank of Alaska, complete with the bank manager wielding a shotgun from the roof of the bank. In the afternoon, the **NOME RIVER RAFT RACE** begins at Mile 13 of the Kougarok Road. Homemade rafts—basically anything that floats—race downriver. The victorious team claims the distinctive trophy, a fur-trimmed honey bucket. ("Honey bucket" is a polite term for a bucket sometimes used in the Bush in lieu of a "loo.") Contact the Bering Sea Lions Club, PO Box 326, Nome, AK 99762; 907/443-5278.

BATHTUB RACE / An annual Labor Day spectacle, with bathtubs mounted on wheels rattling down Front Street. The rules state the tubs must be full of water and bubbles and that the "bather" must wield a bar of soap, a towel, and a bath mat while being propelled by teammates down the course. Tubs must have at least 10 gallons of water left at the finish line to win. Contact Leo Rasmussen at the Music Mart, PO Box 2, Nome, AK 99762; 907/443-2798.

GOLD RUSH CENTENNIAL (1998–2001) / Nome started celebrating its centennial in the summer of 1998, marking its 100th anniversary with a re-enactment of the discovery of gold at Anvil Creek, an old-fashioned parade, and the dedication of a new postal stamp. Don't worry, you haven't missed out. The hoopla is still going on! Probably most immediately noticeable is that the few remaining historic buildings got face-lifts. The **BOARD OF TRADE SALOON**, which originally stood in the village of St. Michael and was moved board by board to Nome to serve the torrent of thirsty miners, got a new paint job, and the weathered, gray old **ST. JOSEPH'S CHURCH** not only got renovated but got its 10-story steeple back with a lighted cross on top, which can be seen for miles. In front of the church are the statues of those "Three Lucky Swedes" who made the big find and put Nome on the map in September 1898. In 1999, Nome celebrated the stampede of prospectors to the Cape, and in the summer of 2000, the town re-enacts the arrival of the legendary lawman

Wyatt Earp, who opened the **DEXTER SALOON** on Front Street. Winding up all the festivities in 2001 will be the 100th anniversary of the incorporation of Nome as a city. As you can see by Nome's other wacky celebrations, there is no lack of imagination when it comes to planning festivities. Check with the Nome Convention and Visitors Bureau (907/443-5535) for a full roster of events, or visit the Nome Centennial Committee's Web site (www.nome100.com).

RESTAURANTS

Fat Freddie's / ★

50 FRONT ST, NOME; 907/443-5899
The food here is solid family fare: cheeseburgers with lots of grease, sandwiches off the grill, homemade soup and chowder, and hearty meat-and-potatoes dinners. Broad windows offer a nice view of the Bering Sea. Fat Freddie's is a popular Nome hangout, and during Iditarod many racers can be found here enjoying a hot meal after their 1,049-mile trek. *$$; AE, DC, MC, V; local checks only; breakfast, lunch, dinner every day; full bar; located next to the Nugget Inn on Front St, across from Nome City Hall.* &

Fort Davis Roadhouse / ★★

MILE 2, NOME-COUNCIL HWY, NOME; 907/443-2660
The Roadhouse brings a taste of Europe to the tundra. Austrian owner and chef Hatto Eberl was formally trained in Heidelberg and has cooked on cruise ships and run his own restaurants. Now he's given Nome diners something to talk about. Friday night's seafood buffet features fresh halibut, Alaska king salmon, shrimp, crab soufflé, and a variety of other seafood dishes. Saturday night, it's prime rib. Sunday brunch ($16) includes crepes, Belgian waffles, eggs Benedict, and other goodies. The lounge upstairs offers live music and dancing. *$$$; MC, V; checks OK; dinner Fri–Sat, brunch Sun; go straight out Front St in Nome, 2 miles south of town.*

The Lucky Swede

FRONT AND BERING STS, NOME; 907/443-3828
No, it's not a casino, just a cozy shop with coffee and fresh flowers (bagels and coffee for two, $20). Named for "The Three Lucky Swedes," the first to find gold at nearby Anvil Creek, the shop serves flavored lattes, cappuccinos, and espresso. The walls are lined with unusual clothing and knickknacks made by Alaska craftspeople. *$; AE, MC, V; local checks only; breakfast, lunch every day; no alcohol; PO Box 234, Nome, AK 99762; downtown Nome.*

LODGINGS

The Aurora Inn / ★★

527 FRONT ST, NOME, AK 99762; 907/443-3838 OR 800/354-4606
Nome's newest entry into the hotel business is also its most posh. The rooms are spacious and most have a sweeping view of the Bering Sea. Four types of rooms are available, from the basic double at $90 per night in the summer to $150 per night for an "executive suite" with a full kitchen. Winter rates are lower. A sauna is available to chase away the chills. The inn's front desk is also a good place to rent pickup trucks or cars from Stampede Auto Rentals. *$$$; AE, MC, V; local checks only; on E Front St, next to the National Guard Armory.* &

Betty's Igloo Bed and Breakfast

1ST AND K STS, NOME, AK 99762; 907/443-2419
Michael and Betty Hannigan have a tidy two-story home a block from shore, with a view of the Bering Sea. The Hannigans live upstairs and rent three rooms downstairs. Room rates are $55 for a single and $70 for a double; a continental breakfast is included. *$; no credit cards; checks OK; PO Box 1784, Nome, AK 99762.*

Chateau de Cape Nome

1376 E 4TH AVE, NOME, AK 99762; 907/443-2083
This could be the biggest house on the Seward Peninsula—a two-story, 4,400-square-foot home with a stretch limousine parked in the garage. Former Nome police chief, now turned wilderness and hunting guide, Bob Kauer and his wife, Cussy, the city comptroller, run their B&B off and on throughout the year in a home full of gold-rush memorabilia and hunting trophies. That is, when they aren't too busy guiding bear hunters. You're most likely to find rooms available June through early September and mid-October through March. *$; no credit cards; checks OK; PO Box 715, Nome, AK 99762.*

Nome Nugget Inn / ★

FRONT ST AND BERING AVE, NOME, AK 99762; 907/443-2323
The Nugget, in the heart of town, has the most character and class. The famous burl arch for the finish line of the Iditarod stood for many years right outside. During the race, it's like Grand Central Station. The Gold Dust Lounge, with friendly bartenders, gold-rush character, and a view of the Bering Sea, is a pleasant place to trade stories and wild rumors of mushers and the trail. Rates are about $100 for a double. *$$; AE, DC, MC, V; full bar in the Gold Dust Saloon; PO Box 430, Nome AK 99762; downtown.*

Bering Land Bridge National Preserve

This national preserve is one of the most remote and least-visited national parks in the country. Yet it is the remains of an ancient First People's highway. Today, Siberia is 55 miles across the Bering Sea. But during the Pleistocene Ice Age, much of the earth's water was locked in ice. The level of the seas fell, exposing a broad bridge of land—1,000 miles wide—between Asia and North America. Most anthropologists believe this is how the First Peoples came to the Americas thousands of years ago.

The Bering Land Bridge is a primitive landscape, with extensive **LAVA FLOWS, LOW SAND DUNES,** and **CRATERS** that have since become lakes. The people who live here follow a traditional subsistence lifestyle. Some are reindeer herders. The area is home to musk oxen, grizzly bears, moose, reindeer, wolves, wolverines, and foxes. In winter, polar bears cruise the coastline and sometimes come ashore. You can get to the preserve by boat or bush plane in the summer or by ski plane, snowmobile, or dog team in the winter.

Be forewarned it has no visitor facilities and no roads. However, the park service did lift the ban on bicycling in the preserve in 1998. So, if you are hardy and don't mind getting mired down in serious muck and mosquitoes, you can try biking the 20-mile trail to Serpentine Hot Springs (see below).

ADVENTURES

SERPENTINE HOT SPRINGS / A natural hot springs within the preserve is surrounded by an other-worldly landscape. The steaming hot springs are circled by granite spires, once a place of power used by shamans for training in traditional medicines. There's a short airstrip, an old bunkhouse, and a small bathhouse with a wooden pool. It's free and open to the public. In winter, access is by snowmobile or dog team. The springs are about 20 miles beyond the end of the Taylor Highway and about 90 miles north of Nome. Contact Bering Land Bridge National Preserve, PO Box 220, Nome, AK 99762; 907/443-2522.

SOUTHWEST ALASKA

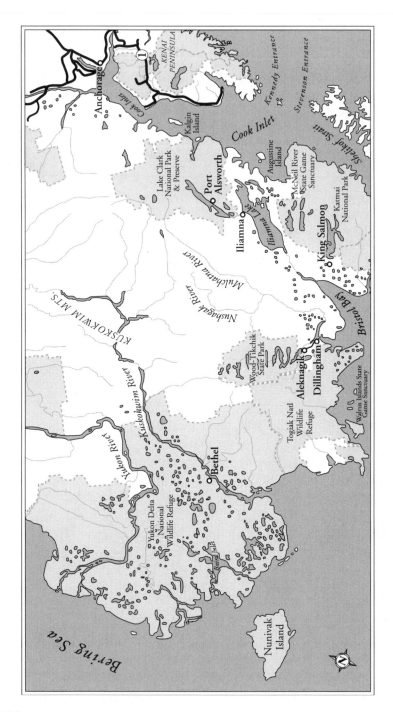

SOUTHWEST ALASKA

Southwest Alaska is best defined by its wildness and biological diversity. The region stretches from Lake Clark down to Bristol Bay, then up the coast to the Yukon-Kuskokwim Delta. It is North America's largest nesting and breeding area for migratory waterfowl. The world's densest population of brown bears and greatest salmon runs are also here. More than 60 communities dot the landscape, most of them small, remote villages whose Athabascan and Yup'ik residents continue to lead subsistence lifestyles heavily dependent on the region's abundant wildlife. Most villages have fewer than 200 people. There is only one paved "highway," 15.5 miles long. Few other roads connect villages. Access is by air, boat, or snowmobile in winter. Scheduled airlines serve only four of the region's towns: Iliamna, King Salmon, Dillingham, and Bethel; local air taxis fly to villages. Fishing is the main work. Bristol Bay, the world's largest sockeye salmon fishery, generates millions of dollars each summer.

This is an angler's paradise—salmon country and rainbow heaven. For the well-to-do, there are luxury fishing lodges ($3,000 to $5,000 per week). If you're not so spendy, do what most Alaskans do—pack your gear and go camping. There's a wealth of areas from which to choose: two national parks, two national wildlife refuges, several Wild and Scenic Rivers, two state game sanctuaries, and the largest state park in the country. Not only do these water-rich habitats sustain incredible salmon migrations, but they also support two of the world's great gatherings of brown bears—at McNeil River State Game Sanctuary and at Brooks Falls in Katmai National Park—with densities of up to 1.4 brown bears per square mile, greater than even Admiralty and Kodiak Islands. The Yukon Delta National Wildlife Refuge is seasonal home to the one of the world's largest nesting populations of geese, ducks, and swans. And thousands of male walrus gather on islands within Bristol Bay.

Though overshadowed by the region's wildlife and fisheries, several of Alaska's most fascinating landscapes occur here. There are two separate lake regions—Lake Iliamna and Lake Clark in the east and the lakes of Wood-Tikchik State Park farther west. Katmai National Park in the south includes 15 active volcanoes and the Valley of Ten Thousand Smokes, site of the largest volcanic eruption in Alaska's recorded history. To the extreme west on the edge of the Bering Sea lies the remote Yukon-Kuskokwim Delta. In summer, visitors can expect wet, cool weather with temperatures around 55°F, overcast skies, and occasionally fierce storms.

Iliamna

Iliamna is an Indian word meaning "big ice" or "big lake." Iliamna Lake is Alaska's largest lake and gives its name to the town on its shores. About 90 people live here year-round. In summer, anglers from around the world come to fish for salmon, Dolly Varden, and especially rainbow trout. The Kvichak River, which flows out of Iliamna Lake, is famous for the largest rainbow trout in the world. The Iliamna–Lake Clark watershed is considered the most important spawning habitat for sockeye salmon in the world and is the major contributor to Bristol Bay's commercial sockeye fishery. Fishing and hunting lodges have operated in the Iliamna Lake region since the 1930s.

ACCESS AND INFORMATION

Located about 100 miles from King Salmon and 225 miles southwest of Anchorage, Iliamna is reached only **BY AIR**. Scheduled passenger service is provided by ERA Aviation (800/866-8394; www.eraaviation.com). Iliamna Air Taxi (907/571-1248, fax 907/571-1244) for local charters.

Iliamna is a short flight from both Lake Clark and Katmai National Parks. A gravel road connects Iliamna to the neighboring Native village of **NEWHALEN**, as well as the Newhalen River, a popular sportfishing stream. Much of the land surrounding Iliamna Lake is privately owned by individuals and Native corporations. **ILIAMNA NATIVES LTD.** (907/ 571-1246) allows camping on its land, but charges a fee. For information, contact **ILIAMNA VILLAGE COUNCIL** (PO Box 245, Iliamna, AK 99606; 907/571-1246, fax 907/571-1256; ilivc@aol.com).

LODGINGS

Airport Hotel / ★

AT THE AIRPORT, ILIAMNA, AK 99606; 907/571-1276, FAX 907/571-1501
For those who cannot afford the thousands of dollars for a fishing lodge, here is a moderately priced option. It has 10 guest rooms and shared bathrooms and offers complimentary rides to the Newhalen River for fishing. The price ($310 for a double) includes lodging plus meals. *$$$; AE, MC, V; checks OK; PO Box 157, Iliamna, AK 99606.*

WILDERNESS LODGES

Iliaska Lodge

PO BOX 228, ILIAMNA, AK 99606; 907/571-1221, JUNE–SEPT; 907/337-9844, OCT–MAY
Iliaska caters particularly to fly-fishers. On the edge of Lake Iliamna, the lodge has private guest rooms for 12 people who come to fish from 3 to

7 days. Guests are flown out daily with experienced guides to the best fishing for rainbows, salmon, grayling, and arctic char. Chief pilot, guide, and owner Ted Gerken has been flying for more than a quarter century and "tying flies for over 40." Cost is from $2,550 per person for 3 days to $5,400 for a week. *No credit cards; checks OK; open early June–late Sept; iliaska@alaska.net; www.alaska.net/~iliaska; winter address: 6160 Farpoint Dr, Anchorage, AK 99517; on the edge of Lake Iliamna, 4 miles from the airport.*

Lake Clark National Park and Preserve

Located on the western side of Cook Inlet, this park and preserve is the quintessential Alaska parkland. Here, wilderness seems to stretch forever, rich with mountains, glaciers, wildlife, wildflowers, forests, tundra, lakes, rivers, and rugged coastal cliffs. There are two active volcanoes, including **MOUNT REDOUBT** (10,197 feet), visible from Anchorage, which last erupted in 1989. The Aleutian and Alaska Ranges join to form rugged peaks, still mostly unclimbed and unexplored. Several major rivers and lakes offer world-class sportfishing for rainbow trout and all five species of Pacific salmon. **LAKE CLARK**, a narrow, 42-mile-long body of water, is the sixth-largest lake in Alaska and the jewel for which the park was named. It is one of the state's least known and least appreciated national parks, in large part because access is only by air. There are no campgrounds, no maintained trails, no visitor centers. But of wildness, there is plenty.

ACCESS AND INFORMATION

From Anchorage, Lake Clark Air (800/662-7661; www.lakeclarkair.com) provides daily commuter flights. Once in Port Alsworth, travel is by foot, boat, or air taxi to outlying areas. For information, contact Superintendent, **LAKE CLARK NATIONAL PARK AND PRESERVE** (4230 University Dr, Ste 311, Anchorage, AK 99508; 907/271-3751, fax 907/271-3707; www.nps.gov\lacl).

Field headquarters for the park is at **PORT ALSWORTH**, a small community (pop. 65) on Lake Clark's southeastern shore. Among the first settlers were bush pilot Leon "Babe" Alsworth and his wife, Mary, who homesteaded 160 acres, built an airstrip, and gave this tiny town its name. The park has no other public facilities, although rangers are often seasonally based at Twin, Telequana, and Crescent Lakes. Visitors exploring the backcountry should plan to be totally self-sufficient and understand how to behave around bears.

FLOAT the Tlikakila, Mulchatna, or Chilikadrotna Rivers (each of them officially designated a Wild and Scenic River). **FISH** for salmon, rainbow trout, or Dolly Varden. Beautiful lakes to explore by **KAYAK** are Lake Clark and Telequana, Turquoise, and Twin Lakes. **BACKPACK** from Turquoise to Twin Lakes.

TUXEDNI BAY, along the coast, is also quite beautiful. **LAKE ILIAMNA**, Alaska's largest lake and another area known for world-class sportfishing, is located just south of the park. Much of the **MULCHATNA** and **CHILIKADROTNA**, two popular fishing and floating rivers, lie outside park boundaries. They feed into the **NUSHAGAK RIVER**, also a popular river-trip destination.

GUIDES AND OUTFITTERS

Guided river trips, as well as hiking opportunities, are offered by **ALASKA ADVENTURES** (907/345-4597; www.ak-adventures.com). **NORTHWARD BOUND** (907/243-3007, fax 907/243-9559; harrower@ alaska.net) guides mountaineering, backpacking, and hiking trips. **OUZEL EXPEDITIONS** (907/783-2216, fax 907/783-3220; www.alaska. net/~ouzel) provides fishing and river trips. Park headquarters has a complete list of Lake Clark's guide and travel services.

WILDERNESS LODGES

Alaska's Wilderness Lodge

WILDERNESS POINT, PORT ALSWORTH, AK 99653; 800/835-8032, FAX 907/781-2223

Nestled among the aspen and spruce on the shores of Lake Clark at Wilderness Point, this lodge run by Pat and Carl Bullo specializes in fly-out fishing adventures with guided trips into the park and surrounding areas. Guests stay in private cabins. Gourmet meals are served in the main lodge. No more than 12 guests at a time for weeklong visits ($5,200 per person for the week with fly-out fishing included). *MC, V (for deposit only); checks OK; open June–Sept; fishawl@worldnet.att.net; www. fishawl.com; winter address: PO Box 700, Sumner, WA 98390.*

Farm Lodge

PORT ALSWORTH, AK 99653; 800/662-7661 OR 907/781-2281, FAX 907/781-2215

The Farm Lodge was built by homesteaders Babe and Mary Alsworth in the 1940s and has been operated as a lodge since 1977 by their son Glen and his wife, Patty. The main lodge (also their home) originally resembled a big red barn, but now is cedar-sided. Home-cooked meals feature wild game, salmon, and vegetables from their garden. The Alsworths also provide flying services (through Lake Clark Air), guided fishing, backpacking drop-offs, and river trips. Full lodging with three meals a day is $80 per person; bed-and-breakfast rates are $60 per person. *DIS, MC, V; checks OK; www.lakeclarkair.com.*

Koksetna Wilderness Lodge

GENERAL DELIVERY, PORT ALSWORTH, AK 99653; 907/781-2227, JUNE–AUG; 530/458-7446, SEPT–MAY
Located on Chulitna Bay, on the shores of Lake Clark, guest accommodations include the main lodge, two cabins with woodstove for heat, two bathhouses, and a steam bath. Accessible by plane, the lodge is a family affair, hosted by Jonathan, Juliann, and Drew Cheney. During the 6-day, 5-night stay ($1,500 per person) activities range from fishing, birdwatching, and wildlife viewing to boating and hiking. Guests also may stay in the cabins and provide their own meals at a lower cost. *No credit cards; checks OK; open June–Aug; koksetna@mako.com; www.homestead.dejanews.com/user.koksetna/koksetna.html; winter address: 1425 5th St, Colusa, CA 95932.*

McNeil River State Game Sanctuary

Created in 1967, McNeil River Sanctuary, located 200 miles southwest of Anchorage, is intended to protect the world's largest gathering of brown bears. The main focus is McNeil Falls, where bears come to feed on chum salmon returning to spawn. During the peak of the chum run (July to August) dozens of brown bears congregate at the falls. As many as 106 bears, including cubs, have been observed along the river in a single day. No more than 10 people a day, always accompanied by one or two state biologists, are allowed to visit bear-viewing sites during the permit period, June 7 through August 25. Because demand is so high, there is an annual drawing to determine permit winners.

The bears begin to arrive at the sanctuary in late May or early June, along tidal mudflats, where they graze on sedges. From mid- to late June they also feast on sockeye salmon that spawn in Mikfik Creek, a neighboring stream of McNeil River, also within the sanctuary. June visitors make daily guided visits to Mikfik to watch the bears. Mikfik's salmon run ends in late June, and the action shifts to McNeil Falls, where humans are restricted to two gravel viewing pads. Located about a mile above the mouth of the river, the falls is actually a series of small waterfalls, pools, and whitewater rapids. One of the great thrills is to watch these magnificent creatures close at hand. It's not uncommon for the most tolerant bears to eat salmon, take naps, or even nurse cubs within 10 feet of the falls' viewing pads.

MCNEIL RIVER BEARS

Brown bears—the coastal equivalents of grizzlies—are solitary creatures by nature. For them to gather in large numbers and close quarters, as they do at McNeil Falls within McNeil River State Game Sanctuary, is exceptional. That they do so while viewed by humans is even more remarkable.

Larry Aumiller, the sanctuary manager since 1976, attributes this phenomenon to several factors: (1) the presence of salmon, an abundant and reliable energy-rich food source; (2) the lack of other good fishing nearby; (3) the presence of McNeil Falls, which acts as a barrier to the chum salmon, making them easy prey for the bears; and (4) the region's high bear density.

The final piece of the puzzle is people management. Visitors are told: "The bears come first at McNeil River. All human use is of secondary importance." That philosophy led to the sanctuary's highly successful permit system, limiting the number of people at the falls each day. Since the state enacted visitor restrictions, the number of bears visiting the falls has increased dramatically. Even more significant: no bears have been killed in self-defense, and no humans have been injured by bears. This despite thousands of bear-human encounters, often at close range.

"It's widely assumed that bears and people don't mix," says Aumiller. "But here, we've shown that they can mix, if you do the right things. To me, that's the most important message of McNeil: humans can coexist with bears. The first day people come here, many are fearful because of things they've heard or read about bears. But after they've seen a few bears up close and the bears go about their business, people begin to relax. The transformation is almost universal." Instead of irrational fear, visitors learn tolerance and healthy respect. They also learn to understand what Aumiller means when he says, "McNeil is an example of what could be."

A summary of bear-safety tips is available in a free brochure, "Bear Facts." Pick one up at the Alaska Public Lands Information Centers in Anchorage, Fairbanks, Ketchikan, or Tok. Another excellent source is Stephen Herrero's book *Bear Attacks: Their Causes and Avoidance*.

—Bill Sherwonit

ACCESS AND INFORMATION

Located near the northern end of the Alaska Peninsula, along Cook Inlet's western shore, McNeil is accessible by either boat or plane, but nearly all visitors fly into the sanctuary on **FLOATPLANES**. Most arrange for air-taxi flights out of Homer, a coastal community on the lower Kenai Peninsula. The two most commonly used are Bill and Barbara DeCreeft's Kachemak Air Service (907/235-8924; www.alaskaseaplanes.com) and

Beluga Lake Floatplane (907/235-8256; berryman@xyz.net). Once in the sanctuary, all travel is on foot. For information, contact **ALASKA DEPARTMENT OF FISH AND GAME**, Division of Wildlife Conservation (333 Raspberry Rd, Anchorage, AK 99518-1599; 907/267-2182; www.state.ak.us/local/akpages/FISH.GAME).

Permit applications are available from the Alaska Department of Fish and Game. They must be postmarked no later than March 1 and accompanied by a $25 nonrefundable fee. The permit drawing occurs on March 15 of each year. **PERMITS** are for 4-day periods. As many as three people may apply as a group. Visitors pay an additional user fee for the sanctuary—$150 for Alaskans and $350 for nonresidents.

All visitors stay in a designated tent-camping area that also has a wood-fired sauna. Food is stored and cooked in a cabin. Bring sturdy camping gear and be prepared for **WILDERNESS CONDITIONS**. Note that the hike to the falls is 4 miles round-trip and is strenuous. Visitors spend approximately 6 to 8 hours viewing bears each day. **WEATHER** at McNeil Sanctuary is often foggy or rainy, and coastal storms are common. Visitors should be prepared for travel delays when planning their trip.

WILDERNESS LODGES

Chenik Camp

KAMISHAK BAY, PO BOX 956, HOMER, AK 99603; 907/235-8910, FAX 907/235-8911

Located on Kamishak Bay within McNeil River State Game Refuge (which borders the sanctuary), the camp was established in 1978, intended for visitors who wanted to watch and photograph brown bears gathering at Chenik Creek, about 8 miles north of McNeil River. The rustic camp has room for eight guests in three cabins (without indoor plumbing or electricity), a sod-roofed sauna, bath house, and small lodge with dining area, fireplace, library, and picture windows that overlook the ocean. Gourmet meals are served three times daily, including fresh halibut, salmon, and crab. Run by Michael and Diane McBride (who also own Kachemak Bay Wilderness Lodge near Homer), Chenik Camp is open from early June through early August. Five-day packages are $2,250 per person. *No credit cards; checks OK; open early June–early Aug; wildrnes@xyz.net; www.xyz.net\~wildrnes.lodge.htm.*

King Salmon

King Salmon was a U.S. Air Force base during World War II and remained a major military installation until 1994, when the base closed down. Now, only a skeleton maintenance crew of nonmilitary people remains. But the community that grew up around the base continues to do just fine, thanks to the superior runway. People stop here en route to other villages or backcountry destinations in nearby parks and refuges. Fewer than 400 people live here year-round (about 15 percent are Alaska Natives). Most are employed by government or transportation agencies, such as the Alaska Department of Fish and Game, U.S. Fish and Wildlife Service, National Park Service, National Weather Service, and Federal Aviation Administration.

The nature of the town changes dramatically in summer, when seasonal workers arrive to work in Bristol Bay's fishing or tourism industries. From June through September, thousands of tourists come here from around the world, bound for fishing, hunting, wildlife viewing, river floating, and backcountry trekking adventures in nearby wilderness areas.

ACCESS AND INFORMATION

Located along the Naknek River, about 20 miles from Bristol Bay and 290 miles from Anchorage, King Salmon has **AIR SERVICE** year-round with Peninsula Airways (800/448-4226) and Reeve Aleutian Airways (800/544-2248). Alaska Airlines (800/426-0333) flies to King Salmon during the summer season.

Once in King Salmon, it's possible to rent a car, catch a cab, or walk. Most everything in town is within walking distance. Several **AIR-TAXI** operators offer transportation to outlying villages, as well as nearby parks and refuges. **CHARTERS** can be arranged with Branch River Air Service (907/246-3437), C-Air (907/246-6318, fax 907/688-3969; flycair@alaskalife.net), Egli Air Haul (907/246-3554), and King's Flying Service (907/246-4414, fax 907/246-4416; kingair@bristolbay.com). For those going to **BROOKS CAMP** in Katmai National Park, Katmai Air Service (907/246-3079 or 800/544-0551, fax 907/246-6263; katmailand@alaska.net; www.katmailand.net) offers regularly scheduled summer flights. Located at the airport, the **KING SALMON VISITORS CENTER** (PO Box 298, King Salmon, AK 99613; 907/246-4250, fax 907/246-8550; angie_terrellwagner@fws.gov) is open daily in summer.

Make **RESERVATIONS** for airlines and hotels well in advance. King Salmon's three hotels are often filled in summer. The same is true for flights.

A paved road connects King Salmon with **NAKNEK** (15 miles away), as well as Naknek Lake, which offers boat access into Katmai National Park and Preserve. Boats can be rented locally.

RESTAURANTS

Quinault Landing Resort / ★

ALONG THE NAKNEK RIVER, NEAR THE AIRPORT, KING SALMON; 800/770-FISH OR 907/246-6200, SUMMER; FAX 907/246-6200
With large windows looking out at the Naknek River, the restaurant offers the most formal and elegant dining experience in King Salmon. White tablecloths, wine lists, gourmet meals, daily specials, advance reservations—everything you'd expect in a big city. It's also seasonal, open only in summer. Fresh fish and other seafood are served daily, in both appetizers and entrees. *$$–$$$; AE, DC, MC, V; checks OK; breakfast, lunch, dinner every day; closed Oct–May; full bar; www. kingsalmonalaska.com; PO Box 418, King Salmon, AK 99613.* ₠

WILDERNESS LODGES

Mike Cusack's King Salmon Lodge

MILE 1, NAKNEK RIVER RD, KING SALMON, AK 99613; 800/437-2464, OUTSIDE ALASKA, OR 907/246-3452, FAX 907/563-7929
Located on a grassy bluff that overlooks the Naknek River, this has evolved into one of the region's premier fishing lodges. Gourmet meals include fresh salmon, Alaska king crab, filet mignon, duck, pheasant, or quail, plus a selection of premium wines. The dining room has views of both the Naknek River and Mount Katmai. Guests may choose to participate in guided fishing trips. Anglers are flown out to world-class fishing streams and lakes anywhere within a 200-mile radius. The lodge offers a 1-week package for $6,100 per person. *AE, MC, V; checks OK; open mid-June–late Sept; winter address: 3601 C St, Suite 1350, Anchorage, AK 99503; along the Naknek River a short distance from the airport.* ₠

Katmai National Park and Preserve

Declared a national monument in 1918 to preserve the "living laboratory" of a violently explosive 1912 volcanic eruption, Katmai—upgraded to national park status in 1980—is perhaps now best known for its abundance of brown bears. The park's premier attractions are the **VALLEY OF TEN THOUSAND SMOKES** and **BROOKS FALLS**, where up to two dozen bears may be observed fishing for sockeye salmon. The salmon start arriving in early July, bound for spawning grounds in Brooks Lake. As they near the end of their journey, they face one final obstacle: 5-foot-high Brooks Falls. Following the salmon to the falls are brown bears, the coastal equivalents of grizzlies. As many as 60 brown bears inhabit the Brooks River drainage in July, although only rarely do more than a dozen fish the falls at any time.

The bears, in turn, attract humans. Hundreds of people come daily from mid-June through early September to Brooks Falls and nearby **BROOKS CAMP**, which is a park field station, campground, and wilderness lodge. They come to see bears and to fish. The Valley of Ten Thousand Smokes, however, makes an interesting side trip; it was formed by the giant volcanic eruption of Novarupta and subsequent collapse of Mount Katmai in 1912.

Despite the monument's volcanic wonders, Katmai received little attention until the 1940s, when entrepreneur and early bush pilot Ray Petersen established five remote sportfishing camps. The largest was Brooks, which remains the focal point of Katmai tourism. Largely overshadowed by Brooks' bears is the rest of Katmai National Park and Preserve, which includes hundreds of miles of rugged, pristine coastline, 15 active volcanoes belonging to the "Pacific Ring of Fire," two officially designated Wild and Scenic Rivers—the Nonvianuk and Alagnak—and a series of large, connected lakes that form a kayak and canoe route called the **SAVONOSKI LOOP**.

ACCESS AND INFORMATION

Located at the northern end of the Alaska Peninsula, Katmai National Park and Preserve is 300 miles southwest of Anchorage. Most visitors fly into the park through **KING SALMON**. There are several **AIR-TAXI OPERATIONS**, including Branch River Air (907/246-3437), C-Air (907/246-6318, fax 907/688-3969; flycair@alaskalife.net), Egli Air Haul (907/246-3554), and Katmailand (800/544-0551; katmailand@alaska.net; www.katmailand.com).

Prime-time bear-viewing is in July and September. For **PERMITS AND INFORMATION**, contact park headquarters at Katmai National Park and Preserve (PO Box 7, King Salmon, AK 99613; 907/246-3305 or 800/365-2267, fax 907/246-4286; www.nps.gov\katm). There's a campground, visitors center, and ranger station at Brooks Camp, as well as viewing platforms to watch the bears at Brooks Falls and the lower Brooks River. The remainder of the park, however, is undeveloped (with the exception of a few privately owned lodges). Camping is by permit only, within 5 miles of Brooks Camp. Sites at the Brooks campground are determined by lottery. Wilderness travelers may camp anywhere in the park but are asked to pick up a backcountry permit at park headquarters. Clean camping is particularly important in bear country.

With the notable exception of Brooks Camp and a 23-mile road to an overlook of the Valley of Ten Thousand Smokes, Katmai is wilderness with no public facilities. Visitors going beyond Brooks must be self-sufficient and prepared for wilderness travel. A brochure, "Traveling the Katmai Backcountry," is available from park headquarters. The Katmai region has one of the world's highest densities of brown bears, and visitors should understand the do's and don'ts of bear encounters.

At Katmai, the main activity is, of course, watching bears. You can also attend **NATURALIST PROGRAMS**, staged nightly at Brooks Camp; **FISH** for salmon and rainbow trout; or **BACKPACK** through the Valley of Ten Thousand Smokes. **DUMPLING MOUNTAIN** (2,440 feet) makes a good day hike and is accessible from Brooks Camp. Possibilities on the water include **CANOEING OR KAYAKING** the Savonoski Loop, floating the Nonvianuk and Alagnak Rivers, or kayaking along Katmai's remote outer coast.

GUIDES AND OUTFITTERS

Guided hiking and/or river-running trips are offered by **ALASKA RIVER ADVENTURES** (888/836-9027 or 907/595-2000, fax 907/595-1533; www.alaska.net/~fishin/), **ALYESKA WILDERNESS GUIDES** (907/345-4470; awg@alaska.com), and **OUZEL EXPEDITIONS** (907/783-2216, fax 907/783-3220; www.alaska.net/~ouzel). For wildlife viewing and photography trips, contact **KATMAILAND** (800/544-0551; katmailand@alaska.net; www.bearviewing.net and www.katmailand.net); and **JOSEPH VAN OS'S TRAVELWILD EXPEDITIONS** (800/368-0077 or 206/463-5362; www.travelwild.com). **LIFETIME ADVENTURES** (907/746-4644; adventures@matnet.com) offers biking, bear viewing, kayaking, and climbing packages.

Three dozen companies and lodges offer guided fishing services, including **ALASKA TROPHY ADVENTURES** (907/246-8280, fax 907/246-7561; aktrophy@bristolbay.com; www.alaskatrophyadventures.com), **FOX BAY LODGE** (907/246-6234; www.foxbaylodge.com), and **MORRISON GUIDE SERVICE** (907/246-3066; morrison@bristolbay.com). A complete list of guide services and air-taxi operators is available from Katmai headquarters.

WILDERNESS LODGES

Katmailand

4125 AIRCRAFT DR, ANCHORAGE, AK 99502; 800/544-0551 OR 907/243-5448, FAX 907/243-0649

Katmailand operates three fly-in lodges within Katmai National Park. **BROOKS LODGE** was built in the 1940s as a fishing camp, though today most of its guests come to see the brown bears that fish for salmon at nearby Brooks Falls. The lodge looks out over Naknek Lake, with 16 small cabins around it that sleep four guests each. Visitors fish for salmon or rainbow trout, watch and photograph bears, or take the day trip to the Valley of Ten Thousand Smokes. The lodge operates from June to September. Prices range from $433 per person for a 1-day tour to $1,472 per person for 5 days. **KULIK LODGE**, on the Kulik River, offers premier fishing for rainbows and salmon. The spruce-log lodge has a large stone fireplace and bar. Multiday packages include transportation from Anchorage and cost between $1,850 and $4,100 per person. **GROSVENOR LODGE**, on the stream that connects Colville and Grosvenor Lakes, is another sportfishing lodge. There is room for only six guests in three guest cabins with shared bathhouse. Prices range from $1,675 to $2,650 per person. *No credit cards; checks OK; open June–mid-Sept for Brooks Lodge, June–early Oct for the others; katmailand@alaska.net; www.bearviewing.net or www.katmailand.net.*

Katmai Wilderness Lodge

PO BOX 4332, KODIAK, AK 99615; 800/488-8767 OR 907/486-8767, FAX 907/486-6798

On property owned by the Russian Orthodox Church, this lodge is located on Kukak Bay along Katmai's remote outer coast. Brown bear viewing, sea kayaking, and fishing for halibut or salmon are the main attractions. Up to 12 guests stay in the lodge's four log cabins. The 3-night "wilderness package" costs $2,000, including round trip from Kodiak, lodging, meals, guided bear viewing, and fishing. Prime time here for bears is August. *No credit cards; checks OK; open May 15–Sept 15; katbears@ptialaska.net; www.katmai-wilderness.com.*

Dillingham

Commercial fishing has been the heartbeat of this town for more than a century. Bristol Bay's first cannery was built in 1884 at the site of present-day Dillingham, and several more were constructed over the next 17 years. Dillingham's population more than doubles in summer with the arrival of Bristol Bay's world-famous salmon runs. The harbor holds more than 500 boats, and the city-run dock handles more than 10,000 tons of fish and freight annually. Traditionally a Native village, Dillingham's year-round population (2,100) includes a mixture of Eskimos, Aleuts, Athabascans, and non-Natives. About 55 percent of the population is Native. Residents retain subsistence lifestyles consisting of hunting, fishing, trapping, and berry picking. The largest community in the Bristol Bay region, Dillingham has eight churches, a hospital, a health clinic, a public library, a community college, four restaurants, several hotels and bed-and-breakfasts, five taxi companies, nine air-taxi operators, and nearly 200 businesses. The region's climate is maritime, and the weather is often foggy, windy, and wet.

ACCESS AND INFORMATION

Alaska Airlines (800/426-0333) and Peninsula Airways (800/448-4226; www.penair.com) have regularly scheduled hourlong flights from Anchorage. Several local **AIR-TAXI OPERATORS** offer access to the region's parks, refuges, and villages. Among them are Bay Air (907/842-2570, fax 907/842-2470; bayair@nushtel.com), Yute Air (907/842-5333, fax 907/842-1001; www.yuteair.com), Tucker Aviation (907/842-1023, fax 907/842-2600), Starflite (907/842-2486, fax 907/842-5863), and Tikchik Airventures (907/842-5841, fax 907/842-3221; grant@nushtel.com).

For information, contact **DILLINGHAM CHAMBER OF COMMERCE** (PO Box 348, Dillingham, AK 99576; 907/842-5115, fax 907/842-4097; dlgchmbr@nushtel.com; www.nushtel.com/~dlgchmbr).

EXPLORING

Dillingham is a jumping-off point for many backcountry destinations, including Wood-Tikchik State Park, Togiak National Wildlife Refuge, Round Island, several popular spots for river running, and numerous fishing lodges. A 22-mile gravel road connects Dillingham with **ALEK-NAGIK LAKE**, the lowermost lake in the Wood River chain. An espresso bar in Dillingham also serves sandwiches; it's named **JUST BECAUSE**. Located in the library building, the **SAMUEL K. FOX MUSEUM** (907/842-5115) features contemporary and traditional Native arts, crafts, and artifacts, and occasionally hosts traveling exhibits (limited hours).

Wood-Tikchik State Park

Despite its inland setting, this is a water-based park dominated by the Wood River and the spectacular Tikchik Lakes. Snowcapped mountains, low tundra, and interconnected clearwater lakes, some 45 miles long, characterize the region. Everything from grizzlies and moose to porcupines, river otters, and loons inhabits the park's forests and tundra, but best known are the fish. Lakes and streams here provide critical spawning habitat for the five species of Pacific salmon. They also support healthy populations of rainbow and lake trout, arctic char, grayling, and pike. This has long been known as a fisherman's paradise. Today it is becoming increasingly popular with water adventurers, such as kayakers and rafters, who travel its interconnected river and lake systems.

ACCESS AND INFORMATION

Located in the Bristol Bay region, 325 miles southwest of Anchorage, Wood-Tikchik is easiest to reach **BY PLANE** through Dillingham. Flying into the park are Bay Air (907/842-2570, fax 907/842-2470; bayair@nushtel.com), Tikchik Airventures (907/842-5841, fax 907/842-3221; grant@nushtel.com), Starflite (907/842-2486, fax 907/842-5863), and Yute Air (907/842-5333, fax 907/842-1001; www.yuteair.com). Once in the park, the easiest way to get around is by boat via the Wood River and Tikchik Lakes systems.

Managed as a wild area, Wood-Tikchik has no trails and only four "developed" camping areas with a total of 12 sites. Most are very primitive. A backcountry cabin, available to visitors on a first-come, first-served basis for up to 3 nights, is located near the mouth of Lake Beverly. For general information, contact **WOOD-TIKCHIK STATE PARK** (summer: PO Box 3022, Dillingham, AK 99576; 907/842-2375. Oct–May: 3601 C St, Ste 1200, Anchorage, AK 99503-5921; 907/269-8698; www.dnr.state.ak.us\parks).

ADVENTURES

You can **FLOAT** either the Wood River or Tikchik Lakes systems and **FISH** for rainbow trout and salmon. The park's most popular fly-in float trip is the 85-mile journey from Lake Kulik to Aleknagik, a Yup'ik Eskimo village east of Dillingham. Though it can be done in less than a week, paddlers are advised to give themselves at least 10 days to 2 weeks. The other popular trip begins at Nishlik Lake and ends at Tikchik Lake, a distance of about 60 miles. Those who float the Nuyakuk River below Tikchik Lake should use extreme caution; portages are necessary to get past the Nuyakuk Rapids and Nuyakuk Falls.

Outfitters that run **GUIDED RIVER TRIPS** through Wood-Tikchik include Alaska River Adventures (907/595-2000, fax 907/595-1533; www.alaskanet/~fishin/) and Wilderness Birding Adventures (907/694-7442; wildbird@alaska.net). Alaska Recreational River Guides (907/376-8655) offers guided fishing trips. Tikchik State Park Tours (907/243-1416 or 888/345-2445; info@tikchik.com; www.tikchik.com) does guided kayaking, trekking, river-floating, and fishing trips in the Tikchik Lakes system.

WILDERNESS LODGES

Royal Coachman Lodge

PO BOX 450, DILLINGHAM, AK 99576; 907/868-6032 OR 907/842-2725, SUMMER; 207/474-8691, WINTER; FAX 907/868-6033, SUMMER, 207/474-3231, WINTER

A floatplane-accessible fishing lodge in the heart of the nation's largest state park, Gary Merrill's Royal Coachman Lodge lies at the outlet of Tikchik Lake, on the Nuyakuk River. Guests stay in comfortable cabins. Experienced fishing guides take guests to streams and lakes throughout the Wood-Tikchik State Park and Togiak Refuge, but there's also excellent fishing right at the lodge. No more than 12 guests at a time are hosted for a week's stay. Cost is $4,950 per person per week. Gary and Heather Merrill also operate Lower Nushagak King Salmon Camp and Kanektok Wilderness Camp, one of only two fishing camps in the Togiak Refuge wilderness. *AE, DIS, MC, V; checks OK; open early June–Sept; gmerrill@somtel.com; www.Royalcoachmanlodge.com; winter address: RFD #1, PO Box 2140, Skowhegan, ME 04976.*

Tikchik Narrows Lodge

PO BOX 220248, ANCHORAGE, AK 99522; 907/243-8450, FAX 907/248-3091
Located on a narrow peninsula between Nuyukuk and Tikchik Lakes, Bud Hodson's lodge has a view of the ruggedly beautiful Kilbuck Mountains. More than 50 miles from the nearest road and accessible only by floatplane, it sits deep within Wood-Tikchik State Park. Guests stay in cabins. The main lodge has a stone fireplace and a panoramic view of the surrounding park. Meals include freshly baked breads and pastries, and entrees ranging from sauteed halibut to roast beef with Yorkshire pudding. Guests fish the waters of this parkland, as well as neighboring Togiak National Wildlife Refuge. The weeklong stay includes daily guided fishing trips and costs $5,400 per person. *No credit cards; checks OK; open mid-June–Sept; info@tikchiklodge.com; www.tikchiklodge.com.*

Walrus Islands State Game Sanctuary

Each year, in spring and summer, thousands of male walrus gather on this group of seven islands in Bristol Bay. The females and young travel north to spend their summers in the Bering and Chukchi Seas. Scientists still aren't sure exactly why males stay behind. However, what is clear is that the walrus bulls use these islands as resting places in between food binges. Because of their importance to these creatures, the seven Walrus Islands and adjacent waters were given special "protected" status in 1960. The centerpiece of the sanctuary is **ROUND ISLAND**, a small (2 miles long by 1 mile wide) and rugged piece of ground where thousands of walrus congregate in spring as the pack ice begins its annual retreat. For the next 7 months, these huge fellows (some weigh up to 2 tons) spend their time alternately gorging on invertebrates such as clams and snails, then hauling out on the rocks and resting up for the next binge.

ACCESS AND INFORMATION

Round Island is located about 30 miles from the mainland. Most visitors get there by **CHARTERING A BOAT** ride with Don Winkelman's Round

Island Boat Charters (907/493-5127; dwinkkyahr@aol.com), based at the Togiak Fisheries cannery, or with Terry Johnson's Walrus Island Expeditions (907/842-2102; www.alaskawalrusisland.com), which operates out of Dillingham. To reach the Togiak cannery, take a plane from Dillingham to either Togiak or Twin Hills. Several airlines and **AIR-TAXI OPERATORS** fly between Dillingham and Togiak, including Peninsula Airways (800/448-4226; www.penair.com), Tucker Aviation (907/842-1023, fax 907/842-2600), and Yute Air (907/842-5333, fax 907/842-1001; www.yuteair.com). The boat ride takes 1 to 3 hours from Togiak, depending on the seas. Johnson's tours combine a plane ride from Dillingham to Togiak with a 1½–2½-hour boat trip into the Walrus Islands sanctuary.

Once at Round Island, visitors are met by sanctuary staff, who assist in transferring people and gear to shore. Travel on the island is entirely by foot. Round Island has by far the largest gathering of walrus of all the islands. The best time is June through August. Only 12 people at a time are allowed to camp on Round Island. Permits for a 5-day block of time are issued on a first-come, first-served basis. Applications must be sent to the Alaska Department of Fish and Game, accompanied by a $50 fee. For **PERMIT APPLICATIONS AND INFORMATION**, contact Alaska Department of Fish and Game, Division of Wildlife Conservation (PO Box 1030, Dillingham, AK 99576-1030; 907/842-2334, fax 907/842-5514; www.state.ak.us/adfg).

Round Island is a rugged, often stormy place, and anyone who goes there should be in good physical condition, prepared for **WILDERNESS CONDITIONS**. Visitors should also anticipate weather delays when making travel plans. Visitors are required to bring their own camping gear. Tents should be expedition quality, capable of withstanding 60mph winds. Two wildlife technicians are stationed on the island to conduct research and enforce sanctuary regulations. They are not tour guides. Visitors should be prepared to fend for themselves. Visitors are expected to stay on the island's trail system and within designated viewing areas. Beaches are off-limits to minimize disturbances to resting walrus.

Bethel

This is not the picture-book part of Alaska with green forests and snow-capped mountains, nor is it part of the popular tourist circuit. The Yukon-Kuskokwim Delta is flat and almost treeless. But the longer you are there, the more extraordinary you'll find its beauty.

This is the home of the most traditional Native population in Alaska—the Yup'ik Eskimos. From Platinum to Kotlik, from Stony River to Tuntutuliak, from Grayling to Emmonak, they live in 46 villages scattered over 76,000 square miles. It is a vast, wet expanse of land with twisted, convoluted rivers and streams, myriad lakes, and soggy tundra. For anyone outside the culture, the names of many of the villages are often unpronounceable—words such as Chuathbaluk, Kwigiumpain-ukamiut, and Mamterillermiut. The last is the original Eskimo name for the town we know today as Bethel.

Bethel (pop. 5,000) is the hub of the region—a ramshackle assort- ment of buildings on the western bank of the Kuskokwim River. Next to the Yukon River, the Kuskokwim is the second-longest river in Alaska. This is bird country, and subsistence fishing is a way of life. In 1885, the Moravian Church sent missionaries to the area to establish a church and school here. They took the name Bethel from the Holy Scriptures. In Hebrew, it means "House of God." But, once here, the missionaries ignored the advice of the local shaman about the siting of their mission. He warned them that the riverbank would fall away underneath their home and the water would sweep it downstream. They thought this was only superstition. But, rather, it was the forces of nature—weather, wind, and water—correctly interpreted. Consequently, over the past 100 years, Bethel residents have been dragging their homes away from the banks of the river on a consistent basis, and the town has moved farther and far- ther inland.

Until about 1984, the most modern attempt at controlling this ero- sion was to take junked cars and push them over the bank to make a type of bulwark. It, too, ultimately failed. But the sight of 1959 Ramblers and Willys jeeps tilted on the bank at 50-degree angles, as if some phantom were about to drive them into the river, made an unforgettable picture. The present seawall, constructed by the Army Corps of Engineers, is more sturdy, but Bethel lost some of its charm with the departure of the junkers.

The river defines the way of life here. Most Native folks spend time at fish camps along its banks in the summer, go duck hunting on the delta in spring, pick berries in the fall, and take their skiffs upriver to hunt moose for the winter. Traditional clothing is still worn.

ACCESS AND INFORMATION

Regularly scheduled daily FLIGHTS are available, winter and summer, to both Bethel and Aniak on Alaska Airlines (800/426-0333). Reeve Aleut- ian Airways (907/543-3154, in Bethel, or 800/544-2248) also flies daily between Anchorage and Bethel. Check the Peninsula Airways (800/448- 4226) flight schedule too.

The CITY OF BETHEL may be reached at PO Box 388, Bethel, AK 99559; 907/543-2047. The YUGTARVIK MUSEUM AND CULTURAL CENTER (907/543-1819) opened in 1995 and features exhibits on the ancient and contemporary times of the Yup'ik and Chup'ik peoples. It is well worth a visit and is open afternoons Tuesday through Saturday. The gift shop has many local arts and crafts of the region.

GUIDES AND OUTFITTERS

LAMONT ALBERTSON / A warm-hearted, no-nonsense, burly fellow, former mayor of Aniak, Lamont Albertson is the best sportfishing guide in the Aniak-Bethel-Kuskokwim region. He has fished, lived, raised his family, and taught school in this part of Alaska for more than 30 years. His guided fishing trips have a naturalist/educational bent to them with strong emphasis on catch-and-release. His tent camp, 45 miles up the beautiful little Aniak River, is reached by jet boat from the village of Aniak. All five species of Pacific salmon and the northernmost population of naturally occurring rainbow trout in the world swim here, as well as Dollies, arctic char, and grayling. Bears, moose, and caribou wander close to camp—sometimes right through. Lamont's wife, Sheryll, does the cooking and you'll eat like a king—salmon, king crab, wild game, and a vast array of local blueberry dishes. Fishing is good mid-June to September. Cost is $250 to $500 per person per day. PO Box 91, Aniak, AK 99557; 907/675-4380, March–Oct; 352/498-0225, Nov–Feb.

FESTIVALS AND EVENTS

THE KUSKOKWIM 300 / Held every year at the end of January, this is one of the most popular sled-dog races in Alaska and a qualifier for the Iditarod Race. It starts in Bethel, runs a course down the Kuskokwim River, turns around in Aniak, and dashes back. With a purse of $100,000, it is the second-richest long-distance dog race in the world, next to the Iditarod. For more information, call headquarters near race time (907/543-3300).

CAMAI DANCE FESTIVAL / Held the last weekend of March, this is a welcoming festival of dances. In the Yup'ik language, *camai* means "hello." This is a regional festival of special importance. Despite the efforts of missionaries to suppress this traditional form of expression, it never disappeared in Southwest Alaska. In the past 15 years, it has seen a resurgence, with many villages sponsoring youth dance groups led by village elders who teach the songs, drumming, and movements. The festival takes place in the Bethel High School gym, which is filled to capacity during the three days and nights of dancing. Each village gets an hour to perform. These are not actors pretending to demonstrate a culture; this is the real thing. Count yourself lucky if you get to witness this festival. For more information, call (907/543-2911).

LODGINGS

Bentley's Porter House Bed and Breakfast

624 1ST AVE, BETHEL, AK 99559; 907/543-3552, FAX 907/543-3230
Bentley's overlooks the Kuskokwim River and is a block from downtown. From the second floor, you can see the famous Bethel seawall, the river, and the start of the Kuskokwim 300, if you're there in the right season. A big, friendly place with 24 rooms, encompassing the main house and three smaller homes, Bentley's serves family-style breakfasts, with good food and plenty of it. Choose rooms upstairs in the main house for the best views and light. Room rates range from $92 for a single to $127 for a double. *$$; AE, DIS, MC, V; checks OK; PO Box 529, Bethel, AK 99559; downtown, on the river.*

Pacifica Guesthouse

1220 HOFFMAN HWY, BETHEL, AK 99559; 907/543-4305
This hotel is a mile or two out of town, on the way in from the airport. There's a simple, Northern European feel to it. There are 35 rooms, some with private bath. If you really want to be luxurious (by Bush standards), go Las Vegas in one of their 10 suites ($150 for a double). Each has a private bath and sitting room with furnishings that once graced the Las Vegas Hilton years ago. A single room with shared bath is $90 and a double room with shared bath is $100. *$$$; AE, DIS, MC, V; checks OK; PO Box 1208, Bethel, AK 99559; 1½ miles from the airport, toward downtown.* &

Yukon Delta National Wildlife Refuge

Each spring, millions of birds return to the Yukon-Kuskokwim Delta, where they nest and raise their young on the wetlands. Birds come from all over North America as well as from continents that border the Pacific Ocean. Most notable are brant, geese, ducks, and swans. This is the nation's largest refuge. Most of it is tundra, interwoven with countless ponds, lakes, sloughs, marshes, and meandering streams, including Alaska's two longest waterways: the **YUKON AND KUSKOKWIM RIVERS**. One-third of the refuge's acreage is water. Not surprisingly, given the abundance of fish, birds, and other wildlife, the delta has been home to Yup'ik Eskimo people for thousands of years.

ACCESS AND INFORMATION

The only companies with permits to operate **AIR TAXIS** in the refuge are Yukon Aviation (907/543-3280, fax 907/543-3244), Ptarmigan Air (888/868-8008, or 907/543-5225), and Kusko Aviation (907/543-3279, fax 907/556-8822). Also offering transportation from Bethel to outlying villages are Yute Air (907/543-3003; www.yuteair.com) and Craig Air (907/543-2575, fax 907/543-3602; craigair@unicom/alaska.com). There are **NO VISITOR FACILITIES** within the refuge itself. For further information, contact **YUKON DELTA NATIONAL WILDLIFE REFUGE** (PO Box 346, Bethel, AK 99559-0346; 907/543-3151, fax 907/543-4413; www.r7.fws.gov/nwr/yd/ydnwr.html).

The prime time to visit the delta is **MID-MAY TO LATE JUNE**, when the weather is best and breeding season is at its peak. Fishing and river floating are best from June to September. Among the outfits who provide guided hunting, birding, or wildlife viewing/photography trips are Yukon Delta Tours (907/949-1928, fax 907/949-1931) and Nunivak Island Experiences (907/827-8512).

Some villages, such as Chevak and Emmonak, are starting up **CULTURAL TOURS** that may include trips into the refuge. Contact the refuge for more information. **MOSQUITOES** and biting insects can sometimes be intolerable, especially in lowland areas, during midsummer.

Besides the Yukon and Kuskokwim, other rivers popular with boaters, anglers, and wildlife watchers are the **KISARALIK RIVER**, a Kuskokwim tributary, and the **ANDREAFSKY RIVER**, a Yukon tributary. Nunivak Island offers opportunities to see musk ox, reindeer, marine mammals, and birds.

ALASKA PENINSULA AND ALEUTIAN ISLANDS

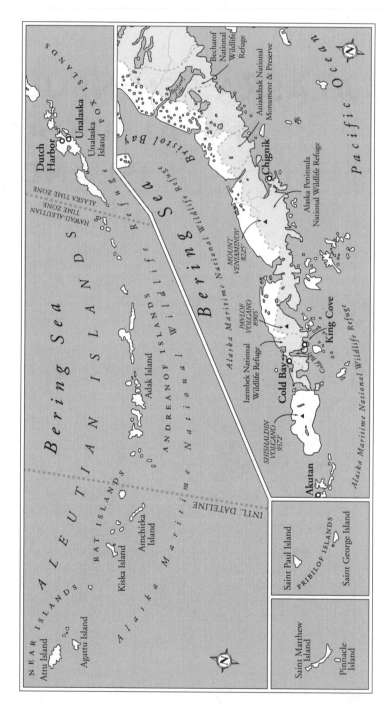

NEAR ISLANDS
Attu Island
Agattu Island

ALEUTIAN ISLANDS

RAT ISLANDS
Kiska Island
Amchitka Island

Alaska Maritime National Wildlife Refuge

INTL. DATELINE

Bering Sea

ANDREANOF ISLANDS
Adak Island

Alaska Maritime National Wildlife Refuge

Bering Sea

FOX ISLANDS

Unalaska
Dutch Harbor
Unalaska Island

HAWAII-ALEUTIAN TIME ZONE
ALASKA TIME ZONE

Akutan

SHISHALDIN VOLCANO 9372'

Cold Bay

Izembek National Wildlife Refuge

King Cove

PAVLOF VOLCANO 8905'

Alaska Maritime National Wildlife Refuge

MOUNT VENIAMINOF 8225'

Alaska Peninsula National Wildlife Refuge

Chignik

Aniakchak National Monument & Preserve

Becharof National Wildlife Refuge

Bristol Bay

Pacific Ocean

Saint Paul Island
PRIBILOF ISLANDS
Saint George Island

Saint Matthew Island
Pinnacle Island

ALASKA PENINSULA AND ALEUTIAN ISLANDS

Sweeping away from Alaska's mainland, the Alaska Peninsula and Aleutian Island Chain stretch more than 1,500 miles toward Siberia, separating the North Pacific Ocean from the Bering Sea. Mere dots in the vast waters of the Bering Sea are the Pribilof Islands, a tiny volcanic archipelago whose geologic origins are tied to the peninsula and the Aleutian Chain. All are part of the Pacific basin's "Ring of Fire."

The region encompasses some of Alaska's most remote, inaccessible, and rugged country. Volcanoes, earthquakes, wind, and oceans carve the landscape. From a seismic and volcanic perspective, this is one of the most turbulent regions in the world. More than 70 volcanoes have been identified, many of them active. Among the most active are Akutan, with 33 eruptions; Shishaldin, which has erupted 35 times; and Pavlof, with 41 eruptions. Pavlof is on the lower Alaska Peninsula, while the other two are in the Aleutians. The Aleutian and Pribilof Islands are actually the tops of large, submerged mountains. Among the most spectacular volcanic landforms in the region are the Aniakchak Caldera, the Aghileen Pinnacles, Ukrinek Maars (craters), and the mountains Pavlof, Veniaminov, and Peulik.

This is the traditional home of the Aleut people, distant cousins of the Eskimos. Many still supplement their income with subsistence lifestyles, dependent on the harvest of fish, wild game, berries, and other foods from the sea. There are few roads (all of them local and isolated, and none more than 50 miles long) and no paved highways. Of the region's two dozen villages, 15 have fewer than 200 year-round residents. The largest community, Unalaska/Dutch Harbor, has a population of less than 4,000.

Biologically, the waters of the North Pacific, the Bering Sea, and Bristol Bay are among the richest on earth. They support a billion-dollar fishing industry (though a growing number of scientists, conservationists, and Natives of the region fear overfishing is taking its toll on the region's sea life). A few coastal villages boom dramatically in summer, as fishermen and cannery workers from Outside arrive for the lucrative salmon and bottomfish harvests. King Cove's population more than doubles during the fishing season. Egegik, on the shores of Bristol Bay, jumps from 120 residents in winter to more than 1,000 in summer. The other main employer since World War II (until recently) was the military. (The Aleutians were the site of one of the bloodiest battles in the Pacific.)

Wildlife, too, arrives in spectacular numbers, all dependent on the ocean's bounty. Forty million seabirds are seasonal residents. The coastal cousin of the grizzly—the brown bear—grows to enormous proportions on a high-protein diet of salmon, which spawn in vast numbers in the clear lakes and streams of the peninsula. The sea coast boasts an abundance of marine mammals—sea lions, seals, otters, whales, and porpoises—yet there are distressing signs that even the rich North Pacific–Bering Sea ecosystem is under stress. Two once-plentiful species—sea lions and harbor seals—have experienced dramatic declines in recent decades.

ACCESS AND INFORMATION

The principal means of travel is **BY AIR**. Alaska Airlines (800/426-0333), Reeve Aleutian Airways (800/544-2248 or 907/243-4700), and Peninsula Airways, (800/448-4226 or 907/243-2323), provide regularly scheduled passenger service to Chignik, Cold Bay, Sand Point, and Dutch Harbor. Round trip costs an average of $500 to $800. Aleutian Air, Ltd. (907/581-1686), in Unalaska, offers charter service to neighboring islands, including the Pribilofs.

For those with flexible schedules, the state ferry MV *Tustumena*, known as "The Trusty Tusty," services Homer and Kodiak from March through October; the trip takes 3 to 4 days, depending on where you embark. En route it stops at five towns—Chignik, Sand Point, King Cove, Cold Bay, and Dutch Harbor. For reservations, call 800/642-0066.

Anyone traveling to this region must be prepared for **WEATHER DELAYS**, sometimes lasting several days. Weather often can be violent and stormy. **BROWN BEARS** are abundant throughout much of the Alaska Peninsula. Take precautions to avoid unwanted encounters. Boil or filter water before drinking to prevent giardia, an intestinal disorder caused by a waterborne parasite. Parks and refuges within this region generally have **NO VISITOR FACILITIES**. If you plan to explore the backcountry, come prepared for wilderness camping and travel.

Unalaska/Dutch Harbor

The history of this far-flung community mirrors the history of Alaska. More than 8,000 years ago, the ancestors of the Aleuts arrived in this new land. Much, much later, in the 18th century, Russian fur hunters discovered a rich treasure chest here in the soft, black, velvety fur of the playful sea otter. By the turn of the century, whales and gold had lured waves of fortune hunters and ships to sail north along this coast.

For a long time, the village of Unalaska on Unalaska Island, with its charming onion-domed church, was the main town on the Aleutian Chain. During the gold-rush era, Unalaska and her little neighbor, Dutch Harbor, swelled with thousands of hopeful gold seekers on their way north. Some called her "the bawdy queen of the Alaska Gold Coast." As the gold began to taper off, though, Unalaska was left almost a ghost town. Business boomed again during World War II, when it became a strategic naval base. After the war, it lay deserted. Not so today. Beginning with the rich and dangerous king crab industry, which took off in the 1960s, the pendulum of history has swung back again. Today fortunes are mined from beneath the sea.

The big money is in fish and crab. The city of Unalaska and the International Port of Dutch Harbor (Unalaska/Dutch Harbor) are the number-one fishing port in the United States, measured in both pounds of fish processed and total dollar value delivered. Unalaska is a working town with an international flavor. On any one day, Russian, Japanese, and Korean vessels are waiting in the harbor to pick up fish products and cargo to freight back home.

For many visitors, the military aspect is perhaps the most interesting. There's a partially sunken war ship in one of the bays left over from World War II. Old trails zigzag up the sides of the mountains, leading to former defense garrisons. (The zigzagging was to avoid strafing by Japanese war planes.)

Weather is characterized by wind and water, fog and ferocious gales. Clear blue skies on average happen about 10 days out of the year. During the war, American forces in the Aleutians lost two men to weather and frostbite to every one killed by enemy gunfire. As the soldiers stationed out here used to say, "It doesn't rain in the Aleutians. It rains in Asia and blows over."

The town is divided into two sections by a bridge known locally as "The Bridge to the Other Side." The Unalaska side, on massive Unalaska Island, is home to the original village site, most homes, businesses, and city offices. The Dutch Harbor side, on neighboring Amaknak Island, is the site of the state airport and most industry. Mariners long ago incorrectly christened the whole community Dutch Harbor, after the place they dropped anchor, and that's what airline schedules and many Outsiders call it, but locals know the city is officially Unalaska. The Chamber of Commerce compromises by calling it "Unalaska/Dutch Harbor"— so, take your pick!

ACCESS AND INFORMATION

For information on fishing excursions, birding, sightseeing tours, historical tours, flight-seeing, hotels, restaurants and special events, visit the **UNALASKA/DUTCH HARBOR CONVENTION & VISITORS BUREAU** (907/581-2612, fax 907/581-2613; updhcvb@arctic.net; www.arctic. net/~updhcvb). See also the Access and Information section at the beginning of this chapter.

HALIBUT, "THE OLD WOMAN OF THE SEA"

Unalaska is one of the best-kept secrets of big-game fishermen. The icy Bering Sea is home to some of the largest halibut in the world, measuring more than 8 feet in length and tipping the scales at 400-plus pounds. These monsters are so big fishermen call them "barn doors," because that's what it feels like when you're pulling one off the bottom of the ocean.

Halibut from Unalaska made headlines in the summer of 1995 when fishermen landed three whoppers, ranging from 347 to 439 pounds. The next summer, a world record was set with a 459-pounder hauled out of Unalaska Bay.

Fishermen out here say it's only a matter of time until someone sets another world record. The visitors bureau is even banking on it. They put up a $100,000 prize in the local halibut derby, held annually from June through September, to lure some lucky fisherman on to glory. All you have to do is top the record halibut of 459 pounds as well as have a derby ticket in your pocket. It's tricky, though. Rules of the International Game Fish Association demand that the fish be gaffed, not shot, before landing. Trying to wrestle a 400-pound fish into your boat is more than challenging. The 1996 derby winner, fishing from a small skiff, solved that problem by towing his 439-pound catch to shore rather than swamping his boat.

If you're just fishing for dinner, the tastiest halibut are actually in the 20- to 60-pound class. Because the largest and oldest fish are the females and thus produce generations more halibut (that's why Native fishermen respectfully called the halibut "the old woman of the sea"), charter owners often will encourage you to release those that aren't derby-winning size. But Unalaska fishermen have dreams that go beyond the derby. They all swear that somewhere out there is "The Ultimate Halibut," a fish that will break the 500-pound mark. Perhaps, she's waiting for *you*.

—Carol M. Sturgulewski

EXPLORING

CHURCH OF THE HOLY ASCENSION / A National Historic Landmark, this Russian Orthodox cathedral has been a symbol of Unalaska and part of its distinctive charm since its construction in 1895. The first church here was built under the sharp eye of Father Veniaminov in 1826. Later canonized as Saint Innocent, he was a singularly impressive fellow who mastered the *baidarka* (an early form of kayak) so that he could paddle a thousand miles through the Aleutians to tend his flock. A recently completed church restoration has brought new luster to the largest collection of Russian Orthodox artifacts in Alaska, including some that date back to Veniaminov's time. Work still continues on restoring church icons and the neighboring Bishop's House. Tours are available by appointment; call 907/581-6404.

MUSEUM OF THE ALEUTIANS / This new museum, opened in 1999, is the first ever to exclusively feature the Aleutian and Pribilof Islands. Many collections that have been scattered at museums around the world are gradually being brought home. Exhibits begin with Aleut prehistory dating back 9,000 years and follow the Russian occupation, gold rush, World War II, and the fisheries of the past century. Located at Salmon Way near the Grand Aleutian Hotel, the museum also sponsors summer **ARCHAEOLOGICAL DIGS**, which you can join for an hour, a week, or a month. No experience is needed; if you'd rather work indoors, the museum also welcomes volunteers to work with the laboratory and collections. Call 907/581-5150.

REMNANTS OF WORLD WAR II / Bunkers, pillboxes, tunnels, the remains of old Quonset huts, zigzag trails all over the hills, and a sunken ship in the harbor are visible reminders of the military presence here and the fierce battle for the Aleutians. Hike up **BUNKER HILL**, visit **MEMORIAL PARK**, walk along **UNALASKA LAKE**, and note where modern Unalaska has converted military leftovers into homes and businesses. There's even a pillbox next to the school playground.

ADVENTURES

HIKING THE MOUNTAINS / On Unalaska there are no bears, no trees to block your view, and bugs tend to get blown away by the sea breezes. The island does have, however, lots of bald eagles and red foxes and a profusion of wildflowers, birds, and berries. Salmonberries are ripe in August, followed by blueberries, which can be picked as late as November some years. **MOUNT MAKUSHIN** (6,680 feet), a steaming volcano, is the highest mountain on the island. Some of the popular hikes close to town are **PYRAMID PEAK** (2,136 feet), rising to the south, and **MOUNT BALLYHOO** (1,589 feet), on the Dutch Harbor side. They say this mountain was named by the famous writer Jack London on his way to the gold fields in Nome around the turn of the century. Every July there's a rigorous scramble up to its summit called the **BALLYHOO RUN**.

Most of the land on the island is privately owned by the Native people. In order to hike, ski, bike, or camp on the land, please first obtain a **PERMIT** from the Ounalashka Corporation (907/581-1276) on Salmon Way, near the Grand Aleutian Hotel. Topo **MAPS** (as well as an espresso bar) are located at **NICKY'S PLACE** (907/581-1570) on the Front Beach. Nicky's also features works by local artists, a surprisingly large and talented pool for such a small community. Open every day, with the exception of "especially sunny days," Nicky's also will open after hours "for coffee emergencies and for those who work late or fish hard."

FISHING / The **ILIULIUK RIVER**, which runs out of Unalaska Lake into Iliuliuk Harbor, teems with salmon in the summer. As it flows past the onion-shaped domes of the cathedral, it is in full view of bald eagles sitting atop the spires, watching their dinner passing by on the fin. The really big fish here, though, are **HALIBUT**. Unalaska is home to the International Game Fish Association's world-champion halibut, weighing in at 459 pounds. Local charter operations make an art of going after the big ones. Fishing licenses may be purchased at local grocery or fish supply stores.

GUIDES AND OUTFITTERS

Bobbie Lekanof's **EXTRA MILE TOURS** (907/581-6171) focuses on birdwatching and wildflowers. Patricia Lekanof-Gregory's **ALEUT TOURS** (907/581-6001) offers a 2-hour bus tour with an emphasis on Aleut and Russian history. **DAN PARRETT PHOTOGRAPHY** (907/581-5175) and Scott Darsney's **WILD MOUNTAIN IMAGES** (907/581-1312) both assist camera bugs in Aleutian photo safaris. Marlaine Skelly offers day trips or longer expeditions in her 45-foot metal motorsailer via **ALEUTIAN SPIRIT ADVENTURES** (907/581-3118). **ALEUTIAN ADVENTURE SPORTS** (888/581-4489) provides guided backpacking and sea kayaking trips around Unalaska and neighboring islands. **VOLCANO BAY ADVENTURES** (907/581-3414) offers guided salmon and trout fishing, hiking, and birdwatching. **FAR WEST OUTFITTERS** (907/581-1647) specializes in marine tours, fishing charters, and sightseeing on the 32-foot boat *Suzanne Marie* or the *Silver Cloud*. Skipper Henry Olsen has overseen the landing of some of the biggest halibut taken in these waters. Other local fishing charters include **AVI CHARTERS** (907/581-5960), with skipper Andy McCracken; **SUREGOOD ADVENTURES** (907/581-2378), with Dan and Chris Graves and Peter Thompson; and **DAN MAGONE'S** 32-foot commercial fishing boat *Lucille* (907/581-5949).

RESTAURANTS

The Chart Room / ★★★

AIRPORT BEACH RD, UNALASKA; 907/581-3844

Located in the Grand Aleutian Hotel with windows overlooking Margaret Bay, the Chart Room is quite posh and no more expensive than a nice restaurant in Anchorage, but you'll rarely see anyone in a tie or high heels. Get a happy start to your evening with a drink by the fireplace in the Cape Cheerful Lounge. It's no big surprise that from this island's vantage point, facing out to the ocean with the Bering Sea in its backyard, halibut, salmon, shrimp, squid, and other fish and shellfish are star players in the Chart Room's North Pacific Rim cuisine. The wine selection is quite good and reasonably priced. Locals crowd in for the lavish Sunday brunch and Wednesday evening seafood buffet. *$$; AE, DC, DIS, MC, V; local checks only; dinner every day, brunch Sun; full bar; Pouch 503, Dutch Harbor, AK 99692; in the Grand Aleutian Hotel on the Dutch Harbor side.* &

Tino's Steakhouse

11 N 2ND ST, DUTCH HARBOR; 907/581-4288
Tino's is an example of the Unalaska melting pot. Its menu includes American steaks and hamburgers, but for locals the big draw is the Mexican side of the menu. Nachos, burritos, tostadas, and chile specialties cover the plates, in hefty servings designed for hardworking, hungry fishermen. *$$; MC, V, local checks only; breakfast, lunch, dinner every day; beer and wine; on Broadway, near the church.*

LODGINGS

Carl's Bayview Inn / ★

606 BAYVIEW, UNALASKA, AK 99685; 907/581-1230 OR 800/581-1230
On the Unalaska side of town, a stone's throw from the Russian Orthodox church, this is a roomy and comfortable inn with homey touches and a well-connected host. Carl Moses is a state legislator in the Alaska House of Representatives, with a district that covers Bristol Bay through the Aleutian Islands. With a view over Iliuliuk Bay (when it's not too foggy), the inn is next door to Carl's general store, which is as general a store as you've ever been in. You can buy anything here from a fishing boat to a thimble. The inn has about 30 rooms. Prices vary: $90 for a basic room with shower; $125 for a studio with kitchenette; $150 for a suite with kitchen, like a small apartment; and $175 for the best suite in the house. The inn also has a live band, playing country and rock 'n' roll, five nights a week. *$$; DIS, MC, V; checks OK; full bar, Bayview Lounge; Bayview@arctic.net.* & *(one room only)*

The Grand Aleutian / ★★★

AIRPORT BEACH RD NEAR MARGARET BAY, DUTCH HARBOR, AK 99692; 907/581-3844 OR 800/891-1194
Some call it "The Grand Illusion"—a fancy hotel seemingly at the end of the world and in another time zone. But it is fancy without pretension and certainly the most comfortable place in Unalaska. From its opening in 1994, it quickly became the hangout for all the local movers and shakers. Here's where you'll find the big muckety-mucks in the fish business. It's also perfect for tourists who want familiarity. Most nights during peak fishing season, there is live music and dancing. All rooms have a view of Margaret Bay, Unalaska Bay, or Mount Ballyhoo. Their tour operation—Grand Aleutian Tours—offers a selection of excursions, such as charter fishing, birding, nature hikes, island tours, marine tours, and

mountain biking. The hotel offers a special package for those wishing to work on the Museum of the Aleutians archaeological dig during the day and relax over gourmet meals at night. *$$; AE, DC, DIS, MC, V; local checks only; full bar; www.ansi.net/~grand_aleutian; 5 minutes from the airport on Airport Beach Rd at Margaret Bay on the Dutch Harbor side.* &

Aniakchak National Monument and Preserve

This is one of the nation's wildest and least-visited parklands. On the Alaska Peninsula, 450 miles southwest of Anchorage, its principal feature and attraction is the **ANIAKCHAK CALDERA**. Six miles across, the caldera was created thousands of years ago by the collapse of a large volcano, following an eruption geologists say was much larger than the one at Mount St. Helens in 1980. Still active, Aniakchak last erupted in 1931.

When first viewed from a plane, the caldera looks like a moonscape, bleak and desolate. But, surprisingly, with a closer view, one finds a myriad of life—plants, mammals, and birds. Sockeye salmon swim up the Aniakchak River into the caldera through a break in the crater wall called "The Gates." They then spawn in the blue-green waters of Surprise Lake.

Even in midsummer, weather in the Aniakchak Caldera may become violent. The caldera creates its own microclimate, and its interior is subject to severe windstorms and heavy rains. Campers have had their tents ripped apart by 100mph gales, and high winds can stir up volcanic ash clouds to an elevation of 6,000 feet.

ACCESS AND INFORMATION

If you visit the caldera, you're likely to have it all to yourself. Fewer than 100 people visit it annually (not including flight-seers). Because of its remote location and fly-in access, Aniakchak is expensive to reach. Park staff discourage solo travel. All visitors are advised to file a trip plan with the National Park Service at park headquarters: **ANIAKCHAK NATIONAL MONUMENT AND PRESERVE HEADQUARTERS** (PO Box 7, King Salmon, AK 99613; 907/246-3305; www.nps.gov/parklists/ak.html). Aniakchak and Katmai National Park share a visitor center and phone number in King Salmon. For **GENERAL INFORMATION** on the park, you also can call the Alaska Public Lands Information Center (907/271-2737) in Anchorage.

AIR TAXIS serving the monument include Egli Air Haul (907/246-3554), King's Flying Service (907/246-4414), and Katmai Air, c/o Katmailand (800/544-0551; katmailand@alaska.net; www.katmailand.com).

OUZEL EXPEDITIONS (800/825-8196 or 907/783-2216; www.ouzel. com) in Girdwood offers wilderness float trips down the Aniakchak River as well as other guided trips in Alaska.

The best things to do are to explore the caldera—CLIMB VENT MOUNTAIN (3,350 feet), a splatter cone formed 1,500 years ago and located inside the caldera—or FLOAT ANIAKCHAK RIVER, which flows out of Surprise Lake within the caldera and offers Class II to Class IV whitewater as it rushes past sharp volcanic boulders in its upper 13 miles. Officially designated a Wild and Scenic River, the Aniakchak offers easier floating and excellent salmon fishing in its lower 14 miles, before emptying into the Pacific Ocean. Floatplane pickups can be made along the coast.

Alaska Peninsula and Becharof National Wildlife Refuges

These two refuges stretch along the Alaska Peninsula and encompass towering volcanic mountains, broad valleys, rugged coastal fjords, rolling tundra, and glacially formed lakes. Fourteen major volcanoes are located here, including nine that have erupted in historic times. MOUNT VENIAMINOV last erupted in 1993. The refuges are best known for sportfishing and trophy hunting. BECHAROF LAKE, 35 miles long, is Alaska's second-largest lake (next to Lake Iliamna) and is the nursery for one of the world's largest runs of salmon. MOUNT PEULIK, UKINREK MAARS, and GAS ROCKS offer a glimpse into the region's volcanism. UGASHIK LAKES are famous for salmon and trophy grayling (the world-record grayling, nearly 5 pounds, was caught at Ugashik Narrows in 1981). The coastline offers rugged scenery and abundant wildlife, although it's often stormy or shrouded in fog. The land is dense with brown bears, and caribou migrate through here annually.

Most visitors fly in from King Salmon, located about 10 air miles from Becharof's northern corner. Air-taxi services include Branch River Air (907/246-3437), Egli Air Haul (907/246-3554), King's Flying Service (907/246-4414), and Katmai Air, c/o Katmailand (800/544-0551; katmailand@alaska.net; www.katmailand.com).

Two of the top wilderness lodges for hunting and fishing in the refuges are BLUE MOUNTAIN LODGE (907/688-2419), in the Ugashik Lakes region, and PAINTER CREEK LODGE (907/344-5181), which is exceptional for sportfishing—rainbows, salmon, arctic char, Dolly Varden, and grayling.

For GENERAL INFORMATION on the refuge, contact the Alaska Public Lands Information Center in Anchorage (907/271-2737; www.

nps.gov/parklists/ak.html). For more in-depth information, contact the Refuge Manager, Alaska Peninsula and Becharof National Wildlife Refuges (PO Box 277, King Salmon, AK 99613; 907/246-3339). Be advised you often will get a recording in summer, though.

Izembek National Wildlife Refuge

An international crossroads for migrating waterfowl and shorebirds, Izembek is Alaska's smallest national wildlife refuge. It's also one of the oldest. Visitors normally fly into the town of **COLD BAY** on regularly scheduled airlines, then arrange transportation into the refuge. Reeve Aleutian Airways (800/544-2248) has package air/motel deals to the refuge, which cost about $600 for transportation from Anchorage to Cold Bay, including two nights in the local motel. You also can rent a car through them to drive into the refuge. Fall is the most spectacular season in the refuge for wildlife viewing.

The heart of the refuge is **IZEMBEK LAGOON**, 30 miles long, which contains one of the world's largest eelgrass beds. Hundreds of thousands of waterfowl converge on the lagoon each fall, including the entire world population of black brant, which feed on Izembek's eelgrass before heading south to warmer climates. Brown bears fish salmon-rich streams. Caribou feed on tundra plants. Among the year-round residents are **TUNDRA SWANS**, the only nonmigratory wild population of this species in the world.

Two of the most prominent features of the land are **FROSTY PEAK** (6,000 feet), accessible from the Cold Bay road system, and **AGHILEEN PINNACLES**, a series of volcanic spires (up to 4,800 feet)—an extreme mountaineering challenge.

Make sure you bring rain gear as it rains at least once a day out there in the summer. Contact **IZEMBEK NATIONAL WILDLIFE REFUGE** (PO Box 127, Cold Bay, AK 99571; 907/532-2445) for more information.

The Pribilof Islands

Five tiny volcanic islands way out in the Bering Sea make up the Pribilofs. The two largest, 40 miles apart, are inhabited—St. Paul (pop. 750) and St. George (pop. 170). Most of the people are Aleut. In the late 1700s, Russians forcibly moved several hundred Aleut people here to harvest fur seals. When the United States purchased Alaska in 1867, relatively little changed out here except the flag. The Aleuts were considered wards of the state. It was only on October 28, 1983, on the long coattails of the civil rights movement, that they gained total autonomy, and that is the

LOOK BACK TO THE FUTURE

One of the most unusual features of the islands that lie at the end of the Aleutian chain—Attu, Kiska, Shemya, and Amchitka—occurred for the first time in recorded history on December 31, 1999.

If it weren't for the United States–Russian Convention signed in 1867 during the United States' purchase of Russian America, these islands would be west of the International Dateline, which lies at 180° longitude. This is the demarcation line separating today from tomorrow.

That old agreement called for bending the dateline so that the tip of the Aleutians would be considered part of North America in reckoning time. Adventurers reluctant to leave the Second Millennium as it slipped into history could use Shemya or Attu as viewing stations for looking from the year 1999 into the year 2000 and the Third Millennium. If the Russians or Japanese were so inclined, they could have used the far-out Aleutians, so close to their homelands, to look from the year 2000 back into 1999.

You can get the same thrill each New Year's Eve on the tip of the Aleutians should you choose such a wild destination for lifting a champagne glass and holding on to the year just a little bit longer or getting a sneak preview of the year to come, although it will be another thousand years before the next time warp comes to look forward to the future or back to the past millennium.

—Edward J. Fortier

day they celebrate. Though their lives have revolved around the fur seal harvest for nearly 200 years, residents are now dependent on two other industries: tourism and commercial fishing. The fur seal harvest today is for subsistence only.

This is as remote as you can get, but the treasure chest of wildlife is rich indeed. Hundreds of visitors come here annually—to watch seals and birds. The islands are part of the **ALASKA MARITIME NATIONAL WILDLIFE REFUGE**. St. Paul is home to the largest northern fur seal colony in the world; more than 800,000 seals gather here annually. St. George has a smaller population, but nearly a quarter of a million fur seals still arrive on its shores every summer.

The seals spend their winters at sea, and begin arriving in the Pribilofs in May. Large male "beachmasters," weighing about 600 pounds, show up first, quickly establishing their territories and building their harems (sometimes up to 100 females). Pregnant females don't arrive until June. They usually give birth to a single pup within 48 hours, then mate again within a week, while still nursing their newborn.

WORLD WAR II IN ALASKA

Many people today are surprised to learn that the United States was occupied by enemy forces during World War II in a far-off corner of Alaska.

The front-page headline in the New York Times on that fateful day—June 4, 1942—read: "Japanese Bomb Dutch Harbor, Alaska, Twice!" The Japanese landed forces on Attu and Kiska, two tiny islands at the end of the Aleutian Chain, and the Rising Sun flag flew on American soil. It took the United States more than a year and hundreds of lives to liberate those islands. On Attu, fighting was in the mountains. Those who lived through it say it was grim. The Japanese retreated just above the fog line and continued to pick off hundreds of American soldiers down below. But the United States forces outnumbered them 10 to 1.

The Japanese who didn't get killed in that final charge died by holding hand grenades to their chests. After the battle, the Americans found the diary of a young Japanese lieutenant. This was his final entry: "The last assault is to be carried out ... Only 33 years of living and I am to die here. I have no regrets. Banzai to the Emperor! ... Good-bye, Tasuka, my beloved wife."

Next to Iwo Jima, Attu was the second-bloodiest battle of the war in the Pacific.

—Nan Elliot

The Pribilofs often have been nicknamed "Islands of the Seals," but they could just as easily be called "Islands of the Birds." This remote Bering Sea archipelago is widely recognized as a birder's paradise.

The best time to visit is mid-May through August, when migratory birds and marine mammals are most abundant. Each month is "a season of its own," say locals. The best time for birders interested in a glimpse of the accidental Asian songbird blown off-course by westerly winds is mid-May to early June. Best time for viewing both seals and seabirds is June through August. And the most colorful time, the peak of the wild-flower blooms, is late June through mid-July.

ACCESS AND INFORMATION

Located 300 miles from mainland Alaska and nearly 800 miles from Anchorage, St. Paul and St. George are accessible by air or boat. But nearly all visitors fly due to the distances involved and island-tour arrangements. The largest of the Pribilofs, St. Paul has **AIR SERVICE** by Reeve Aleutian Airways (800/544-2248 or 907/243-4700) in Anchorage. Peninsula Airways (800/448-4226), in Anchorage, flies to both islands and is the only airline to fly to St. George; round-trip airfare is about $800.

For **PACKAGE AIR-LAND TOURS** to St. Paul, choose Reeve Aleutian Airways. There are no tours to St. George. For information about the island, contact the **CITY OF ST. GEORGE** (PO Box 929, St. George, AK 99591; 907/859-2263). The **CITY OF ST. PAUL** (PO Box 901, St. Paul, AK 99660; 907/546-2331) may also be reached.

Be sure to bring foul-weather clothing. Summer temperatures rarely rise above 60°F. Plan for **WEATHER DELAYS**, both coming and going.

The majority of visitors go to **ST. PAUL** and arrive on a package or guided tour, but it's possible to explore the islands on your own, if planning is done well in advance. On St. Paul, **VEHICLES** may be rented from the Tanadgusix (TDX) Native Corporation (907/546-2312); independent travelers may also join daily guided tours of the island. With its 45 miles of volcanic-cinder roads, an excellent way to explore St. Paul is by mountain bike. No rentals are available, but bikes can be brought on airlines as excess baggage.

ST. GEORGE is much less frequently visited. There are no package tours or land-based tours. And while it has a hotel, there is no restaurant. But there is a kitchen available for use and one store for groceries, beer, and wine. However, be aware that the weather can be unflyable for many days in a row, which means you will want to pad your visit on either end as well as bring extra food from home because the store can easily run out if the planes don't get in for a while. No camping is allowed anywhere on St. Paul or St. George Island.

ADVENTURES

ISLAND EVENTS / Watch St. Paul Island's **FUR SEALS** from viewing blinds—a couple are within walking distance of town. Participate in the village's many summertime **CULTURAL EVENTS**, including Aleut dances, parades, and Native games. Smell the **FLOWERS**—dozens of species bloom here each summer. Look for **BIRDS**—more than 200 species have been sighted on St. Paul. Watch for the island's small **REINDEER HERD**, about 700 strong, transplanted here decades ago.

ST. PAUL ISLAND TOUR / Tours of St. Paul Island are arranged through Reeve Aleutian Airways (800/544-2248) in cooperation with Tanadgusix Native Corporation. Packages range from 3 days/2 nights to 8 days/7 nights, offered from late May through late August. Prices range from $950 to $1,700. Tour price includes round-trip transportation from Anchorage, guide services (tour participants are escorted to both seal and seabird rookeries), ground transportation on St. Paul Island, sightseeing, and shared accommodations at the hotel. Meals are not included. Breakfast, lunch, and dinner are available at extra cost.

JOSEPH VAN OS PHOTO SAFARIS / This outfit will plan tours to St. Paul Island for the independent traveler who is either a serious amateur photographer or a professional photographer. A 4-day package is about $2,500, including meals, lodging, round-trip airfare from Anchorage, guide service, and island transportation. 206/463-5383; www.photosafaris.com.

LODGINGS

King Eider Hotel

ST. PAUL ISLAND, AK 99660; 907/546-2477

A distinctive robin's-egg blue color, the King Eider Hotel is right in the middle of town. The only hotel on St. Paul, it has 25 rooms with shared baths, many of them reserved in advance during the summer season by tour groups. As there is no restaurant in town, guests may bring food or take their meals at the local cannery at extra cost. The cannery is a short walk from the hotel and serves quite sumptuous meals cafeteria-style. If you are an independent traveler, the cost of the hotel is $80 for a double, and you can join the daily land tours at extra cost. Nonsmoking. $$; MC, V; checks OK; Box 88, St. Paul Island, AK 99660; about 5 miles from the airport.

St. George Tanaq Hotel

GEORGE ISLAND, AK 99591; 907/272-9886 OR 907/859-2255

A National Historic Landmark, this is St. George's only hotel. With 10 rooms, it can accommodate up to 18 people. Advance reservations are especially encouraged in July. The hotel has four shared bathrooms and a shared kitchen, as there is no restaurant on the island. No bar or restaurant here, either, but there is one store in town with groceries, beer, and wine. Advice: Do allow extra time on either end as weather delays are frequent, and be sure to bring extra food. $$$; MC, V; no checks; Box 939, St. George Island, AK 99591; 5 miles from the airport.

YUKON TERRITORY

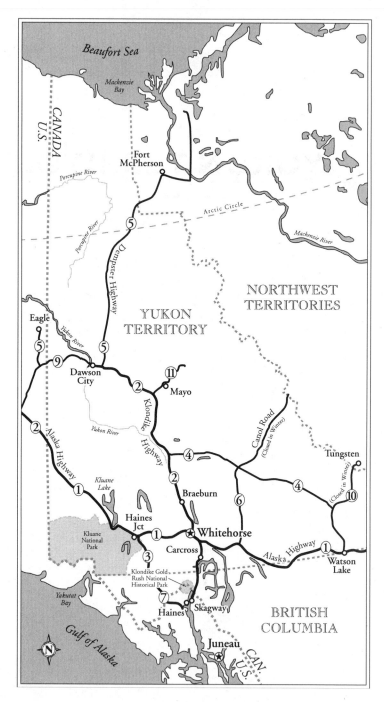

YUKON TERRITORY

The discovery of gold more than 100 years ago in the cold streams and tributaries of the Klondike River electrified the world and forever linked the fortunes and romance of Alaska and the Yukon Territory.

Before the Klondike Gold Rush of 1898, the north country was seen more as a frozen wasteland by both governments of Canada and the United States. Yet, it was far from barren, peopled by remarkable cultures who had lived in these harsh extremes for countless centuries. Today in Canada, they are known as "First Nations" people. The major groups in the Yukon are the Gwich'in people in Old Crow, north of Dawson City on the Porcupine River; the Han people from Dawson to Eagle, Alaska; the Northern and Southern Tutchone people, widely spread from Burwash Landing, across Whitehorse and up to Pelly Crossing; the Kaska people living around Watson Lake; the Upper Tanana people of Beaver Creek near the Alaska border; and the Tlingits in the area around Carcross and Teslin.

The Yukon is richly marbled with mountain ranges. Mount Logan (19,500 feet), the highest mountain in Canada and second-highest in North America (next to Mount McKinley in Alaska) rises in the southwest part of the territory in the St. Elias Range. Nearby Kluane National Park offers attractions for outdoor enthusiasts. The pale glacial blue waters of Kluane Lake are most spectacular in June when the deep purple and blue lupine flowers bloom and in September when the leaves turned golden.

Furs and whales first lured white men to arctic Alaska and northwest Canada. But it was the discovery of gold that fired the world's imagination and brought fortune seekers into the north en masse.

In August 1896, George Carmack, a Californian prospecting for gold, and his two Tagish Indian brothers-in-law, Dawson Charlie and Skookum (meaning "strong") Jim, were panning for color on Rabbit Creek, off the Klondike River, a few miles upstream from Dawson City. In exposed bedrock, they found gold lying thick between the slabs of rock like hunks of cheese in a sandwich, Carmack later reported. Each of their original claims produced more than $1 million. Appropriately, they renamed it Bonanza Creek.

A year later, the steamships *Excelsior* and *Portland* chugged into San Francisco and Seattle carrying enough gold on board to touch off an epidemic of gold fever and jump-start the Klondike Gold Rush. The *Portland* held more than a ton of gold, and 5,000 people crowded, open-mouthed, on the dock to watch the miners drag down the gangway battered suitcases, satchels, tin cans, socks, jars, and a whole array of other odd containers full of the precious yellow metal.

Gold fever swept 'round the world. From every walk of life, men and women left their jobs bound for the Klondike to strike it rich. They had no idea where they were going or what hardships they would endure. Escaping a depressed economy, they carried with them the fervent hope of a more prosperous life. Only a few ever found gold or got rich, and many who did squandered it away. In the end those who supported the miners' lives, like the grocers, outfitters, and "good-time" gals, probably made out a whole lot better.

What the Klondike stampede did do was swell the North's population in such a way that law and order, government, and inevitable bureaucracy were soon to follow. The Northwest Mounted Police, with their distinctive red uniforms and strict code of honor, became the stuff of legends. They patrolled the mountain passes during the stampede and turned back all who were not carrying at least 1 ton of provisions for the long winter ahead, thus preventing mass starvation.

Dawson became a lively town during those years, but when the gold petered out, so did the people. Yet some stayed, enraptured by this wild place and the rewards of a life lived amid such overwhelming beauty. Many of the descendants of those early adventurers are still here. And you can meet them—Yukoners are hospitable, friendly folks.

Like Alaska, the Yukon has lots of land and not many people—a population of 32,000 spread across 186,000 square miles. Alaskans and Yukoners share many similarities. They'll greet you with an open and ready warmth and take you for who you are. They work hard and play hard. Watch out—these folks can party! Just try to keep up.

ACCESS AND INFORMATION

The Yukon, like Alaska, has few roads. The major roads from the United States and southern Canada are the **ALASKA HIGHWAY**, starting in Dawson Creek, British Columbia; the somewhat parallel Stewart/Cassiar Highway from Prince Rupert, British Columbia; and the Taylor/Dempster Highway, which runs east from Alaska to Dawson City and then north to above the Arctic Circle, dead-ending in Inuvik, Northwest Territories.

The **ALASKA MARINE HIGHWAY SYSTEM** (800/526-6731), a ferry service, carries passengers and vehicles from Bellingham, Washington, and docks in Haines and Skagway, both in Alaska. From either port you can drive to the Yukon via the **HAINES HIGHWAY** or the **KLONDIKE HIGHWAY**. From Skagway the route winds through spectacular White Pass and a glacially created, high alpine plateau.

Canada provides **24-HOUR ROAD REPORTS** for the Yukon highways (867/667-8215), the British Columbia section of the Alaska Highway (250/774-7447), and the Stewart/Cassiar Highway (604/771-3000).

TIPS FOR AMERICANS CROSSING THE BORDER

Take **proof of citizenship**, such as a passport or birth certificate. You are going into another country. A valid driver's license or voting card may be sufficient, but come prepared with enough paperwork to satisfy the most officious gatekeeper. That goes for the kids too. If you're divorced, carry proof-of-custody papers or a letter from your former spouse. Children under 18 years old, when not accompanied by a parent, should have a letter of permission.

Driving with your **headlights** on is mandatory, as visibility is often limited by blowing snow or dust-covered windows. You must also wear a seat belt. Once across the border, you will be faced with the **metric system.** Gas is in liters (about a quarter gallon) and distances are in kilometers (0.621 mile).

In recent years, the **Canadian dollar** has been weak next to the American dollar, which makes many things seem like a bargain to Americans. **"Loonies"** are the Canadian one-dollar coin with a loon on the back, and **"Twonies"** are the two-dollar coins with a copper center. They're both big and heavy. Pennies, nickels, and dimes are about the same, but Canadian currency will not work in U.S. vending machines, and vice versa. However, nickels and dimes will work in parking meters. Go figure. Exchange rates fluctuate; take roughly a third off your purchase and you have the U.S. equivalent.

The Canadian government also has a refund program on the 7 percent **Goods and Services Tax** that visitors pay. To qualify you cannot be a resident of Canada. You must spend more than $100 CDN on goods purchased and/or accommodations. You must take the goods out of Canada within 60 days of purchase, and you must present your original receipts (credit card slips are not acceptable). Apply at any Canadian Duty Free Shop for a cash refund up to $500 CDN or mail a completed application form within a year to Revenue Canada, Customs and Excise, Visitors Rebate Program, Ottawa, ON, K1A 1J5 Canada.

—Dimitra Lavrakas

The main airport for the Yukon is in Whitehorse, which has limited **JET SERVICE.** You can catch a plane from Anchorage on ERA Aviation (800/866-8394), or connect through Vancouver via Canada 3000 Airlines (604/647-3117) from May to September, or Canadian Airlines (403/294-2058). In summer, Condo Air has direct flights from Germany.

An excellent source of information is the tour planner from **TOURISM YUKON** (Government of the Yukon, PO Box 2703, Whitehorse, YT Y1A 2C6, Canada; 867/667-5340; www.touryukon.com).

Whitehorse

Situated on the banks of the Yukon River, Whitehorse is the largest city in the territory (pop. 23,000). Named by stampeders for a series of tumultuous rapids that looked like the flowing manes of dozens of wild, white horses, the town sits in a bowl surrounded by hills. The gold seekers of 1898 had to maneuver the treacherous rapids of the Yukon River in their crudely built boats. Many didn't make it. In 1958, the river's wild horses were calmed by the building of a hydroelectric dam.

In 1950, Whitehorse became the territorial seat of government, usurping the position Dawson City once held. It was an act of convenience—a road now connected it to the rest of the country and the Lower 48. After the bombing of Pearl Harbor during World War II, the U.S. Army decided to build the Alaska-Canada Highway, also known as "The Alcan." As Alaska was strategically located in the Pacific, the road was designed to supply operations there during the ensuing war years. But the road also brought lots of Americans north and an infusion of money that Whitehorse sorely needed at the time. Sadly, with the Yankees came disease—influenza and measles—against which Native peoples had no immunity. All along the route north, villages were deeply affected, and many people died.

The road made Whitehorse a destination. The support services brought prosperity. People came in from remote areas to buy supplies and enjoy a movie or a night on the town.

ACCESS AND INFORMATION

The **INFORMATION CENTRE** (Hanson St and 2nd Ave; 867/667-3084; www.touryukon.com) is lovely, with light streaming through stained-glass windows. There, they'll point you in the right direction and offer plenty of excellent brochures on what to see and do.

EXPLORING

SS KLONDIKE NATIONAL HISTORIC SITE / The largest and most modern stern-wheeler of its time (launched in 1937), the SS *Klondike* is dry-docked on the west bank of the Yukon River in Whitehorse. It is a living museum and tribute to the important job stern-wheelers performed in transporting people and supplies up and down the Yukon River during the gold rush. By 1899, 60 steamboats, 8 tugs, and 20 barges plied the waters of the Yukon between Whitehorse and Dawson City. With the building of the Alaska Highway in 1942, the old stern-wheeler began to fade into history. Maintained by Parks Canada, the stern-wheeler offers tours every half hour and is open May through mid-September. For information, call Canadian Heritage (867/667-3970).

MACBRIDE MUSEUM / The "Rivers of Gold" exhibit here features the largest collection of Yukon gold anywhere. Covering half of a city block, the museum is chock-full of exhibits on the prehistory and history of the Yukon. Great gift shop. Open daily in summer; call for winter hours. 1st Ave and Wood St; 867/667-2709.

YUKON BERINGIA INTERPRETIVE CENTRE / If you're a prehistory buff, just look for the giant mastodon on the Alaska Highway, next to the Yukon Transportation Museum, and you'll find the Beringia Interpretive Centre (867/667-8855). The center details the Yukon's Ice Age history. Open daily, May to mid-September.

ADVENTURES

TAKHINI HOT SPRINGS / A welcome respite to weary travelers, Takhini Hot Springs is north of Whitehorse at Mile 6.2 on the Takhini Hot Springs Road, just off the North Klondike Highway. It recently was purchased by a consortium of Whitehorse families who plan to add cabins in addition to the tent sites, laundry, RV park, cafe, and sauna already there. Bring a towel and a bathing suit to swim in the outdoor pool (100°F; 38°C). For more information, call 867/633-2706.

CARCROSS / An abbreviation of "Caribou Crossing," Carcross is a small Tlingit Native village (pop. 431) an hour's drive south from Whitehorse along the South Klondike Highway. **THE CARIBOU HOTEL** (867/821-4501) is the oldest business in the Territory. The **CARCROSS BARRACKS** (867/821-4372) sells locally made Native crafts, ice cream, and fresh baked goods in summer.

ATLIN / The town of Atlin, on the shores of beautiful **ATLIN LAKE**, just over the border into British Columbia, is an old gold-mining town that still has several active claims. It's a 3-hour drive from Whitehorse. At the end of the Klondike Gold Rush, it attracted a number of stampeders. Between 1910 and the mid-1920s it was a tourist destination by way of Skagway, first by train, then by steamship. One old steamship, the MV *Tarahne*, now sits on the shores of Atlin Lake and is the site of dinner-theater performances in summer, featuring a salmon dinner and a mystery performance, *Murder on the MV Tarahne*. Every Saturday; 250/651-0076.

FESTIVALS AND EVENTS

YUKON QUEST INTERNATIONAL SLED DOG RACE / Temperatures in February can dip into serious below-zero weather when mushers take off on "the toughest sled-dog race in the world." Each year, Whitehorse alternates with Fairbanks, Alaska, as the start or finish of this grueling 1,000-mile sled-dog race, which runs along the Yukon River through Dawson City, then traverses trails once used by miners and trappers. No matter how frigid, fans always turn out to "watch them doggies run." 867/668-4711; www.yukonquest.net.

FROSTBITE MUSIC FESTIVAL / This brings in the best national and local talent. Performances, workshops, dances, and an acoustic stage encompass all types of music from jazz to folk. Held in mid-February at the Yukon College Arts Center (867/668-4921).

YUKON SOURDOUGH RENDEZVOUS / The city's gold-rush past is remembered with games and events for the entire family the last week in February. Don't be alarmed to see your bank teller costumed as a can-can dancer! Toe-tapping fiddling happens at the Yukon College Arts Center, and out on the streets there's heavy competition in the flour-packing and whipsaw contests. 867/667-2148; www.rendezvous.yukon.net/.

YUKON RIVER QUEST CANOE RACE / If you can't come north in winter for the dog-sled races, come north for the summer solstice. On June 21, 1999, the first Yukon River Quest Canoe Race—a tribute to the early stampeders—was held from Whitehorse to Dawson City, a distance of 460 miles. The winners collected $5,000 U.S. for a first-place finish. The race is sponsored by the Yukon Quest Sled Dog Race. For information on either race, check www.polarcom.com/~riverquest.

ANNUAL GOLD RUSH BATHTUB RACE / In the third week of August, you can participate in one of the wackier races on the Yukon—the world's longest and toughest bathtub race, from Whitehorse to Dawson City. The winners make it in about 48 hours; all others must finish in at least 3 days. Organized by the folks at Sourdough Rendezvous, the tubs compete for prize money of $5,000 CDN.

KLONDIKE TRAIL OF '98 INTERNATIONAL ROAD RELAY / If you like to race on terra firma, there's the grueling relay run from Skagway, Alaska, to Whitehorse in September. This 161-mile race goes up and over White Pass, closely following one of the routes of the Klondike Gold Rush. Teams split the mileage by running different legs of the journey—in the foggy mists at the top of the pass, they appear as apparitions. Teams come up with some fetching names like Chocolate Claim Jumpers, Medicine Chests (women who work at the clinic), Trial Runners (a lawyers' team), and Klondike Keystone Kops (members of the Royal Canadian Mounted Police). Call 867/668-4236.

FRANCOFETE FESTIVAL / October highlights the contributions of the French Canadians who plowed their way across the heavily forested continent as *coeureurs de bois*—a combination of packer, trapper, and adventurer. The festivities celebrate the culture, sports, arts, and renowned culinary talents of the French community in Canada. Call 867/668-2663.

RESTAURANTS

Antonio's Vineyard / ★

202 STRICKLAND ST, WHITEHORSE; 867/668-6266
If you're on a quest for good Greek cooking in the north, Antonio's stands out. The lunch buffet offers a savory choice of delicacies—lamb with greens, moussaka, pizza, and a "real Greek salad" (i.e., no filler lettuce— just a delicious combination of tomatoes, cucumbers, onions, olives, and feta cheese). *$; MC, V; no checks; lunch Mon–Fri, dinner every day; full bar; antonios@hypertech.yk.ca; downtown, just off 2nd Ave.*

Tagish Lake Resort Restaurant / ★★★

ON TAGISH RD, JUST OFF THE ALASKA HWY, CARCROSS;
867/668-1009
You'll be surprised to find such fine gourmet cooking in a place so remote—a taste of Switzerland in the wilds of the Yukon! The Wiener schnitzel is perfect. The New York steak with pears and blue cheese on top is a yin-yang treat for the tongue. The chocolate mousse is unparalleled, and the homemade Bailey's Cream ice cream is pure heaven. The resort offers six choices of single-malt Scotch and a solid wine and beer list. If you've been traveling in the north country for a while, this will surpass your expectations, even after listening to rave reviews from friends and strangers alike. The lodging is bunkhouse, rooms, or log cabins. *$$; V; local checks only; breakfast, lunch, dinner every day; full bar; www.Tagishlake.com; from Carcross on the Tagish Rd, take a right at the sign for Tagish Lake Resort and proceed 8 miles. The resort also can be reached by turning off the Alaska Hwy at Jake's Corner and onto Tagish Rd.*

Talisman Cafe / ★

2112 2ND AVE, WHITEHORSE; 867/667-2736
This casual cafe offers tasty sandwiches, a diverse selection of quiches, and good, hearty soups. The turkey sandwich (with real turkey and cranberry sauce) is a heavy-hitting favorite. You can even choose dark or light meat and have Thanksgiving every day of the week. To top it off, there's a wide variety of desserts and specialty teas. *$; MC, V; no checks; lunch, dinner every day; beer and wine; downtown near the main shopping center.*

THE MIGHTY YUKON

The mighty Yukon River is the fifth-longest river in North America, flowing 1,920 miles from its headwaters in the Yukon, through Dawson City, and across Alaska to meet the Bering Sea. Its headwaters are the glacier-fed lakes and streams of White Pass on the border of Canada and Alaska.

The Gwich'in called the Yukon River *Yu-kun-ah*, meaning "great river." For the people who live along its banks, it is a daily thoroughfare—by boat in summer and by dogsled or snowmachine in winter.

To paddle the Yukon is every river lover's dream. From Whitehorse to Dawson City, a journey following in the footsteps of the 1898 stampeders, it takes about 7 to 10 days. The river flows about 6mph and every bend offers a surprising new vista—and maybe a bear, moose, or wolf. Keep your eyes peeled.

WHITEHORSE OUTFITTERS will guide, rent gear, and pick you up wherever you pull out of the river. Contact Up North (867/667-7905; www.yukonweb. com/tourism/upnorth) or Kanoe People (867/668-4899). Experience Yukon Inc. (867/863-6021) in Carmacks, 104 miles north of Whitehorse, offers a Yukon riverboat tour to Five Finger Rapids and Fort Selkirk. Canoe rentals are also available. In winter, they'll take you on ice-fishing or snowmobiling excursions. For those who like being on the water but don't want to paddle, there are float trips through Miles Canyon near Whitehorse. Call Scenic Gold Rush Raft Tours (867/633-4836) in Whitehorse.

—Dimitra Lavrakas

LODGINGS

A Country Cabin Bed and Breakfast / ★★

MILE 5.5, TAKHINI HOT SPRINGS RD, WHITEHORSE, YT, Y1A 5X9; 867/633-2117

A short drive out of town, three cozy log cabins with wrought-iron bedsteads, kerosene lamps, and woodstoves sit peacefully in the woods—a perfect place for the weary traveler. A dip in the Takhini Hot Springs pool nearby will unkink your driving knots and soothe the spirit. Listen for the hoot of an owl and the swish of its wings as it chases a snowshoe hare in the night. There are outhouses and a quaint pitcher and bowl for washing up. In the morning, owner Bona Cameron-Lambert leaves a breakfast basket full of homemade muesli, yogurt, dried fruit, muffins, and coffee or tea. *$; no credit cards; local checks only; no alcohol; off the Klondike Hwy heading to Dawson City, look for Takhini Hot Springs Rd.*

Hawkins House Bed & Breakfast / ★★

303 HAWKINS ST, WHITEHORSE, YT, YIA IX5; 867/668-7638, FAX 867/668-7632
A bright, cheerful home with Victorian charm located a few blocks from the Yukon River and Main Street shops of downtown Whitehorse, Hawkins House has four guest rooms with private balconies, bathrooms, and work tables with computer jacks for business folks. Rooms are tailored colorfully along cultural and historical themes. Breakfast (an extra $7 CDN) is a sumptuous affair, including homemade moose sausage, crepes, waffles, jams, and salmon pâté, and also features themes from French Canadian to First Nations. Room rates range, winter to summer, from $100 to $150 CDN. The proprietors speak both French and German. *$–$$; MC, V; no checks; cpitzel@internorth.com; www.hawkinshouse.yk.ca/; downtown.*

Dawson City

Dawson City was the epicenter of the Klondike Gold Rush, and you will be reminded of it every time you turn a corner. Wild tales and legends abound here. Stroll down wooden boardwalks and into many restored historic buildings. The streets are still unpaved.

Dawson City throws open the doors and rolls out the welcome mat for tourists from mid-May through mid-September. The pace slows a little and there are fewer places open in winter. Wintertime population is about 2,000. For the locals, the time is a welcome breather from the hustle and bustle of summer.

ACCESS AND INFORMATION

To reach Dawson City, turn off the Alaska Highway, west of Whitehorse, onto the Klondike Highway. Or approach from the Taylor/Dempster Highway off the Alaska Highway near Tok, Alaska, at Teslin Junction. The **GEORGE BLACK FERRY** will carry you and your vehicle free of charge across the Yukon River (May–Sept, 24 hours a day, except Wed mornings, 5–7 am, when it is serviced). There is no air service to Dawson. The **KLONDIKE VISITORS ASSOCIATION** can be reached at 867/993-5575.

EXPLORING

BRAEBURN is a small settlement on the way to Dawson City from Whitehorse. It has a gas station and, if you're getting hungry, the **BRAEBURN LODGE** (Mile 43.8 on the Klondike Highway) serves gigantic, Frisbee-size cinnamon buns. Their sandwiches are equally large, made with fresh bread baked on the premises.

DIAMOND TOOTH GERTIE'S CASINO has three nightly music and dance performances, as well as gambling. You can play blackjack or poker, spin the wheel, or become mesmerized for hours at the one-arm bandit. Or enjoy the GASLIGHT FOLLIES, a vaudeville-style show at the Palace Grand Theatre. The DAWSON CITY MUSEUM (403/993-5291) is open during the summer season and holds a treasure trove of Klondike Gold Rush and Han Native people artifacts with good interpretive exhibits. KLONDIKE NATIONAL HISTORIC SITES (867/993-7200) offers a city walking tour. The COMMISSIONER'S RESIDENCE (867/993-7200), a splendid old turn-of-the century building, holds polite Victorian teas during the summer.

Literary types can go to ROBERT SERVICE'S CABIN, where daily readings of the "Bard of the North" are held. JACK LONDON'S original cabin—well, half of it—is also here. The other half is in Jack London Square in Oakland, California. The cabin features daily readings from London's work, as well as an account of London's life. The BERTON CABIN is the boyhood home of Pierre Berton, who wrote Klondike Fever and many other popular books on the Klondike.

FESTIVALS AND EVENTS

YUKON GOLD PANNING CHAMPIONSHIP / Open to cheechakos and sourdoughs alike. All events are timed—see how fast you can pan! Always held on July 1, Canada Day. Contact the Klondike Visitors Association, 867/993-5575.

DAWSON CITY MUSIC FESTIVAL / In the third week of July, Dawson is overrun with music lovers. Headline acts from all over North America come to play. There are special workshops, as well as events for children. Tickets go fast; contact 867/993-5584; www.dcmf.com.

GREAT KLONDIKE INTERNATIONAL OUTHOUSE RACE / Canoes, bicycles, skis, bathtubs, outhouses—Yukoners will race *in* or *on* anything! During the first week of September, teams race fancifully decorated outhouses through downtown streets. Watch out for flying TP. Call 867/993-5575.

RESTAURANTS

Klondike Kate's / ★★

3RD AVE AND KING ST, DAWSON CITY; 867/993-6527

Prepare for a real taste of the North. You can order arctic grayling here—something rarely seen on a menu but a tasty fish nonetheless, more often caught on your own fishing pole while out camping. Flavors from the Mediterranean such as hummus, tzatziki, and tabouli are featured. Or go south of the border with huevos rancheros. A big breakfast special of eggs, sausage, home fries, and bacon is $3.99 CDN. Located in an old gold-rush building, the restaurant is named for one of the Klondike's most celebrated dance-hall girls. If the wind is not blowing too hard, dine alfresco on the outdoor, covered patio. *$; MC, V; local checks only; breakfast, lunch, dinner every day; open May–Oct; full bar; in the heart of downtown.*

LODGINGS

Dawson City River Hostel / ★★

ACROSS THE RIVER, DAWSON CITY, YT, Y0B 1G0; 867/993-6823

Welcome to Dieterland. This is Dieter Reinmuth's own hostel that he built by hand. Look around at the unique use of old bicycle parts and recycled junk. A fertile mind put this all together. As in any sovereignty, there are laws. Don't worry, you won't have to memorize them, they're posted everywhere. You can camp here or rent a cabin for two to four people. It's a fairly basic setup with outhouses and a "prospector's bath house." Campers come here in droves for the Dawson City Music Festival. Dieter also offers bicycle and canoe rentals. Take the George Black Ferry from Dawson City over to the hostel. *$; no credit cards; checks OK; open mid-May–Sept; PO Box 32, Dawson City, Yukon Y0B 1G0.*

White Ram Bed and Breakfast / ★★

7TH AVE AND HARPER ST, DAWSON CITY, YT, Y0B 1G0; 867/993-5772

It's hard to miss. Look to the hillside above the city: it's the pink building still within walking distance of downtown. The White Ram is bright, cozy, and squeaky clean; you can either share a bathroom or have one of your own, depending on your budget. There's a laundry, barbecue area, a big kitchen, and a hot tub out back. The chalkboard out front lists the rooms available. You write down the one you want, after checking it out. Full breakfast (eggs and pancakes) is included. *$; MC, V; no checks; Box 302, Dawson City, YT, Y0B 1G0.*

Haines Junction and Kluane National Park

Nestled into one of the world's most dramatic settings, Haines Junction is a small town of 800, located in the Yukon at the junction of the Haines and Alaska Highways. From here to Haines, Alaska, it's 150 miles south through equally stunning country. (Haines is at the head of Lynn Canal at the northern end of the Inside Passage of Southeast Alaska; see Southeast Alaska chapter.) Whitehorse in the Yukon is 100 miles down the Alaska Highway from Haines Junction.

This beautiful little crossroads is located on the eastern border of **KLUANE NATIONAL PARK AND RESERVE**. The park was established first as a game sanctuary in the 1940s and formally as a national park in the 1970s. Together with bordering Wrangell-St. Elias National Park in Alaska, these two parks represent extraordinary wilderness, including some of the highest mountains on the continent, huge glaciers, remote Bush areas, and abundant wildlife. In 1980, they were declared by the United Nations to be a joint World Heritage Site. The Kluane National Park Visitor Information Centre (867/634-2345) has interpretive displays, schedules of guided hikes, and more. It's located just off the Alaska Highway, about 0.2 miles east of the junction. It's open every day in summer and Monday through Friday the rest of the year.

Haines Junction is also headquarters for the newly created (1993) **TATSHENSHINI-ALSEK WILDERNESS PARK**, international protection for the wilderness surrounding two spectacular rivers—the "Tat" and the Alsek (see Guides and Outfitters in the Haines section of the Southeast Alaska chapter).

RESTAURANTS AND LODGINGS

The Raven / ★★★

ALASKA HWY AT VISITOR CENTRE ACCESS, HAINES JUNCTION, YT,
Y0B 1L0; 867/634-2500, FAX 867/634-2804
Surrounded by the spectacular St. Elias Mountains, on the border of Kluane National Park, this wonderful little European oasis of gourmet dining and lovely, spacious, clean rooms has old-hat travelers on the road from Haines to Anchorage all abuzz. The hosts, Christine and Hans Nelles, are German and serve a variety of European and German specialties, make their own pasta, and change the menu daily, just in case you fall in love and want to spend the summer here. There are only 12 rooms, so book early. Guests are treated to a sumptuous German breakfast with homemade black bread, cheeses, fresh fruit, and different meats, including special German sausage. Even if you can't stay, make a point to stop for one of their elegant dinners. Nonsmoking. *$$; AE, MC, V; no checks; open April 1–Sept 27; beer and wine; www.yukonweb.com/tourism/raven; Box 5470, Haines Junction, YT, Y0B 1L0.* ♿ *(one room only)*

We Stand By Our Reviews

Sasquatch Books is proud of *Alaska Best Places*. Our editors and contributors go to great lengths and expense to see that all of the restaurant and lodging reviews are as accurate, up-to-date, and honest as possible. If we have disappointed you, please accept our apologies; however, if a recommendation in this 2nd edition of *Alaska Best Places* has seriously misled you, Sasquatch Books would like to refund your purchase price. To receive your refund:

1. Tell us where and when you purchased your book and return the book and the book-purchase receipt to the address below.
2. Enclose the original restaurant or lodging receipt from the establishment in question, including date of visit.
3. Write a full explanation of your stay or meal and how *Alaska Best Places* misled you.
4. Include your name, address, and phone number.

Refund is valid only while this 2nd edition of *Alaska Best Places* is in print. If the ownership, management, or chef has changed since publication, Sasquatch Books cannot be held responsible. Tax and postage on the returned book is your responsibility. Please allow six to eight weeks for processing.

Please address to Satisfaction Guaranteed, *Alaska Best Places*, and send to:

Sasquatch Books
615 Second Avenue, Suite 260
Seattle, WA 98104

Alaska Best Places Report Form

Based on my personal experience, I wish to nominate the following restaurant, place of lodging, shop, nightclub, sight, or other as a "Best Place"; or confirm/correct/disagree with the current review.

_____

_____

_____

_____

(Please include address and telephone number of establishment, if convenient.)

REPORT

Please describe food, service, style, comfort, value, date of visit, and other aspects of your experience; continue on another piece of paper if necessary.

_____

_____

_____

_____

_____

_____

_____

I am not concerned, directly or indirectly, with the management or ownership of this establishment.

_____

SIGNED

_____

ADDRESS

_____

_____

PHONE   **DATE**

Please address to Alaska Best Places and send to:
SASQUATCH BOOKS
615 SECOND AVENUE, SUITE 260
SEATTLE, WA 98104
Feel free to email feedback as well: **BOOKS@SASQUATCHBOOKS.COM**